In Heavenly Places

In
Heavenly
Places

Ellen G. White

Review and Herald® Publishing Association
Hagerstown, MD 21740

FOREWORD

This devotional book has been compiled largely from unpublished and out-of-print Spirit of Prophecy materials. Its inspirational truths have been drawn from the deep reservoir of accumulated Ellen G. White articles, which through the years appeared in the journals of the church, and from many, many letters of admonition, encouragement, and instruction written to both youthful and mature Advent pilgrims pressing on their journey to the kingdom. As the verities of the message are presented first from one approach and then from another, they appear with new beauty and added luster.

The Ellen G. White statements that comment on the texts of Scripture were selected and assembled in the offices of the Ellen G. White Estate. This was done in harmony with Mrs. White's instruction to the trustees, with whom she left the responsibility of the care of her writings.

To provide devotional readings of uniform length it has been necessary, at times, to drop out portions of some of the materials selected, which are repetitive or less pertinent to the topic presented, but in each case this has been indicated by marks of ellipsis. Such omissions have in no way distorted or altered the meaning of the original passage. References directing the reader to the original source of each selection appear at the close of the volume. The Scripture Index includes not only all verses quoted but also those alluded to, thus providing a reference help that may be used, to a limited extent, as a Subject Index.

We believe that this volume, presenting in a fresh setting encouraging counsels and basic principles vital to successful Christian experience and living, is a worthy addition to the Spirit of Prophecy books. That it may lift the reader in his devotional moments to *Heavenly Places,* is the prayerful wish of the publishers and

THE TRUSTEES OF THE ELLEN G. WHITE ESTATE

Silver Spring, MD 20904-6600

"In Heavenly Places"

Eph. 2:6

"In heavenly places"—can it be
This glorious promise is for me?
Raised up by Heaven's boundless might,
To sit with Christ in realms of light
      In heavenly places?

O wondrous love, that paid the price
Redemption claimed, by sacrifice
Of God's own Son! What bitter cup
My Saviour drank to lift me up
      To heavenly places!

Up from a life defiled by sin,
Washed in His blood, made pure within,
Robed in His righteousness, freed of blame,
Fitted to bear my Saviour's name
      In heavenly places.

Joint heir with Christ, I sit with Him,
I walk and talk and work with Him;
Above this world, sin's battlefield,
I rest in Him, His truth my shield,
      In heavenly places—
      In Christ Jesus.

         —BESSIE MOUNT

"IN HEAVENLY PLACES"—OUR EXALTED PRIVILEGE

But God, who is rich in mercy, for his great love wherewith he loved us, even when we were dead in sins, hath quickened us together with Christ, . . . and hath raised us up together, and made us sit together in heavenly places in Christ Jesus. Eph. 2:4-6.

As God raised Christ from the dead, that He might bring life and immortality to light through the gospel, and thus save His people from their sins, so Christ has raised fallen human beings to spiritual life, quickening them with His life, filling their hearts with hope and joy. [1]

Christ gave Himself for the redemption of the race, that all who believe in Him may have everlasting life. Those who appreciate this great sacrifice receive from the Saviour that most precious of all gifts —a clean heart. They gain an experience that is more valuable than gold or silver or precious stones. They sit together in heavenly places in Christ, enjoying in communion with Him the joy and peace that He alone can give. They love Him with heart and mind and soul and strength, realizing that they are His blood-bought heritage. Their spiritual eyesight is not dimmed by worldly policy or worldly aims. They are one with Christ as He is one with the Father. [2]

Christ "gave himself for us, that he might redeem us from all iniquity, and purify unto himself a peculiar people, zealous of good works" (Titus 2:14). He made an offering so complete that through His grace every one may reach the standard of perfection. Of those who receive His grace and follow His example it will be written in the book of life, "Complete in Him—without spot or stain." [2]

"Blessed be the God and Father of our Lord Jesus Christ," . . . "who hath blessed us with all spiritual blessings in heavenly places in Christ" (Eph. 1:3). What is there left for us to ask, that is not included in this merciful, abundant provision? Through the merits of Christ we are blessed with all spiritual blessings in heavenly places in Christ. It is our privilege to draw nigh to God, to breathe in the atmosphere of His presence. . . . Nothing short of abiding in the presence of Christ will bring peace, freedom, courage, and power. [3]

GETTING ACQUAINTED WITH GOD

Acquaint now thyself with him, and be at peace: thereby good shall come unto thee. Receive, I pray thee, the law from his mouth, and lay up his words in thine heart. Job 22:21, 22.

From the beginning it has been Satan's studied plan to cause men to forget God, that he might secure them to himself. Therefore he has sought to misrepresent the character of God, to lead men to cherish a false conception of Him. The Creator has been presented to their minds as clothed with the attributes of the prince of evil himself—as arbitrary, severe, and unforgiving—that He might be feared, shunned, and even hated by men. . . .

Christ came to reveal God to the world as a God of love, a God of mercy, tenderness, and compassion. By the world's Redeemer the thick darkness with which Satan had enshrouded the throne of the Deity was swept away, and the Father was again manifest to men as the Light of life. . . .

Christ is saddened by the sight of men so absorbed in worldly cares and business perplexities that they have no time to become acquainted with God. To them heaven is a strange place; for they have lost it out of their reckoning. Not familiar with heavenly things, they tire of hearing about them. They dislike to have their minds disturbed in regard to their need of salvation. But the Lord desires to disturb their minds, that they may become acquainted with Him in time to accept His offer of salvation. . . .

The day will come when the awful denunciation of God's wrath will be uttered against those who have persisted in their disloyalty to Him. . . . But you need not be among those who will come under His wrath. We are living in the day of His salvation. The light from the cross of Calvary is shining forth in clear, bright rays, revealing Jesus, our sacrifice for sin. "We have redemption through his blood, the forgiveness of sins" (Eph. 1:7).

God desires to restore His image in you. Believe that He is your Helper. Resolve to become acquainted with Him. As you draw nigh to Him with confession and repentance, He will draw nigh to you with mercy and forgiveness.[4]

8

LEARNING OF GOD THROUGH HIS WORKS

The Lord is good to all: and his tender mercies are over all his works. All thy works shall praise thee, O Lord; and thy saints shall bless thee. Ps. 145:9, 10.

We love to contemplate the character and love of God in His created works. What evidences has He given the children of men of His power, as well as of His parental love! He has garnished the heavens and made grand and beautiful the earth.

"O Lord our Lord, how excellent is thy name in all the earth! . . . When I consider thy heavens, the work of thy fingers, the moon and the stars, which thou hast ordained; what is man, that thou art mindful of him? and the son of man, that thou visitest him?" "All thy works praise thee, O Lord; and thy saints shall bless thee" (Ps. 8:1, 3, 4; 145:10).

Had our world been formed with a perfectly level surface the monotony would have fatigued the eye and wearied the senses. God has adorned our world with grand mountains, hills, valleys, and ranges of mountains. The rugged granite, bare mountains, also the mountains decorated with evergreens and verdure, and the valleys with their softened beauty make the world a mirror of loveliness. The goodness, wisdom, and power of God are manifest everywhere. In mountains, rocks, hills, and valleys, I see the works of divine power. I can never be lonely while viewing the grand scenery of nature. On the journey over the plains and mountains I have had feelings of the deepest reverence and awe while viewing the frowning precipice and snow-capped mountain heights.

The mountains, hills, and valleys should be to us as schools in which to study the character of God in His created works. The works of God which we may view in the ever-varying scenes—in mountains, hills, and valleys, in trees, shrubs, and flowers, in every leaf, every spire of grass—should teach us lessons of the skill and love of God and of His infinite power.

Those who study nature cannot be lonesome. They love the quiet hours of meditation, for they feel that they are brought in close communion with God while tracing His power in His created works.[5]

9

LOVE THAT IS MEASURELESS

The Lord hath appeared of old unto me, saying, Yea, I have loved thee with an everlasting love: therefore with lovingkindness have I drawn thee. **Jer. 31:3.**

Those who know not God cannot by their learning or science find out God. Christ does not try to prove the great mystery, but reveals a love that is beyond measurement. He does not make God's power and greatness the chief theme of His discourses. He speaks of Him oftenest as *our Father*. . . . He desires our minds, weakened by sin, to be encouraged to grasp the idea that God is love. . . .

The father of the prodigal son is the type that Christ chooses as a representation of God. This father longs to see and receive once more the son who has left him. He waits and watches for him, yearning to see him, hoping that he will come. When he sees a stranger approaching, poor and clothed with rags, he goes out to meet him, if perchance it may be his son. And he feeds and clothes him as if he were indeed his son. By and by he has his reward, for his son comes home, on his lips the beseeching confession, "Father, I have sinned against heaven, and in thy sight, and am no more worthy to be called thy son." And the father says to the servants, "Bring forth the best robe, and put it on him; and put a ring on his hand, and shoes on his feet; and bring hither the fatted calf, and kill it; and let us eat, and be merry" (Luke 15:21-23).

There is no taunting, no casting up to the prodigal of his evil course. The son feels that the past is forgiven and forgotten, blotted out forever. And so God says to the sinner, "I have blotted out, as a thick cloud, thy transgressions, and as a cloud thy sins" (Isa. 44:22). "I will forgive their iniquity, and I will remember their sin no more" (Jer. 31:34). . . .

Heaven is waiting and yearning for the return of the prodigals who have wandered far from the fold. Many of those who have strayed away may be brought back by the loving service of God's children. . . .

Think of the Father subjecting Himself to sorrow, sparing not His own Son, but freely delivering Him up for us all. . . . O that we had a better understanding of His love! [6]

10

GIFT OF GOD'S LOVE

For God so loved the world, that he gave his only begotten Son, that whosoever believeth in him should not perish, but have everlasting life. John 3:16.

How can we understand God? How are we to know our Father? We are to call Him by the endearing name of Father. And how are we to know Him and the power of His love? It is through diligent search of the Scriptures. We cannot appreciate God unless we take into our souls the great plan of redemption. We want to know all about these grand problems of the soul, of the redemption of the fallen race. It is a wonderful thing that after man had violated the law of God and separated himself from God, was divorced, as it were, from God —that after all this there was a plan made whereby man should not perish, but that he should have everlasting life. . . . God gave His only-begotten Son to die for us. . . . When our minds are constantly dwelling upon the matchless love of God to the fallen race, we begin to know God, to become acquainted with Him. . . .

Right here on this little atom of a world were enacted the grandest scenes that were ever known to humanity. All the universe of heaven was looking on with intense interest. Why? The great battle was to be fought between the power of darkness and the Prince of light. Satan's work was to magnify his power constantly. . . . He was all the time placing God in a false light. He was presenting Him as a God of injustice, and not a God of mercy. He was constantly stirring up their minds so that they would have an incorrect view of God.

How was God to be rightly represented to the world? How was it to be known that He was a God of love, full of mercy, kindness, and pity? How was the world to know this? God sent His Son, and He was to represent to the world the character of God. . . .

We want to keep this perfect Pattern before us. God was so good as to send a representation of Himself in His Son Jesus Christ, and we want to get the mind and heart to unfold and reach upward. . . . Let yours be the prayer, Reveal Thyself to me, that in Thy matchless grace I may lay hold on the golden link, Christ, which has been let down from heaven to earth, that I may grasp it and be drawn upward.[7]

11

A LOVE BORN OF MERCY

I will be merciful to their unrighteousness, and their sins and their iniquities will I remember no more. Heb. 8:12.

God's love for the fallen race is a peculiar manifestation of love—a love born of mercy; for human beings are all undeserving. Mercy implies the imperfection of the object toward which it is shown. It was because of sin that mercy was brought into active exercise.

Sin is not the object of God's love, but of His hatred. But He loves and pities the sinner. The erring sons and daughters of Adam are the children of His redemption. Through the gift of His Son He has revealed toward them His infinite love and mercy.[8]

God proposes cooperation with His frail, erring creatures, whom He has placed on vantage ground. On the one side there are infinite wisdom, goodness, compassion, power; on the other, weakness, sinfulness, absolute helplessness, poverty, dependence. . . . Man is given the privilege of working with God in the saving of his own soul. He is to receive Christ as his personal Saviour and believe in Him. Receiving and believing is his part of the contract. . . .

The plan of redemption was arranged in the counsels between the Father and the Son. Then Christ pledged Himself to render an account for man if he proved disloyal. He pledged Himself to make an atonement which would unite every believing soul to God. He who lays his sins upon the substitute and surety . . . can unite with the apostle in saying: "Blessed be the God and Father of our Lord Jesus Christ, who hath blessed us with all spiritual blessings in heavenly places." "That in the ages to come he might shew the exceeding riches of his grace in his kindness toward us through Christ Jesus" (Eph. 1:3; 2:7).

In His infinite love Christ devised the plan of salvation. This plan He stands ready to fulfill in behalf of all who will cooperate with Him. In their behalf He says to the Father, Do not impute their sins to them, but lay them on Me. Be merciful to their unrighteousness, and their sins and their iniquities remember no more. They have accepted My merits and made peace with Me. . . . My righteousness is theirs, and for My sake bless them with all spiritual blessings.[9]

12

ONLY ONE REDEEMER

God commendeth his love toward us, in that, while we were yet sinners, Christ died for us. Rom. 5:8.

As soon as there was sin, there was a Saviour. Christ knew that He would have to suffer, yet He became man's substitute. As soon as Adam sinned, the Son of God presented Himself as surety for the human race.[10]

Think of how much it cost Christ to leave the heavenly courts, and take His position at the head of humanity. Why did He do this? Because He was the only one who could redeem the fallen race. There was not a human being in the world who was without sin. The Son of God stepped down from His heavenly throne, laid off His royal robe and kingly crown, and clothed His divinity with humanity. He came to die for us, to lie in the tomb as human beings must, and to be raised for our justification. He came to become acquainted with all the temptations wherewith man is beset. He rose from the grave and proclaimed over the rent sepulcher of Joseph, "I am the resurrection, and the life." One equal with God passed through death in our behalf. He tasted death for every man, that through Him every man might be a partaker of eternal life.

Christ ascended to heaven, bearing a sanctified, holy humanity. He took this humanity with Him into the heavenly courts, and through the eternal ages He will bear it as the One who has redeemed every human being in the city of God, the One who has pleaded before the Father, "I have graven thee upon the palms of my hands." The palms of His hands bear the marks of the wounds that He received. If we are wounded and bruised, if we meet with difficulties that are hard to manage, let us remember how much Christ suffered for us. . . .

Our Saviour bore all that we are called upon to bear, so that no human being could say, "He does not know my suffering and my trials." In all our afflictions He was afflicted. . . .

Satan declared that human beings could not live without sin. Christ passed over the ground where Adam stumbled and fell, and by a sinless life placed the human race on vantage ground, that every one might stand before the Father, accepted in the Beloved.[11]

13

THE MOST EXALTED THEME

In this was manifested the love of God toward us, because that God sent his only begotten Son into the world, that we might live through him. 1 John 4:9.

The plan of redemption, by which the merciful divine-human Redeemer rescued man from the thralldom of sin, is beyond the comprehension of men or of angels. It is indeed a mystery so surpassing, so grand, so sublime, that we can never hope fully to understand it.

Christ's sacrifice for fallen man has no parallel. It is the most exalted, sacred theme on which we can meditate. Every heart that is enlightened by the grace of God is constrained to bow with inexpressible gratitude and adoration before the Redeemer for His infinite sacrifice.

In His life Jesus of Nazareth differed from all other men. . . . He is the only true model of goodness and perfection. From the beginning of His ministry men began more clearly to comprehend the character of God. . . . Christ's mission on earth was to reveal to men that God was not a despot, but a heavenly Father, full of love and mercy for His children. He spoke of God by the endearing title of "My Father." . . .

In all the sufferings and afflictions of man there is an Eye to pity, a Heart to love. "Like as a father pitieth his children, so the Lord pitieth them that fear him" (Ps. 103:13). God's tenderest care is exercised over us. He pities us in our weakness and in our sorrow. We may be despondent, even despairing; the heavy clouds of affliction may be over us; but there is light ahead. Beyond the gloom is a sympathetic, compassionate Friend, One who does not willingly grieve or afflict the children of men.[12]

In the gracious blessings which our heavenly Father has bestowed upon us we may discern innumerable evidences of a love that is infinite, and a tender pity surpassing a mother's yearning sympathy for her wayward child. When we study the divine character in the light of the cross we see mercy, tenderness, and forgiveness blended with equity and justice. In the language of John we exclaim: "Behold, what manner of love the Father hath bestowed upon us, that we should be called the sons of God" (1 John 3:1).[13]

14

RIGHTEOUSNESS THROUGH CHRIST

For he hath made him to be sin for us, who knew no sin; that we might be made the righteousness of God in him. 2 Cor. 5:21.

The God of justice did not spare His Son. . . . The whole debt for the transgression of God's law was demanded from our Mediator. A full atonement was required. How appropriate are the words of Isaiah, "It pleased the Lord to bruise him; he hath put him to grief." His soul was made "an offering for sin." "He was wounded for our transgressions, he was bruised for our iniquities" (Isa. 53:10, 5).

Jesus suffered the extreme penalty of the law for our transgression, and justice was fully satisfied. The law is not abrogated; it has not lost one jot of its force. Instead, it stands forth in holy dignity, Christ's death on the cross testifying to its immutability. Its demands have been met, its authority maintained.

God spared not His only-begotten Son. To show the depth of His love for man, He delivered Him up for us all. "Behold the Lamb of God, which taketh away the sin of the world" (John 1:29). Behold Him dying on the cross. Behold Him who was equal with God, mocked and derided by the mob. Behold Him in Gethsemane, bowed under the burden of the sins of the whole world.

Was the penalty remitted because He was the Son of God? Were the vials of wrath withheld from Him who was made sin for us? Without abatement the penalty fell upon our divine-human Substitute.

Hear His cry, "My God, my God, why hast thou forsaken me?" (Mark 15:34). He was treated as a sinner, that we might be treated as righteous, that God might be just, and yet the justifier of the sinner. . . .

The love existing between the Father and His Son cannot be portrayed. It is measureless. In Christ, God saw the beauty and perfection of excellence that dwells in Himself. Wonder, O heavens, and be astonished, O earth, for God spared not His own Son, but gave Him up to be made sin for us, that those who believe may be made the righteousness of God in Him. . . .

Language is too feeble for us to attempt to portray the love of God. We believe it, we rejoice in it, but we cannot comprehend it.[14]

NOT TO CONDEMN BUT TO SAVE

For God sent not his Son into the world to condemn the world; but that the world through him might be saved. John 3:17.

There are souls who are trembling in unbelief. They ask, "How can I know that God is reconciled to me? How can I be assured that He loves and pardons me?" It is not for you, dear youth, to make yourselves just with God. Jesus invites you to come to Him with all your burdens and perplexities. . . . Accept the promise and the provision that God has made. . . . Look away from self to Jesus; for in Christ the character of the Father is revealed.[15]

The blood of Christ in ever-abiding efficacy is our only hope, for through His merits alone we have pardon and peace.[16]

The character of God as revealed by Christ invites our faith and love, for we have a Father whose mercy and compassion fail not. At every step of our journey heavenward He will be with us to guide in every perplexity, to give us help in every temptation.[15]

Your reason and imagination should be touched with the life-giving power of Christ, that forms of beauty and truth may be impressed thereon. There are great and precious truths that demand your contemplation, in order that you may have a sound foundation for your faith by having a correct knowledge of God. O that the superficial, vain seeker for truth would learn that the world by wisdom, however much acquired, knew not God.

It is proper to seek to learn all that is possible from nature, but do not fail to look from nature to Christ for the complete representation of the character of the living God. By contemplation of Christ, by conformity to the divine likeness, your conceptions of the divine character will expand, and your mind and heart will be elevated, refined, and ennobled. Let the youth aim high, not relying upon human wisdom, but living day by day as seeing Him who is invisible, doing their work as in the sight of the intelligences of heaven. . . .

He who constantly depends upon God through simple trust and prayerful confidence, will be surrounded by the angels of heaven. He who lives by faith in Christ, will be strengthened and upheld, able to fight the good fight of faith, and lay hold upon eternal life.[16]

INFINITE POWER

Who is this that cometh from Edom, with dyed garments from Bozrah? this that is glorious in his apparel, travelling in the greatness of his strength? I that speak in righteousness, mighty to save. Isa. 63:1.

The only-begotten Son of God came to this world to redeem the fallen race. He has given us evidence of His great power. He will enable those who receive Him to build up characters free from all the tendencies that Satan reveals. We can resist the enemy and all his forces. The battle will be won, the victory gained, by him who chooses Christ as his leader, determined to do right because it is right.

Our divine Lord is equal to any emergency. With Him nothing is impossible. He has shown His great love for us by living a life of self-denial and sacrifice and by dying a death of agony. Come to Christ just as you are. . . . Cast yourself wholly on His mercy. There is no difficulty within or without that cannot be surmounted in His strength.

Some have stormy tempers; but He who calmed the stormy Sea of Galilee will say to the troubled heart, "Peace, be still." There is no nature so rebellious that Christ cannot subdue it, no temper so stormy that He cannot quell it, if the heart is surrendered to His keeping.

He who commits his soul to Jesus need not despond. We have an all-powerful Saviour. Looking to Jesus, the author and finisher of your faith, you can say, "God is our refuge and strength, a very present help in trouble. Therefore will not we fear, though the earth be removed, and though the mountains be carried into the midst of the sea" (Ps. 46:1, 2). . . .

Let us have more confidence in our Redeemer. Turn not from the waters of Lebanon to seek refreshment at broken cisterns, which can hold no water. Have faith in God. Trustful dependence on Jesus makes victory not only possible but certain. Though multitudes are pressing on in the wrong way, though the outlook be ever so discouraging, yet we may have full assurance in our Leader; for "I am God," He declares, "and there is none else" (Isa. 45:22). He is infinite in power, and able to save all who come to Him. There is no other in whom we can safely trust.[17]

CHRIST THE REVELATION OF GOD

For the Father himself loveth you, because ye have loved me, and have believed that I came out from God. John 16:27.

In viewing the holiness and glory of the God of the universe, we are terrified, for we know that His justice will not permit Him to clear the guilty. But we need not remain in terror; for Christ came to the world to reveal the character of God, to make plain to us His paternal love toward His adopted children. We are not to estimate the character of God by the stupendous works of nature alone, but by the simple, lovely life of Jesus, who presented Jehovah as more merciful, more compassionate, more tender, than our earthly parents.

Jesus presented the Father as one to whom we could give our confidence and present our wants. When we are in terror of God, and overwhelmed with the thought of His glory and majesty, the Father points us to Christ as His representative. What you see revealed in Jesus, of tenderness, compassion, and love, is the reflection of the attributes of the Father. The cross of Calvary reveals to man the love of God. Christ represents the Sovereign of the universe as a God of love. By the mouth of the prophet He said, "I have loved thee with an everlasting love: therefore with loving-kindness have I drawn thee" (Jer. 31:3).

We have access to God through the merits of the name of Christ, and God invites us to bring to Him our trials and temptations; for He understands them all. He would not have us pour out our woes to human ears. Through the blood of Christ we may come to the throne of grace and find grace to help in time of need. We may come with assurance, saying, "My acceptance is in the Beloved." "For through him we both have access by one Spirit unto the Father." "In whom we have boldness and access with confidence by the faith of him" (Eph. 2:18; 3:12).

As an earthly parent encourages his child to come to him at all times, so the Lord encourages us to lay before Him our wants and perplexities, our gratitude and love. Every promise is sure. Jesus is our Surety and Mediator, and has placed at our command every resource, that we may have a perfect character.[18]

A MUTUAL CONTRACT

But as many as received him, to them gave he power to become the sons of God, even to them that believe on his name. John 1:12.

Salvation is secured by a mutual contract. "As many as *received him,* to them gave he power to become the sons of God." Will you, with all your heart and mind and soul, enter into this contract? [19]

Look to your Redeemer in faith and loving trust, for power and wisdom to do the work of character building. He sits as a refiner, to purify the gold and silver from all dross. Then look continually unto Him, and no cheap or worthless material will be brought into the structure of your character building.

By faith you may accept the merits of the blood of the Son of God, which He has shed that the sinner might not perish, but have everlasting life. God has laid upon Him all power, that He may impart help to every one who will break with Satan and acknowledge Christ as his only hope. . . . When you are ready to cooperate with Him who can keep you from falling, your resolutions will be of some value. Christ, the chief Healer, will make you whole. He works mightily with every one who is in earnest. He will give strength and victory. All the mean and wicked traits of character can be taken away by the One who has purchased you as His property. . . .

Make a break with the enemy. Cast yourselves loose from the prince of the power of the air and from the legion of his associates.

Satan will resist the efforts of those who choose to stand on the Lord's side. He will resort to every kind of deception to frustrate their efforts. But God has given His Son to bear the sins of those who seek His truth and righteousness. He stands ready to impart grace to every one who looks to Him in faith. . . .

The exercise of faith and manly courage will enlarge the comprehension of what it means to be a Christian. We are to seek for that faith which works by love and purifies the soul. We shall have severe conflicts with our hereditary and cultivated tendencies to evil. There must be a firm dependence upon the Captain of our salvation. He will not fail to do His part. [19]

19

A CHANGE OF HEART

Repent ye therefore, and be converted, that your sins may be blotted out, when the times of refreshing shall come from the presence of the Lord. Acts 3:19.

In order to be saved, we must know by experience the meaning of true conversion. It is a fearful mistake for men and women to go on day by day professing to be Christians yet having no right to the name. In God's sight profession is nothing, position is nothing. He asks, Is the life in harmony with My precepts? There are many who suppose that they are converted but who are not able to bear the test of character presented in the Word of God. . . .

Conversion is a change of heart, a turning from unrighteousness to righteousness. Relying upon the merits of Christ, exercising true faith in Him, the repentant sinner receives pardon for sin. As he ceases to do evil and learns to do well, he grows in grace and in the knowledge of God. He sees that in order to follow Jesus he must separate from the world, and after counting the cost, he looks upon all as loss if he may but win Christ. He enlists in His army and bravely and cheerfully engages in the warfare, fighting against natural inclinations and selfish desires and bringing the will into subjection to the will of Christ. Daily he seeks the Lord for grace, and he is strengthened and helped. Self once reigned in his heart, and worldly pleasure was his delight. Now self is dethroned, and God reigns supreme. His life reveals the fruit of righteousness. The sins he once loved he now hates. Firmly and resolutely he follows in the path of holiness. This is genuine conversion. . . .

Let us not forget that in his conversion and sanctification man must cooperate with God. "Work out your own salvation with fear and trembling," the Word declares. "For it is God which worketh in you both to will and to do of his good pleasure" (Phil. 2:12, 13). Man cannot transform himself by the exercise of his will. He possesses no power by which this change may be effected. The renewing energy must come from God. The change can be made only by the Holy Spirit. He who would be saved, high or low, rich or poor, must submit to the working of this power.[20]

GOD'S GRACE TRANSFORMS THE LIFE

Marvel not that I said unto thee, Ye must be born again.
John 3:7.

The great truth of the conversion of the heart by the Holy Spirit is presented in Christ's words to Nicodemus: "Verily, verily I say unto thee, Except a man be born from above [margin], he cannot see the kingdom of God. . . . That which is born of the flesh is flesh; and that which is born of the Spirit is spirit" (John 3:3-6).[21]

It is by the renewing of the heart that the grace of God works to transform the life. No mere external change is sufficient to bring us into harmony with God. There are many who try to reform by correcting this bad habit or that bad habit, and they hope in this way to become Christians, but they are beginning in the wrong place. Our first work is with the heart. . . .

The leaven of truth works secretly, silently, steadily, to transform the soul. The natural inclinations are softened and subdued. New thoughts, new feelings, new motives, are implanted. A new standard of character is set up—the life of Christ. The mind is changed; the faculties are aroused to action in new lines. Man is not endowed with new faculties, but the faculties he has are sanctified. The conscience is awakened.

The Scriptures are the great agency in this transformation of character. Christ prayed, "Sanctify them through thy truth: thy word is truth" (John 17:17). If studied and obeyed, the Word of God works in the heart, subduing every unholy attribute. The Holy Spirit comes to convict of sin, and the faith that springs up in the heart works by love to Christ, conforming us, body, soul, and spirit, to His will.

A man sees his danger. He sees that he needs a change of character, a change of heart. He is stirred; his fears are aroused. The Spirit of God is working in him, and with fear and trembling he works for himself, seeking to find out his defects of character and to see what he can do to bring about the needed change in his life. . . . He confesses his sins to God, and if he has injured anyone, he confesses the wrong to the one he has injured. . . . He acts in harmony with the Spirit's working, and his conversion is genuine.[21]

21

A MIGHTY UNSEEN POWER

The wind bloweth where it listeth, and thou hearest the sound thereof, but canst not tell whence it cometh, and whither it goeth: so is every one that is born of the Spirit. John 3:8.

The Holy Spirit strives with every man. It is the voice of God speaking to the soul.[22]

No human reasoning of the most learned man can define the operations of the Holy Spirit upon human minds and characters, yet they can see the effects upon the life and actions. . . .

Though we cannot see the Spirit of God, we know that men who have been dead in trespasses and sins become convicted and converted under its operations. The thoughtless and wayward become serious. The hardened repent of their sins, and the faithless believe. The gambler, the drunkard, the licentious, become steady, sober, and pure. The rebellious and obstinate become meek and Christlike.

When we see these changes in the character, we may be assured that the converting power of God has transformed the entire man. We saw not the Holy Spirit, but we saw the evidence of its work on the changed character of those who were hardened and obdurate sinners. As the wind moves in its force upon the lofty trees and brings them down, so the Holy Spirit can work upon human hearts, and no finite man can circumscribe the work of God. . . .

You cannot see the operating agency, but you can see its effects.[23]

Those who not only hear but do the words of Christ, make manifest in character the operation of the Holy Spirit. The result of the internal operation of the Holy Spirit is demonstrated in the outward conduct. The life of the Christian is hid with Christ in God, and God acknowledges those who are His, declaring, "Ye are my witnesses." They testify that divine power is influencing their hearts and shaping their conduct. Their works give evidence that the Spirit is moving upon the inward man; those who are associated with them are convinced that they are making Jesus Christ their pattern.

Those who are in connection with God are channels for the power of the Holy Spirit. . . . The inner life of the soul will reveal itself in the outward conduct.[24]

SURE REMEDY FOR SIN

Come now, and let us reason together, saith the Lord: though your sins be as scarlet, they shall be as white as snow; though they be red like crimson, they shall be as wool. Isa. 1:18.

That which should cause us the deepest joy is the fact that God forgives sin. If we take Him at His word and forsake our sins, He is ready and willing to cleanse us from all unrighteousness. He will give us a pure heart and the abiding presence of His Spirit, for Jesus lives to intercede for us. But . . . spiritual things are spiritually discerned. It is a living, active, abiding faith that discerns the will of God, that appropriates the promises, and profits by the truths of His word. It is not because we are righteous, but because we are dependent, faulty, erring, and helpless ourselves, that we must rely upon Christ's righteousness, and not upon our own.[25]

When you receive the words of Christ as if they were addressed to you personally, when each applies the truth to himself as if he were the only sinner on the face of the earth for whom Christ died, you will learn to claim by faith the merits of the blood of a crucified and risen Saviour. . . .

Many feel that their faults of character make it impossible for them to meet the standard that Christ has erected, but all that such ones have to do is to humble themselves at every step under the mighty hand of God. Christ does not estimate the man by the amount of work he does, but by the spirit in which the work is performed.

When He sees men lifting the burdens, trying to carry them in lowliness of mind, with distrust of self and with reliance upon Him, He adds to their work His perfection and sufficiency, and it is accepted of the Father. We are accepted in the Beloved. The sinner's defects are covered by the perfection and fullness of the Lord our Righteousness. Those who with sincere will, with contrite heart, are putting forth humble efforts to live up to the requirements of God, are looked upon by the Father with pitying, tender love; He regards such as obedient children, and the righteousness of Christ is imputed unto them.[25]

23

A NEW CREATION

Create in me a clean heart, O God; and renew a right spirit within me. Ps. 51:10.

*Let your cry be to God, Convert my inmost soul. Plead with God for the transforming power of His grace. Hold fast to your Saviour as did Jacob, until God shall not only reveal to you yourself but shall reveal to you Himself and you shall see in Jesus a strength and support, a brightness and power, you have never sensed and realized. Your soul's salvation is in great peril, and now do not, I plead with you, deceive your own soul. If your faith perseveringly grasps the promises, you will prevail. This is the victory that overcometh the world, even our faith.

As long as you are true to yourself, no adverse power of earth or hell will be able to destroy your peace or interrupt your communion with God. If you fear God you need not walk in uncertainty. If you please Him you will secure everything which your soul requires. The language of an eminent Christian was, "There is nothing in the universe I fear but that I shall not know all my duty, or shall fail to do it." . . .

Stand up for Jesus, though it may require any sacrifice, any self-denial. Stand up for Jesus; anywhere, anywhere, stand up for Jesus. Do all your work as though you could see through the veil and God's eye were directed full upon you, taking cognizance of every action. He hath purchased you with His own blood, and when you need His help, call upon Him and you will have it. It is then Jesus will stand up for you.

Let your short, uncertain life be a continual preparation for the future immortal life. Temptation is allowed to come upon us to discover the character we possess and to improve our defects. There are continual solicitations to sin which are disguised to deceive and allure the soul to ruin. Satan will transform himself into an angel of light, and he is constantly plotting to rob God of His glory in the destruction of souls. I beseech of you for your soul's sake to resist the devil that he may flee from you. Hang your helpless soul on God.[20]

---

* From a letter of personal appeal.

THE SHEPHERD'S TENDER CARE

I say unto you, that likewise joy shall be in heaven over one sinner that repenteth, more than over ninety and nine just persons, which need no repentance. Luke 15:7.

The beautiful parable that Christ gave of the one lost sheep, of the shepherd that left the ninety and nine to go in search of that which was lost, illustrates the care of the great Shepherd. He did not look carelessly over the sheep of the fold, and say, "I have ninety and nine, and it will cost me too much trouble to go in search of the straying one; let him come back, and I will open the door of the sheepfold and let him in; but I cannot go after him." No. . . . He counts and recounts the flock, and when he is certain that one sheep is lost, he slumbereth not. He leaves the ninety and nine within the fold; however dark and tempestuous the night, however perilous and unpleasant the way, however long and tedious the search, he does not weary, he does not falter, until the lost is found.

But when it is found, does he act indifferently? Does he call the sheep, and command the straying one to follow him? Does he threaten and beat it, or drive it before him, recounting the bitterness and discomfiture and anxiety that he has had on its account? No; he lays the weary, exhausted, wandering sheep on his shoulder, and . . . returns it to the fold. His gratitude finds expression in melodious songs of rejoicing, and heavenly choirs respond to the shepherd's note of joy. . . . For "joy shall be in heaven over one sinner that repenteth, more than over ninety and nine just persons which need no repentance." Jesus says, "I am the good shepherd, and know my sheep, and am known of mine" (John 10:14). Just as a shepherd of earth knows his sheep, so does the chief Shepherd know His flock that are scattered throughout the whole world. . . . "And ye, my flock, the flock of my pasture, are men, and I am your God, saith the Lord God" (Eze. 34:31).[27]

However lowly, however elevated we may be, whether we are in the shadow of adversity or in the sunshine of prosperity, we are His sheep, the flock of His pasture, and under the care of the chief Shepherd.[27]

25

GOD HAS CHOSEN ME

God hath from the beginning chosen you to salvation through sanctification of the Spirit and belief of the truth. 2 Thess. 2:13.

In this text the two agencies in the salvation of man are revealed —the divine influence, the strong, living faith of those who follow Christ. . . .

Sanctification is the work, not of a day or of a year, but of a lifetime. The struggle for conquest over self, for holiness and heaven, is a lifelong struggle. . . . Paul's sanctification was the result of a constant conflict with self. He said, "I die daily" (1 Cor. 15:31). . . . It is by unceasing endeavor that we maintain the victory over the temptations of Satan. Christian integrity must be sought with resistless energy, and maintained with a resolute fixedness of purpose.

There is a science of Christianity to be mastered—a science as much deeper, broader, higher, than any human science as the heavens are higher than the earth. The mind is to be disciplined, educated, trained; for we are to do service for God in ways that are not in harmony with inborn inclination. There are hereditary and cultivated tendencies to evil that must be overcome. Our hearts must be educated to become steadfast in God. We are to form habits of thought that will enable us to resist temptation. By a life of holy endeavor and firm adherence to the right the children of God are to seal their destiny. . . .

The word that was spoken to Jesus at the Jordan embraces humanity. God spoke to Jesus as our representative. With all our sins and weaknesses, we are not cast aside as worthless. "He hath made us accepted in the beloved" (Eph. 1:6). The glory that rested upon Christ is a pledge of the love of God for us. It tells us of the power of prayer—how the human voice may reach the ear of God and our petitions find acceptance in the courts of heaven. . . . The light which fell from the open portals upon the head of our Saviour will fall upon us as we pray for help to resist temptation. The voice which spoke to Jesus says to every believing soul, "This is my beloved child, in whom I am well pleased." [28]

26

COOPERATING WITH HEAVEN

Work out your own salvation with fear and trembling. For it is God which worketh in you both to will and to do of his good pleasure. Phil. 2:12, 13.

Man, in the work of saving of the soul, is wholly dependent upon God. He cannot of himself move one step toward Christ unless the Spirit of God draws him, and this drawing is ever, and will continue until man grieves the Holy Ghost by his persistent refusal. . . .

The Spirit is constantly showing to the soul glimpses of the things of God, and then a divine presence seems to hover near, and if the mind responds, if the door of the heart is opened, Jesus abides with the human agent. . . .

The Spirit of God does not propose to do our part, either in the willing or the doing. . . . As soon as we incline our will to harmonize with God's will, the grace of Christ stands ready to cooperate with the human agent; but it will not be the substitute to do our work independent of our resolving and decidedly acting. Therefore it is not the abundance of light, and evidence piled upon evidence, that will convert the soul. It is only the human agent accepting the light, arousing the energies of the will, realizing and acknowledging that which he knows is righteousness and truth, and thus cooperating with the heavenly ministrations appointed of God in the saving of the soul.

If the sinner or the backslider settles himself in disobedience and sin, the light may flash from heaven all about him, . . . without breaking the bewitching power of falsehood and the spell of the world's deception. . . .

Obey not the voice of the deceiver, which is in harmony with the unsanctified will, but obey the impulse that God has given. . . . Everything is at stake. Will the human agent cooperate with the divine "to will and to do"? If man places his will on God's side, fully surrendering self to God's will, the high and holy endeavor of the human agent takes down the obstruction he himself has erected, the rubbish is cleared away from the door of the heart, the defiance barricading the soul is broken down. The door of the heart is opened and Jesus enters, to abide as a welcome guest.[29]

27

IN THE HANDS OF THE POTTER

But now, O Lord, thou art our father; we are the clay, and thou our potter; and we all are the work of thy hand. Isa. 64:8.

In His Word God compares Himself to a potter and His people to the clay. His work is to mold and fashion them after His own similitude. The lesson they are to learn is the lesson of submission. Self is not to be made prominent. If due attention is given to the divine instruction, if self is surrendered to the divine will, the hand of the Potter will produce a shapely vessel.[30]

The excellence of a genuine connection with Christ comes with obedience to the words, "Take my yoke upon you, and learn of me. . . ." The worker who has this experience has an intense longing to know the fullness of the love that passes knowledge. His capacity to enjoy the love of God constantly increases. Learning daily in the school of Christ he has a constantly increasing capacity to grasp the meaning of the sublime truths that are as far-reaching as eternity. . . .

He realizes that he is material with which God is working, and that he must be passive in the Master's hands. Trials come to him, for unless tested by trial and disappointment he would never know his lack of wisdom and experience.

If he seeks the Lord with humility and trust, every trial will work for his good. He may sometimes seem to fail, but his supposed failure to reach the place where he hoped to stand may be God's way of bringing his advancement. He thinks that he has failed, but his supposed failure means a better knowledge of himself and a firmer trust in God. . . . He may make mistakes, but he learns not to repeat these mistakes. United with Christ, the True Vine, he is enabled to bear fruit to the glory of God. . . .

The Lord desires us to be meek and lowly and contrite, yet filled with the assurance that comes from a knowledge of the will of God. He "hath not given us the spirit of fear; but of power, and of love, and of a sound mind. . . . Who hath saved us, and called us with an holy calling, not according to our works, but according to his own purpose and grace . . ." (2 Tim. 1:7-9).[31]

THE HEAVENLY ELECTION

Wherefore the rather, brethren, give diligence to make your calling and election sure: for if ye do these things, ye shall never fall. 2 **Peter** 1:10.

This is the only election regarding which the Bible speaks. Fallen in sin, we may become partakers of the divine nature and attain to a knowledge far in advance of any scientific learning. By partaking of the flesh and the blood of our crucified Lord, we shall gain life eternal. In the sixth of John we read: "Whoso eateth my flesh, and drinketh my blood, hath eternal life" (John 6:54). "It is the spirit that quickeneth; the flesh profiteth nothing: the words that I speak unto you, they are spirit, and they are life" (verse 63).

None need lose eternal life. Everyone who chooses daily to learn of the heavenly Teacher will make his calling and election sure. Let us humble our hearts before God and follow on to know Him whom to know aright is life eternal.

"Give diligence to make your calling and election *sure:* for if ye do these things, ye shall never fall: for so an entrance shall be ministered unto you abundantly into the everlasting kingdom of our Lord and Saviour Jesus Christ" (2 Peter 1:10, 11).

Here are your life-insurance papers. This is not an insurance policy the value of which someone else will receive after your death; it is a policy that assures *you* a *life* measuring with the life of God—even eternal life. O what an assurance! what a hope! Let us ever reveal to the world that we are seeking for a better country, even a heavenly. Heaven has been made for us, and we want a part in it. We cannot afford to allow anything to separate us from God and heaven. In this life we must be partakers of the divine nature. Brethren and sisters, you have only one life to live. O let it be a life of virtue, a life hid with Christ in God!

Unitedly we are to help one another gain perfection of character. To this end, we are to cease all criticism. Onward and still onward we may advance toward perfection, until at last there will be ministered unto us an abundant entrance into the heavenly kingdom.[32]

29

A LITTLE HEAVEN HERE

Seek ye the Lord, all ye meek of the earth, which have wrought his judgment; seek righteousness, seek meekness: it may be ye shall be hid in the day of the Lord's anger. Zeph. 2:3.

In view of what is soon to come upon the earth, I entreat you, brethren and sisters, to walk before God in all meekness and lowliness of mind, remembering the care that Jesus has for you. All the meek of the earth are exhorted to seek Him. . . . Let self break in pieces before God. It is hard to do this; but we are warned to fall upon the Rock and be broken, else it will fall upon us, and grind us to powder. It is to the humble in heart that Jesus speaks; His everlasting arms encircle them, and He will not leave them to perish by the hands of the wicked.

What is it to be a Christian? It is to be Christlike; it is to do the works of Christ. Some fail on one point, some on another. Some are naturally impatient. Satan understands their weakness and manages to overcome them again and again. But let none be discouraged by this. Whenever little annoyances and trials arise, ask God in silent prayer to give you strength and grace to bear them patiently. There is a power in silence; do not speak a word until you have sent up your petition to the God of heaven. If you will always do this, you will soon overcome your hasty temper, and you will have a little heaven here to go to heaven in.

God wants His people to cleanse their hands and purify their hearts. Will it make them unhappy to do this? Will it bring unhappiness into their families if they are kind and patient, courteous and forbearing? Far from it. The kindness they manifest toward their families will be reflected upon themselves. This is the work that should be carried forward in the home. If the members of a family are not prepared to dwell in peace here, they are not prepared to dwell in the family that shall gather around the great white throne. . . .

We must seek to separate sin from us, relying upon the merits of the blood of Christ; and then in the day of affliction, when the enemy presses us, we shall walk among the angels. They will be like a wall of fire about us, and we shall one day walk with them in the city of God.[33]

30

BUILDING FOR ETERNITY

That ye may stand perfect and complete in all the will of God.
Col. 4:12.

The Infinite One—He who alone was able to bring order and beauty out of the chaos and confusion of nature's darkness—is able to subdue the rebellious heart of man and bring his life into conformity to the divine will. His Spirit can quell man's rebellious temper. . . .

Day by day we are building characters, and we are building for eternity. God desires us in our lives to give the people of the world an example of what they should be and of what they can be through obedience to the gospel of Christ. Let us place ourselves in God's hands, to be dealt with as He sees best. . . . "Ye are God's husbandry, ye are God's building" (1 Cor. 3:9). If we build in cooperation with Him, the structure that we rear will day by day grow more beautiful and more symmetrical under the hand of the Master Builder, and through all eternity it will endure.

Sanctification is a progressive work. It is a continuous work, leading human beings higher and still higher. It does not leave love behind, but brings it into the life as the very essence of Christianity.

Christ says to us, "Be ye therefore perfect, even as your Father which is in heaven is perfect" (Matt. 5:48). He is our example. During His life on earth He was ever kind and gentle. His influence was ever fragrant, for in Him dwelt perfect love. He was never sour and unapproachable, and He never compromised with wrong to obtain favor. If we have His righteousness, we shall be like Him in gentleness, in forbearance, in unselfish love. Shall we not, by dwelling in the sunshine of His presence, become mellowed by His grace?

Let us honor our profession of faith. Let us adorn our lives with beautiful traits of character. Harshness of speech and action is not of Christ, but of Satan. Shall we, by clinging to our imperfections and deformities, make Christ ashamed of us? His grace is promised to us. If we will receive it, it will beautify our lives. . . . Deformity will be exchanged for goodness, perfection. Our lives will be adorned with the graces that made Christ's life so beautiful.[34]

31

IN RIGHT RELATION TO GOD

Jesus answered and said unto him, If a man love me, he will keep my words: and my Father will love him, and we will come unto him, and make our abode with him. John 14:23.

Consider the familiar relation Christ here brings to view as existing between the Father and His children. His presence and guardianship are an abiding thing. While we trust in Christ's saving power, all the arts and wiles of the fallen host can do nothing to harm us. Heavenly angels are constantly with us, guiding and protecting. God has ordained that we shall have His saving power with us, to enable us to do all His will. Let us grasp the promises and cherish them moment by moment. Let us believe that God means just what He says.[35]

There is a possibility of the believer in Christ obtaining an experience that will be wholly sufficient to place him in right relation to God. Every promise that is in God's Book holds out to us the encouragement that we may be partakers of the divine nature. This is the possibility—to rely upon God, to believe His Word, to work His works; and this we can do when we lay hold of the divinity of Christ.

This possibility is worth more to us than all the riches in the world. There is nothing on earth that can compare with it. As we lay hold of the power thus placed within our reach, we receive a hope so strong that we can rely wholly upon God's promises; and laying hold of the possibilities there are in Christ, we become the sons and daughters of God.[36]

There are high attainments for the Christian. He may ever be rising to higher attainments. John had an elevated idea of the privilege of a Christian. He says, "Behold, what manner of love the Father hath bestowed upon us, that we should be called the sons of God" (1 John 3:1). It is not possible for humanity to rise to a higher dignity than is here implied. To man is granted the privilege of becoming an heir of God and a joint heir with Christ. To those who have been thus exalted, are unfolded the unsearchable riches of Christ, which are of a thousandfold more value than the wealth of the world. Thus, through the merits of Jesus Christ, finite man is elevated to fellowship with God and with His dear Son.[37]

32

FELLOWSHIP WITH CHRIST

God is faithful, by whom ye were called unto the fellowship of his Son Jesus Christ our Lord. 1 Cor. 1:9.

The true Christian keeps the windows of the soul open heavenward. He lives in fellowship with Christ. His will is conformed to the will of Christ. His highest desire is to become more and more Christlike, that he may say with Paul: "I am crucified with Christ: nevertheless I live; yet not I, but Christ liveth in me . . ." (Gal. 2:20).

Earnestly and untiringly we are to strive to reach God's ideal for us. Not as a penance are we to do this, but as the only means of gaining true happiness. The only way to gain peace and joy is to have a living connection with Him who gave His life for us, who died that we might live, and who lives to unite His power with the efforts of those who are striving to overcome.

Holiness is constant agreement with God. Shall we not strive to be that which Christ so greatly desires us to be—Christians in deed and in truth—that the world may see in our lives a revelation of the saving power of truth? This world is our preparatory school. While here we shall meet with trials and difficulties. Continually the enemy of God will seek to draw us away from our allegiance. But while we cleave to Him who gave Himself for us we are safe.

The whole world was gathered into the embrace of Christ. He died on the cross to destroy him who had the power of death and to take away the sin of every believing soul. He calls upon us to offer ourselves on the altar of service, a living, consuming sacrifice. We are to make an unreserved consecration to God of all that we have and are.

In this lower school of earth we are to learn the lessons that will prepare us to enter the higher school, where our education will continue under the personal instruction of Christ. Then He will open to us the meaning of His word. Shall we not, in the few days of probation remaining to us, act like men and women who are seeking for life in the kingdom of God, even an eternity of bliss? We cannot afford to miss the privilege of seeing Christ face to face and of hearing from His lips the story of redemption.[38]

AMAZING GRACE!

Grace be to you, and peace, from God our Father, and from the Lord Jesus Christ. Eph. 1:2.

"Grace be to you." We owe everything to God's free grace. Grace in the covenant ordained our adoption. Grace in the Saviour effected our redemption, our regeneration, and our exaltation to heirship with Christ. Not because we first loved Him did God love us; but "while we were yet sinners," Christ died for us. . . . Although by our disobedience we have merited God's displeasure and condemnation, yet He has not forsaken us, leaving us to grapple with the power of the enemy. Heavenly angels fight our battles for us, and cooperating with them, we may be victorious over the powers of evil.

We should never have learned the meaning of this word "grace" had we not fallen. God loves the sinless angels, who do His service and are obedient to all His commands, but He does not give them grace. These heavenly beings know nought of grace; they have never needed it, for they have never sinned. Grace is an attribute of God shown to undeserving human beings. We ourselves did not seek after it, but it was sent out in search of us. God rejoices to bestow this grace upon all who hunger for it, not because we are worthy, but because we are so utterly unworthy. Our need is the qualification which gives us the assurance that we shall receive this gift.[39]

God's supply of grace is waiting the demand of every sinsick soul. It will heal every spiritual disease. By it hearts may be cleansed from all defilement. It is the gospel remedy for everyone who believes.[40]

We may make daily progress in the upward path to holiness and yet we find still greater heights to be reached; but every stretch of the spiritual muscles, every taxation of heart and brain, brings to light the abundance of the supply of grace essential for us as we advance.

The more we contemplate these riches, the more we will come into possession of them, and the more we shall reveal the merits of Christ's sacrifice, the protection of His righteousness, His inexpressible love, the fullness of His wisdom, and His power to present us before the Father without spot or wrinkle or any such thing.[41]

THE GIFT OF PEACE

And the peace of God, which passeth all understanding, shall keep your hearts and minds through Christ Jesus. Phil. 4:7.

Sin has destroyed our peace. While self is unsubdued we can find no rest. The masterful passions of the heart no human power can control. We are as helpless here as were the disciples to control the raging storm. But He who spoke peace to the billows of Galilee has spoken the word of peace for every soul. However fierce the tempest, those who turn to Jesus with the cry, "Lord, save us," will find deliverance. His grace, which reconciles the soul to God, quiets the strife of human passion, and in His love the heart is at rest. . . . "Being justified by faith, we have peace with God through our Lord Jesus Christ" (Rom. 5:1). "The work of righteousness shall be peace; and the effect of righteousness quietness and assurance for ever" (Isa. 32: 17).

Whoever consents to renounce sin and open his heart to the love of Christ, becomes a partaker of this heavenly peace. There is no other ground of peace than this. The grace of Christ, received into the heart, subdues enmity; it allays strife and fills the soul with love. He who is at peace with God and his fellow men cannot be made miserable. Envy will not be in his heart; evil surmisings will find no room there; hatred cannot exist. The heart that is in harmony with God is a partaker of the peace of heaven and will diffuse its blessed influence on all around. The spirit of peace will rest like dew upon hearts weary and troubled with worldly strife.

Christ's followers are sent to the world with the message of peace. Whoever, by the quiet, unconscious influence of a holy life, shall reveal the love of Christ; whoever, by word or deed, shall lead another to renounce sin and yield his heart to God is a peacemaker.

And "blessed are the peacemakers: for they shall be called the children of God" (Matt. 5:9). The spirit of peace is evidence of their connection with heaven. The sweet savor of Christ surrounds them. The fragrance of the life, the loveliness of the character, reveal to the world the fact that they are children of God. Men take knowledge of them that they have been with Jesus.[42]

35

FROM DESPAIR TO HOPE AND JOY

Now the God of hope fill you with all joy and peace in believing, that ye may abound in hope, through the power of the Holy Ghost. Rom. 15:13.

If Jesus had not died our sacrifice and risen again, we should never have known peace, never have felt joy, but only experienced the horrors of darkness and the miseries of despair. Then let only praise and gratitude be the language of our hearts. All our lives we have been partakers of His heavenly benefits, recipients' of the blessings of His priceless atonement. Therefore it is impossible for us to conceive the low and helpless state . . . from which Christ has raised us. When we feel the pains, the sorrows and bereavements to which we are subject, let not one murmuring thought dishonor our Redeemer. . . . We cannot determine how much less we suffer than our sins deserve. . . .

Can we look upon Him whom our sins have pierced and not be willing also to drink of the cup of humiliation? Our sins mingled the bitter cup which He removed from our lips and drank Himself, that in its place He might put to our lips the cup of blessing. . . .

The language of the soul should be that of joy and gratitude. If any have dark chapters in their experience let them bury them. Let this history not be kept bright by repetition. . . . Cultivate only those thoughts and those feelings which will produce gratitude and praise. . . .

I entreat of you never to utter one word of complaint, but to cherish feelings of gratitude and thankfulness. By so doing you will be learning to make melody in your hearts. Weave into your experience the warp and woof, the golden threads, of gratitude. Contemplate the better land, where tears are never shed, where temptations and trials are never experienced, where losses and reproaches are never known, where all is peace and joy and happiness. Here your imagination may have full scope. These thoughts will make you more heavenly-minded, will endue you with heavenly vigor, will satisfy your thirsty soul with rivers of living waters, and will set upon your heart the seal of the divine image. They will fill you with joy and hope in believing and will abide with you as a comforter forever.[43]

36

THE PERIL OF NEGLECT

How shall we escape, if we neglect so great salvation; which at the first began to be spoken by the Lord, and was confirmed unto us by them that heard him? Heb. 2:3.

No greater gift can be bestowed upon man than that which is comprehended in Christ. . . . A neglect to lay hold of the priceless treasure of salvation means the eternal ruin of your soul. The peril of indifference to God and neglect of His gift is measured by the greatness of salvation. God has done to the uttermost of His almighty power. The resources of infinite love have been exhausted in devising and executing the plan of redemption for man. God has revealed His character in the goodness, the mercy, compassion, and love manifested to save a race of guilty rebels. What could be done that has not been done in the provisions of the plan of salvation? If the sinner remains indifferent to the manifestation of the goodness of God, if he neglects so great a salvation, . . . what can be done to touch his hard heart? [44]

What importance, what magnitude, it gives to the theme of redemption, that He who has undertaken the salvation of man was the brightness of the Father's glory, the express image of His person! How, then, can Heaven regard those who neglect so great a salvation, wrought out for man at such infinite cost? To neglect to lay hold on the rich blessings of Heaven is to refuse, to set at nought, Him who was equal with the Father, the only One who could save fallen man. Oh, shall we through neglect of Christ throw away our one chance for eternal life? . . .

What love, what wonderful love, was displayed by the Son of God! The death we deserved was suffered to come upon Him that immortality might be given to us, who could never merit such a reward. Is not salvation great in its simplicity and wonderful in its comprehensiveness? . . . Contemplating the fullness of the provision that God has made whereby every son and daughter of Adam may be saved, we are led to exclaim with John, "Behold, what manner of love the Father hath bestowed upon us, that we should be called the sons of God" (1 John 3:1). . . . The plan of redemption provides for every emergency and for every want of the soul. [45]

CHRIST EXEMPLIFIED GOD'S LAW

Then said I, Lo, I come: in the volume of the book it is written of me, I delight to do thy will, O my God: yea, thy law is within my heart. Ps. 40:7, 8.

In the councils of heaven it was determined that there must be given to mankind a living exemplification of the law. Having decided to make this great sacrifice, God left nothing obscure, nothing indefinite, in regard to the salvation of the human race. He gave to mankind a standard by which to form character. With an audible voice and in awful grandeur He spoke His law from Mount Sinai. Distinctly He stated what we must do in order to render acceptable obedience to Him and . . . remain loyal to His law. "Thou shalt love the Lord thy God with all thy heart, and with all thy soul, and with all thy mind. This is the first and great commandment. And the second is like unto it, Thou shalt love thy neighbour as thyself. On these two commandments hang all the law and the prophets" (Matt. 22:37-40).

So deep was the Lord's interest in the beings He had created, so great His love for the world, that He "gave his only begotten Son, that whosoever believeth in him should not perish, but have everlasting life" (John 3:16). Christ came to bring moral power to man, to elevate, ennoble, and strengthen him, enabling him to be a partaker of the divine nature, having escaped the corruption that is in the world through lust. He proved to the inhabitants of the unfallen worlds and to human beings that the law can be kept. While possessing the nature of man, He obeyed the law of God, vindicating God's justice in demanding that it be obeyed. In the judgment His life will be an unanswerable argument in favor of God's law.

All who possess the faculty of reason may learn the measure of their duty. Christ is our pattern. In humanity He lived a spotless life. He was merciful, compassionate, obedient—full of goodness and truth. By His life of obedience He gave a true representation of the law. By uniting with Christ, fallen, sinful human beings may conform the life to the divine precepts. By keeping the commandments of God, they become laborers together with Him who came to the world to represent the Father by keeping all His commandments.[1]

OUR LINK WITH HEAVEN

And lo a voice from heaven, saying, This is my beloved Son, in whom I am well pleased. Matt. 3:17.

After Christ was baptized of John in Jordan, He came up out of the water, and bowing upon the banks of the river He prayed with fervency to His heavenly Father for strength to endure the conflict with the prince of darkness in which He was about to engage. The heavens were opened to His prayer, and the light of God's glory, brighter than the sun at noonday, came from the throne of the Eternal, and assuming the form of a dove with the appearance of burnished gold, encircled the Son of God, while the clear voice from the excellent glory was heard in terrible majesty, saying, "This is my beloved Son, in whom I am well pleased."

Here was the assurance to the Son of God that His Father accepted the fallen race through their representative and that He had granted them a second trial. The communication between heaven and earth, between God and man, which had been broken by the fall of Adam, was resumed. He who knew no sin became sin for the race, that His righteousness might be imputed to man. Through the perfection of Christ's character, man was elevated in the scale of moral value with God; and through the merits of Christ, finite man was linked to the Infinite. Thus the gulf which sin had made was bridged by the world's Redeemer.

But few have a true sense of the great privileges which Christ gained for man by thus opening heaven before him. The Son of God was then the representative of our race; and the special power and glory which the Majesty of heaven conferred upon Him, and His words of approval, are the surest pledge of His love and good will to man. As Christ's intercessions in our behalf were heard, the evidence was given to man that God will accept our prayers in our own behalf through the name of Jesus. The continued, earnest prayer of faith will bring us light and strength to withstand the fiercest assaults of Satan. . . . The life of a living Christian is a life of living prayer. . . . Our great Leader points us to the open heavens as the only source of light and strength.[2]

WONDERFUL CONDESCENSION!

For ye know the grace of our Lord Jesus Christ, that, though he was rich, yet for your sakes he became poor, that ye through his poverty might be rich. 2 Cor. 8:9.

We visited the buildings which were formerly the palaces of kings when France was under kingly rule. . . . My thoughts were first upon the kings who had once traversed these grand halls and figured in these galleries. Where is their human greatness now? . . .

Then we remember Jesus, who came to our world with His blessed purposes of love, divesting Himself of His royal robe, His royal crown, stepping down from the royal throne, clothing His divinity with humanity, and coming to our world to be a Man of sorrows and acquainted with grief. We see Him among the poor, blessing the afflicted, healing the sick, soothing the infirmities of age, reaching with His divine pity the very depths of human woe and misery. He even noticed the sorrows and needs of little children. . . .

Angels have been sent as messengers of mercy to the distressed, to the suffering. These angels from the world of light, from the infinite glory of God before the throne, are on missions of love, of care, of mercy for the suffering ones of humanity. But there is a picture of greater condescension than this: the Lord, the Son of the Infinite Father, . . . the Prince of the kings of the earth. . . .

What is the work of angels in comparison with His condescension? His throne is from everlasting. He has reared every arch and pillar in nature's great temple. Behold Him, the beginning of the creation of God, who numbers the stars, who created the worlds— among which this earth is but a small speck, and would scarcely be missed from the many worlds more than a tiny leaf from the forest trees. The nations before Him are but "as a drop of a bucket," and "as the small dust of the balance" . . . (Isa. 40:15).

Contemplate Him, the Lord, the all-glorious Redeemer, an inhabitant of the world He has created, and yet unacknowledged by the very ones He manifested so great interest to bless and save. . . . What condescension to the fallen men of earth! What wondrous love! [3]

MYSTERY OF ALL MYSTERIES

Who, being in the form of God, thought it not robbery to be equal with God: but made himself of no reputation, and took upon him the form of a servant, and was made in the likeness of men: and being found in fashion as a man, he humbled himself, and became obedient unto death, even the death of the cross. Phil. 2:6-8.

Christ was Himself without spot or stain of sin, but having taken the nature of man, He was exposed to the fiercest assaults of the enemy, to his sharpest temptations, to the keenest of sorrow. He suffered being tempted. He was made like unto His brethren, that He might show that through the grace given, humanity could overcome the temptations of the enemy. . . . Listen to His words, "Lo, I come: in the volume of the book it is written of me, I delight to do thy will, O my God: yea, thy law is within my heart" (Ps. 40:7, 8). Who is it that thus announces His purpose of coming to this earth? Isaiah tells us: "Unto us a child is born, unto us a son is given: and the government shall be upon his shoulder; and his name shall be called Wonderful, Counsellor, The mighty God, The everlasting Father, The Prince of Peace" (Isa. 9:6).

"In the beginning was the Word, and the Word was with God, and the Word was God. . . . All things were made by him; and without him was not any thing made that was made. In him was life; and the life was the light of men." "And the Word was made flesh, and dwelt among us" (John 1:1-3, 14). . . .

"Without controversy great is the mystery of godliness: God was manifest in the flesh, justified in the Spirit, seen of angels, preached unto the Gentiles, believed on in the world, received up into glory." "Wherefore God also hath highly exalted him, and given him a name which is above every name: that at the name of Jesus every knee should bow, of things in heaven, and things in earth, and things under the earth; and that every tongue should confess that Jesus Christ is Lord, to the glory of God the Father." ". . . Who is the image of the invisible God, the firstborn of every creature" (1 Tim. 3:16; Phil. 2:9-11; Col. 1:14, 15).

The incarnation of Christ is the mystery of all mysteries.[4]

41

CHRIST OUR SACRIFICE AND SURETY

Who his own self bare our sins in his own body on the tree, that we, being dead to sins, should live unto righteousness: by whose stripes ye were healed. 1 Peter 2:24.

If for some crime that you had committed you were incarcerated within prison walls, with the sentence of death passed upon you, and a friend should come to you and say, "I will take your place, and you may go free," would not your heart be filled with gratitude for such unselfish love? Christ has done infinitely more than this for us. We were lost; the sentence of death had been passed upon us; and Christ died for us, and thus set us free. He said, "I will take upon Myself the guilt of the sinner, that he may have another trial. I will put within his reach power that will enable him to overcome in the struggle with evil."

This is where human beings stand today. Christ has bought us with His life, and we belong to Him. All our powers, physical, mental, and spiritual, belong to Him; and to withhold from Him that which is His own is robbery.[5]

Imagine, if possible, the nature and degree of Christ's sufferings. This suffering in humanity was to prevent the outpouring of the wrath of God upon the whole of those for whom Christ died. Yea, for the church this great sacrifice will be efficacious throughout eternity. Can we compute the amount of her transgression in figures? Impossible. Then who can approach unto a conception of what Christ has endured when standing in the place of surety for His church . . . ? . . . [He was] the only One who could bear the strokes in behalf of the sinner and because of His innocence not be consumed. . . . In the sacrifice of God's only-begotten Son is demonstrated the awful glory of divine justice and holiness.[6]

By pledging His own life Christ has made Himself responsible for every man and woman on the earth. He stands in the presence of God, saying, "Father, I take upon Myself the guilt of that soul. It means death to him if he is left to bear it. If he repents he shall be forgiven. My blood shall cleanse him from all sin. I gave My life for the sins of the world."[7]

A VOLUNTARY SACRIFICE

For ye are bought with a price: therefore glorify God in your body and in your spirit, which are God's. 1 Cor. 6:20.

How earnestly Christ prosecuted the work of our salvation! What devotion His life revealed as He sought to give value to fallen man by imputing to every repenting, believing sinner the merits of His spotless righteousness! How untiringly He worked! In the Temple and the synagogue, in the streets of the cities, in the market place, in the workshop, by the seaside, among the hills, He preached the gospel and healed the sick. He gave all there was of Himself, that He might work out the plan of redeeming grace.

Christ was under no obligation to make this great sacrifice. Voluntarily He pledged Himself to bear the punishment due to the transgressor of His law. His love was His only obligation, and without a murmur He endured every pang and welcomed every indignity that was part of the plan of salvation.

The life of Christ was one of unselfish service, and His life is our lesson book. The work that He began we are to carry forward. With His life of toil and sacrifice before them, can those who profess His name hesitate to deny self, to lift the cross and follow Him? He humbled Himself to the lowest depths that we might be lifted to the heights of purity and holiness and completeness. He became poor that He might pour into our poverty-stricken souls the fullness of His riches. He endured the cross of shame, that He might give us peace and rest and joy and make us partakers of the glories of His throne. . . .

Should we not give back to God all that He has redeemed, the affections He has purified, and the body that He has purchased, to be kept unto sanctification and holiness? . . .

True Christianity diffuses love through the whole being. It touches every vital part—the brain, the heart, the helping hands, the feet—enabling men to stand firmly where God requires them to stand. . . . We can, *we can,* reveal the likeness of our divine Lord. We can know the science of spiritual life. We can glorify God in our bodies and in our spirits, which are His.[8]

43

BREAKING THE POWER OF DEATH

I will ransom them from the power of the grave; I will redeem them from death: O death, I will be thy plagues; O grave, I will be thy destruction. Hosea 13:14.

Well might all heaven be astonished at the reception their loved Commander received in the world! . . . He made the world, and yet the world knew Him not. Friends denied Him, forsook Him, and betrayed Him. He was assailed by temptation. Human agony convulsed His divine soul. He was lacerated with cruel scourgings. His hands were pierced with nails, His holy temples were crowned with thorns. . . . It was the working of Satan's machinations that made the life of Christ one dark series of afflictions and sadness; and at last he compassed Christ's death. . . .

In the act of dying, Christ was destroying him who had the power of death. He carried out the plan, finished the work which from Adam's fall He had covenanted to undertake. By dying for the guilt of a sinful world, He reinstated fallen man, on condition of obedience to God's commandments, in the position from which he had fallen in consequence of disobedience. And when He broke the fetters of the tomb and rose triumphant from the dead He answered the question, "If a man die, shall he live again?" (Job 14:14). Christ made it possible that every child of Adam might, through a life of obedience, overcome sin and rise also from the grave to his heritage of immortality purchased by the blood of Christ.

Our salvation was wrought out by infinite suffering to the Son of God. His divine bosom received the anguish, the agony, the pain that the sinfulness of Adam brought upon the race. The heel of Christ was indeed bruised when His humanity suffered, and grief heavier than that which ever oppressed the beings He had created weighed down His soul as He was engaged in paying the vast debt which man owed to God.[9]

The question, "If a man die, shall he live again?" has been answered. . . . God in human form has brought life and immortality to light through the gospel. In dying, Christ secured eternal life for all who believe in Him.[10]

44

A FRIEND IN THE HEAVENLY COURT

Blessed be the God and Father of our Lord Jesus Christ, which according to his abundant mercy hath begotten us again unto a lively hope by the resurrection of Jesus Christ from the dead, to an inheritance incorruptible, and undefiled, and that fadeth not away, reserved in heaven for you. 1 Peter 1:3, 4.

Is there any reason why this lively hope should not give us as much confidence and joy at this time as it gave the disciples in the early church? Christ is not enclosed in Joseph's new tomb. He is risen, and has ascended up on high, and we are to act out our faith, that the world may see that we have a lively hope. . . .

Our hope is not without foundation; our inheritance is not corruptible. It is not the subject of imagination.[11]

We read in the Bible about the resurrection of Christ from the dead, but do we act as though we believed it? Do we believe that Jesus is a living Saviour, that He is not in Joseph's new tomb, with the great stone rolled before it, but that He has risen from the dead and ascended on high . . . ? He is there to plead our cases in the courts of heaven. He is there because we need a friend in the heavenly court, One who is to be our advocate and intercessor. Then let us rejoice in this. We have everything for which to praise God.

Many judge of their religious state by their emotions, but these are not a safe criterion. Our Christian life does not depend upon our feelings, but upon our having a right hold from above. We must believe the words of God just as He has spoken them; we must take Christ at His word, believe that He came to represent the Father, and that the Father, as is represented in Christ, is our friend, and that He desires not that we should perish, or He would never have given His Son to die our sacrifice. The cross of Calvary is an eternal pledge to every one of us that God wants us to be happy, not only in the future life but in this life.[12]

The death of Christ brings to the rejector of His mercy the wrath and judgments of God, unmixed with mercy. This is the wrath of the Lamb. But the death of Christ is hope and eternal life to all who receive Him and believe in Him.[13]

AN HONORED GUEST

Behold, I stand at the door, and knock: if any man hear my voice, and open the door, I will come in to him, and will sup with him, and he with me. Rev. 3:20.

All who will open their hearts to receive Him may have Jesus as an honored guest.[14]

Jesus is the perfect pattern. Instead of trying to please self and have our own way, let us seek to reflect His image. He was kind and courteous, compassionate and tender. Are we like Him in these respects? Do we seek to make our lives fragrant with good works? . . .

It is not enough that we merely profess the faith; something more than a nominal assent is wanted. There must be a real knowledge, a genuine experience in the principles of the truth as it is in Jesus. The Holy Spirit must work within, bringing these principles into the strong light of distinct consciousness, that we may know their power and make them a living reality. . . .

God has honored His Son by making Him the model after which He molds the characters of all who believe on Him. He takes of the things of Christ and reveals them to us, that we may catch His temper and bear His likeness. . . .

The obstacles, provocations, and hardships that we meet, may prove to us, not a curse, but the greatest blessings of our lives; for the grandest characters are built amid hardships and trials. But they must be received as practical lessons in the school of Christ. Every temptation resisted, every trial bravely borne, gives us a new experience and advances us in the work of character building. We have a better knowledge of the working of Satan, and of our own power to defeat him through divine grace.

Jesus was the light of the world. . . . It is our privilege to walk in the sunshine of His presence and to weave into the characters we are forming the golden threads of cheerfulness, gratitude, forbearance, and love. We may thus show the power of divine grace and reflect light from Heaven amid all the frets and irritations that come to us day by day.[14]

OUR SURE FOUNDATION

For other foundation can no man lay than that is laid, which is Jesus Christ. Now if any man build upon this foundation gold, silver, precious stones, wood, hay, stubble; every man's work shall be made manifest: for the day shall declare it, because it shall be revealed by fire; and the fire shall try every man's work of what sort it is. 1 Cor. 3:11-13.

As fire reveals the difference between gold, silver, and precious stones, and wood, hay, and stubble, so the day of judgment will test characters, showing the difference between characters formed after Christ's likeness and characters formed after the likeness of the selfish heart. All selfishness, all false religion, will then appear as it is. The worthless material will be consumed; but the gold of true, simple, humble faith will never lose its value. It can never be consumed; for it is imperishable.[15]

Anyone can be just what he chooses to be. Character is not obtained by receiving an education. Character is not obtained by amassing wealth or by gaining worldly honor. Character is not obtained by having others fight the battle of life for us. It must be sought, worked for, fought for; and it requires a purpose, a will, a determination. To form a character which God will approve, requires persevering effort. It will take a continual resisting of the powers of darkness to . . . have our names retained in the book of life. Is it not worth more to have our names registered in that book, have them immortalized among the heavenly angels, than to have them sounded in praise throughout the whole earth?[16]

In the probationary time granted us here we are each building a structure that is to have the inspection of the Judge of all the earth. This work is the molding of our characters. Every act of our lives is a stone in that building, every faculty is a worker, every blow that is struck is for good or for evil. The words of inspiration warn us to take heed how we build, to see that our foundation is sure. If we build upon the solid rock, pure, noble, upright deeds, the structure will go up beautiful and symmetrical, a fit temple for the indwelling of the Holy Spirit.[17]

47

UNDER WHICH STANDARD?

No man can serve two masters: for either he will hate the one, and love the other; or else he will hold to the one, and despise the other. Ye cannot serve God and mammon. Matt. 6:24.

Every individual in our world will be arrayed under one of two banners—the chosen and loyal under the blood-stained banner of Prince Immanuel, and all others under Satan's standard. . . .

There is to be no compromise with the powers of darkness. Individually we must take our stand. If we are not at enmity with the prince of darkness, the serpent, his folds encircle us and all our powers; his sting is in our hearts. All who range themselves under the blood-stained banner of the Prince of Life will henceforth count Satan as a foe, and will in God's strength oppose him as a deadly enemy. They will take the helmet of salvation and the sword of the Spirit, which is the Word of God. And what will they do in order to hold vantage ground? "Praying always with all prayer and supplication in the Spirit, and watching thereunto with all perseverance" (Eph. 6:18). . . .

We should be quick to discern danger. We should see the hateful character of sin and should expel it from the soul. The doers of the Word know that in Jesus there is strength, which becomes their own by faith. They are clothed with righteousness that God will accept, for it is the righteousness of Christ. Clad in this armor of God, the panoply of heaven, they successfully resist the serpent's wiles. Not one soul has a moment to lose. . . . The concerns of eternity are of sufficient importance to take precedence over every other enterprise. "What must I do to be saved?" should be the great and solemn question with us now.[18]

I wish that all could appreciate the wonderful working of God in behalf of man. For fallen angels there has been no atonement; but for fallen man a full and ample offering has been made, to save to the uttermost all who shall come unto God by Him.[18]

God beholds in all His children the image of His only-begotten Son. He looks upon them with a love greater than any language can express. He enfolds them in the arms of His love. The Lord rejoices over His people.[18]

48

INESTIMABLE TREASURE

The kingdom of heaven is like unto a merchantman, seeking goodly pearls: who, when he had found one pearl of great price, went and sold all that he had, and bought it. Matt. 13:45, 46.

When Christ compared the kingdom of heaven to a pearl of great price He desired to lead every soul to appreciate that pearl above all else. The possession of the pearl, which means the possession of Christ as a personal Saviour, is a symbol of the highest riches. It is a treasure above every earthly treasure. . . .

There are some who are seeking, always seeking, for the goodly pearl. But they do not make an entire surrender of their wrong habits. They do not die to self that Christ may live in them. Therefore they do not find the precious pearl. . . . They never know what it is to have peace and harmony in the soul; for without entire self-surrender there is no rest, no joy. Almost Christians, yet not fully Christians, they seem near the kingdom of heaven, but they cannot enter there. Almost but not wholly saved means to be not almost but wholly lost. . . .

In the parable the merchantman is represented as selling all that he had to gain possession of one pearl of great price. This is a beautiful representation of those who appreciate the truth so highly that they give up all they have to come into possession of it. They lay hold by faith of the salvation provided for man at the sacrifice of the only-begotten Son of God. The righteousness of Christ, as a pure, white pearl, has no defect, no guilt, no stain. No work of man can improve the great and precious truths of God's Word. They are not a mixture of truth and error. They are without a flaw. . . .

Christ is ready to receive all who come to Him in sincerity. But He will not tolerate one particle of pretense or hypocrisy. He is our only hope. He is our Alpha and Omega. He is our sun and our shield, our wisdom, our sanctification, our righteousness. Only by His power can our hearts be kept daily in the love of God. . . .

Salvation, with its blood-bought, inestimable treasures, is the pearl of great price. It may be searched for and found. But all who really find it will sell all they have to buy it.[19]

49

ABUNDANTLY PARDONED

Let the wicked forsake his way, and the unrighteous man his thoughts: and let him return unto the Lord, and he will have mercy upon him: and to our God, for he will abundantly pardon. Isa. 55:7.

Many do not move in the confidence of a living assurance that Christ is pleading before the Father as our Intercessor. Christ has identified Himself with our necessities, and is able to supply every peculiar need of our weakness. During His life on this earth He took the attitude of a suppliant, an earnest petitioner, seeking at the hand of the Father a fresh supply of strength, that He might be invigorated and refreshed and come forth with words of encouragement and lessons of consolation to impart to human beings. His words are to brace every soul for duty and strengthen every soul for trial.

As Christ in His humanity sought strength from His Father, that He might be enabled to endure trial and temptation, so are we to do. We are to follow the example of the sinless Son of God. Daily we need help and grace and power from the Source of all power. We are to cast our helpless souls upon the One who is ready to help us in every time of need. Too often we forget the Lord. Self gives way to impulse, and we lose the victories that we should gain.

If we are overcome let us not delay to repent, and to accept the pardon that will place us on vantage ground. If we repent and believe, the cleansing power from God will be ours. His saving grace is freely offered. His pardon is given to all who will receive it. . . .

God will always accept confession if the evil that has been done is repented of. Our heavenly Father makes the declaration, "As I live, . . . I have no pleasure in the death of the wicked; but that the wicked should turn from his way and live" (Eze. 33:11). Over every sinner that repents the angels of God rejoice with songs of joy. Not one sinner need be lost. Full and free is the gift of saving grace. . . .

We are living in the day of preparation. We must obtain a full supply of grace from the divine storehouse. The Lord has made provision for every day's demand.[20]

ROBED IN CHRIST'S RIGHTEOUSNESS

Blessed are they whose iniquities are forgiven, and whose sins are covered. Blessed is the man to whom the Lord will not impute sin. Rom. 4:7, 8.

Well may our hearts turn to our Redeemer with the most perfect trust when we think of what He has done for us, even when we were sinners. Through faith we may rest in His love. "Him that cometh to me," He says, "I will in no wise cast out" (John 6:37).

It would be a terrible thing to stand before God clothed in sinful garments, with His eye reading every secret of our lives. But through the efficacy of Christ's sacrifice we may stand before God pure and spotless, our sins atoned for and pardoned. "If we confess our sins, he is faithful and just to forgive us our sins, and to cleanse us from all unrighteousness" (1 John 1:9). The redeemed sinner, clothed in the robes of Christ's righteousness, may stand in the presence of a sin-hating God, made perfect by the merits of the Saviour.[21]

Only through faith in Christ's name can the sinner be saved. . . . Faith in Christ is not the work of nature, but the work of God on human minds, wrought in the very soul by the Holy Spirit, who reveals Christ, as Christ revealed the Father. Faith is the substance of things hoped for, the evidence of things not seen. With its justifying, sanctifying power, it is above what men call science. It is the science of eternal realities. Human science is often deceptive and misleading, but this heavenly science never misleads. It is so simple that a child may understand it, and yet the most learned men cannot explain it. It is inexplainable and immeasurable, beyond all human expression.[22]

What inexpressible love has the Saviour manifested toward the children of men! Not only does He take off the brand of sin, but He cleanses and purifies the soul, clothing it in the robe of His own righteousness, which is without spot, woven in the loom of heaven. He not only lifts the curse from the sinner, but brings him into oneness with Himself, reflecting upon him the bright beams of His righteousness. He is welcomed by the heavenly universe, accepted in the beloved Son of God. What glory can fallen man, through repentance and faith, bring back to God![23]

51

IN THE SUNLIGHT OF THE CROSS

Looking unto Jesus the author and finisher of our faith; who for the joy that was set before him endured the cross, despising the shame, and is set down at the right hand of the throne of God. Heb. 12:2.

The cross speaks life, and not death, to the soul that believes in Jesus. Welcome the precious life-giving rays that shine from the cross of Calvary. Reach up for the blessing, believe for the blessing. . . .

Walk not in the shadow of the cross. Do not give expression to weeping, lamentation, and woe; but encourage your soul to hope and joy. The cross points upward to a living Saviour, who is your advocate, and is pleading in your behalf. . . . When you are deeply shadowed it is because Satan has interposed himself between you and the bright rays of the Sun of Righteousness. . . .

I have indeed been halting under the shadow of the cross. It is not a common thing for me to be overpowered and to suffer so much depression of spirits as I have suffered for the last few months. I would not be found to trifle with my own soul and thus trifle with my Saviour. I would not teach that Jesus is risen from the tomb, and that He is ascended on high and lives to make intercession for us before the Father, unless I carry out my teachings by practice and believe in Him for His salvation, casting my helpless soul upon Jesus for His grace, for righteousness, for peace and love.

I must trust in Him irrespective of the changes of my emotional atmosphere. I must show forth the praises of Him who has called me out of darkness into His marvelous light. My heart must be steadfast in Christ, my Saviour, beholding His love and gracious goodness. I must not trust Him now and then, but always, that I may manifest the results of abiding in Him who has bought me with His precious blood. We must learn to believe the promises, to have an abiding faith. . . .

Let us live in the sunlight of the cross of Calvary. Let us no longer dwell in the shadow, complaining of our sorrows, for this only deepens our trouble. Let us never forget, even when we walk in the valley, that Christ is as much with us when we walk trustingly there as when we are on the mountaintop.[24]

UNDER CHRIST'S YOKE

Come unto me, all ye that labour and are heavy laden, and I will give you rest. Take my yoke upon you, and learn of me; for I am meek and lowly in heart: and ye shall find rest unto your souls. Matt. 11:28, 29.

Our Saviour purchased the human race by humiliation of the very severest kind. . . . He points us to the only path that will lead to the strait gate, opening into the narrow way, beyond which lie broad and pleasant pastures. He has marked out every step of the way; and that no one may make a mistake, He tells us just what to do. "Take my yoke upon you, and learn of me; for I am meek and lowly in heart: and ye shall find rest unto your souls. For my yoke is easy, and my burden is light" (Matt. 11:29, 30). This is the only way in which sinners can be saved. Knowing that no one can obey this command in his own strength, Christ tells us not to be worried nor afraid, but to remember what He can do if we come to Him, trusting in His strength. He says, If you yoke up with Me, your Redeemer, I will be your strength, your efficiency.

The blessings connected with Christ's invitation can be realized and enjoyed by those only who wear Christ's yoke. Accepting this invitation, you withdraw your sympathy, your affections, from the world, and place them where you can enjoy the blessing of close fellowship and communion with God. By coming to Christ, you bind up your interests with His.

The Lord has determined that every soul who obeys His word shall have His joy, His peace, His continual keeping power. Such men and women are brought near Him always, not only when they kneel before Him in prayer, but when they take up the duties of life. He has prepared for them an abiding place with Himself, where the life is purified from all grossness, all unloveliness. By this unbroken communion with Him, they are made colaborers with Him in their lifework. . . .

He invites us, Come unto Me. Take My yoke upon you. I require you to do nothing that I have not done before you. All I ask you to do is to follow My example. Walk in the path I have marked out. Place your feet in My footsteps.[25]

53

ONLY ONE PATTERN

But we all, with open face beholding as in a glass the glory of the Lord, are changed into the same image from glory to glory, even as by the Spirit of the Lord. 2 Cor. 3:18.

If we gaze even a moment upon the sun in its meridian glory, when we turn away our eyes, the image of the sun will appear in everything upon which we look. Thus it is when we behold Jesus; everything we look upon reflects His image, the Sun of Righteousness. We cannot see anything else, or talk of anything else. His image is imprinted upon the eye of the soul, and affects every portion of our daily life, softening and subduing our whole nature. By beholding, we are conformed to the divine similitude, even the likeness of Christ. To all with whom we associate we reflect the bright and cheerful beams of His righteousness.[26]

Jesus was a perfect pattern of what we should be. He was the strictest observer of His Father's law, yet He moved in perfect freedom. He had all the fervor of the enthusiast, yet He was calm, sober, and self-possessed. He was elevated above the common affairs of the world, yet He did not exclude Himself from society. He dined with publicans and sinners, played with little children, and took them in His arms and blessed them. He graced the wedding feast with His presence. He shed tears at the grave of Lazarus. He was a lover of the beautiful in nature and used the lilies to illustrate the value of natural simplicity in the sight of God, above artificial display. He used the occupation of the husbandman to illustrate the most sublime truths. . . .

His zeal never degenerated into passion nor His consistency into selfish obstinacy. His benevolence never savored of weakness nor His sympathy of sentimentalism. He combined the innocence and simplicity of the child with manly strength, all-absorbing devotion to God with tender love for man. He possessed commanding dignity combined with winning grace of humility. He manifested unyielding firmness with gentleness. May we live daily in close connection with this perfect, faultless character.[27]

We have not six patterns to follow, nor five; we have only one, and that is Christ Jesus.[28]

54

ABIDING IN CHRIST

Abide in me, and I in you. As the branch cannot bear fruit of itself, except it abide in the vine; no more can ye, except ye abide in me. John 15:4.

It is not a casual touch with Christ that is needed, but it is to abide with Him. He called you to abide with Him. He does not propose to you a short-lived blessedness that is realized occasionally through earnest seeking of the Lord and passes away as you engage in the common duties of life. Your abiding with Christ makes every necessary duty light, for He bears the weight of every burden. He has prepared for you to abide with Him. This means that you are to be conscious of an abiding Christ, that you are continually with Christ, where your mind is encouraged and strengthened. . . .

Do not stand outside of Christ, as many professed Christians of today. To "abide in me, and I in you" is a possible thing to do, and the invitation would not be given if you could not do this. Jesus our Saviour is constantly drawing you by His Holy Spirit, working with your mind that you will abide with Christ. . . . The blessings He bestows are all connected with your own individual action. Shall Christ be refused? He says, "Him that cometh to me I will in no wise cast out" (John 6:37). Of another class He says, "Ye will not come to me, that ye might have life" (John 5:40). . . .

Have you, have I, fully comprehended the gracious call, "Come unto me"? He says, "Abide *in* me," not Abide *with* Me. "Do understand My call. Come to Me to stay with Me." He will freely bestow all blessings connected with Himself upon all who come to Him for life. He has something better for you than a short-lived blessedness that you feel when you seek the Lord in earnest prayer. That is but as a drop in the bucket, to have a word with Christ. You are privileged with His abiding presence in the place of a short-lived privilege that is not lasting as you engage in the duties of life. . . . Will anxiety, perplexity, and cares drive you away from Christ? Are we less dependent upon God when in the workshop, in the field, in the market-place? . . . The Lord Jesus will abide with you and you with Him in every place.[29]

55

ONE WITH CHRIST

I am the vine, ye are the branches. He that abideth in me, and I in him, the same bringeth forth much fruit; for without me ye can do nothing. John 15:5.

Christ's connection with His believing people is illustrated by this parable as by no other.[30]

All who receive Christ by faith become one with Him. The branches are not tied to the vine; they are not joined to it by any mechanical process of artificial fastening. They are united to the vine, so as to become part of it. They are nourished by the roots of the vine. So those who receive Christ by faith become one with Him in principle and action. They are united to Him, and the life they live is the life of the Son of God. They derive their life from Him who is life.

Baptism may be repeated over and over again, but of itself it has no power to change the human heart. The heart must be united with Christ's heart, the will must be submerged in His will, the mind must become one with His mind, the thoughts must be brought into captivity to Him. . . . The regenerated man has a vital connection with Christ. As the branch derives its sustenance from the parent stock and, because of this, bears much fruit, so the true believer, united with Christ, reveals in his life the fruits of the Spirit. The branch becomes one with the vine; storm cannot carry it away; frost cannot destroy its vital properties. Nothing is able to separate it from the vine. It is a living branch, and it bears the fruit of the vine. So with the believer. By good words and good actions he reveals the character of Christ. . . .

Christ has provided means whereby our whole life may be an unbroken communion with Himself; but the sense of Christ's abiding presence can come only through living faith. . . .

Let all contemplate the completeness it is their privilege to have and ask themselves the question, Is my will submerged in Christ's will? Is the fullness and richness of the Living Vine—His goodness, His mercy, His compassion and love—seen in my life and character? [30]

56

TRUE TO OUR NAME

He that saith he abideth in him ought himself also so to walk, even as he walked. 1 John 2:6.

We bear the name of Christian. Let us be true to this name. To be a Christian means to be Christlike. It means to follow Christ in self-denial, bearing aloft His banner of love, honoring Him by unselfish words and deeds. In the life of the true Christian there is nothing of self—self is dead. There was no selfishness in the life that Christ lived while on this earth. Bearing our nature, He lived a life wholly devoted to the good of others. . . . In word and deed Christ's followers are to be pure and true. In this world—a world of iniquity and corruption—Christians are to reveal the attributes of Christ. All they do and say is to be free from selfishness. . . .

Said the great apostle to the Gentiles, "I live; yet not I, but Christ liveth in me: and the life which I now live in the flesh I live by the faith of the Son of God, who loved me, and gave himself for me" (Gal. 2:20). By faith Paul appropriated the grace of Christ, and this grace supplied the necessities of his soul. By faith he received the heavenly gift, and imparted it to souls longing for light. This is the experience we need. . . . Pray for this faith. Strive for it. Believe that God will give it to you. . . .

Learn of Him who has said, "I am meek and lowly in heart" (Matt. 11:29). Learning of Him, you will find rest. Day by day you will gain an experience in the things of God, day by day realize the greatness of His salvation and the glory of a union with Him. Constantly you will learn better how to live Christlike, and constantly you will grow more like the Saviour.

If we will die to self, if we will enlarge our idea of what Christ can be to us and what we can be to Him, if we will unite with one another in the bonds of Christian fellowship, God will work through us with mighty power. Then we shall be sanctified through the truth. We shall indeed be chosen by God and controlled by His Spirit. Every day of life will be precious to us, because we shall see in it an opportunity to use our entrusted gifts for the blessing of others.[31]

HOW MUCH DOES GOD LOVE US?

I in them, and thou in me, that they may be made perfect in one; and that the world may know that thou hast sent me, and hast loved them, as thou hast loved me. John 17:23.

It seems almost too good to believe that the Father can and does love any member of the human family as He loves His Son. But we have the assurance that He does, and this assurance should bring joy to every heart, awakening the highest reverence and calling forth unspeakable gratitude. God's love is not uncertain and unreal, but a living reality.[32]

The Creator of all worlds proposes to love those who believe in His only-begotten Son as their personal Saviour, even as He loves His Son. Even here and now His gracious favor is bestowed upon us to this marvelous extent. . . . Much as He has promised us for the life to come, He also bestows princely gifts upon us in this life, and as subjects of His grace, He would have us enjoy everything that will ennoble, expand, and elevate our characters. It is His design to fit us for the heavenly courts above.[33]

Those who live in close fellowship with Christ will be promoted by Him to positions of trust. The servant who does the best he can for his master is admitted to familiar intercourse with one whose commands he loves to obey. In the faithful discharge of duty we may become one with Christ, for those who are obeying God's commands may speak to Him freely. The one who talks most familiarly with his divine Leader has the most exalted conception of His greatness and is the most obedient to His commands.[34]

In the life of man things sacred and secular are to be done, some in business lines, some in the ministry of the Word, and some in various trades; but when a man gives himself to Christ and loves God with the whole heart, mind, soul, and strength, he serves with a devotion that takes his whole being. . . . He recognizes the ownership of his powers and the ownership of himself. This consecration invests his whole life with a sacredness which makes him gentle, kind, and courteous. His every act is a consecrated act. . . . He is under Christ, being trained for the higher grade above.[35]

58

"PARTAKERS OF THE DIVINE NATURE"

Whereby are given unto us exceeding great and precious promises: that by these ye might be partakers of the divine nature, having escaped the corruption that is in the world through lust. 2 Peter 1:4.

"Partakers of the divine nature." Is this possible? Of ourselves we can do no good thing. How, then, can we be partakers of the divine nature? By coming to Christ just as we are, needy, helpless, dependent. He died to make it possible for us to be partakers of the divine nature. He took humanity upon Himself that He might reach humanity. With the golden chain of His matchless love He has bound us to the throne of God. We are to have power to overcome as He overcame.

To all He gives the invitation: "Come unto me. . . . Take my yoke upon you, and learn of me; for I am meek and lowly in heart: and ye shall find rest unto your souls . . ." (Matt. 11:28-30).

We have a part to act in this work. Let none think that men and women are going to be taken to heaven without engaging in the struggle here below. We have a battle to fight, a victory to gain. God says to us, "Work out your own salvation." How? "With fear and trembling. For it is God which worketh in you both to will and to do of His good pleasure" (Phil. 2:12, 13). God works, and man works. . . . Thus only can we be partakers of the divine nature.

Here is the consistency of true religion. We are to be "labourers together with God," working in harmony with Him. "Ye are God's husbandry, ye are God's building" (1 Cor. 3:9). This figure represents human character, which is to be wrought upon point by point. Each day God works on His building to perfect the structure, that it may become a holy temple for Him. Man is to cooperate with God, striving in His strength to make himself what God designs him to be, building his life with pure, noble deeds. . . .

God asks us to live only one day at a time. You need not look a week or a month ahead. *Today* do your best. Today speak and act in a way that will honor God. The promise is, "As thy days, so shall thy strength be" (Deut. 33:25).[36]

59

LIVING ABUNDANTLY

I am come that they might have life, and that they might have it more abundantly. John 10:10.

There can be no such thing as a narrow life for any soul connected with Christ. Those who love Jesus with heart and mind and soul and their neighbor as themselves have a broad field in which to use their ability and influence. There is no talent to be used for selfish gratification. Self must die, and our lives be hid with Christ in God. . . .

The Lord would have us value our souls according to the estimate —as far as we can comprehend it—that Christ has placed upon them. . . . Jesus died that He might redeem man from eternal ruin. Then we are to hold ourselves as property purchased. "Ye are not your own." "Ye are bought with a price: therefore glorify God in your body, and in your spirit, which are God's" (1 Cor. 6:19, 20). All our powers of mind and soul and body are the Lord's. Our time belongs to Him. We are to place ourselves in the very best possible condition to do His service, keeping constantly in connection with Christ, and considering daily the costly sacrifice made for us that we should be made the righteousness of God in Him. . . .

Those who are emptied of self, the thoughtful and conscientious, cannot raise their eyes to Christ, the living Saviour, without feelings of awe and the deepest humility. To behold Jesus continually will make the soul alive unto God. We shall love Jesus, we shall love the Father who sent Him into the world, for we see Him in a wondrous light, full of grace and truth. Jesus declares, "All things are delivered unto me of my Father" (Matt. 11:27); . . . "All power is given unto me in heaven and in earth" (Matt. 28:18). What for? That He may give gifts unto men, that they may lay all their powers under tribute to make known the wondrous love wherewith He hath loved us. . . .

When we estimate all our talents in the light of the cross of Calvary, we shall so live for Christ and so let our light shine before men that our lives will never again seem narrow. Who can estimate the value of the soul? [37]

"WITHOUT OFFENCE"

That ye may approve things that are excellent; that ye may be sincere and without offence till the day of Christ; being filled with the fruits of righteousness, which are by Jesus Christ, unto the glory and praise of God. Phil. 1:10, 11.

The Lord presents before His finite creatures no impossibilities. . . . The power of a higher, purer, nobler life is our great need. God's people are to be filled with holy joy, that its radiance may shine forth from them, brightening the pathway of others. What power, what peace, what joy the soul may have that is united with Christ! The divine splendor is revealed to those who commune with Him who is the source of power.

We know little of the peace and happiness and joy of heaven. We need more efficiency. We need to receive from Christ the water of life, that it may be in us a well of water, refreshing all who come within the sphere of our influence. . . .

At our baptism we pledged ourselves to break all connection with Satan and his agencies, and to put heart and mind and soul into the work of extending the kingdom of God. All heaven is working for this object. The Father, the Son, and the Holy Spirit are pledged to cooperate with sanctified human instrumentalities. If we are true to our vow, there is opened to us a door of communication with heaven —a door that no human hand or satanic agency can close. . . .

Moral and spiritual perfection, through the grace and power of Christ, is promised to all who believe. At every step we are to ask for the help of Christ. He is the model we are to follow in character building. He calls for deeds, not words, saying, "Let your light so shine before men, that they may see your good works, and glorify your Father which is in heaven" (Matt. 5:16). . . .

Christ is the source of light, the fountain of life. . . . It is His purpose that human beings, purified and sanctified, shall be His helping hand. He leads us to the throne of God and gives us a prayer to offer to Him. When we live this prayer we are brought into close contact with Christ; at every step we touch His living power. In our behalf He sets in operation the all-powerful agencies of heaven.[38]

61

THE HAPPIEST PEOPLE

Thou wilt shew me the path of life: in thy presence is fulness of joy; at thy right hand there are pleasures for evermore. Ps. 16:11.

Do not think that when you walk with Jesus you must walk in the shadow. The happiest people in the world are those who trust in Jesus and gladly do His bidding. From the lives of those who follow Him, unrest and discontent are banished. . . . They may meet with trial and difficulty, but their lives are full of joy; for Christ walks beside them, and His presence makes the pathway bright. . . .

When you arise in the morning, rise with the praise of God on your lips, and when you go out to work, go with a prayer to God for help. . . . Wait for a leaf from the tree of life. This will soothe and refresh you, filling your heart with peace and joy. Fix your thoughts upon the Saviour. Go apart from the bustle of the world and sit under Christ's shadow. Then, amid the din of daily toil and conflict, your strength will be renewed. It is positively necessary for us to sit down sometimes and think of how the Saviour descended from heaven, from the throne of God, to show what human beings may become if they will unite their weakness to His strength. Having gained renewal of strength by communion with God, we may go on our way rejoicing, praising Him for the privilege of bringing the sunshine of Christ's love into the lives of those we meet. . . .

Heavenly intelligences are waiting to cooperate with human instrumentalities, that the world may see what human beings may become through a union with the divine. Those who consecrate body, soul, and spirit to God's service will constantly receive a new endowment of physical, mental, and spiritual power. The inexhaustible supplies of heaven are at their command. Christ gives them the life of His life. The Holy Spirit puts forth its highest energies to work in mind and heart. Through the grace given us we may achieve victories which, because of our defects of character and the smallness of our faith, may have seemed to us impossible.

To every one who offers himself to the Lord for service, withholding nothing, is given power for the attainment of measureless results.[39]

GRACE AND DIGNITY IN DAILY DUTIES

His speech [margin] is most sweet: yea, he is altogether lovely.
S. of Sol. 5:16.

Study the life that Christ lived while on this earth. He did not neglect the smallest, simplest duty. Perfection marked all that He did. Look to Him for help, and you will be enabled to perform your daily duties with the grace and dignity of one who is seeking for the crown of immortal life.

We dwell much on the grandeur of Christ's life. We speak of the great things that He accomplished, of the miracles He wrought, of how He spoke peace to the tempestuous waters, restored sight to the blind and hearing to the deaf, and raised the dead to life. But His attention to small things is even higher proof of His greatness. Listen to Him speaking to Martha as she comes to Him with the request that He bid her sister help her with the serving. He tells her not to allow the cares of the household to disturb the peace of her soul. "Martha, Martha," He says, "thou art careful and troubled about many things: but one thing is needful: and Mary hath chosen that good part, which shall not be taken away from her" (Luke 10:41, 42).

Listen to the words that He spoke as the weary mothers brought their children to Him to be blessed. The disciples, unwilling that their Master should be disturbed, were sending the women away, but Christ said, "Suffer the little children to come unto me, and forbid them not: for of such is the kingdom of God" (Mark 10:14). And taking them in His arms, He blessed them. Could the future of these children be opened before us we could see the mothers recalling to the minds of the children the scene of that day and repeating the loving words of the Saviour. . . . This same Jesus is your Saviour.[40]

The divine beauty of the character of Christ, of whom the noblest and most gentle among men are but a faint reflection; of whom Solomon by the Spirit of inspiration wrote, He is "the chiefest among ten thousand. . . . Yea, he is altogether lovely"; . . . the self-denying Redeemer, throughout His pilgrimage of love on earth was a living representation of the character of the law of God.[41]

"MORE THAN CONQUERORS"

In all these things we are more than conquerors through him that loved us. Rom. 8:37.

Through the power that Jesus gives, we can be "more than conquerors." But we cannot manufacture this power. Only through the Spirit of God can we receive it.

We need a deep insight into the nature of Christ and into the mystery of His love, "which passeth knowledge" (Eph. 3:19). We are to live in the warm, genial rays of the Sun of Righteousness. Nothing but Christ's loving compassion, His divine grace, His almighty power, can enable us to baffle the relentless foe and subdue the opposition of our own hearts. What is our strength? The joy of the Lord. Let the love of Christ fill our hearts, and then we shall be prepared to receive the power that He has for us.

Let us thank God every day for the blessings that are ours. If the human agent will humble himself before God, . . . realizing his utter inability to do the work that needs to be done in order that his soul may be purified; if he will cast away his own righteousness, Christ will abide in his heart. He will put His hand to the work of creating him anew, and will continue the work till he is complete in Him. . . .

Beholding Christ for the purpose of becoming like Him, the seeker after truth sees the perfection of the principles of God's law, and he becomes dissatisfied with everything but perfection. . . . But he knows that with the Redeemer there is saving power that will gain for him the victory in the conflict. The Saviour will strengthen and help him as he comes pleading for grace and efficiency.[42]

Christ will never neglect the work that has been placed in His hands. He will inspire the resolute disciple with a sense of the perversity, the sin-stained condition, the depravity, of the heart upon which He is working. The true penitent learns the uselessness of self-importance. Looking to Jesus, comparing his own defective character with the Saviour's perfect character, he says only—

"In my hand no price I bring;
Simply to Thy cross I cling."[42]

THE CHRISTIAN'S ALL IN ALL

But Christ is all, and in all. Col. 3:11.

Christ, the precious Saviour, is to be the Christian's all in all. Every holy thought, every pure desire, every godlike purpose, is from Him who is the light, the truth, and the way. Christ is to live in His representatives by the Spirit of truth. . . . Paul says, "I am crucified with Christ: nevertheless I live; yet not I, but Christ liveth in me: and the life which I now live in the flesh I live by the faith of the Son of God, who loved me, and gave himself for me" (Gal. 2:20). . . .

Under the mighty impulse of His love He took our place in the universe and invited the Ruler of all things to treat Him as a representative of the human family. He identified Himself with our interests, bared His breast for the stroke of death, took man's guilt and its penalty, and offered in man's behalf a complete sacrifice to God. By virtue of this atonement He has power to offer to man perfect righteousness and full salvation. Whosoever shall believe on Him as a personal Saviour shall not perish but have everlasting life.[43]

Jesus identifies His interest with His chosen and tried people. He represents Himself as personally affected with all that concerns them. . . . After presenting His relation to His people in various lights, He finally declares that in the great day He will judge of every action as if it had been done unto Himself.

His sympathy with His people is without a parallel. He will not simply remain a spectator, indifferent to what His people may suffer, but identifies Himself with their interests and sorrows. If His people are wronged, maligned, treated with contempt, their sufferings are registered in the books of heaven as done unto Him.[43]

The privileges, the blessings, of the child of God are represented by the apostle in the following language: "To whom God would make known what is the riches of the glory of this mystery among the Gentiles; which is Christ in you, the hope of glory" (Col. 1:27). When we realize that our hope of glory is Christ, that we are complete in Him, we shall rejoice with joy unspeakable and full of glory.[43]

"COMPLETE IN HIM"

And ye are complete in him, which is the head of all princi-pality and power. Col. 2:10.

Christ's likeness in us is a grand truth, a practical truth. I am not merely a thing that God loves, made to be left the sport of Satan's temptations; I am a child of God, begotten unto a lively hope, big with immortality and full of glory. We are to dwell in God, and God in us. Purity in us is like purity in God; love in my heart is a living principle, like the love in the heart of God; and all the treasures of heaven are at my command because I am redeemed by the blood of the Lamb. . . .

We are sons and daughters of God. Satan is the destroyer and Christ is the restorer. He will make us partakers of His holiness. God does not make light of sin, but He seeks to rescue us from sin. There is not in Jesus Christ harsh, stern repulsiveness or resentment; and if we have the character of Christ we shall have His mold. There is no forcing us to holiness, but . . . He wishes us to imitate His character, to admire Him—true, pure, generous, and loving. . . .

Happiness is composed of little things and great things. . . . If we would become like Christ and receive His fashion of character, we must in little things train the soul to daily progressive sanctification. We have no time to lose. Would you impress the seal to obtain a clear impression upon the wax, you do not dash it on by a violent action, but you place the seal carefully and firmly and press it down until the wax receives the mold. Just so the Lord is dealing with our souls. . . . Not now and then, but constantly the new life is implanted by the Holy Spirit after Christ's likeness.

Acts make habits and habits constitute character. There is no fear of overlooking great things, but there is peril in overlooking and undervaluing little things. God is the God of the whole man, and the little things are essential. God is a god of the whole man, and not a God of the part. He made all, He redeemed all, and He must be served in all, and then He will bless all, soul and body. Our entire life will then be glorified, and every breath, every sound, every touch will be peace and light and happiness.⁴⁴

LET US ASK OF GOD

If any of you lack wisdom, let him ask of God, that giveth to all men liberally, and upbraideth not; and it shall be given him. James 1:5.

It is the privilege of every believer first to talk with God in his closet, and then as God's mouthpiece to talk with others. In order that we may have something to impart, we must daily receive light and blessing. Men and women who commune with God, who have an abiding Christ, who, because they cooperate with holy angels, are surrounded with holy influences, are needed at this time. The cause needs those who have power to draw with Christ, power to express the love of God in words of encouragement and sympathy.

As the believer bows in supplication before God, and in humility and contrition offers his petition from unfeigned lips, he loses all thought of self. His mind is filled with the thought of what he must have in order to build up a Christlike character. He prays, "Lord, if I am to be a channel through which Thy love is to flow day by day and hour by hour, I claim by faith the grace and power that Thou hast promised." He fastens his hold firmly on the promise, "If any of you lack wisdom, let him ask of God, . . . and it shall be given him."

How this dependence pleases the Master! How He delights to hear the steady, earnest pleading! . . . With wonderful and ennobling grace the Lord sanctifies the humble petitioner, giving him power to perform the most difficult duties. All that is undertaken is done unto the Lord, and this elevates and sanctifies the lowliest calling. It invests with new dignity every word, every act, and links the humblest worker . . . with the highest of the angels in the heavenly courts. . . .

The sons and daughters of God have a great work to do in the world. They are to accept the Word of God as the man of their counsel and to impart it to others. They are to diffuse light. All who have received the engrafted word will be faithful in giving that word to others. They will speak the words of Christ. In conversation and in deportment they will give evidence of a daily conversion to the principles of truth. Such believers will be a spectacle to the world, to angels, and to men, and God will be glorified in them.[1]

67

WHOM GOD ACCEPTS

To this man will I look, even to him that is poor and of a contrite spirit, and trembleth at my word. Isa. 66:2.

Those who search for worldly distinction and glory make a sad mistake. It is the one who denies self, giving to others the preference, who will sit nearest to Christ on His throne. He who reads the heart sees the true merit possessed by His lowly, self-sacrificing disciples, and because they are worthy He places them in positions of distinction, though they do not realize their worthiness and do not seek for honor. . . .

God places no value on outward display or boasting. Many who in this life are looked upon as superior to others will one day see that God values men according to their compassion and self-denial. . . . Those who follow the example of Him who went about doing good, who help and bless their fellow men, trying always to lift them up, are in God's sight infinitely higher than the selfish ones who exalt themselves.

God does not accept men because of their capabilities, but because they seek His face, desiring His help. God sees not as man sees. He judges not from appearances. He searches the heart, and judges righteously. "To this man will I look," He declares, "even to him that is poor and of a contrite spirit, and trembleth at my word." He accepts and communes with His lowly, unpretentious followers; for in them He sees the most precious material, which will stand the test of storm and tempest, heat and pressure.

Our object in working for the Master should be that His name may be glorified in the conversion of sinners. Those who labor to gain applause are not approved of God. . . .

Humble workers, who do not trust in their great gifts, but who work in simplicity, trusting always in God, will share in the joy of the Saviour. Their persevering prayers will bring souls to the cross. Heavenly angels will respond to their self-sacrificing efforts. . . .

These workers are trees of the Lord's planting. In a peculiar sense they bear fruit equal to the fruit borne by the apostles. A rich reward awaits them in the future life.[2]

68

STRENGTH THROUGH PRAYER

O come, let us worship and bow down: let us kneel before the Lord our maker. **Ps. 95:6.**

Christ has given His disciples assurance that special seasons for devotion are necessary. Prayer went before and sanctified every act of His ministry. . . . The night seasons of prayer which the Saviour spent in the mountain or in the desert were essential to prepare Him for the trials He must meet in the days to follow. He felt the need of the refreshing and invigorating of soul and body, that He might meet the temptations of Satan; and those who are striving to live His life will feel this same need. . . .

Christ has pledged Himself to be our substitute and surety, and He neglects no one. There is an inexhaustible fund of perfect obedience accruing from His obedience. In heaven His merits, His self-denial and self-sacrifice, are treasured up as incense to be offered up with the prayers of His people. As the sinner's sincere, humble prayers ascend to the throne of God, Christ mingles with them the merits of His life of perfect obedience. Our prayers are made fragrant by this incense. . . .

Let all remember that the mysteries of God's kingdom cannot be learned by reasoning. True faith, true prayer—how strong they are! The prayer of the Pharisee had no value, but the prayer of the publican was heard in the courts above, because it showed dependence reaching forth to lay hold of Omnipotence. Self was to the publican nothing but shame. Thus it must be with all who seek God. Faith and prayer are the two arms which the needy suppliant lays upon the neck of infinite Love. . . .

We speak with Jesus Christ as we walk by the way, and He says, "I am at thy right hand." We may walk in daily companionship with Christ. When we breathe out our desire, it may be inaudible to any human ear, but that word cannot die away into silence nor can it be lost, though the activities of business are going on. Nothing can drown the soul's desire. It rises above the din of the street, above the noise of machinery, to the heavenly courts. It is God to whom we are speaking, and the prayer is heard. Ask then; "Ask, and it shall be given you." [3]

STANDING IN THE LIGHT OF HEAVEN

For God, who commanded the light to shine out of darkness, hath shined in our hearts, to give the light of the knowledge of the glory of God in the face of Jesus Christ. 2 Cor. 4:6.

Provision has been made whereby the communication between heaven and our souls may be free and open. Finite man can place himself where rays of light and glory from the throne of God will be given him in abundance. The light of the knowledge of the glory of God which shines in the face of Jesus Christ may shine upon him. He may stand where it can be said of him, "Ye are the light of the world." Were it not for the communication between heaven and earth there would be no light in the world. Like Sodom and Gomorrah, all men would perish beneath the just judgment of God. But the world is not left in darkness. The long-suffering mercy of God is still extended to the children of men, and it is His design that the rays of light which emanate from the throne of God shall be reflected by the children of light. . . .

It is our privilege to stand with the light of heaven upon us. It was thus that Enoch walked with God. It was no easier for Enoch to live a righteous life than it is for us at the present time. The world in his time was no more favorable to growth in grace and holiness than it is now.

It was by prayer and communion with God that Enoch was enabled to escape the corruption that is in the world through lust. We are living in the perils of the last days, and we must receive our strength from the same Source. We must walk with God. A separation from the world is required of us, for we cannot remain free from its pollution unless we follow the example of the faithful Enoch. . . .

Those who profess the religion of Christ should understand the responsibility resting upon them. They should feel that this is an individual work, an individual preaching of Christ. If each would realize this and take hold of the work, we should be as mighty as an army with banners. The heavenly Dove would hover over us. The light of the glory of God would be no more shut away from us than it was from the devoted Enoch.[4]

LETTERS TO HEAVEN

Let us therefore come boldly unto the throne of grace, that we may obtain mercy, and find grace to help in time of need. Heb. 4:16.

Prayer is not an expiation for sin. It is not a penance. We need not come to God as condemned criminals, for Christ has paid the penalty of our transgression. He has made an atonement for us. His blood cleanses from sin. Our prayers are as letters sent from earth, directed to our Father in heaven. The petitions that ascend from sincere, humble hearts will surely reach Him. He can discern the sincerity of His adopted children. He pities our weakness and strengthens our infirmities. He has said, "Ask, and ye shall receive."

Many of the human family know not what they should ask for as they ought. But the Lord is kind and tender. He helps their infirmities by giving them words to speak. He who comes with sanctified desire has access through Christ to the Father. Christ is our intercessor. The prayers that are placed in the golden censer of the Saviour's merits are accepted by the Father.

Every promise in the Word of God is for us. In your prayers, present the pledged word of Jehovah and by faith claim His promises. His word is the assurance that if you ask in faith, you will receive all spiritual blessings. Continue to ask, and you will receive exceeding abundantly above all that you ask or think. Educate yourself to have unlimited confidence in God. Cast all your care upon Him. Wait patiently for Him, and He will bring it to pass.

We are to come to God, not in a spirit of self-justification, but with humility, repenting of our sins. He is able to help us, willing to do for us more than we ask or think. He has the abundance of heaven wherewith to supply our necessities. . . . God is holy, and we must pray, "lifting up holy hands, without wrath and doubting" (1 Tim. 2:8). . . .

We are to seek "first the kingdom of God, and his righteousness" (Matt. 6:33). We are to be ready to receive the blessing which God will bestow upon those who seek Him with the whole heart, in sincerity and truth. We must keep the heart open if we would receive of the grace of Christ.[5]

SWEET COMMUNION WITH OUR SAVIOUR

That which we have seen and heard declare we unto you, that ye also may have fellowship with us: and truly our fellowship is with the Father, and with his Son Jesus Christ. 1 John 1:3.

It is our privilege to taste the sweetness of communion with a crucified and risen Saviour. But in order for this to be, self must be surrendered to God. Self-indulgence means that Christ is not followed in self-denial and cross bearing. When self strives for the highest place, the spiritual perceptions become dimmed. The eyes are turned from Christ to the poor picture of self. We cannot afford to become separated from Christ. We must keep looking unto Jesus, the author and finisher of our faith. . . .

It is as we commune with Christ that precious, holy light shines into our souls, until every chamber is lighted up and we become bright lights in the world, reflecting to others the glory of Christ. We are to keep Christ before us as the example of perfection.[6]

Communion with God is the life of the soul. It is not a something which we can interpret, a something which we can clothe with beautiful words, but which does not give us the genuine experience that makes our words of real value. Communion with God gives us a daily experience that does indeed make our joy full.

Those who have this union with Christ will declare it in spirit and word and work. Profession is nothing unless, in word and work, good fruit is manifest. Unity, fellowship with one another and with Christ—this is the fruit borne on every branch of the living vine. The cleansed soul, born again, has a clear, distinct testimony to bear. . . .

To know God is, in the scriptural sense of the term, to be one with Him in heart and mind, having an experimental knowledge of Him, holding reverential communion with Him as the Redeemer. Only through sincere obedience can this communion be obtained. . . .

Following Christ's example of unselfish service, trusting like little children in His merits, and obeying His commands, we shall receive the approval of God. Christ will abide in our hearts, and our influence will be fragrant with His righteousness.[7]

FERVENT PRAYER

Trust in him at all times; ye people, pour out your heart before him: God is a refuge for us. Ps. 62:8.

Prayer is the opening of the heart to God as to a friend. The eye of faith will discern God very near, and the suppliant may obtain precious evidence of the divine love and care for him. But why is it that so many prayers are never answered? . . . The Lord gives us the promise: "Ye shall seek me, and find me, when ye shall search for me with all your heart" (Jer. 29:13). Again, He speaks of some who "have not cried unto me with their heart" (Hosea 7:14). Such petitions are prayers of form, lip service only, which the Lord does not accept. . . .

There is need of prayer—most earnest, fervent, agonizing prayer—such prayer as David offered when he exclaimed: "As the hart panteth after the water brooks, so panteth my soul after thee, O God." "I have longed after thy precepts"; "I have longed for thy salvation." "My soul longeth, yea, even fainteth for the courts of the Lord: my heart and my flesh crieth out for the living God." "My soul breaketh for the longing that it hath unto thy judgments" (Ps. 42:1; 119:40, 174; 84:2; 119:20). This is the spirit of wrestling prayer, such as was possessed by the royal psalmist. . . .

Of Christ it is said: "And being in an agony he prayed more earnestly" (Luke 22:44). In what contrast to this intercession by the Majesty of heaven are the feeble, heartless prayers that are offered to God. Many are content with lip service, and but few have a sincere, earnest, affectionate longing after God.

Communion with God imparts to the soul an intimate knowledge of His will. . . . True prayer engages the energies of the soul and affects the life. He who thus pours out his wants before God feels the emptiness of everything else under heaven. "All my desire is before thee," said David, "and my groaning is not hid from thee." "My soul thirsteth for God. . . ." "When I remember these things, I pour out my soul in me" (Ps. 38:9; 42:2, 4).[8]

Your prayers may rise with an importunity that will not accept denial. That is faith.[9]

73

NOTHING TOO SMALL

The Lord is good unto them that wait for him, to the soul that seeketh him. Lam. 3:25.

There are few who rightly appreciate or improve the precious privilege of prayer. We should go to Jesus and tell Him all our needs. We may bring Him our little cares and perplexities as well as our greater troubles. Whatever arises to disturb or distress us, we should take it to the Lord in prayer.[10]

We lose many precious blessings by failing to bring our needs and cares and sorrows to our Saviour. He is the wonderful Counselor. He looks upon His church with intense interest and with a heart full of tender sympathy. He enters into the depth of our necessities. But our ways are not always His ways. He sees the result of every action, and He asks us to trust patiently in His wisdom, not in the supposedly wise plans of our own making.

Do not cease to pray. If the answer tarry, wait for it. Lay all your plans at the feet of the Redeemer. Let your importunate prayers ascend to God. If it be for His name's glory, the soothing words will be spoken, "Be it unto thee according to thy word."

We can never weary Christ by earnest supplications. We do not depend on God as we should. Let us leave unsaid every word of complaint. Talk faith and courage while waiting for God. . . . Be afraid to doubt, lest this become a habit that will destroy faith. The dealing of the heavenly Father may seem dark and mysterious and unexplainable; nevertheless we are to trust in Him.[11]

Oh, how precious is Jesus to the soul who trusts in Him! But many are walking in darkness because they bury their faith in the shadow of Satan. . . . Never for a moment should we allow Satan to think that his power to distress and annoy is greater than the power of Christ to uphold and strengthen. . . .

Every sincere prayer that is offered is mingled with the efficacy of Christ's blood. If the answer is deferred, it is because God desires us to show a holy boldness in claiming the pledged word of God. He is faithful who hath promised. He will never forsake the soul who is wholly surrendered to Him.[12]

74

PRAYER MOVES HEAVEN

Ask, and it shall be given you; seek, and ye shall find; knock, and it shall be opened unto you. Matt. 7:7.

Why is it that we do not receive more from Him who is the source of light and power? We expect too little. . . .

We do not value as we should the power and efficacy of prayer. "The Spirit also helpeth our infirmities: for we know not what we should pray for as we ought: but the Spirit itself maketh intercession for us with groanings which cannot be uttered" (Rom. 8:26). God desires us to come to Him in prayer, that He may enlighten our minds. He alone can give clear conceptions of truth. He alone can soften and subdue the heart. He can quicken the understanding to discern truth from error. He can establish the wavering mind and give it a knowledge and a faith that will endure the test. Pray, then; pray without ceasing. The Lord who heard Daniel's prayer will hear yours if you will approach Him as Daniel did.

Let us live in close communion with God. The joy of the Christian arises from a sense of God's love and care for His children and the assurance that He will not leave them alone in their weakness.[13]

We need to know how to pray. It is not tame, spiritless prayers that take hold of the divine attributes. Prayer is heard by God when it comes from a heart broken by a sense of unworthiness. Prayer was instituted for our comfort and salvation, that through faith and hope we may lay hold on the rich promises of God. Prayer is the expression of the desires of a soul hungering and thirsting for righteousness.[14]

Prayer is a heaven-ordained means of success. Appeals, petitions, entreaties, between man and man, move men and act a part in controlling the affairs of nations. But prayer moves heaven. That power alone that comes in answer to prayer will make men wise in the wisdom of heaven and enable them to work in the unity of the Spirit, joined together by the bonds of peace. Prayer, faith, confidence in God, bring a divine power that sets human calculations at their real worth—nothingness. . . . He who places himself where God can enlighten him, advances, as it were, from the partial obscurity of dawn to the full radiance of noonday.[15]

JESUS THE MIGHTY PETITIONER

Neither pray I for these alone, but for them also which shall believe on me through their word. John 17:20.

Think of Christ, the adored of angels, in the attitude of a suppliant. He was a mighty petitioner, seeking at the hands of the Father fresh supplies of grace, and coming forth invigorated and refreshed, to impart His lessons of assurance and hope. Look at His kneeling form, as in the moonlit hours He pours forth His soul to the Father. Behold the angels watching the earnest suppliant. His prayer rises to all heaven in our behalf. . . .

The disciples often witnessed Christ kneeling in prayer, their hearts broken and humbled. As their Lord and Saviour arose from His knees, what did they read in His countenance and bearing? That He was braced for duty and prepared for trial. Prayer was a necessity of His humanity, and His petitions were often accompanied with strong crying and with agony of soul as He saw the necessities of His disciples, who, not understanding their own dangers, were often, under Satan's temptations, led away from duty into wrongdoing.

Christ's life was pure and undefiled. He refused to yield to the temptations of the enemy. Had He yielded on one point, the human family would have been lost. Who can tell the agony that He endures as He sees Satan playing the game of life for the souls of those who claim to be His disciples, and sees them yielding point after point, allowing the soul's defenses to be broken down? We can form no conception of the agony that He endures at this sight. One soul lost, one soul given up to Satan's power, means more to Him than the whole world. . . . What an argument of power in the prayer, "That they all may be one; as thou, Father, art in me, and I in thee, that they also may be one in us; that the world may believe that thou hast sent me. And the glory which thou gavest me I have given them; that they may be one, even as we are one" (John 17:21, 22).[16]

Christ is represented as hunting, searching, for the sheep that was lost. It is His love that encircles us, bringing us back to the fold, giving us the privilege of sitting together with Him in heavenly places.[17]

ASKING IN CHRIST'S NAME

And whatsoever ye shall ask in my name, that will I do, that the Father may be glorified in the Son. John 14:13.

I am so thankful that we can trust in God. And the Lord is honored when we trust in Him, bringing to Him all our perplexities. . . . The Lord Jehovah did not deem the principles of salvation complete while invested only with His own love. By His own appointment He has placed at His altar an Advocate clothed in our nature. As our Intercessor, His office work is to introduce us to God as His sons and daughters. Christ intercedes in behalf of those who have received Him. To them He gives power, by virtue of His own merits, to become members of the royal family, children of the heavenly King. And the Father demonstrates His infinite love for Christ, who paid our ransom by His blood, by receiving and welcoming Christ's friends as His friends. He is satisfied with the atonement made. He is glorified by the incarnation, the life, death, and mediation of His Son.

In Christ's name our petitions ascend to the Father. He intercedes in our behalf, and the Father lays open all the treasures of His grace for our appropriation, to enjoy and communicate to others. Ask in My name, Christ says. I do not say that I will pray the Father for you, for the Father Himself loveth you, because you have loved Me. Make use of My name. This will give your prayers efficiency, and the Father will give you the riches of His grace. Wherefore ask and ye shall receive, that your joy may be full.

What condescension! What a privilege is granted us! Christ is the connecting link between God and man. . . . As we approach God through the virtue of Christ's merits, we are clothed with His priestly vestments. He places us close by His side, encircling us with His human arm, while with His divine arm He grasps the throne of the Infinite. He puts His merits as sweet incense in a censer in our hands in order to encourage our petitions. He promises to hear and answer our supplications. Yes; Christ has become the medium of prayer between man and God. He also has become the medium of blessing between God and man. He has combined divinity and humanity.[18]

OUR ACCESS TO THE FATHER

Verily, verily, I say unto you, Whatsoever ye shall ask the Father in my name, he will give it you. John 16:23.

We are to pray in the name of Christ, our Mediator. Our petitions are of value only as they are offered in His name. He has bridged the gulf that sin has made. By His atoning sacrifice He has bound to Himself and His Father those who believe in Him. His is the only name under heaven whereby we may be saved. . . .

We are not to be so overwhelmed with the thought of our sins and errors that we shall cease to pray. Some realize their great weakness and sin, and become discouraged. Satan casts his dark shadow between them and the Lord Jesus, their atoning sacrifice. They say, It is useless for me to pray. My prayers are so mingled with evil thoughts that the Lord will not hear them.

These suggestions are from Satan. In His humanity Christ met and resisted this temptation, and He knows how to succor those who are thus tempted. In our behalf, He "offered up prayers and supplications with strong crying and tears" (Heb. 5:7).

Many, not understanding that their doubts come from Satan, become fainthearted and are defeated in the conflict. Do not, because your thoughts are evil, cease to pray. If we could in our own wisdom and strength pray aright, we could also live aright, and would need no atoning sacrifice. But imperfection is upon all humanity. Educate and train the mind that you may in simplicity tell the Lord what you need. As you offer your petitions to God, seeking for forgiveness for sin, a purer and holier atmosphere will surround your soul.[19]

The Lord desires us to improve in prayer and to offer our spiritual sacrifices with increased faith and power. . . . He has given His own Son for our redemption. If by living faith we accept Him as our Saviour, we are placed on vantage ground with God; for Christ stands before His Father, saying, "Lay their sins on me. I will bear their guilt. They are my property. I have graven them upon the palms of my hands." In our behalf He presents before His Father the marks of the crucifixion which He will bear throughout eternity.[20]

OUR PERSONAL INTERCESSOR

Who is he that condemneth? It is Christ that died, yea rather, that is risen again, who is even at the right hand of God, who also maketh intercession for us. Rom. 8:34.

The Lord Jesus is your personal intercessor. . . . Repeat over and over many times through the day, "Jesus has died for me. He saw me in peril, exposed to destruction, and poured out His life to save me. He does not behold the soul as a trembling suppliant prostrate at His feet without pity, and He will not fail to raise me up." He has become the advocate for man. He has lifted up those who believe in Him and placed a treasurehouse of blessing at their demand. Men cannot bestow one blessing upon their fellows, they cannot remove one stain of sin. It is only the merit and righteousness of Christ that will avail anything, but this is placed to our account in rich fullness. We may draw upon God every moment. As we turn to Him, He answers, "Here I am."

Christ proclaims Himself our Intercessor. He would have us know that He has graciously engaged to be our Substitute. He places His merit in the golden censer to offer up with the prayers of His saints, so that the prayers of His dear children may be mingled with the fragrant merit of Christ as they ascend to the Father in the cloud of incense.

The Father hears every prayer of His contrite children. The voice of supplication from the earth unites with the voice of our Intercessor, who pleads in heaven, whose voice the Father always hears. Let our prayers therefore continually ascend to God. Let them not come up in the name of any human being, but in the name of Him who is our Substitute and Surety. Christ has given us His name to use. . . .

Jesus receives and welcomes you as His own friend. He loves you; He has pledged Himself to open before you all the treasures of His grace for your appropriation. He says, "At that day ye shall ask in my name: and I say not unto you, that I will pray the Father for you: for the Father himself loveth you, because ye have loved me, and have believed that I came out from God" (John 16:26, 27). He virtually says, Make use of My name, and it will be your passport to the heart of My Father, and to all the riches of His grace.[21]

79

THE SPIRIT'S INTERCESSION

Likewise the Spirit also helpeth our infirmities: for we know not what we should pray for as we ought: but the Spirit itself maketh intercession for us with groanings which cannot be uttered. Rom. 8:26.

We must not only pray in Christ's name, but by the inspiration of the Holy Spirit. This explains what is meant when it is said that the Spirit "maketh intercession for us, with groanings which cannot be uttered." Such prayer God delights to answer. When with earnestness and intensity we breathe a prayer in the name of Christ, there is in that very intensity a pledge from God that He is about to answer our prayer "exceeding abundantly above all that we ask or think." [22]

The Holy Spirit will be given to those who seek for its power and grace and will help our infirmities when we would have an audience with God. Heaven is open to our petitions, and we are invited to come "boldly unto the throne of grace, that we may obtain mercy, and find grace to help in time of need" (Heb. 4:16). We are to come in faith, believing that we shall obtain the very things we ask of Him. [23]

We may commit the keeping of our souls to God as unto a faithful Creator, not because we are sinless, but because Jesus died to save just such erring, faulty creatures as we are, thus expressing His estimate of the value of the human soul. We may rest upon God, not because of our own merit, but because the righteousness of Christ will be imputed to us. . . .

There are rich promises for us in the Word of God. The plan of salvation is ample. It is no narrow, limited provision that has been made for us. We are not obliged to trust in the evidence that we had a year or a month ago, but we may have the assurance today that Jesus lives and is making intercession for us. [24]

God does not leave His erring children who are weak in faith, and who make mistakes. The Lord hearkens and hears their prayer and their testimony. Those who look unto Jesus day by day and hour by hour, who watch unto prayer, are drawing nigh to Jesus. Angels with wings outspread wait to bear their contrite prayers to God, and to register them in the books of heaven. [25]

ASK IN FAITH

Therefore I say unto you, What things soever ye desire, when ye pray, believe that ye receive them, and ye shall have them. Mark 11:24.

"If ye then, being evil, know how to give good gifts unto your children, how much more shall your Father which is in heaven give good things to them that ask him?" (Matt. 7:11). These gifts are freely given to us by God. Oh, how weak is our faith, that we do not avail ourselves of the rich, glorious promises of God! It is His nature to bestow His gifts upon us. All-wise and all-powerful, He will give liberally to all who ask in faith. He is more merciful, more tender, more patient and loving than any earthly parent.[26]

The believer in Christ is consecrated to high and holy purpose. . . . Called according to God's purpose, set apart by grace divine, invested with Christ's righteousness, imbued with the Holy Spirit, offering up the sacrifices of a broken and contrite heart, the true believer is indeed a representative of the Redeemer.

Upon such a worshiper, God looks with delight. He will let His light shine into the chambers of the mind and into the soul temple if men, when they lack wisdom, will go to their closets in prayer and ask wisdom from Him who gives to all men liberally and upbraids not. The promise is, "It shall be given him. But let him ask in faith, nothing wavering. For he that wavereth is like a wave of the sea driven with the wind and tossed" (James 1:5, 6). . . . Show a firm, undeviating trust in God. Be ever true to principle. Waver not. . . .

All things are possible to those that believe. No one coming to the Lord in sincerity of heart will be disappointed. How wonderful it is that we can pray effectually, that unworthy, erring mortals possess the power of offering their requests to God!

What higher power can man require than this—to be linked with the infinite God? Feeble, sinful man has the privilege of speaking to his Maker. We utter words that reach the throne of the Monarch of the universe. We pour out our heart's desire in our closets. Then we go forth to walk with God as did Enoch.[26]

ACCORDING TO GOD'S WILL

And this is the confidence that we have in him, that, if we ask any thing according to his will, he heareth us: and if we know that he hear us, whatsoever we ask, we know that we have the petitions that we desired of him. 1 John 5:14, 15.

When you pray for temporal blessings, remember that the Lord may see that it is not for your good or for His glory to give you just what you desire. But He will answer your prayer, giving you just what is best for you.

When Paul prayed that the thorn in his flesh might be removed, the Lord answered his prayer, not by removing the thorn, but by giving him grace to bear the trial. "My grace," He said, "is sufficient for thee." Paul rejoiced at this answer to his prayer, declaring, "Most gladly therefore will I rather glory in my infirmities, that the power of Christ may rest upon me" (2 Cor. 12:9). When the sick pray for the recovery of health, the Lord does not always answer their prayer in just the way they desire. But even though they may not be immediately healed, He will give them that which is of far more value —grace to bear their sickness.[27]

Make your requests known to your Maker. Never is one repulsed who comes to Him with a contrite heart. Not one sincere prayer is lost. Amid the anthems of the celestial choir, God hears the cries of the weakest human being. We pour out our heart's desire in our closets, we breathe a prayer as we walk by the way, and our words reach the throne of the Monarch of the universe. They may be inaudible to any human ear, but they cannot die away into silence, nor can they be lost through the activities of business that are going on. Nothing can drown the soul's desire. It rises above the din of the street, above the confusion of the multitude, to the heavenly courts. It is God to whom we are speaking, and our prayer is heard. You who feel the most unworthy, fear not to commit your case to God.[28]

There is a mighty power in prayer. Our great adversary is constantly seeking to keep the troubled soul away from God. An appeal to Heaven by the humblest saint is more to be dreaded by Satan than the decrees of cabinets or the mandates of kings.[29]

THE SECRET OF SPIRITUAL POWER

They that wait upon the Lord shall renew their strength; they shall mount up with wings as eagles; they shall run, and not be weary; and they shall walk, and not faint. Isa. 40:31.

Much prayer is necessary to successful effort. Prayer brings power. Prayer has "subdued kingdoms, wrought righteousness, obtained promises, stopped the mouths of lions, quenched the violence of fire, . . . turned to flight the armies of the aliens" (Heb. 11:33, 34).

Jesus lived in dependence upon God and communion with Him. To the secret place of the Most High, under the shadow of the Almighty, men now and then repair; they abide for a season, and the result is manifest in noble deeds; then their faith fails, the communion is interrupted, and the lifework marred. But the life of Jesus was a life of constant trust, sustained by continual communion; and His service for heaven and earth was without failure or faltering.

Christian workers can never attain the highest success until they learn the secret of strength. They must give themselves time to think, to pray, to wait upon God for a renewal of physical, mental, and spiritual power. They need the uplifting of His Spirit. Receiving this, they will be quickened by fresh life. The wearied frame and tired brain will be refreshed, the burdened heart will be rested.[30]

Prayer is the breath of the soul. It is the secret of spiritual power. No other means of grace can be substituted, and the health of the soul be preserved. Prayer brings the heart into immediate contact with the Well-spring of life, and strengthens the sinew and muscle of the religious experience.[31]

Family prayer and public prayer have their place, but it is secret communion with God that sustains the soul-life. It was in the mount with God that Moses beheld the pattern of that wonderful building which was to be the abiding-place of His glory. It is in the mount with God—the secret place of communion—that we are to contemplate His glorious ideal for humanity. Thus we shall be enabled so to fashion our character-building that to us may be fulfilled the promise, "I will dwell in them, and walk in them; and I will be their God, and they shall be my people" (2 Cor. 6:16).[32]

THE SILENT HEART CRY

Thou shalt hide them in the secret of thy presence from the pride of man: thou shalt keep them secretly in a pavilion from the strife of tongues. Ps. 31:20.

When men and women are in the busy activities of life and are pressed with numerous cares, they cannot live upon their knees. But even in the market place there is a watcher constantly present to witness every transaction, and the books of heaven record every penny of unlawful gain as fraud. While men cannot live upon their knees in the market place, yet the silent heart's earnest desire presented to heaven finds access to the Father through the watchers. The way to the throne of God is open, and all who have the fear of God before them and desire to walk in His counsel will seek His strength to do His will in crowded companies as well as in the chapel. . . .

There is a chance for every man who loves and fears God, with every temptation that shall come in the business transactions of life, to know how to retreat into the secret place of the Most High's pavilion, so that he can remain there and be safe. Then he will honor God because he feels the strength and fullness of power of Him who is back of the promises. He communes with God where no eye sees and no ear hears but His.

All the Lord requires is a willing mind to walk in the way of the Lord. If there be a pure heart he shall see God and will feel His keeping power even in the busiest, most excitable crowd, if duty requires him to be there. . . . In such places every true, genuine receiver of Christ . . . carries the lamp of life. . . .

We must not have a religion that is retained only in favorable circumstances. A religion dependent on circumstances will surely fail when it is most needed, in the most difficult surroundings. The religion of the Bible will require the gospel lamp to be kept burning brightly in unfavorable surroundings—in the market place, in the workshop— just as verily as in the place where prayer is wont to be made. Purest Christian principles may be preserved in every place. Loving and believing in Christ as our personal Saviour, we can claim His grace and His guardian care wherever we may be.[33]

GUARD JEALOUSLY YOUR HOURS FOR PRAYER

As the hart panteth after the water brooks, so panteth my soul after thee, O God. Ps. 42:1.

He who is a citizen of the heavenly kingdom will be constantly looking at things not seen. The power of earth over the mind and character is broken. He has the abiding presence of the heavenly Guest, in accordance with the promise, "I will love him, and will manifest myself to him" (John 14:21). He walks with God as did Enoch, in constant communion. . . .

Daily beset by temptation, constantly opposed by the leaders of the people, Christ knew that He must strengthen His humanity by prayer. In order to be a blessing to men He must commune with God, pleading for energy, perseverance, and steadfastness. Thus He showed His disciples where His strength lay. Without this daily communion with God no human being can gain power for service. It is the privilege of every one to commit himself, with all his trials and temptations, his sorrows and disappointments, to the loving heavenly Father. No one who does this, who makes God his confidant, will fall a prey to the enemy.

"We have not an high priest which cannot be touched with the feeling of our infirmities; but was in all points tempted like as we are, yet without sin. Let us therefore come boldly unto the throne of grace, that we may obtain mercy, and find grace to help in time of need" (Heb. 4:15, 16). . . .

Guard jealously your hours for prayer and self-examination. Set apart some portion of each day for a study of the Scriptures and communion with God. Thus you will obtain spiritual strength and grow in grace and favor with God. He alone can direct our thoughts aright. He alone can give us noble aspirations and fashion our characters after the divine similitude. If we draw near to Him in earnest prayer, He will fill our hearts with high and holy purposes and with deep, earnest longing for purity and cleanness of thought. . . .

He imparts the richest blessings to those who serve Him with a pure heart. He teaches each one who opens the heart to His instruction and obeys His voice.[34]

85

THE SECRET PLACE OF PRAYER

He that dwelleth in the secret place of the most High shall abide under the shadow of the Almighty. Ps. 91:1.

The way to the throne of God is always open. You cannot always be on your knees in prayer, but your silent petitions may constantly ascend to God for strength and guidance. When tempted, as you will be, you may flee to the secret place of the Most High. His everlasting arms will be underneath you.[35]

We come to God by special invitation, and He waits to welcome us to His audience chamber. . . . We may be admitted into closest intimacy and communion with God.[36]

Pray with humble hearts. Seek the Lord often in prayer. In the secret place, alone, the eye sees Jesus and the ear is opened to Jesus. You come forth from the secret place of prayer to abide under the shadow of the Almighty. Temptations come, but you press closer and still closer to the side of Jesus and place your hand in His hand. Then you gain a rich experience, resting in His love and rejoicing in His mercy. The worries and perplexities and cares are gone, and you rejoice in Jesus Christ. The soul is quick to hear the Father's voice, and you will commune with God. All criticism is banished, all judging of others has been expelled from the soul. . . .

In Jesus Christ there is fragrance of character. There is the developing of nobleness of character, of refinement and purity, for by beholding you reflect the image of Christ. Sons of God, daughters of God, we must be like Him, and in this close relationship to God we receive power and heavenly endowment that we may work the works of God. . . .

Oh, what joy we experience in the service of God! What peace, what contentment and rest! Members of the royal family, children of the heavenly king! "It doth not yet appear what we shall be: but we know that, when he shall appear, we shall be like him . . ." (1 John 3:2). With such a hope, such a relationship, with all the great and precious possibilities, should not our faith grasp much more than it does? Should we not be inspired with hope and courage that will not fail nor be discouraged under any difficulties? [37]

"WITH ALL YOUR HEART"

And ye shall seek me, and find me, when ye shall search for me with all your heart. Jer. 29:13.

Many have not had that religious experience that is essential for them, that they may stand without fault before the throne of God. The furnace fires of affliction He permits to be kindled upon them to consume the dross, to refine, to purify and cleanse them from the defilement of sin, of self love, and to bring them to know God and to become acquainted with Jesus Christ by walking with Him as did Enoch. . . .

That which is called praying morning and evening, according to custom, is not always fervent and effectual. It is with many a sleepy, dull, and heartless repetition of words, and does not reach the ear of the Lord. God does not need or require your ceremonial compliments, but He will respect the broken heart, the confession of sins, the contrition of the soul. The cry of the humble, broken heart He will not despise. . . .

We must have such love for Jesus that we will consider it a privilege to suffer and even die for His sake. We may tell the Lord all our trials, tell Him all our weaknesses, tell Him all our dependence upon His might and His power. This is true prayer. If ever there was a time when the Spirit of grace and supplication was needed to be poured out upon us, God Himself inditing our prayers, it is now. And the promise is to be brought before every church, and the simplicity of truth dwelt upon. "Ask, and ye shall receive" (John 16: 24). It is faith, living faith that we need. . . .

The Lord will lead His people and guide them. The commandment will go forth from God as to Daniel, to help those making earnest intercession to the throne of His grace in their time of need.[38]

We need to open the heart to Christ. We need much firmer faith and more fervent devotion. We need to die to self, and in mind and heart to cherish an adoring love for our Saviour. When we will seek the Lord with all the heart we shall find Him, and our hearts will be all aglow with His love. Self will sink into insignificance, and Jesus will be all and in all to the soul.[39]

FAITH THAT WILL NOT LET GO

And he said, I will not let thee go, except thou bless me.
Gen. 32:26.

You who love to speak of the faults of others, arouse, and look into your own hearts. Take your Bibles, and go to God in earnest prayer. Ask Him to teach you to know yourself, to understand your weakness, your sins and follies, in the light of eternity. Ask Him to show you yourself as you stand in the sight of Heaven. This is an individual work. . . . In humility send your petition to God, and do not rest day nor night until you can say, Hear what the Lord hath done for me—until you can bear a living testimony and tell of victories won.

Jacob wrestled with the Angel all night before he gained the victory. When morning broke, the Angel said, "Let me go, for the day breaketh." But Jacob answered, "I will not let thee go, except thou bless me." Then his prayer was answered. "Thy name shall be called no more Jacob," said the Angel, "but Israel: for as a prince hast thou power with God and with men, and hast prevailed" (Gen. 32:26-28).

We need the perseverance of Jacob and the unyielding faith of Elijah. Time after time Elijah sent his servant to see if the cloud was rising, but no cloud was to be seen. At last, after seven times, the servant returned with the word, "There ariseth a little cloud out of the sea, like a man's hand" (1 Kings 18:44). Did Elijah stand back and say, I will not receive this evidence; I will wait till the heavens gather blackness? No. He said, It is time for us to be going. He ventured all upon that token from God and sent his messenger before him to tell Ahab that there was the sound of abundance of rain.

It is such faith as this that we need, faith that will take hold and will not let go. Inspiration tells us that Elijah was a man subject to like passions as we are. Heaven heard his prayer. He prayed that rain might cease, and there was no rain. Again he prayed for rain, and rain was sent. And why should not the Lord be entreated in behalf of His people today? O that the Lord would imbue us with His Spirit! O that the curtain might be rolled back that we might understand the mystery of godliness! [40]

THE SPIRIT OF SUBMISSION

Pray without ceasing. 1 Thess. 5:17.

Pray often to your heavenly Father. The oftener you engage in prayer, the closer your soul will be drawn into a sacred nearness to God. The Holy Spirit will make intercession for the sincere petitioner with groanings which cannot be uttered, and the heart will be softened and subdued by the love of God. The clouds and shadows which Satan casts about the soul will be dispelled by the bright beams of the Sun of Righteousness, and the chambers of mind and heart will be illuminated by the light of Heaven.

But be not discouraged if your prayers do not seem to obtain an immediate answer. The Lord sees that prayer is often mixed with earthliness. Men pray for that which will gratify their selfish desires, and the Lord does not fulfill their requests in the way which they expect. He takes them through tests and trials, He brings them through humiliations, until they see more clearly what their necessities are. He does not give to men those things which will gratify a debased appetite and which will prove an injury to the human agent and make him a dishonor to God. He does not give men that which will gratify their ambition and work simply for self-exaltation. When we come to God we must be submissive and contrite of heart, subordinating everything to His sacred will.

In the Garden of Gethsemane, Christ prayed to His Father, saying, "O my Father, if it be possible, let this cup pass from me" (Matt. 26:39). The cup which He prayed should be removed from Him, that looked so bitter to His soul, was the cup of separation from God in consequence of the sin of the world. . . . "Nevertheless not what I will, but what thou wilt" (Matt. 26:39). The spirit of submission that Christ manifested in offering up His prayer before God is the spirit that is acceptable to God. Let the soul feel its need, its helplessness, its nothingness; let all its energies be called forth in an earnest desire for help, and help will come. . . . Let faith pierce the darkness. Walk with God in the dark as well as in the light, repeating the words, "He is faithful that promised" (Heb. 10:23). Through the trial of our faith we shall be trained to trust in God.[41]

PRAYER IN THE HOME

Praying always with all prayer and supplication in the Spirit, and watching thereunto with all perseverance and supplication for all saints. Eph. 6:18.

If ever there was a time when every house should be a house of prayer, it is now. Infidelity and skepticism are prevailing. Iniquity abounds, and in consequence the love of many waxes cold. . . .

And yet in this time of fearful peril some who profess to be Christians have no family altar. They do not honor God in the home nor teach their children to love and fear Him. . . .

The idea that prayer is not essential is one of Satan's most successful devices to ruin souls. Prayer is addressing the mind to God, the Fountain of wisdom, the Source of strength and peace and happiness. Prayer includes acknowledgement of the divine perfections, gratitude for mercies received, penitential confession of sins, and earnest entreaty for the blessing of God, both for ourselves and for others.

Jesus prayed to the Father with strong crying and tears. Paul exhorts believers to "pray without ceasing" (1 Thess. 5:17). "In every thing, by prayer and supplication with thanksgiving let your requests be made known unto God" (Phil. 4:6). . . . God has a right to command our devotions; His authority is sacred and unquestionable. We are under obligation to pray because He requires it; and in obeying His requirements we shall receive a gracious and precious reward. . . .

Parents should make a hedge about their children by prayer; they should pray with full faith that God will abide with them and that holy angels will guard themselves and their children from Satan's cruel power. . . .

Fathers and mothers, at least morning and evening lift up your hearts to God in humble supplication for yourselves and your children. Your dear ones are exposed to temptations and trials. There are frets and irritations that daily beset the path of old and young; and those who would live patient, loving, cheerful lives amid daily annoyances must pray. This victory can be gained only by a resolute and unwavering purpose, constant watchfulness, and continual help from God.[42]

THE PRAYER MEETING A PRECIOUS SEASON

Again I say unto you, That if two of you shall agree on earth as touching any thing that they shall ask, it shall be done for them of my Father which is in heaven. For where two or three are gathered together in my name, there am I in the midst of them. Matt. 18:19, 20.

The Lord has promised that where two or three are met together in His name, there will He be in the midst. Those who meet together for prayer will receive an unction from the Holy One. There is great need of secret prayer, but there is also need that several Christians meet together and unite with earnestness their petitions to God.[43]

Seek every opportunity to go where prayer is wont to be made. Those who are really seeking for communion with God will be seen in the prayer meeting, faithful to do their duty, and earnest and anxious to reap all the benefits they can gain. They will improve every opportunity of placing themselves where they can receive the rays of light from heaven.[44]

We meet together to edify one another by an interchange of thoughts and feelings, to gather strength, and light, and courage by becoming acquainted with one another's hopes and aspirations; and by our earnest, heartfelt prayers, offered up in faith, we receive refreshment and vigor from the Source of our strength. These meetings should be most precious seasons. . . .

All have not the same experience in their religious life. But those of diverse exercises come together and with simplicity and humbleness of mind talk out their experience. All who are pursuing the onward Christian course should have, and will have, an experience that is living, that is new and interesting. A living experience is made up of daily trials, conflicts, and temptations, strong efforts and victories, and great peace and joy gained through Jesus. A simple relation of such experiences gives light, strength, and knowledge that will aid others in their advancement in the divine life.[45]

Educate your mind to love the Bible, to love the prayer meeting, to love the hour of meditation, and, above all, the hour when the soul communes with God.[46]

91

THE BLESSINGS OF FELLOWSHIP IN PRAYER

Then they that feared the Lord spake often one to another: and the Lord hearkened, and heard it, and a book of remembrance was written before him for them that feared the Lord, and that thought upon his name. Mal. 3:16.

If Christians would associate together, speaking to each other of the love of God, and of the precious truths of redemption, their own hearts would be refreshed, and they would refresh one another. We may be daily learning more of our heavenly Father, gaining a fresh experience of His grace; then we shall desire to speak of His love; and as we do this, our own hearts will be warmed and encouraged. If we thought and talked more of Jesus, and less of self, we should have far more of His presence.[47]

Let small companies assemble in the evening, at noon, or in the early morning to study the Bible. Let them have a season of prayer, that they may be strengthened, enlightened, and sanctified by the Holy Spirit. . . . If you yourselves will open the door to receive it, a great blessing will come to you. Angels of God will be in your assembly. You will feed upon the leaves of the tree of life.[48]

The fact that the Lord has been represented as hearkening to the words spoken by His witnesses, tells us that Jesus is in our very midst. He says, "Where two or three are gathered together in my name, there am I in the midst." One person is not to do all the witnessing for Jesus, but every one who loves God is to testify of the preciousness of His grace and truth.[49]

Praying together will bind hearts to God in bonds that will endure; confessing Christ openly and bravely, exhibiting in our characters His meekness, humility, and love, will charm others with the beauty of holiness.[50]

God will remember those who have met together and thought upon His name, and He will spare them from the great conflagration. They will be as precious jewels in His sight. . . . It is not a vain thing to serve God. There is a priceless reward for those who devote their life to His service.[51]

A CHAIN OF EARNEST, PRAYING BELIEVERS

Finally, brethren, pray for us, that the word of the Lord may have free course, and be glorified, even as it is with you. 2 Thess. 3:1.

Among God's people there should be at this time frequent seasons of sincere, earnest prayer. The mind should constantly be in a prayerful attitude. In the home and in the church let earnest prayers be offered in behalf of those who have given themselves to the preaching of the Word. Let believers pray as did the disciples after the ascension of Christ.

A chain of earnest, praying believers should encircle the world. Let all pray in humility. A few neighbors may meet together to pray for the Holy Spirit. Let those who cannot leave home, gather in their children, and unite in learning to pray together. They may claim the promise of the Saviour: "Where two or three are gathered together in my name, there am I in the midst of them" (Matt. 18:20). [52]

There is nothing more needed in the work than the practical results of communion with God. We should hold convocations for prayer, asking the Lord to open the way for the truth to enter the strongholds where Satan has set up his throne, and dispel the shadow he has cast athwart the pathway of those whom he is seeking to deceive and destroy. We have the assurance, "The effectual fervent prayer of a righteous man availeth much" (James 5:16). [53]

In the Lord's Prayer we have an example of a perfect petition. How simple, yet how comprehensive it is! This prayer should be taught to the children. Let all study carefully the principles contained in it. In response to the prayers of God's people, angels are sent with heavenly blessings. . . . Through daily prayer and consecration all may so relate themselves to their heavenly Father that He can bestow upon them rich blessings. . . .

Oh, how differently many would act were God to draw aside the veil that hides Him from our eyes, and reveal Himself seated on His throne in the high and holy place, not in silent grandeur, but surrounded with ten thousand times ten thousand, and thousands of thousands of holy, happy beings, waiting to do His bidding! [54]

93

REFLECTING GOD'S LOVE

Let the people praise thee, O God; let all the people praise thee. Ps. 67:3.

As Christians we ought to praise God more than we do. We ought to bring more of the brightness of His love into our lives. As by faith we look to Jesus His joy and peace are reflected from the countenances. How earnestly we should seek so to relate ourselves to God that our faces may reflect the sunshine of His love! When our own souls are vivified by the Holy Spirit, we shall exert an uplifting influence upon others who know not the joy of Christ's presence.[55]

The Lord is not pleased to have His people a band of mourners. He wants them to repent of their sins, that they may enjoy the liberty of the sons of God. Then they will be filled with the praises of God, and will be a blessing to others.

The Lord Jesus was anointed also "to appoint unto them that mourn in Zion, to give unto them beauty for ashes, the oil of joy for mourning, the garments of praise for the spirit of heaviness; that they might be called trees of righteousness, the planting of the Lord, that He might be glorified" (Isa. 61:3).

"That he," Christ Jesus, "might be glorified." O that this might be the purpose of our lives! Then we should have regard even to the expression of our countenance, to our words, and even to the tone of our voice when we speak.[56]

The melody of praise is the atmosphere of heaven; and when heaven comes in touch with the earth, there is music and song—"thanksgiving, and the voice of melody" (Isa. 51:3). . . . Let there be singing in the home, of songs that are sweet and pure, and there will be fewer words of censure and more of cheerfulness and hope and joy. . . .

As our Redeemer leads us to the threshold of the Infinite, flushed with the glory of God, we may catch the themes of praise and thanksgiving from the heavenly choir round about the throne; and as the echo of the angels' song is awakened in our earthly homes, hearts will be drawn closer to the heavenly singers. Heaven's communion begins on earth. We learn here its keynote.[57]

SONGS OF PRAISE

And he hath put a new song in my mouth, even praise unto our God: many shall see it, and fear, and shall trust in the Lord. Ps. 40:3.

I have thought with what joy the angels would look down from heaven upon us if we were all praising God and abiding in Christ. If, indeed, there is joy to the full for the Christian, why should we not possess it, and manifest it to the world? . . .

In just a little time Christ will come in power and great glory, and what a terrible thing it would be if we should not be ready! Let us get ready at once. Separate evil from you, begin to sing the song of praise and rejoicing here below. . . . Let your lips be tuned to praise God. . . . Angels in heaven are praising God all the time, and here are mortals for whom Christ left the heavenly home and suffered mockery, insult, and death, that He might lift us up to sit in heavenly places, and they offer no song of praise.

If you sit in heavenly places with Christ, you cannot refrain from praising God. Begin to educate your tongues to praise Him and train your hearts to make melody to God; and when the evil one begins to settle his gloom about you, sing praise to God. When things go crossways at your homes, strike up a song about the matchless charms of the Son of God, and I tell you, when you touch this strain, Satan will leave you. You can drive out the enemy with his gloom; . . . and you can see, oh, so much clearer, the love and compassion of your heavenly Father.[58]

Those who come into sacred relation with the God of heaven are not left to the natural weakness and infirmity of their natures. . . . The world loses all attraction for them; for they seek a better country, an eternal world, a life that is to continue through never-ending ages. This is the theme of their thought and conversation. The Word of God becomes exceedingly precious. They discern spiritual things. They rejoice in "that blessed hope, and the glorious appearing of the great God and our Saviour Jesus Christ" (Titus 2:13). They long to see the King in His beauty, the angels that have never fallen, and the land of unfading bloom.[59]

PRAISING GOD BEFORE THE WORLD

By him therefore let us offer the sacrifice of praise to God continually, that is, the fruit of our lips giving thanks to his name.
Heb. 13:15.

We need to offer praise and thanksgiving to God, not only in the congregation, but in the home life. Let the voices of His heritage be heard recounting the works of the Lord. Speak of His goodness, tell of His power. . . .

We feel depressed, greatly depressed, as we see the world and its wickedness. The professed Christian world is enveloped in the darkness that covers the earth. We sigh and cry for the abominations that are done in the land. Why is it that all this wickedness does not break forth in decided violence against righteousness and truth? It is because the four angels are holding the four winds, that they shall not blow upon the earth. But human passions are reaching a high pass, and the Spirit of the Lord is being withdrawn from the earth. Were it not that God has commanded angelic agencies to control the satanic agencies that are seeking to break loose and to destroy, there would be no hope. But the winds are to be held until the servants of God are sealed in their foreheads. . . .

Amid the moral darkness light is to shine forth in clear, distinct rays. . . . But every soul needs to turn his face toward the light that he may reflect this light. We need to praise God much more than we do. We are to show that we have cause for rejoicing. "Ye are a chosen generation, a royal priesthood, an holy nation, a peculiar people; that ye should shew forth the praises of him who hath called you out of darkness into his marvellous light" (1 Peter 2:9). Are we doing this as fully as we should? Are we revealing that love in the home that will honor and glorify our Redeemer?

However black the clouds that roll upon the world at the present time, there is light beyond. Ignorance, superstition, darkness, unbelief strong and masterful, will meet us at every step we advance. But our faith must soar above all and see the bow of promise encircling the throne. We must reflect the light with pen and voice, praising God before the world.[60]

96

WATCH AND PRAY

Watch and pray, that ye enter not into temptation: the spirit indeed is willing, but the flesh is weak. Matt. 26:41.

We are pilgrims and strangers in this world, traveling a path beset with dangers from those who have rejected the only One who could save them. Ingenious subterfuges and scientific problems will be held out before us, to tempt us to swerve from our allegiance, but we are not to heed them. Let every soul be on the alert. The adversary is on your track. Be vigilant, watching carefully lest some masterly snare shall take you unaware. . . .

The experience of the disciples in the Garden of Gethsemane contains a lesson for the Lord's people today. . . . They did not realize the necessity of watchfulness and earnest prayer in order to withstand temptation. Many today are fast asleep, as were the disciples. They are not watching and praying lest they enter into temptation. Let us often read and give careful study to those portions of God's Word that have special reference to these last days, pointing out the dangers that will threaten God's people.

We need keen, sanctified perception. This perception is not to be used in criticizing and condemning one another, but in discerning the signs of the times. We are to keep our hearts with all diligence that we may not make shipwreck of faith. Those who neglect to watch and pray in these days of peril; those who neglect to unite with their brethren in seeking the Lord, but who stand aloof from God's appointed agencies in the church, are in grave danger of strengthening themselves in their own way, following the impulses of their own minds, and of refusing to heed the admonitions of the Lord. . . .

Let every believer closely examine himself to ascertain what are his weak points. Let him cherish a spirit of humility and plead with the Lord for grace and wisdom and for the faith that works by love and purifies the soul. Let him cast away all self-confidence. . . . Self-confidence leads to a lack of watchfulness. . . . Those who walk humbly before God, distrustful of their own wisdom, will realize their danger and will know the power of God's keeping care.[61]

ANGEL GUARDS

The angel of the Lord encampeth round about them that fear him, and delivereth them. Ps. 34:7.

If the curtain could be rolled back, and each one could discern the constant activities of the heavenly family to preserve the inhabitants of the earth from Satan's seductive wiles, lest in their careless attitude they should be led astray through satanic strategy, they would lose a large degree of their self-confidence and self-assurance. They would see that the armies of heaven are in continual warfare with satanic agencies, to obtain victories in behalf of those who do not sense their danger, and who are passing on in unconscious indifference.[1]

Angels are belting the world, refusing Satan his claims to supremacy, made because of the vast multitude of his adherents. We hear not the voices, we see not with the natural sight the work of these angels, but their hands are linked about the world, and with sleepless vigilance they are keeping the armies of Satan at bay till the sealing of God's people shall be accomplished.

The ministers of Jehovah, angels have skill and power and great strength, being commissioned to go forth from heaven to earth to minister to His people. They are given the work of keeping back the raging power of him who has come down like a roaring lion, seeking whom he may devour.[2]

When we surrender all we have and are to God, and are placed in trying and dangerous positions, coming in contact with Satan, we should remember that we shall have victory in meeting the enemy in the name and power of the Conqueror. Every angel would be commissioned to come to our rescue, when we thus depend upon Christ, rather than that we should be permitted to be overcome. But we need not expect to get the victory without suffering; for Jesus suffered in conquering for us.[3]

The angels of God are communicating with and guarding His people, and are pressing back the powers of darkness that they shall not have any control over those who shall be heirs of salvation. Are we working in harmony with the angels? This is the line of communication the Lord has established with the children of men.[4]

ANGELS IN THE HOME

For he shall give his angels charge over thee, to keep thee in all thy ways. They shall bear thee up in their hands, lest thou dash thy foot against a stone. **Ps. 91:11, 12.**

Angels of God are watching over us. Upon this earth there are thousands and tens of thousands of heavenly messengers commissioned by the Father to prevent Satan from obtaining any advantage over those who refuse to walk in the path of evil. And these angels who guard God's children on earth are in communication with the Father in heaven. "Take heed that ye despise not one of these little ones," Christ said; "for I say unto you, That in heaven their angels do always behold the face of my Father which is in heaven" (Matt. 18:10).[5]

Scarcely any of us realize that angels are about us; and these precious angels, who minister to those who shall be heirs of salvation, are saving from us many, many temptations and difficulties. The whole family of heaven is interested in the families here below; and how thankful we should be for this interest manifested for us day and night.

Words spoken in our homes which are impatient and unkind, angels hear; and do you want to find in the books of heaven a record of the impatient and passionate words you have uttered in your family? Impatience brings the enemy of God and man into your family and drives out the angels of God. If you are abiding in Christ, and Christ in you, you cannot speak angry words.

Fathers and mothers, I beseech you for Christ's sake, to be kind, tender, and patient in your homes. Then light and sunshine will enter your homes, and you will feel that bright beams from the Sun of Righteousness are indeed shining into your hearts.[6]

It is the absence of the graces of God's Spirit that leaves the home in a dark, unhappy condition. Your home should be a blessed sanctuary where God can come in, and where His holy angels can minister unto you. If impatience and unkindness are manifested one to another, angels cannot be attracted to your home; but where love and peace abide, these heavenly ones love to come and bring still more of the holy influence of the home above.[6]

99

SPECIAL CARE FOR THE WEAK

Take heed that ye despise not one of these little ones; for I say unto you, That in heaven their angels do always behold the face of my Father which is in heaven. Matt. 18:10.

Man is God's property, and angels are looking with intense interest to see how man will deal with his fellow man. When heavenly intelligences see those who claim to be the sons and daughters of God putting forth Christlike efforts to help the erring, manifesting a tender, sympathetic spirit for the repentant and the fallen, angels press close to them and bring to their remembrance the very words that will soothe and uplift the soul. Holy angels are on the track of every one of us. We are not to despise the least of God's little ones. . . .

Jesus has given His precious life, His personal attention, to the least of God's little ones; and angels that excel in strength encamp round about them that fear God. Then let us be upon our guard, and never permit one contemptuous thought to occupy the mind in regard to one of the little ones of God. We should look after the erring with solicitude, and speak encouraging words to the fallen, and fear lest by some unwise action we shall turn them away from the pitying Saviour. . . .

All heaven is interested in the work of saving the lost. Angels watch with intense interest to see who will leave the ninety and nine and go out in tempest and storm and rain into the wild desert to seek the lost sheep. The lost are all around us, perishing and sadly neglected. But they are of value to God, the purchase of the blood of Christ.[7]

By all that has given us advantage over another—be it education and refinement, nobility of character, Christian training, religious experience—*we are in debt to those less favored;* and, so far as lies in our power, we are to minister unto them. If we are strong, we are to stay up the hands of the weak. Angels of glory, that do always behold the face of the Father in heaven, make such their special charge. Angels are ever present where they are most needed, with those who have the hardest battle with self to fight and whose surroundings are the most disagreeable. And in this ministry Christ's true followers will cooperate.[8]

I HAVE A GUARDIAN ANGEL

Bless the Lord, ye his angels, that excel in strength, that do his commandments, hearkening unto the voice of his word. Ps. 103:20.

Today, as in the past, all heaven is watching to see the church develop in the true science of salvation. The Lord Jesus is among men. His angels walk among us unrecognized and unacknowledged. We are saved from many snares and unseen dangers that through the machinations and hostility of our foe are placed in our path to destroy us. O that our eyes might be open to discern the watchful solicitude and tender care of the messengers of light! If those who politely acknowledge the favors which they receive from earthly friends would realize how much they owe to God, their hearts would respond in grateful thanks for precious favors that are now unnoticed.[9]

We do not recount God's mercies often enough. . . . By our failure to express gratitude we are dishonoring our Maker. His angels, thousands upon thousands and ten thousand times ten thousand, are commissioned to minister to those who shall be heirs of salvation. They guard us against temporal evil and press back the powers of darkness, else we should be destroyed. Why do we not value God's watchcare? If Satan had his way and carried out his designs, destruction would be seen on every hand. Why do we not remember that we are mercifully shielded from peril? Have we not reason to be thankful every moment, thankful even when there are apparent difficulties in our pathway? Cannot we trust our heavenly Father?[10]

We shall never know what dangers, seen and unseen, we have been delivered from through the interposition of the angels until we shall see in the light of eternity the providences of God. Then we shall better understand what God has done for us all the days of our life. We shall know then that the whole heavenly family watched to see our course of action from day to day.[11]

Every believer who constantly realizes his dependence on God has his appointed angel, sent from heaven to minister to him. The ministry of these angels is especially essential now, for Satan is making his last desperate effort to secure the world.[12]

WORKING WITH THE ANGELS

Are they not all ministering spirits, sent forth to minister for them who shall be heirs of salvation? Heb. 1:14.

One part of the ministry of heavenly angels is to visit our world and oversee the work of the Lord which is in the hands of His stewards. In every time of necessity they minister to those who as co-workers with God are striving to carry forward His work in the earth. . . . The angelic hosts rejoice whenever any part of God's work prospers.

Angels are interested in the spiritual welfare of all who are seeking to restore the moral image of God in man, and the human family are to connect with the heavenly family in binding up the wounds and bruises that sin has made. Angelic agencies, though invisible, are cooperating with visible human agencies, forming a relief association with men. The very angels who, when Satan was seeking the supremacy, fought the battle in the heavenly courts and triumphed on the side of God, the very angels who shouted for joy over the creation of our world and over the creation of our first parents to inhabit the earth, the angels who witnessed the fall of man and his expulsion from his Eden home—these very heavenly messengers are most intensely interested to work in union with the fallen, redeemed race for the salvation of human beings perishing in their sins.

Human agencies are the hands of heavenly instrumentalities, for heavenly angels employ human hands in practical ministry. . . . By uniting with these powers that are omnipotent, we are benefited by their higher education and experience. Thus, as we become partakers of the divine nature and separate selfishness from our lives, special talents for helping one another are granted us. . . .

With what joy and delight Heaven looks upon these blended influences! All heaven is watching those agencies that are as the hand to work out the purposes of God in the earth, thus doing the will and purpose of God in heaven. Such cooperation accomplishes a work that brings honor and glory and majesty to God. Oh, if all would love as Christ has loved, that perishing men might be saved from ruin, what a change would come to our world! [13]

ANGEL GUIDANCE

And the angel of the Lord spake unto Philip, saying, Arise, and go toward the south unto the way that goeth down from Jerusalem unto Gaza, which is desert. Acts 8:26.

God has recorded many narratives in His Inspired Word to teach us that the human family is the object of the special care of heavenly angels. Man is not left to become the sport of Satan's temptations. All heaven is actively engaged in the work of communicating light to the inhabitants of the world, that they may not be left without spiritual guidance. An eye that never slumbers nor sleeps is guarding the camp of Israel. Ten thousand times ten thousand and thousands of thousands of angels are ministering to the needs of the children of men. Voices inspired by God are crying, This is the way, walk ye in it. If men will hear the voice of warning, if they will trust to God's guidance and not to finite judgment, they will be safe. . . .

Heavenly angels watch those who are seeking for enlightenment, and cooperate with those who try to win souls to Christ. This is shown in the experience of Philip and the Ethiopian.

A heavenly messenger was sent to Philip to show him his work for the Ethiopian. . . . Angels of God were taking notice of this seeker for light. . . . Today, as then, angels are leading and guiding those who will be led and guided. The angel sent to Philip could himself have done the work for the Ethiopian, but this was not God's way of working. As God's instruments, men must work for others.

When God pointed out to Philip his work, the disciple did not say, as many are saying today, God does not mean that. I will not be too confident, or I shall make a mistake. Philip that day learned a lesson of conformity to God's will that was worth everything to him. He learned that every soul is precious in the sight of God and that angels will bring light to those who are in need of it. Through the ministration of angels God sends light to His people, and through His people this light is to be given to the world. . . .

Faithful sentinels are on guard, to direct souls in right paths.[14]

THE ACT OF FAITH

Now faith is the substance of things hoped for, the evidence of things not seen. Heb. 11:1.

Faith is not the ground of our salvation, but it is the great blessing —the eye that sees, the ear that hears, the feet that run, the hand that grasps. It is the means, not the end. If Christ gave His life to save sinners, why shall I not take that blessing? My faith grasps it, and thus my faith is the substance of things hoped for, the evidence of things unseen. Thus resting and believing, I have peace with God through the Lord Jesus Christ.[15]

Faith, saving faith . . . is the act of the soul by which the whole man is given over to the guardianship and control of Jesus Christ. He abides in Christ and Christ abides in the soul by faith as supreme. The believer commits his soul and body to God, and with assurance may say, Christ is able to keep that which I have committed unto Him against that day. All who will do this will be saved unto life eternal. There will be an assurance that the soul is washed in the blood of Christ and clothed with His righteousness and precious in the sight of Jesus.[16]

Remember that the exercise of faith is the one means of preserving it. Should you sit always in one position, without moving, your muscles would become strengthless and your limbs would lose the power of motion. The same is true in regard to your religious experience. You must have faith in the promises of God. . . . Faith will perfect itself in exercise and activity.[17]

It is of the greatest importance to us that we surround the soul with the atmosphere of faith. Every day we are deciding our own eternal destiny in harmony with the atmosphere that surrounds the soul. We are individually accountable for the influence that we exert, and consequences that we do not see will result from our words and actions. If God would have saved Sodom for the sake of ten righteous persons, what would be the influence for good that might go out as the result of the faithfulness of the people of God if every one who professed the name of Christ were also clothed with His righteousness?[18]

FAITH VERSUS SIGHT

For we are saved by hope: but hope that is seen is not hope: for what a man seeth, why doth he yet hope for? Rom. 8:24.

Our Saviour asks the question, "When the Son of man cometh, shall he find faith on the earth?" (Luke 18:8), implying that true faith would be almost extinct. It is too true that the spirit of doubt, criticism, and faultfinding is destroying confidence in God's Word and in His work. It is impossible for the carnal mind to understand or appreciate the work of God. All who desire to doubt or cavil will find occasion. . . . Those who in humility of heart follow the light as it shines upon them will receive clearer light, while those who refuse to obey till they can see all occasion for doubt removed, will be left in darkness.[19]

God gives us sufficient evidence to enable us to accept the truth understandingly, but He does not propose to remove all occasion for doubt and unbelief. Should He do this, there would no longer be a necessity for the exercise of faith; for we would be able to walk by sight. All who with a teachable spirit study the Word of God may learn therefrom the way of salvation, yet they may not be able to understand every portion of the Sacred Record. . . . Whatever is clearly established by the Word of God we should accept, without attempting to meet every doubt which Satan may suggest, or with our finite understanding to fathom the counsels of the infinite One, or to criticize the manifestations of His grace or power. . . .

If we seek in humility to learn the will of God as revealed in His Word, and then obey that will as it is made plain to our understanding, we shall become rooted and grounded in the truth. Said Christ: "If any man will do his will, he shall know of the doctrine" (John 7:17). . . .

Let us draw nearer and nearer to the pure light of Heaven, remembering that divine illumination will increase according to our onward movements, qualifying us to meet new responsibilities and emergencies. The path of the just is progressive, from strength to strength, from grace to grace, and from glory to glory.[20]

THE DANGEROUS SEEDS OF DOUBT

God is not a man, that he should lie; neither the son of man, that he should repent: hath he said, and shall he not do it? or hath he spoken, and shall he not make it good? Num. 23:19.

Those who are perpetually talking doubts and demanding additional evidence to banish their cloud of unbelief do not build on the Word. Their faith rests on circumstances; it is founded in feeling. But feeling, be it ever so pleasing, 'is not faith. God's Word is the foundation upon which our hopes of heaven must be built.

It is a great misfortune to be a chronic doubter, keeping the eye and thoughts on self. While you are beholding self, while this is the theme of thought and conversation, you cannot expect to be conformed to the image of Christ. Self is not your saviour. You have no redeeming qualities in yourself. "I" is a very leaky boat for your faith to embark in. Just as surely as you trust yourself in it, it will founder. The lifeboat, to the lifeboat! This is your only safety. Jesus is the captain of the lifeboat, and He has never lost a passenger.[21]

We need a more heavenly atmosphere to surround our souls. We need to have our lips touched with a live coal from off the altar. We need to hear the word from Christ, "Be thou clean." If we have scattered darkness, if we have accumulated rubbish and hoarded doubts, if we have planted seeds of doubt and discouragement in the minds of others, may God help us to see our sin. We cannot afford to drop a single word of doubt, for it will germinate and grow and bring forth a bitter harvest. We should take heed to the exhortation, "Be ye holy in all manner of conversation" (1 Peter 1:15). One seed of doubt sown, and it is beyond the power of man to kill it. God alone can pluck it from the soul. . . .

The great field of the promises of God has been presented before us, and by these we are to lay hold of faith, hope, and love. In these graces the church may shine forth and present to the world a living representation of the righteousness of Christ. Living faith grasps the hand of divine power, and faith is as an anchor to the soul, sure and steadfast. . . . John says, "This is the victory that overcometh the world, even our faith" (1 John 5:4).[22]

106

WE EXPECT TOO LITTLE

According to your faith be it unto you. Matt. 9:29.

Faith is the medium of connection between human weakness and divine power. . . . We must seek to have our faith strengthened. The iniquity that abounds must not for one moment lessen our faith and love for God or weaken our trust in His sure promises, else some mighty storm of temptation will sweep us away from the true foundation. We have a great work to do, and we need greater faith. . . . Through communion with God our faith will be strengthened, and the trial of our faith may prove our signal triumph.[23]

There is a real work to be wrought in us. Constantly we must submit our will to God's will, our way to God's way. . . . By beholding as in a glass the glory of the Lord, we are actually changed into the same image, from glory to glory, even as by the Spirit of the Lord. We expect too little, and we receive according to our faith. We are not to cling to our own ways, our own plans, our own ideas. . . . Besetting sins are to be conquered and evil habits overcome. Wrong dispositions and feelings are to be rooted out, and holy tempers and emotions begotten in us by the Spirit of God. . . .

Faith, living faith, we must have, a faith that works by love and purifies the soul. We must learn to take everything to the Lord with simplicity and earnest faith. The greatest burden we have to bear in this life is self. Unless we learn in the school of Christ to be meek and lowly, we shall miss precious opportunities and privileges for becoming acquainted with Jesus. Self is the most difficult thing we have to manage. In laying off burdens, let us not forget to lay self at the feet of Christ.

Hand yourself over to Jesus, to be molded and fashioned by Him, that you may be made vessels unto honor. Your temptations, your ideas, your feelings, must all be laid at the foot of the cross. Then the soul is ready to listen to words of divine instruction. Jesus will give you to drink of the water which flows from the river of God. Under the softening and subduing influence of His Spirit your coldness and listlessness will disappear. Christ will be in you a well of water, springing up into everlasting life.[24]

THE FAITH THAT AVAILS

And Jesus said, Somebody hath touched me: for I perceive that virtue is gone out of me. Luke 8:46.

There are two kinds of connection between the branches and the vine. The one is deceptive, superficial.

The crowd pressing upon Christ had no living union with Him by genuine faith. But a poor woman who had been many years a great sufferer and had spent all her living upon physicians but was made no better, but rather worse, thought if she could get within reach of Him, if she could only touch the hem of His garment, she would be made whole. Christ understood all that was in her heart, and He placed Himself where she could have the opportunity she desired. He would use that act to distinguish the touch of genuine faith from the casual contact of those who were crowding about Him. . . .

When the woman reached forth her hand and touched the hem of His garment, she thought this stealthy touch would not be known by anyone; but Christ recognized that touch and responded to her faith by His healing power. She realized in a moment that she was made whole, and the Lord Jesus would not let such faith pass unnoticed. He turned Him about quickly and said, "Who touched me?" All the disciples were pressing close around Him, and Peter said, "The multitude throng thee and press thee, and sayest thou, Who touched me? And Jesus said, Somebody hath touched me: for I perceive that virtue is gone out of me" (Luke 8:45, 46).

When the woman saw that she was not hid she came tremblingly and cast herself at His feet, telling the whole story. For twelve years she had been afflicted, but as soon as her finger touched the hem of His garment she was made whole. Jesus said to her, "Daughter, be of good comfort: thy faith hath made thee whole; go in peace" (verse 48). The mere touch of faith brought its reward.[25]

The faith which avails to bring us in vital contact with Christ expresses on our part supreme preference, perfect reliance, entire consecration. . . . It works in the life of the follower of Christ true obedience to God's commandments, for love to God and love to man will be the result of vital connection with Christ.[26]

A WORKING FAITH

And be found in him, not having mine own righteousness, which is of the law, but that which is through the faith of Christ, the righteousness which is of God by faith. Phil. 3:9.

It is one thing to read and teach the Bible, and another thing to have by practice its life-giving, sanctifying principles engrafted on the soul. . . . "By grace are ye saved through faith" (Eph. 2:8). The mind should be educated to exercise faith rather than to cherish doubt, suspicion, and jealousy. We are too prone to regard obstacles as impossibilities. To have faith in the promises of God, to go forward by faith, pressing on without being governed by circumstances, is a lesson hard to learn. Yet it is a positive necessity that every child of God should learn this lesson. The grace of God through Christ is ever to be cherished, for it is given us as the only way of approaching God. . . .

The faith mentioned in God's Word calls for a life in which faith in Christ is an active, living principle. It is God's will that faith in Christ shall be made perfect by works; He connects the salvation and eternal life of those who believe, with these works, and through them provides for the light of truth to go to all countries and peoples. This is the fruit of the workings of God's Spirit.

We show our faith in God by obeying His commands. Faith is always expressed in words and actions. It produces practical results, for it is a vital element in the life. The life that is molded by faith develops a determination to advance, to go forward, following in the footsteps of Christ.[27]

We have been taken as rough stones out of the quarry of the world by the cleaver of truth and placed in the workshop of God. He who has genuine faith in Christ as his personal Saviour will find that the truth accomplishes a definite work for him. His faith is a working faith. . . . We cannot create our faith, but we can be colaborers with Christ in promoting the growth and triumph of faith.[28]

The faith that works by love and purifies the soul produces the fruit of humility, patience, forbearance, long-suffering, peace, joy, and willing obedience.[29]

HOW FAITH WORKS

For in Jesus Christ neither circumcision availeth any thing, nor uncircumcision; but faith which worketh by love. Gal. 5:6.

Christ has shown His great love for us by giving His life that we should not perish in our sins, that He might clothe us with His salvation. If this divine love is cherished in our hearts, it cements and strengthens our union with those of like faith. "He that dwelleth in love dwelleth in God, and God in him" (1 John 4:16). The strengthening of our love for our brethren and sisters strengthens our love for Christ. This principle of love for God and for those for whom Christ died, needs to be quickened by the Holy Spirit and cemented with brotherly kindness, tenderness; it needs to be strengthened by acts which testify that God is love. This union, which joins heart with heart, is not the result of sentimentalism, but the working of a healthful principle. Faith works by love, and purifies the soul from all selfishness. Thus the soul is perfected in love. And having found grace and mercy through Christ's precious blood, how can we fail to be tender and merciful? . . .

Faith in Jesus Christ as our personal Saviour, the One who pardons our sins and transgressions, the One who is able to keep us from sin and lead us in His footsteps, is set forth in the fifty-eighth chapter of Isaiah. Here are presented the fruits of a faith that works by love and purifies the soul from selfishness. Faith and works are here combined.

"Is not this the fast that I have chosen? to loose the bands of wickedness, to undo the heavy burdens, and to let the oppressed go free, and that ye break every yoke? Is it not to deal thy bread to the hungry, and that thou bring the poor that are cast out to thy house? when thou seest the naked, that thou cover him; and that thou hide not thyself from thine own flesh? Then shall thy light break forth as the morning, and thine health shall spring forth speedily: and thy righteousness shall go before thee; the glory of the Lord shall be thy rereward. . . . And the Lord shall guide thee continually, and satisfy thy soul in drought, and make fat thy bones: and thou shalt be like a watered garden, and like a spring of water, whose waters fail not." [30]

110

TRUST YOURSELF WITH GOD

But the Lord is faithful, who shall stablish you, and keep you from evil. 2 Thess. 3:3.

How many there are who go through life under a cloud of condemnation! They do not believe God's word. They have no faith that He will do as He has said. Many who long to see others resting in the pardoning love of Christ do not rest in it for themselves. But how can they possibly lead others to show simple, childlike faith in the heavenly Father when they measure His love by their feelings?

Let us trust God's word implicitly, remembering that we are His sons and daughters. Let us train ourselves to believe His word. We hurt the heart of Christ by doubting, when He has given such evidence of His love. He laid down His life to save us. He says to us: "Come unto me, . . . and I will give you rest. . . ." Do you believe He will do as He has said? Then, after you have complied with the conditions, carry no longer the burden of your sins. Let it roll upon the Saviour. Trust yourself with Him. Has He not promised to give you rest? But to many He is obliged to say sorrowfully, "Ye will not come to me, that ye might have life" (John 5:40).[31]

Behold Christ. Dwell upon His love and mercy. This will fill the soul with abhorrence for all that is sinful and will inspire it with an intense desire for the righteousness of Christ. The more clearly we see the Saviour, the more clearly shall we discern our defects of character. Confess your sins to Christ, and with true contrition of soul cooperate with Him by putting these sins away. Believe that they are pardoned. The promise is positive, "If we confess our sins, he is faithful and just to forgive us our sins, and to cleanse us from all unrighteousness" (1 John 1:9). Be assured that the word of God will not fail. He who has promised is faithful. It is as much your duty to believe that God will fulfill His word and forgive you as it is to confess your sins. . . .

Look steadfastly to Jesus. Behold Him, full of grace and truth. He will make His goodness pass before you while He hides you in the cleft of the rock. You will be enabled to endure the seeing of Him who is invisible, and by beholding you will be transformed.[31]

A TEST OF FAITH

By faith Abraham, when he was called to go out into a place which he should after receive for an inheritance, obeyed; and he went out, not knowing whither he went. Heb. 11:8.

God selected Abraham as His messenger through whom to communicate light to the world. The word of God came to him, not with the presentation of flattering prospects in this life of large salary, of great appreciation and worldly honor. "Get thee out of thy country, and from thy kindred, and from thy father's house, unto a land that I will shew thee" (Gen. 12:1), was the divine message to Abraham. The patriarch obeyed. . . . He forsook his country, his home, his relatives, and all pleasant associations connected with his early life, to become a pilgrim and a stranger.[32]

Abraham . . . might have reasoned and questioned the purposes of God in this. But he showed that he had perfect confidence that God was leading him; he did not question whether it was a fertile, pleasant country or whether or not he should have ease. He went at God's bidding. This is a lesson to every one of us. . . .

There are those who may be in favorable positions . . . in all the things of this life, but God may have a work for them to do elsewhere, a work that they could not do among their relatives and friends. The very position of ease and the relatives who surround them may prevent them from developing the very traits of character which God would have them develop. But God sees that to change their position and to send them where their surroundings will be entirely different will be the very best place for them to develop a character which will glorify Him. . . .

When we set ourselves where all is convenience and ease, we do not feel so much the necessity of depending moment by moment upon God. God in His providence brings us into positions where we shall feel our necessity of His help and strength. . . .

It is stated of Abraham that he looked for a city whose builder and maker is God. . . . So with every one of us. We are only pilgrims and strangers in this world. We are seeking the city which Abraham looked for, whose builder and maker is God.[33]

112

SHUN NEEDLESS WORRY

Therefore I say unto you, Take no thought for your life, what ye shall eat, or what ye shall drink; nor yet for your body, what ye shall put on. Is not the life more than meat, and the body than raiment? Matt. 6:25.

While you do your best, weary not your body and mind with the cares of this life. Do not spoil your religious experience by worry, but trust the Lord to work for you and to do for you what you cannot do for yourself. The life is more than meat. . . .

There is much needless worrying, much trouble of mind, over things that cannot be helped. The Lord would have His children put their trust fully in Him. Our Lord is a just and righteous God; His children should acknowledge His goodness and His justice in the large and small things of life. Those who cherish the spirit of worry and complaint are refusing to recognize His guiding hand.

Needless anxiety is a foolish thing, and it hinders us from standing in a true position before God. When the Holy Spirit comes into the soul, there will be no desire to complain and murmur because we do not have everything we want. Rather, we will thank God from a full heart for the blessings that we have. . . .

There is one blessing that all may have who seek for it in the right way. It is the Holy Spirit of God, and this is a blessing that brings all other blessings in its train. If we will come to God as little children, asking for His grace and power and salvation, not for our own uplifting, but that we may bring blessing to those around us, our petitions will not be denied. Then let us study the Word of God that we may know how to take hold of His promises and claim them as our own. Then we shall be happy. . . .

Christ came to earth and gave His life that we might have eternal salvation. He wants to encircle each of us with the atmosphere of heaven, that we may give to the world an example that will honor the religion of Christ. . . . In this life we are to be controlled by the spirit that rules in the heavenly courts. Righteousness and truth are to go before us. And the glory of the Lord will be the rereward of all who serve Him acceptably. They obtain Christ's righteousness.[34]

GOD CARES FOR YOU

Behold the fowls of the air: for they sow not, neither do they reap, nor gather into barns; yet your heavenly Father feedeth them. Are ye not much better than they? Matt. 6:26.

As we look upon the lofty trees waving with fresh, green foliage, and the earth covered with its green velvet carpet, and the flowers and shrubs springing from the earth, we should remember that all these beauties of nature have been used by Christ in teaching His grand lessons of truth. As we look upon the fields of waving grain, and listen to the merry songsters in their leafy homes, and view the boats upon the water of the lake, we should remember the words of Christ upon the lakeside, in the groves, and on the mountains, and the lessons there taught by Him should be repeated to us by the similar objects of nature which surround us.[35]

He made use of the lofty trees, the cultivated soil, the barren rocks, the flowers of beauty struggling through the clefts, the everlasting hills, the glowing flowers of the valley, the birds caroling their songs in the leafy branches, the spotless lily resting in purity upon the bosom of the water. All these objects that made up the living scene around them were made the medium by which His lessons were impressed upon the minds of His hearers. They were thus brought home to the hearts of all, . . . leading them gently up from the contemplation of the Creator's works in nature to nature's God. . . .

In one of His most impressive lessons Christ says, "Behold the fowls of the air; for they sow not, neither do they reap, nor gather into barns; yet your heavenly Father feedeth them. . . ."

The Great Teacher is here leading out minds to understand the parental care and love which God has for His children. He directs them to observe the birds flitting from tree to tree, or skimming upon the bosom of the lake, without a flutter of distrust or fear. God's eye is upon these little creatures; He provides them food; He answers all their simple wants. Jesus inquires, "Are ye not much better than they?" . . .

If God cares for and preserves the little birds, will He not have far greater love and care for the creatures formed in His image? [36]

EXPRESSIONS OF GOD'S LOVE

And why take ye thought for raiment? Consider the lilies of the field, how they grow; they toil not, neither do they spin: and yet I say unto you, That even Solomon in all his glory was not arrayed like one of these. Matt. 6:28, 29.

The courtly robes of the greatest king that ever sat upon an earthly throne could not compare, in their artificial splendor, with the spotless beauty of the lilies fashioned by the divine hand. This is an example of the estimate which the Creator of all that is beautiful places upon the artificial in comparison with the natural.

God has given us these things of beauty as an expression of His love, that we may obtain correct views of His character. We are not to worship the things of nature, but in them we are to read the love of God. Nature is an open book, from the study of which we may gain a knowledge of the Creator and be attracted to Him by the things of use and beauty which He has provided. . . .

"Wherefore, if God so clothe the grass of the field, which today is, and tomorrow is cast into the oven, shall he not much more clothe you, O ye of little faith? Therefore take no thought, saying, What shall we eat? or, What shall we drink? or, Wherewithal shall we be clothed?" (verses 30, 31). Much unnecessary care and anxiety is felt in regard to our future, concerning what we shall eat and drink and wherewithal we shall be clothed. The labor and worry of needless display in apparel causes much fatigue and unhappiness and shortens our lives. Our Saviour would not only have us discern the love of God displayed in the beautiful flowers about us, but He would have us learn from them lessons of simplicity and of perfect faith and confidence in our heavenly Father.

If God cares to make these inanimate things so beautiful, that will be cut down and perish in a day, how much more careful will He be to supply the needs of His obedient children, whose lives may be as enduring as eternity. How readily will He give them the adornment of His grace, the strength of wisdom, the ornament of a meek and quiet spirit. The love of God to man is incomprehensible, broad as the world, high as heaven, and as enduring as eternity.[37]

115

TAKE GOD'S WORD ON TRUST

I, even I, am he that blotteth out thy transgressions for mine own sake, and will not remember thy sins. Put me in remembrance: let us plead together: declare thou, that thou mayest be justified. Isa. 43:25, 26.

Satan will come to you saying, You are a sinner. But do not let him fill your mind with the thought that, because you are sinful, God has cast you off. Say to him, Yes; I am a sinner, and for that reason I need a Saviour. I need forgiveness and pardon, and Christ says that if I come to Him I shall not perish. In His letter to me I read, "If we confess our sins, he is faithful and just to forgive us our sins, and to cleanse us from all unrighteousness" (1 John 1:9). I will believe the word He has left for me. . . .

The moment you grasp God's promises by faith and say, I am the lost sheep that Jesus came to save, a new life will take possession of you, and you will receive strength to resist the tempter. But faith to grasp the promises does not come by feeling. "Faith cometh by hearing, and hearing by the word of God" (Rom. 10:17). You must not look for some great change to take place; you must not expect to feel some wonderful emotion. . . .

Take God's word on trust, saying, He loves me: He gave His life for me; and He will save me. . . . Look away from yourself to Jesus. Embrace Him as your Saviour. Cease to bemoan your helpless condition. Looking to Jesus, the author and finisher of your faith, you will be inspired with hope and will see the salvation of God. When you feel tempted to mourn, force your lips to utter the praises of God. "Rejoice in the Lord alway" (Phil. 4:4). Is He not worthy of praise? Then educate your lips to talk of His glory and to magnify His name. . . .

Today the Lord says to you, Be not discouraged, but cast your burdens upon Me. You cannot carry your own sins. I will take them all. . . . If you will trust in Me, you will not want any good thing. . . .

Never has a soul that trusts in Jesus been left to perish. "I, even I, am he," the Lord declares, "that blotteth out thy transgressions for mine own sake, and will not remember thy sins." [38]

BATTLES TO FIGHT

Fight the good fight of faith, lay hold on eternal life, where-unto thou art also called, and hast professed a good profession before many witnesses. 1 Tim. 6:12.

There are continuous battles to fight, and we are not safe a moment unless we place ourselves under the guardianship of One who gave His own precious life to make it possible for everyone who will believe in Him as the Son of God, while meeting the strain of Satan's varied science, to escape the corruptions that are in the world through lust. He is fully able, in response to our faith, to unite our human with His divine nature. We are, while trusting in and partaking of the divine nature and strengthening our own efforts, proclaiming Christ's mission on earth to be peace on earth and good will toward men. We are bound to speak of the dangers of the warfare with invisible foes, and to keep the armor on, for we war not merely against flesh and blood but against principalities and powers and spiritual wickedness in high places. . . . Therefore we need to keep under the constant guardianship of holy angels.

To follow Christ is not freedom from conflict. It is not child's play. It is not spiritual idleness. All the enjoyment in Christ's service means sacred obligations in meeting oft stern conflicts. To follow Christ means stern battles, active labor, warfare against the world, the flesh, and the devil. Our enjoyment is the victories gained for Christ in earnest, hard, warfare. . . . We are enlisted for labor, "not for the meat which perisheth, but for that meat which endureth unto everlasting life" (John 6:27). . . .

Every soul must count the cost. Not one will succeed but by strenuous effort. We must spiritually exercise all our powers and crucify the flesh with its affections and lusts. Crucifixion means much more than many suppose. . . .

It is a constant watchfulness to be faithful unto death, to fight the good fight of faith until the warfare is ended and as overcomers we shall receive the crown of life.[39]

I can see my Redeemer, in whom I have fresh encouragement to trust as a never-failing Source of strength.[39]

A NOMINAL FAITH NOT SUFFICIENT

For I the Lord thy God will hold thy right hand, saying unto thee, Fear not; I will help thee. Isa. 41:13.

For a few weeks past I have had a deep sense of the promises of God and the hope of the Christian. The Bible never seemed to me so full of rich gems of promise as within the last few weeks. It seems that the dews of heaven are ready to fall upon us and refresh us, if we will only take the promises to ourselves. We can never overcome our own natural tendencies without the help of Heaven, and the precious Jesus places Himself right by our side to help us in this work. He says, "Lo, I am with you alway, even unto the end of the world" (Matt. 28:20). We want to believe just what Christ has said. We want that our faith shall compass the promises. . . .

It is a great thing to believe in Jesus. We hear many say, "Believe, believe; all that you have to do is to believe in Jesus." But it is our privilege to inquire, What does this belief take in? and what does it comprehend? There are many of us who have a nominal faith but we do not bring that faith into our characters. . . . We must have that faith which works by love and purifies the soul, that this belief in Christ will lead us to put away everything that is offensive in His sight. Unless we have this faith that works, it is of no advantage to us. You may admit that Christ is the Saviour of the world, but is He your Saviour? Do you believe today that He will give you strength and power to overcome every defect in your character? . . .

We have individually this lesson to learn of special trust in our Saviour. We are to trust our heavenly Father just as a child trusts its earthly parents, and believe that He is working for our good in all things; and that every struggling cry and every effort against the adversary of our soul enters into the ears of the God of Sabaoth, and that He will send us help every time we need it. He will help us over every temptation if we call upon Him in faith. Now this is the lesson we must learn.

I can trust my Saviour; He saves me today; and while I am struggling to overcome the temptations of the enemy He will give me grace to conquer.[40]

118

ABUNDANT MERCY

They that know thy name will put their trust in thee: for thou, Lord, hast not forsaken them that seek thee. Ps. 9:10.

A soul whom God had forsaken would never feel as you* have felt and would never love the truth and salvation as you have loved it. Oh, if God's Spirit ceases to strive with a soul it is left in an indifferent state, and all the time thinks that it is well enough off. . . . You must not gratify the enemy in the least by doubting and casting away your confidence. Said the angel, "God leaves not His people, even if they err. He turns not from them in wrath for any light thing. If they sin they have an advocate with the Father, Jesus Christ the righteous."

This Advocate pleads for sinners and the Father accepts His prayer. He turns not away the request of His beloved Son. He who so loved you as to give His own life for you will not turn you off and forsake you unless you willfully, determinedly forsake Him to serve the world and Satan. Jesus loves to have you come to Him just as you are, hopeless and helpless, and cast yourself upon His all-abundant mercy and believe that He will receive you just as you are.

You dwell upon the dark side. You must turn your mind away, and instead of thinking all the time upon the wrath of God, think of His abundant mercy, His willingness to save poor sinners, and then believe He saves you. You must in the name of God break this spell that is upon you. You must cry out, "I will, I do believe!" Jesus retains your name upon His breastplate and pleads for you before His Father, and if your eyes could be opened you would see heavenly angels ministering unto you, hovering about and driving back the evil angels that they should not utterly destroy. . . .

God calls upon you to believe. Heed His voice. Cease talking of the wrath of God and talk of His compassion and His abundant mercy. Jesus sits as a refiner and purifier of silver. The furnace in which you may be placed may be very hot, yet you will come forth as gold seven times purified, reflecting the image of Jesus. Have courage. Look up, believe, and you shall see of the salvation of God.[41]

---

* From a letter of comfort to a troubled heart.

TRUST IN TIME OF TRIAL

Cast thy burden upon the Lord, and he shall sustain thee: he shall never suffer the righteous to be moved. Ps. 55:22.

The Lord's care is over all His creatures. He loves them all, and makes no difference, except that He has the most tender pity for those who are called to bear life's heaviest burdens. God's children must meet trials and difficulties. But they should accept their lot with a cheerful spirit, remembering that for all that the world neglects to bestow, God Himself will make up to them in the best of favors.[42]

We are in danger, by worrying, of manufacturing yokes for our necks. Let us not worry, for thus we make the yoke more severe and the burden heavy. Let us do all we can without worrying, trusting in Christ.[43]

With the continual change of circumstances, changes come in our experience; and by these changes we are either elated or depressed. But the change of circumstances has no power to change God's relation to us. He is the same yesterday, today, and forever; and He asks us to have unquestioning confidence in His love.

Satan watches his opportunity to bring about circumstances that will tend to arouse unbelief, hoping to lead us to doubt God. We cannot afford to cherish one thought of unbelief. When we are tempted to look on the dark side, let us open the windows of the soul heavenward, that the bright beams of the Sun of Righteousness may shine in. Let us draw near to God. He has promised that as we do this He will draw near to us and lift up for us a standard against the enemy. The efficiency of His keeping power has in no wise decreased. Let faith stand its trial without wavering, for Christ is a perfect Saviour.

You may look upon your plans as perfect, but God may see that it is essential for you to suffer disappointment in order that your plans may be brought into harmony with His plan. His way is always the right way. He seeth and knoweth all things. We do not always see as He sees. . . .

Take your stand on the word of God. Whatever may occur, hold fast the beginning of your confidence firm unto the end.[44]

TRUST IN TIMES OF AFFLICTION

*My soul shall be satisfied as with marrow and fatness; and my
mouth shall praise thee with joyful lips: when I remember thee
upon my bed, and meditate on thee in the night watches.*
Ps. 63:5, 6.

*Many hours I have passed in wakefulness and pain, but I have
had the precious promises of God brought so fresh and with reviving
power to my mind. The dear Saviour has been very near to me, and I
love to meditate upon the love of Jesus. His tender compassion and
the lessons which He gave to His disciples become clear and so full
of meaning that they are the feeding of the soul upon heavenly
manna. . . . When the Lord sees fit to say, "Lie there patiently, and
reflect"; and when the Holy Spirit brings many things to my memory, precious beyond expression, I do not know what reason I have
to complain. . . . I call to mind the verses which have been a comfort
to me many times in my affliction:

"I see not a step before me as I tread on another year;
 But the past is in God's keeping, the future His mercy shall clear,
 And what looks dark in the distance may brighten as I draw near.

"O restful, blissful ignorance; 'tis blessed not to know;
 It stills me in those mighty arms, which will not let me go,
 And hushes my sad soul to rest on the bosom which loves me so.

"So I go on, not knowing, I would not if I might.
 I would rather walk in the dark with God, than go alone in the light.
 I would rather walk with Him by faith, than walk alone by sight.

"My heart shrinks back from trial which the future may disclose,
 Yet I never have a sorrow but what the dear Lord chose.
 So I send the coming teardrops back with the whispered word,
 'He knows.' " [45]

---

* Written during a long period of illness and suffering, while the author was in
Australia.

TRUST WHEN YOU HAVE FAILED

Not as though I had already attained, either were already perfect: but I follow after, if that I may apprehend that for which also I am apprehended of Christ Jesus. Phil. 3:12.

In order to fight successfully in the battle against sin, you must keep close to Jesus. Do not talk unbelief; you have no excuse for doing this. . . . Unbelief always separates the soul from Christ.

It is not praiseworthy to talk of our weakness and discouragement. Let each one say, "I am grieved that I yield to temptation, that my prayers are so feeble, my faith so weak. I have no excuse to plead for being dwarfed in my religious life. But I am seeking to obtain completeness of character in Christ. I have sinned, and yet I love Jesus. I have fallen many times, and yet He has reached out His hand to save me. I have told Him all about my mistakes. I have confessed with shame and sorrow that I have dishonored Him. I have looked to the cross, and have said, All this He suffered for me. The Holy Spirit has shown me my ingratitude, my sin in putting Christ to open shame. He who knows no sin has forgiven my sin. He calls me to a higher, nobler life, and I press on to the things that are before." . . .

The humility that bears fruit, filling the soul with a sense of the love of God, will speak for the one who has cherished it, in the great day when men will be rewarded according as their works have been. Happy will be the one of whom it can be said, "The Spirit of God never stirred this man's soul in vain. He went forward and upward from strength to strength. Self was not woven into his life. Each message of correction, warning, and counsel he received as a blessing from God. Thus the way was prepared for him to receive still greater blessings, because God did not speak to him in vain. Each step upward on the ladder of progress prepared him to climb still higher. From the top of the ladder the bright beams of God's glory shone upon him. He did not think of resting, but sought constantly to attain the wisdom and righteousness of Christ. Ever he pressed toward the mark for the prize of the high calling of God in Christ Jesus."

This experience every one who is saved must have.[46]

TRUST IN TIME OF DIFFICULTY

Although the fig tree shall not blossom, neither shall fruit be in the vines; the labour of the olive shall fail, and the fields shall yield no meat; the flock shall be cut off from the fold, and there shall be no herd in the stalls: yet I will rejoice in the Lord, I will joy in the God of my salvation. Hab. 3:17, 18.

The children of God may rejoice in all things and at all times. When troubles and difficulties come, believing in the wise providence of God, you may rejoice. You need not wait for a happy flight of feeling, but by faith you may lay hold of the promises and lift up a hymn of thanksgiving to God. . . .

Memory's hall should be hung with sacred pictures, with views of Jesus, with lessons of His truth, with revealings of His matchless charms. If memory's hall were thus furnished, we would not look upon our lot as intolerable. We would not talk of the faults of others. Our souls would be full of Jesus and His love. We would not desire to dictate to the Lord the way that He should lead. We would love God supremely and our neighbor as ourselves. When the joy of the Lord is in the soul, you will not be able to repress it; you will want to tell others of the treasure you have found; you will speak of Jesus and His matchless charms. We should devote all to Him. Our minds should be educated to dwell upon those things that will glorify God; and if our mental powers are dedicated to God, our talents will improve, and we shall have more and more ability to render to the Master. We shall become channels of light to others.

We can have a close connection with God and with our Saviour; and when we are connected with God, we shall be all light in the Lord, for in Him is no darkness at all.[47]

As we learn of Christ, we shall understand how to keep our spiritual strength, we shall feed on the Word of God, and we shall have the blessed experience described by the apostle in these words: "Whom having not seen, ye love; in whom, though now ye see him not, yet believing, ye rejoice with joy unspeakable and full of glory" (1 Peter 1:8).[47]

TRUST WHEN YOU MAKE MISTAKES

My soul, wait thou only upon God; for my expectation is from him. He only is my rock and my salvation: he is my defence; I shall not be moved. Ps. 62:5, 6.

To each one of us has been given the inestimable privilege of being a child of God. Why, then, should we be unhappy? We are all sinful, but we have a Saviour who can take away our sins, for in Him is no sin. We all have many difficulties to meet, many perplexing problems to solve. But we have an all-powerful Helper, who will listen to our requests as willingly and gladly as He listened to the requests of those who, when He was on this earth in person, came to Him for help. . . .

Do you make mistakes? Do not let this discourage you. The Lord may permit you to make small mistakes in order to save you from making larger mistakes. Go to Jesus, and ask Him to forgive you, and then believe that He does. "If we confess our sins, he is faithful and just to forgive us our sins, and to cleanse us from all unrighteousness" (1 John 1:9).[48]

When discouragement presses heavily upon you, read the following scriptures: . . .

"Deep calleth unto deep at the noise of thy waterspouts: all thy waves and thy billows are gone over me. Yet the Lord will command his lovingkindness in the daytime, and in the night his song shall be with me, and my prayer unto the God of my life. I will say unto God my rock, Why hast thou forgotten me? why go I mourning because of the oppression of the enemy? . . . Why art thou cast down, O my soul? and why art thou disquieted within me? hope thou in God: for I shall yet praise him, who is the health of my countenance, and my God" (Ps. 42:7-11).

"God is our refuge and strength, a very present help in trouble. Therefore will not we fear, though the earth be removed, and though the mountains be carried into the midst of the sea; though the waters thereof roar and be troubled, though the mountains shake with the swelling thereof." "For this God is our God for ever and ever: he will be our guide even unto death" (Ps. 46:1-3; 48:14).[48]

THE GARDEN OF GOD'S PROMISES

For ye have need of patience, that, after ye have done the will of God, ye might receive the promise. Heb. 10:36.

The promises of God are like precious flowers scattered through a garden. The Lord would have us linger over them, looking closely into them, taking in their loveliness, and appreciating the favor that God has bestowed upon us by making such rich provisions for our needs. Were it not for contemplation of the promises of God, we could not understand the gracious love and compassion of God toward us or realize how rich were the treasures prepared for those who ,love Him. He would have the soul encouraged to repose in faith upon Him, the only sufficiency of the human agent.

We are to send our petitions through the darkest clouds that Satan may cast over us, and let our faith pierce to the throne of God encircled by the rainbow of promise, the assurance that God is true, that in Him is no variableness neither shadow of turning. The answer may appear to be delayed, but it is not so. The petition is accepted, and the answer given when it is essential for the best good of the petitioner and when the fulfillment of the request will work most for our eternal interest. God scatters His blessings all along our path to brighten our heavenward journey. . . .

We are to come before the mercy seat with reverence, calling up to our mind the promises that God has given, contemplating the goodness of God, and offering up thankful praises for His unchangeable love. We are not to trust in our finite prayers, but in the word of our heavenly Father, in His assurance of His love for us. Believing the promise of His unchanging love, we press our petitions to the throne of grace. Our faith may be tested by delay, but the prophet has given instruction as to what we should do. He says, "Who is among you that feareth the Lord, that obeyeth the voice of his servant, that walketh in darkness, and hath no light? let him trust in the name of the Lord, and stay upon his God" (Isa. 50:10).

Wait upon the Lord; He has made the promise and is back of the assurance. . . . He who hungers and thirsts after righteousness will be filled.[49]

FEELINGS NOT A TEST

Let us hold fast the profession of our faith without wavering; (for he is faithful that promised). Heb. 10:23.

The religion of Christ is not a religion of mere emotion. You cannot depend upon your feelings for an evidence of acceptance with God, for feelings are variable. You must plant your feet on the promises of God's Word . . . and learn to live by faith.[50]

As soon as one begins to contemplate his feelings he is on dangerous ground. If he feels happy and joyous, then he is very confident and has very pleasing emotions. The change will come. There are circumstances that occur which bring depression and sad feelings; then the mind will naturally begin to doubt whether the Lord is with him or not.

Now, the feelings must not be made the test of the spiritual state, be they good or be they discouraging. The word of God is to be our evidence of our true standing before Him. Many are bewildered on this point. . . .

If you confess your sins, believe they are pardoned, because the promise is positive. "If we confess our sins, he is faithful and just to forgive us our sins, and to cleanse us from all unrighteousness" (1 John 1:9). Why, then, dishonor God by doubting His pardoning love? Having confessed your sins, believe that the word of God will not fail, but that He is faithful that hath promised. It is just as much your duty to believe that God will fulfill His word and forgive your sins as it is your duty to confess your sins. Your faith must be exercised in God as one who will do just as He has said He would do—pardon all your transgressions. . . .

Oh, how very many go mourning, sinning and repenting, but always under a cloud of condemnation! They do not believe the word of the Lord. They do not believe that He will do just as He said He would do. . . . You hurt the heart of Christ by doubting, when He has given us such evidences of His love in giving His own life to save us that we should not perish but have everlasting life.[51]

We must trust; we must educate and train our souls to believe the word of God implicitly.[51]

THE SURE ANCHOR OF FAITH

Beloved, now are we the sons of God, and it doth not yet appear what we shall be: but we know that, when he shall appear, we shall be like him; for we shall see him as he is. And every man that hath this hope in him purifieth himself, even as he is pure. 1 John 3:2, 3.

Here the eye of faith is directed to God, to look to the unseen, not upon the things that are now apparent. Faith lives in expectation of a future good; it discerns inexpressible advantages in the heavenly gift. The hope of the future life is an essential part of our Christian faith. When we allow worldly attractions to come in between the soul and God, the world is all we can discern. . . . Look up higher, fix the eye of faith upon things unseen, and you will become strong in the divine strength.

Our faith increases by beholding Jesus, who is the center of all that is attractive and lovely. The more we contemplate the heavenly, the less we see desirable and attractive in the earthly. The more continually we fix the eye of faith on Christ, in whom our hopes of eternal life are centered, the more our faith grows; our hope strengthens, our love becomes more intense and fervent, with the clearness of our spiritual insight, and our spiritual intelligence increases. More and more we realize the positive claim of God upon us to purify ourselves from the customs and practices of a world that knows not God, nor Jesus Christ whom He has sent.

The more we behold Christ, talk of His merits, and tell of His power, the more fully we shall reflect His image in our own characters and the less we shall submit our minds and affections to the paralyzing influences of the world. The more our minds dwell upon Jesus, the less they will be enveloped in the fog of doubt, and the more easily shall we lay all our trials, all our burdens, upon the Burden Bearer. . . .

Let faith pierce through the hellish shadow of Satan and center in Jesus, our high priest, who hath entered for us within the veil. Whatever clouds overcast the sky, whatever storms surge around the soul, this anchor holds firm, and we may be sure of victory.[52]

THE HEAVENLY FATHER'S CLAIM

O that there were such an heart in them, that they would fear me, and keep all my commandments always, that it might be well with them, and with their children for ever! Deut. 5:29.

God stands toward His people in the relation of a father, and He has a father's claim to our faithful service. Consider the life of Christ. Standing at the head of humanity, serving His Father, He is an example of what every son should and may be. The obedience that Christ rendered, God requires from human beings today. He served His Father in love, with willingness and freedom. "I delight to do thy will, O my God," He declared: "yea, thy law is within my heart" (Ps. 40:8). Christ counted no sacrifice too great, no toil too hard, in order to accomplish the work which He came to do. At the age of twelve He said, "Wist ye not that I must be about my Father's business?" (Luke 2:49). He had heard the call, and had taken up the work. "My meat," He said, "is to do the will of him that sent me, and to finish his work" (John 4:34).

Thus we are to serve God. He only serves who acts up to the highest standard of obedience. All who would be sons and daughters of God must prove themselves co-workers with Christ and God and the heavenly angels. This is the test for every soul. . . .

God's great object in the working out of His providences is to try men, to give them opportunity to develop character. Thus He proves whether they are obedient or disobedient to His commands. Good works do not purchase the love of God, but they reveal that we possess that love. If we surrender the will to God, we shall not work in order to earn God's love. His love as a free gift will be received into the soul, and from love to Him we shall delight to obey His commandments.

There are only two classes in the world today, and only two classes will be recognized in the judgment—those who violate God's law and those who obey it. Christ gives the test by which we prove our loyalty or disloyalty. "If ye love me," He says, "keep my commandments. . . . He that hath my commandments, and keepeth them, he it is that loveth me . . ." (John 14:15-21).[1]

128

OUR EXAMPLE IN OBEDIENCE

For even hereunto were ye called: because Christ also suffered for us, leaving us an example, that ye should follow his steps: who did no sin, neither was guile found in his mouth. **1 Peter 2:21, 22.**

Before us is held out the wonderful possibility of being like Christ —obedient to all the principles of the law of God. But of ourselves we are utterly powerless to attain to this condition. All that is good in man comes to him through Christ. The holiness that God's Word declares we must have before we can be saved is the result of the working of divine grace as we bow in submission to the discipline and restraining influence of the Spirit of truth.

Man's obedience can be made perfect only by the incense of Christ's righteousness, which fills with divine fragrance every act of true obedience. The part of the Christian is to persevere in overcoming every fault. Constantly he is to pray to the Saviour to heal the disorders of his diseased soul. He has not the wisdom and strength without which he cannot overcome. They belong to the Lord, and He bestows them on those who in humiliation and contrition seek Him for help.

The work of transformation from unholiness to holiness is a continuous work. Day by day God labors for man's sanctification, and man is to cooperate with Him by putting forth persevering efforts in the cultivation of right habits. . . .

God will more than fulfill the highest expectations of those who put their trust in Him. He desires us to remember that when we are humble and contrite, we stand where He can and will manifest Himself to us. He is well pleased when we urge past mercies and blessings as a reason why He should bestow on us higher and greater blessings. He is honored when we love Him and bear testimony to the genuineness of our love by keeping His commandments. He is honored when we set apart the seventh day as sacred and holy. To those who do this, the Sabbath is a sign, . . . God declares, "that I am the Lord that sanctify them" (Eze. 20:12). Sanctification means habitual communion with God. There is nothing so great and powerful as God's love for those who are His children.[2]

BUILDING ON CHRIST

Therefore thus saith the Lord God, Behold, I lay in Zion for a foundation a stone, a tried stone, a precious corner stone, a sure foundation: he that believeth shall not make haste. Isa. 28:16.

"Other foundation can no man lay than that is laid, which is Jesus Christ" (1 Cor. 3:11). "There is none other name under heaven given among men, whereby we must be saved" (Acts 4:12). Christ the Word, the revelation of God—the manifestation of His character, His law, His love, His life—is the only foundation upon which we can build a character that will endure.

We build on Christ by obeying His word. It is not he who merely enjoys righteousness, that is righteous, but he who does righteousness. Holiness is not rapture; it is the result of surrendering all to God; it is doing the will of our heavenly Father.

Religion consists in doing the words of Christ; not doing to earn God's favor, but because, all undeserving, we have received the gift of His love. Christ places the salvation of man, not upon profession merely, but upon faith that is made manifest in works of righteousness. "As many as are led by the Spirit of God, they are the sons of God" (Rom. 8:14). Not those whose hearts are touched by the Spirit, not those who now and then yield to its power, but they that are led by the Spirit, are the sons of God.[3]

We are to be sons and daughters of God, growing into a holy temple in the Lord. "No more strangers and foreigners, but fellow-citizens with the saints, and of the household of God; . . . built upon the foundation of the apostles and prophets, Jesus Christ himself being the chief corner stone" (Eph. 2:19, 20). This is our privilege. . . .

Every character is to be weighed in the balances of the sanctuary; if the moral character and spiritual advancement do not correspond with the opportunities and blessings, "wanting" is written against the name. The Light of the world is our leader, and the path has been growing brighter and brighter as we have advanced in the footsteps of Jesus. O that we may keep close to our Leader! . . . Those who humbly study the character of Jesus will reflect His image more and more.[4]

OBEDIENCE THE TEST OF TRUE RELIGION

Every tree is known by his own fruit. For of thorns men do not gather figs, nor of a bramble bush gather they grapes. Luke 6:44.

"Examine yourselves, whether ye be in the faith" (2 Cor. 13:5). Some conscientious souls, on reading this, immediately begin to criticize their every feeling and emotion. But this is not correct self-examination. It is not the petty feelings and emotions that are to be examined. The life, the character, is to be measured by the only standard of character, God's holy law. The fruit testifies to the character of the tree. Our works, not our feelings, bear witness of us.

The feelings, whether encouraging or discouraging, should not be made the test of the spiritual condition. By God's Word we are to determine our true standing before Him. Many are bewildered on this point. When they are happy and joyous, they think that they are accepted of God. When a change comes, and they feel depressed, they think that God has forsaken them. . . . God does not desire us to go through life with a distrust of Him. . . . While we were yet sinners, God gave His Son to die for us. Can we doubt His goodness? . . .

But a faithful performance of duty goes hand in hand with a right estimate of the character of God. There is earnest work to do for the Master. Christ came to preach the gospel to the poor, and He sent His disciples forth to do the same work He came to do. So He sends forth His workers today. Sheaves are to be gathered for Him from the highways and hedges.

The tremendous issues of eternity demand of us something besides an imaginary religion, a religion of words and forms, where the truth is kept in the outer court, to be admired as we admire a beautiful flower; they demand something more than a religion of feeling, which distrusts God when trials and difficulties come. Holiness does not consist in profession, but in lifting the cross, doing the will of God. . . . "He that saith, I know him, and keepeth not his commandments, is a liar, and the truth is not in him. But whoso keepeth his word, in him verily is the love of God perfected" (1 John 2: 4, 5).[5]

131

GOD'S WORD OUR GUIDE AND COUNSELOR

For thou wilt light my candle: the Lord my God will enlighten my darkness. Ps. 18:28.

God's Word is our light. It is Christ's message to His heritage, who have been bought with the price of His blood. It was written for our guidance, and if we make this Word our counselor, we shall never walk in strange paths. Our words, whether we are in the home or associating with those outside the home, will be kind, affectionate, and pure. If we study the Word and make it a part of our lives, we shall have a wholesome experience, which will always speak forth the truth. We shall search our hearts diligently, comparing our daily speech and tenor of life with the Word, that we may make no mistake.[6]

There are many in this age of the world who act as if they were at liberty to question the words of the Infinite, to review His decisions and statutes, endorsing, revising, reshaping, and annulling at their pleasure. We are never safe while we are guided by human opinions, but we are safe when we are guided by a "Thus saith the Lord." We cannot trust the salvation of our souls to any lower standard than the decisions of an infallible Judge.

Those who make God their guide and His Word their counselor, behold the lamp of life. God's living oracles guide their feet in straight paths. Those who are thus led do not dare to judge the Word of God, but ever hold that His Word judges them. They get their faith and religion from the Word of the living God. It is the guide and counselor that directs their path. The Word is indeed a light to their feet and a lamp to their path. They walk under the direction of the Father of light, with whom is no variableness, neither shadow of turning. He whose tender mercies are over all His works makes the path of the just as a shining light, which shineth more and more unto the perfect day.[7]

The Bible is the voice of God to His people. As we study the living oracles, we are to remember that God is speaking to His people out of His Word. . . . If we realized the importance of searching the Scriptures, how much more diligently we would study them![8]

THE GREAT STANDARD OF RIGHT AND WRONG

All scripture is given by inspiration of God, and is profitable for doctrine, for reproof, for correction, for instruction in righteousness: that the man of God may be perfect, throughly furnished unto all good works. 2 Tim. 3:16, 17.

In the Word of God is contained everything essential to the perfecting of the man of God. It is like a treasure house, full of valuable and precious stores, but we do not appreciate its riches nor realize the necessity of equipping ourselves with the treasures of truth. We do not realize the great necessity of searching the Scriptures for ourselves. Many neglect the study of the Word of God in order to pursue some worldly interest or to indulge in some trifling pleasure. . . . Oh, we might better put off anything of an earthly character than the investigation of the Word of God, which is able to make us wise unto life eternal. "Given by inspiration of God," . . . the Book of books has the highest claims to our reverent attention. . . .

In searching for Heaven-revealed truths, the Spirit of God is brought into close connection with the sincere searcher of the Scriptures. An understanding of the revealed will of God enlarges the mind, expands, elevates, and endows it with new vigor by bringing its faculties into contact with stupendous truth. . . .

The understanding takes the level of the things with which it becomes familiar. If all would make the Bible their study, we would see a people who were better developed, who were capable of thinking more deeply, who would manifest greater intelligence than those who have earnestly studied apart from the Bible the sciences and histories of the world. The Bible gives the true seeker for truth an advanced mental discipline, and he comes from contemplation of divine things with his faculties enriched; self is humbled, while God and His revealed truth are exalted.[9]

The Bible is the great standard of right and wrong, clearly defining sin and holiness. Its living principles, running through our lives like threads of gold, are our only safeguard in trial and temptation.[10]

AN AUDIENCE WITH THE MOST HIGH

For this cause also thank we God without ceasing, because, when ye received the word of God which ye heard of us, ye received it not as the word of men, but as it is in truth, the word of God, which effectually worketh also in you that believe. 1 Thess. 2:13.

The Bible is God's voice speaking to us just as surely as though we could hear Him with our ears. The word of the living God is not merely written, but spoken. Do we receive the Bible as the oracle of God? If we realized the importance of this Word, with what awe would we open it, and with what earnestness would we search its precepts. The reading and contemplating of the Scriptures would be regarded as an audience with the Most High.

God's Word is a message to us to be obeyed, a volume to be perused diligently, and with a spirit willing to take in the truths written for the admonition of those upon whom the ends of the world are come. It must not be neglected for any other book. . . . When we open the Bible, let us compare our lives with its requirements, measuring our character by the great moral standard of righteousness.[11]

The life of Christ, that gives life to the world, is in His Word. It was by His word that Jesus healed disease and cast out demons; by His word He stilled the sea, and raised the dead; and the people bore witness that His word was with power. He spoke the Word of God, as He had spoken to all the prophets and teachers of the Old Testament. The whole Bible is a manifestation of Christ. It is our source of power.

As our physical life is sustained by food, so our spiritual life is sustained by the Word of God. . . . As we must eat for ourselves in order to receive nourishment, so we must receive the Word for ourselves. We are not to obtain it merely through the medium of another mind.

Yes, the Word of God is the bread of life. . . . It gives immortal vigor to the soul, perfecting the experience, and bringing joys that will abide forever.[12]

JOY AND CONSOLATION

How sweet are thy words unto my taste! yea, sweeter than honey to my mouth! Ps. 119:103.

God has given us His Word as a lamp to our feet and a light to our path. Its teachings have a vital bearing on our prosperity in all the relations of life. Even in our temporal affairs it will be a wiser guide than any other counselor. . . .

The appreciation of the Bible grows with its study. Whichever way the student may turn he will find displayed the infinite wisdom and love of God. To him who is truly converted the Word of God is the joy and consolation of the life. The Spirit of God speaks to him, and his heart becomes like a watered garden.

There is nothing more calculated to strengthen the intellect than a study of the Bible. No other book is so potent to elevate the thoughts, to give vigor to the faculties, as the broad, ennobling truths of the Bible. If God's Word were studied as it should be, men would have a breadth of mind, a nobility of character, that is rarely seen in these times.

No knowledge is so firm, so consistent, so far reaching, as that obtained from a study of the Word of God. If there were not another book in the wide world, the Word of God, lived out through the grace of Christ, would make man perfect in this world, with a character fitted for the future, immortal life. Those who study the Word, taking it in faith as the truth and receiving it into the character, will be complete in Him who is all in all. Thank God for the possibilities set before humanity.

"Whatsoever things were written aforetime were written for our learning, that we through patience and comfort of the scriptures might have hope" (Rom. 15:4). "Meditate upon these things; give thyself wholly to them; that thy profiting may appear to all" (1 Tim. 4:15). "For all flesh is as grass, and all the glory of man as the flower of grass. The grass withereth, and the flower thereof falleth away: but the word of the Lord endureth for ever" (1 Peter 1:24, 25).

The time devoted to a study of God's Word and to prayer will bring a hundredfold return.[13]

A SAFEGUARD AGAINST THE ENEMY

The law of his God is in his heart; none of his steps shall slide.
Ps. 37:31.

Many are surprised into the commission of sin because of a failure to study the Scriptures. They were off their guard, and Satan found them an easy prey.[14]

Wonderful possibilities are open to those who lay hold of the divine assurances of God's word. There are glorious truths to come before the people of God. Privileges and duties which they do not even suspect to be in the Bible will be laid open before them. As they follow on in the path of humble obedience, doing His will, they will know more and more of the oracles of God. . . .

The precious faith inspired of God imparts strength and nobility of character. As His goodness, His mercy, and His love are dwelt upon, clearer and still clearer will be the perception of truth; higher, holier, the desire for purity of heart and clearness of thought. The soul dwelling in the pure atmosphere of holy thought is transformed by intercourse with God through the study of His Word. Truth is so large, so far reaching, so deep, so broad, that self is lost sight of. The heart is softened and subdued into humility, kindness, and love. And the natural powers are enlarged because of holy obedience. From the study of the words of life students may come forth with minds expanded, elevated, ennobled.[15]

Youthful minds fail to reach their noblest development when they neglect the highest source of wisdom—the Word of God. That we are in God's world, in the presence of the Creator; that we are made in His likeness; that He watches over us and loves us and cares for us—these are wonderful themes for thought and lead the mind into broad, exalted fields of meditation. He who opens mind and heart to the contemplation of such themes as these will never be satisfied with trivial, sensational subjects. . . .

The Bible has the highest claim to our reverent attention. We should not be satisfied with a superficial knowledge, but should seek to learn the full meaning of the words of truth, to drink deep of the spirit of the Holy Oracles.[16]

THE SOURCE OF WISDOM

The fear of the Lord is the beginning of wisdom: a good understanding have all they that do his commandments: his praise endureth for ever. Ps. 111:10.

It is a great thing to be wise toward God. The fear of the Lord is the beginning of wisdom. This is heart education, and is of more importance than the education gained merely from books. It is well and essential to obtain a knowledge of the world in which we live, but if we leave eternity out of our reckoning, we shall make a failure from which we can never recover. It will be as the knowledge gained by eating of the fruit of the forbidden tree. . . .

What can the most learned in book lore know aright without a knowledge of the Word of God? Without the education found in the Bible, how shall we reach the next world, where we shall enter the presence of God and see His face? Nothing of this world's wisdom, the knowledge gained from books, presents a true and sure foundation upon which we can build for eternity. Nothing but the bread that comes down from heaven satisfies spiritual hunger. "For the bread of God is he which cometh down from heaven, and giveth life unto the world." . . . The words that I speak unto you, they are spirit, and they are life" (John 6:33, 63). . . . As we eat the words of Christ we are eating the bread of life, which gives spiritual vitality.

The Word of the only true God is infallible. Infinite wisdom, holiness, power, and love are blended in pointing us to the standard by which God measures character. God's Word so plainly defines the laws of His kingdom that none need to walk in darkness. His law is the transcript of His character. It is the standard that all must reach if they would enter the kingdom of God. No one need walk in uncertainty. . . . The law of God is not abolished. It will live through the eternal ages. By Christ's death it was magnified, and sin was exposed in its true light.

What a salvation is revealed in the covenant by which God promised to be our Father, His only-begotten Son our Redeemer, and the Holy Spirit our Comforter, Counselor, and Sanctifier! Upon no lower ground than this is it safe for us to place our feet.[17]

HOW TO STUDY THE BIBLE

Search the scriptures; for in them ye think ye have eternal life: and they are they which testify of me. John 5:39.

It is not enough to study the Bible as other books are studied. In order for it to be understood savingly, the Holy Spirit must move on the heart of the searcher. The same Spirit that inspired the Word must inspire the reader of the Word. Then will be heard the voice of heaven. . . .

The mere reading of the Word will not accomplish the result designed of heaven; it must be studied and cherished in the heart. The knowledge of God is not gained without mental effort. We should diligently study the Bible, asking God for the aid of the Holy Spirit, that we may understand His Word. We should take one verse and concentrate the mind on the task of ascertaining the thought which God has put in that verse for us. We should dwell on the thought till it becomes our own, and we know "what saith the Lord."

There is but little benefit derived from a hasty reading of the Scriptures. One may read the Bible through and yet fail to see its beauty or to comprehend its deep and hidden meaning. One passage studied until its significance is clear to the mind and its relation to the plan of salvation is evident, is of more value than the perusal of many chapters with no definite purpose in view and no positive instruction gained. Keep your Bible with you. As you have opportunity, read it; fix the texts in your memory. Even while you are walking the streets you may read a passage and meditate upon it, thus fixing it in mind.[18]

Times that will try men's souls are just before us, and those who are weak in the faith will not stand the test of those days of peril. The great truths of revelation are to be carefully studied, for we shall all want an intelligent knowledge of the word of God. By Bible study and daily communion with Jesus we shall gain clear, well-defined views of individual responsibility and strength to stand in the day of trial and temptation. He whose life is united to Christ by hidden links will be kept by the power of God through faith unto salvation.[19]

A DIVINE HELPER

But God hath revealed them unto us by his Spirit: for the Spirit searcheth all things, yea, the deep things of God. 1 Cor. 2:10.

The more closely we adhere to the simplicity of truth, the more surely do we comprehend its deep meaning. Then if the heart is under the inspiration of the Spirit of God, it can say, "The entrance of thy words giveth light; it giveth understanding to the simple" (Ps. 119:130). This means the word is interpreted by the Holy Spirit, not merely as perused by the student.

It is not the mere letter of the words which gives the light and the understanding, but the Word is in a special manner written upon the heart, applied by the Holy Spirit. To the mind and heart consecrated to God, an increased measure of understanding is given as the light is communicated to others. . . .

The more room one shall give for the entrance of the Word of God, the more he is enriched intellectually as well as spiritually. He will have a clearer and less biased judgment and his views will be more comprehensive. His estimates of spiritual things will be more correct. His understanding, under the working power of the Holy Spirit, is exercised to digest the truth by making it a personal benefit by the strengthening of the soul to do self-denying works.

Oh, I thank the Lord with heart and soul and voice that the Lord can, by the entrance of the Word into the heart, enlarge our faculties of understanding distinctly and clearly, not only spiritual things but the temporal things with which we are connected.

The sanctifying grace of God upon the human mind sanctifies the reasoning powers. This will be kept before the mind, Will this action that I propose to enter into glorify God? There will be an humble spirit of deep humility, and less dependence will be placed upon human wisdom and far more confidence to reach out after God with the humble prayer, Teach me Thy way and Thy will. And the Lord will create a train of thought that will be safe to follow. Past experiences will be revived, and the safe way will be fastened in the mind.[20]

The divine power cooperates with the human.[20]

HEART WORK

Behold, thou desirest truth in the inward parts: and in the hidden part thou shalt make me to know wisdom. **Ps. 51:6.**

Truth must become truth to the receiver, to all intents and purposes. It must be stamped on the heart. "With the heart man believeth unto righteousness; and with the mouth confession is made unto salvation" (Rom. 10:10). "Thou shalt love the Lord thy God with all thy heart, and with all thy soul, and with all thy mind, and with all thy strength" (Mark 12:30). This is the service that God accepts. . . . The heart is the citadel of the being, and until that is wholly on the Lord's side the enemy will gain constant victories over us through his subtle temptations. . . .

Full and abundant is the provision that has been made that we may have mercy, grace, and peace. Why, then, do human beings act as if they entertained the idea that the truth is a yoke of bondage? It is because the heart has never tasted and seen that the Lord is good.[21]

The world is full of false teaching; and if we do not resolutely search the Scriptures for ourselves, we shall accept the world's errors for truth, adopt its customs, and deceive our own hearts. Its doctrines and customs are at variance with the truth of God. . . .

It is a matter of the highest importance and interest to us that we understand what truth is, and our petitions should go forth with intense earnestness that we may be guided into all truth.[22]

Truth is sacred, divine. It is stronger and more powerful than anything else in the formation of a character after the likeness of Christ. In it there is fullness of joy. When it is cherished in the heart the love of Christ is preferred to the love of any human being. This is Christianity. This is the love of God in the soul. Thus pure, unadulterated truth occupies the citadel of the being. . . .

When the truth as it is in Jesus molds our characters it will be seen to be truth indeed. As it is contemplated by the believer it will grow brighter, shining with its original beauty. It will increase in value, quickening and vivifying the mind and subduing selfish, un-Christlike coarseness of character. It will elevate our aspirations, enabling us to reach the perfect standard of holiness.[23]

THE HIGHEST CULTURE

Happy is the man that findeth wisdom, and the man that getteth understanding. **Prov. 3:13.**

The fear of the Lord is the beginning of wisdom, and the man who consents to be molded and fashioned after the divine similitude is the noblest specimen of the work of God. . . .

The experimental knowledge of true godliness, in daily consecration and service to God, ensures the highest culture of the mind, soul, and body. . . . The impartation of divine power honors our sincere striving after wisdom for the conscientious use of our highest faculties to honor God and bless our fellow men. As these faculties are derived from God, and not self-created, they should be appreciated as talents from God to be employed in His service.

The Heaven-entrusted faculties of the mind are to be treated as the higher powers, to rule the kingdom of the body. The natural appetites and passions are to be brought under the control of the conscience and the spiritual affections. . . .

The religion of Jesus Christ never degrades the receiver; it never makes him coarse or rough, discourteous or self-important, passionate or hardhearted. On the contrary, it refines the taste, sanctifies the judgment, purifies and ennobles the thoughts by bringing them into captivity to Jesus Christ.

God's ideal for His children is higher than the highest human thought can reach. The living God has given in His holy law a transcript of His character. The greatest Teacher the world has ever known is Jesus Christ. And what is the standard He has given for all who believe in Him to reach? "Be ye therefore perfect, even as your Father which is in heaven is perfect" (Matt. 5:48). As God is perfect in His high sphere of action, so man may be perfect in his human sphere. The ideal of Christian character is Christlikeness. There is opened before us a path of continual advancement. We have an object to reach, a standard to gain which includes everything good and pure and noble and elevated. There should be continual striving and constant progress onward and upward toward perfection of character.[24]

THE ROYAL PATH

Whom have I in heaven but thee? and there is none upon earth that I desire beside thee. Ps. 73:25.

The soul that cherishes the love of Christ is full of freedom, light, and joy in Christ. In such a soul there are no divided thoughts. The whole man yearns after God. He goes not to men for counsel, to know what is duty, but to the Lord Jesus, the source of all wisdom. He searches the Word of God that he may find out what standard has been set up.

Can we ever find a surer guide than the Lord Jesus? True religion is embodied in the Word of God and consists in being under the guidance of the Holy One in thought, word, and deed. He who is the way, the truth, and the life takes the humble, earnest, wholehearted seeker and says, Follow Me. He leads him in the narrow way to holiness and heaven. Christ has opened this way for us at great cost to Himself. We are not left to stumble our way along in darkness. Jesus is at our right hand, proclaiming, I am the way. And all who decide to follow the Lord fully will be led in the royal path, yea more, the divine path cast up for the ransomed of the Lord to walk in.[25]

The more we learn of Christ through His Word, the more we feel our need of Him in our experience. We should not rest until we can rest in wearing the yoke of Christ and lifting His burdens. The more faithful we are in service to Him, the more we shall love Him, the more we shall magnify Him. Every duty, large or small, that we perform, will be done with faithfulness, and as we follow on to know the Lord the greater will be our desire to glorify Him.[26]

We are individually now testifying to the world of the power of the grace of Christ in the transformation of human character from glory to glory, from character to character. In beholding Christ our pattern, who is pure and holy and undefiled, we are being prepared for the society of the heavenly angels. If Christ is to be our head and Prince in the heavenly courts, it becomes us to inquire, What is Christ to us now? Can we say as we contemplate our Redeemer, "Whom have I in heaven but thee? and there is none upon earth that I desire beside thee"?[26]

142

IN TOUCH WITH THE INFINITE

Thus saith the Lord, Let not the wise man glory in his wisdom, neither let the mighty man glory in his might, let not the rich man glory in his riches: but let him that glorieth glory in this, that he understandeth and knoweth me, that I am the Lord which exercise lovingkindness, judgment, and righteousness, in the earth: for in these things I delight, saith the Lord. Jer. 9:23, 24.

There is an education which is essentially worldly. Its aim is success in the world, the gratification of selfish ambition. To secure this education many students spend time and money in crowding their minds with unnecessary knowledge. The world accounts them learned; but God is not in their thoughts. . . .

There is another kind of education that is very different. Its fundamental principle, as stated by the greatest Teacher the world has ever known, is, "Seek ye first the kingdom of God, and his righteousness" (Matt. 6:33). Its aim is not selfish; its purpose is to honor God. . . . God is the source of all wisdom. He is infinitely wise and just and good. Apart from Christ, the wisest men that ever lived cannot comprehend Him. They may profess to be wise; they may glory in their attainments; but mere intellectual knowledge, aside from the great truths that center in Christ, is as nothingness. . . .

If men could see for a moment beyond the range of finite vision, if they could catch a glimpse of the Eternal, every mouth would be stopped in its boasting. Men living in this little atom of a world are finite; God has unnumbered worlds that are obedient to His laws, and are conducted with reference to His glory. When men have gone as far in scientific research as their limited powers will permit, there is still an infinity beyond what they can apprehend.

Before men can be truly wise, they must realize their dependence upon God, and be filled with His wisdom. God is the source of intellectual as well as spiritual power. The greatest men who have reached what the world regards as wonderful heights in science are not to be compared with the beloved John or the apostle Paul. It is when intellectual and spiritual power are combined that the highest standard of manhood is attained.[27]

143

THE WITNESS OF THE SPIRIT

The Spirit itself beareth witness with our spirit, that we are the children of God. Rom. 8:16.

You may have the witness of the Spirit that your ways please God. This is obtained by believing in the Word of God, by appropriating that Word to your own soul. This is eating the bread of life, and this will bring eternal life. Compare scripture with scripture. Study the representation of the life of a true Christian as delineated in the Word of God.

The law of God is the great standard of righteousness. This the apostle declares is holy, just, and good. David says, "The law of the Lord is perfect, converting the soul" (Ps. 19:7). Christ says, "If ye love me, keep my commandments." . . . "He that hath my commandments, and keepeth them, he it is that loveth me: and he that loveth me shall be loved of my Father, and I will love him, and will manifest myself to him" (John 14:15, 21). This is most assuredly the witness of the Spirit. . . . "If ye keep my commandments"—from the heart—"ye shall abide in my love; even as I have kept my Father's commandments, and abide in his love" (John 15:10).

Those who are obedient to the will of God will not have a hard and miserable time in this life. Hear again the words of Christ: "These things have I spoken unto you, that my joy might remain in you, and that your joy might be full" (verse 11). This is the witness which it is the privilege of all to have—the joy of Christ in the soul through appropriating the word of God . . . and bringing the requirements of Christ into the practical life. There is full assurance of hope in believing every word of Christ, believing in Him, being united to Him by living faith. When this is his experience, the human being is no longer under the law, for the law no longer condemns his course of action. . . .

To them that believe, Christ is precious. His Spirit moving upon the mind and heart of the believer is in perfect agreement with that which is written in the Word. The Spirit and the Word agree perfectly. Thus the Spirit beareth witness with our spirit that we are born of God.[28]

SANCTIFYING POWER

Sanctify them through thy truth: thy word is truth. John 17:17.

The truth which we profess will be of no avail to us unless we are sanctified through it. . . . While error is prevailing to such an extent in our land, we want to know what is truth, because we cannot be sanctified by error. The better we understand the truth as it is in God's Word, the better we shall know how to sanctify our lives through God's Word.

We are in this world as probationers, and God is proving us by giving us an opportunity to obey His truth. It is a very solemn thing to live in this age of the world, and we should not be satisfied unless we have a living connection with the God of heaven, and we should have a sense of our accountability to Him every day of our lives. . . .

There are voices that we shall hear all around us to divert us away from the truth, but if we have an eye single to the glory of God and are striving to do His will, we shall hear His voice and know it is the voice of the Good Shepherd. It is very important that we understand the voice that speaks to us. . . .

There are temptations that will come to every one of us. We all have our different dispositions to overcome, and how are we to know that we are doing this work day by day? We must look into the mirror—God's holy law—and there discover the defects in our characters. It is a very difficult thing for one to understand himself. We must examine closely to see if there is not something that must be laid aside, and then as we make an effort to put away self, our precious Saviour will give us the help we need that we may be overcomers. . . .

This world is not heaven, it is the preparation place; it is the workshop of God where we are to be hewed and chiseled and fitted up for the heavenly mansions. Then do not be satisfied with a mere sense of the truth; God calls for a reformation at every step. It is to have a fitness for the mansions that Christ has gone to fit up for us. And if we can only be of the heavenly family in the kingdom of glory then we shall have the eternal reward. May God help us to overcome by the blood of the Lamb and the word of His testimony.[29]

145

FREEDOM THROUGH CHRIST

Stand fast therefore in the liberty wherewith Christ hath made us free, and be not entangled again with the yoke of bondage. Gal. 5:1.

In the beginning God placed man under law as an indispensable condition of his very existence. He was a subject of the divine government, and there can be no government without law. . . .

God is omnipotent, omniscient, immutable. He always pursues a straightforward course. His law is truth—immutable, eternal truth. His precepts are consistent with His attributes. But Satan makes them appear in a false light. By perverting them, he seeks to give human beings an unfavorable impression of the Lawgiver. Throughout his rebellion he has sought to represent God as an unjust, tyrannical being. . . .

As a result of Adam's disobedience every human being is a transgressor of the law, sold under sin. Unless he repents and is converted, he is under bondage to the law, serving Satan, falling into the deceptions of the enemy, and bearing witness against the precepts of Jehovah. But by perfect obedience to the requirements of the law, man is justified. Only through faith in Christ is such obedience possible. Men may comprehend the spirituality of the law, they may realize its power as a detector of sin, but they are helpless to withstand Satan's power and deceptions, unless they accept the atonement provided for them in the remedial sacrifice of Christ, who is our Atonement—our At-one-ment—with God.

Those who believe on Christ and obey His commandments are not under bondage to God's law; for to those who believe and obey, His law is not a law of bondage, but of liberty. Everyone who believes on Christ, everyone who relies on the keeping power of a risen Saviour that has suffered the penalty pronounced upon the transgressor, everyone who resists temptation and in the midst of evil copies the pattern given in the Christ life, will through faith in the atoning sacrifice of Christ become a partaker of the divine nature, having escaped the corruption that is in the world through lust. Everyone who by faith obeys God's commandments will reach the condition of sinlessness in which Adam lived before his transgression.[30]

146

GOD'S WAY, NOT MINE

Shew me thy ways, O Lord; teach me thy paths. Lead me in thy truth, and teach me: for thou art the God of my salvation; on thee do I wait all the day. **Ps. 25:4, 5.**

The direction given to Moses was, "See . . . that thou make all things according to the pattern shewed to thee in the mount" (Heb. 8:5). Although Moses was full of zeal to do God's work, and he could have the most skillful, talented men to carry out any suggestions he should make, he must not make a single thing, a bell, a pomegranate, a tassel, or a fringe, or a curtain, or any vessel except according to the pattern showed to him as God's ideal. . . . Forty days the communications were given to him, and when he descended to the foot of the mount he was ready to give the exact pattern that was shown to him in the mount. . . .

Where many have erred, was in not being careful in following God's ideas, but their own. Christ Himself declared, "The Son can do nothing of himself, but what he seeth the Father do" (John 5:19). So utterly was He emptied of Himself that He made no schemes and plans. He lived accepting God's plans for Him, and the Father day by day unfolded His plans. If Jesus was so wholly dependent, and declared, "Whatsoever I see the Father do, that I do," how much more should human agents depend upon God for constant instruction, so that their lives might be the simple working out of God's plans! . . .

Our own way must be overcome. Pride, self-sufficiency, must be crucified and the vacuum supplied with the Spirit and power of God. . . . Did Jesus Christ, the Majesty of heaven, have His way? Behold Him in travail of soul in Gethsemane, praying to His Father. What forces these blood drops of agony from His holy brow? Oh, the sins of the whole world are upon Him! It was separation from the Father's love that forced from His pale and quivering lips the cry, "Father, if it be possible, let this cup pass from me" (Matt. 26: 39). Three times was the prayer offered, but followed by "Nevertheless not my will, but thine, be done" (Luke 22:42). This must be our attitude—Not my will, but Thine, O God, be done. This is true conversion."[31]

THE HIGHEST STANDARD

For not the hearers of the law are just before God, but the doers of the law shall be justified. Rom. 2:13.

In the lives of many whose names are on the church books there has been no genuine change. The truth has been kept in the outer court. There has been no genuine conversion, no positive work of grace done in the heart. . . .

He who would build up a strong, symmetrical character must give all and do all for Christ. The Redeemer will not accept divided service. Daily he must learn the meaning of self-surrender. He must study the Word of God, getting its meaning and obeying its precepts. Thus he may reach the highest standard of Christian excellence. There is no limit to the spiritual advancement that he may make if he is a partaker of the divine nature. Day by day God works in him, perfecting the character that is to stand in the day of final test. Each day of his life he ministers to others. The light that is in him shines forth and stills the strife of tongues. Day by day he is working out before men and angels a vast, sublime experiment, showing what the gospel can do for fallen human beings.

Let us not spare ourselves, but carry forward in earnest the work of reform that must be done in our lives. Let us crucify self. Unholy habits will clamor for the mastery, but in the name and through the power of Jesus we may conquer. To him who daily seeks to keep his heart with all diligence, the promise is given, "Neither death, nor life, nor angels, nor principalities, nor powers, nor things present, nor things to come, nor height, nor depth, nor any other creature, shall be able to separate us from the love of God, which is in Christ Jesus our Lord" (Rom. 8:38, 39). . . . God Himself is "the justifier of him which believeth in Jesus." And "whom he justified, them he also glorified" (verse 30).

Great as is the shame and degradation through sin, even greater will be the honor and exaltation through redeeming love. To human beings, striving for conformity to the divine image, there is imparted an outlay of heaven's treasure, an excellency of power that will place them higher than even the angels who have never fallen.[32]

LOYAL TO GOD OR TO MEN?

We ought to obey God rather than men. Acts 5:29.

Daniel and his companions had a conscience void of offense toward God. But this is not preserved without a struggle. What a test was brought on the three associates of Daniel when they were required to worship the great image set up by King Nebuchadnezzar in the plains of Dura! Their principles forbade them to pay homage to the idol, for it was a rival to the God of heaven. They knew that they owed to God every faculty they possessed, and while their hearts were full of generous sympathy toward all men, they had a lofty aspiration to prove themselves entirely loyal to their God. . . .

The king declared to the three Hebrew youth, if "ye fall down and worship the image which I have made; well: but if ye worship not, ye shall be cast the same hour into the midst of a burning fiery furnace; and who is that God that shall deliver you out of my hands?" The youth said to the king, "O Nebuchadnezzar, we are not careful to answer thee in this matter. If it be so, our God whom we serve is able to deliver us from the burning fiery furnace, and he will deliver us out of thine hand, O king. But if not, be it known unto thee, O king, that we will not serve thy gods, nor worship the golden image which thou hast set up. . . ." (Dan. 3:15-19). . . . Those faithful youth were cast into the fire, but God manifested His power for the deliverance of His servants. One like unto the Son of God walked with them in the midst of the flame, and when they were brought forth, not even the smell of fire had passed on them. . . .

Thus these youth, imbued with the Holy Spirit, declared to the whole nation their faith, that He whom they worshiped was the only true and living God. This demonstration of their own faith was the most eloquent presentation of their principles. In order to impress idolaters with the power and greatness of the living God, His servants must reveal their own reverence for God. They must make it manifest that He is the only object of their honor and worship, and that no consideration, not even the preservation of life itself, can induce them to make the least concession to idolatry. These lessons have a direct and vital bearing upon our experience in these last days.[33]

GOD'S TEST OF LOYALTY

The Lord hath avouched thee this day to be his peculiar people, as he hath promised thee, and that thou shouldest keep all his commandments. Deut. 26:18.

God has a test for us, and if we come up to the standard we shall be a peculiar people. The Sabbath draws a separating line between us and the world, not faintly but in plain, distinct colors. To those who have received the light of this truth the Sabbath is a test; it is not a human requirement, but God's test. It is what will distinguish between those who serve God and those who serve Him not, and upon this point will come the last great conflict between truth and error. All who profess to keep God's law should stand united in the sacred observance of His holy Sabbath. . . .

When the destroying angel was about to pass through the land of Egypt and smite the first-born of both man and beast, the Israelites were directed to bring their children into the house with them and to strike the doorpost with blood; and none were to go out of the house, for all that were found among the Egyptians would be destroyed with them.

We should take this lesson to ourselves. Again the destroying angel is to pass through the land. There is to be a mark placed upon God's people, and that mark is the keeping of His holy Sabbath. We are not to follow our own will and judgment and flatter ourselves that God will come to our terms. . . . That which looks unimportant to you may be of the highest consequence in God's special plans for the preservation of your life or the salvation of your soul. God tests our faith by giving us some part to act in connection with His interposition in our behalf. To those who comply with the conditions His promise will be fulfilled. . . .

We are faithfully to teach our children God's commandments; we should bring them into subjection to parental authority; and then by faith and prayer commit them to God, and He will work with our efforts, for He has promised it. And when the overflowing scourge shall pass through the land, they, with us, may be hidden in the secret of the Lord's pavilion.[34]

"REMEMBER THE SABBATH DAY"

Remember the sabbath day, to keep it holy. Six days shalt thou labour, and do all thy work: but the seventh day is the sabbath of the Lord thy God: in it thou shalt not do any work, thou, nor thy son, nor thy daughter, thy manservant, nor thy maidservant, nor thy cattle, nor thy stranger that is within thy gates: for in six days the Lord made heaven and earth, the sea, and all that in them is, and rested the seventh day: wherefore the Lord blessed the sabbath day, and hallowed it. Ex. 20:8-11.

The fourth commandment is explicit. We are not to do our own work upon the Sabbath. God has given man six days for labor, but He has reserved the seventh to Himself, and He has pronounced a blessing upon those who keep it holy. On the sixth day all needful preparation for the Sabbath is to be made. . . . All purchases should be made and all our cooking should be done on Friday. Let baths be taken, shoes be blacked, and clothing be put in readiness. The sick require care upon the Sabbath, and whatever it may be necessary to do for their comfort is an act of mercy, and not a violation of the commandment. . . . But nothing of our own work should be permitted to encroach upon holy time.

Sunday is generally made a day of feasting and pleasure seeking, but the Lord would have His people give the world a higher, holier example. Upon the Sabbath there should be a solemn dedication of the family to God. . . . Let all unite to honor God upon His holy day. . . .

If you go forward toward heaven, the world will rub hard against you. . . . Earthly authorities will interpose. You will meet tribulations, bruising of the spirit, hard speeches, ridicule, persecutions. Men will require your conformity to laws and customs that would render you disloyal to God. Here is where God's people find the cross in the way to life. But if the Sabbath of the fourth commandment is sacred, if it is indeed, as brought to view in the third angel's message, the sign between God and His people, we must be careful in every word and in every act to show God honor. . . .

The strong force of the downward current will sweep you off your feet unless you are united to Christ as the limpet to the rock.[35]

151

DAY OF DELIGHT AND BLESSING

If thou turn away thy foot from the sabbath, from doing thy pleasure on my holy day; and call the sabbath a delight, the holy of the Lord, honourable; and shalt honour him, not doing thine own ways, nor finding thine own pleasure, nor speaking thine own words: then shalt thou delight thyself in the Lord; and I will cause thee to ride upon the high places of the earth, and feed thee with the heritage of Jacob thy father. Isa. 58:13, 14.

The Sabbath . . . is God's time, not ours; when we trespass upon it we are stealing from God. . . . God has given us the whole of six days in which to do our work, and has reserved only one to Himself. This should be a day of blessing to us—a day when we should lay aside all our secular matters and center our thoughts upon God and heaven.

But while we worship God, we are not to consider this a drudgery. The Sabbath of the Lord is to be made a blessing to us and to our children. They are to look upon the Sabbath as a day of delight, a day which God has sanctified; and they will so consider it if they are properly instructed. . . . They can be pointed to the blooming flowers and the opening buds, the lofty trees and beautiful spires of grass, and taught that God made all these in six days and rested on the seventh day and hallowed it. Thus the parents may bind up their lessons of instruction to their children so that when these children look upon the things of nature they will call to mind the great Creator of them all. . . .

We are not to teach our children that they must not be happy on the Sabbath, that it is wrong to walk out of doors. Oh, no. Christ led His disciples out by the lakeside on the Sabbath day and taught them. His sermons on the Sabbath were not always preached within enclosed walls. . . .

Many say they would keep the Sabbath if it were convenient to do so. But this day is not yours; it is God's day, and you have no more right to take it than you have to steal my purse. God has reserved it, sanctified and blessed it; and it is your duty to devote this time to His service, to make it honorable, to call it a delight.[38]

THE MEASURE OF RESPONSIBILITY

If we say that we have fellowship with him, and walk in darkness, we lie, and do not the truth: but if we walk in the light, as he is in the light, we have fellowship one with another, and the blood of Jesus Christ his Son cleanseth us from all sin. 1 John 1:6, 7.

The degree of light given is the measure of responsibility. The path to heaven will be made plain to all who are faithful in the use of the knowledge they may obtain in regard to the future life. . . . Look at the first act of transgression in the Garden of Eden. To Adam and Eve were plainly stated the laws of Paradise, with the penalty for willful disobedience. They disobeyed, and disobedience brought its sure result. Death entered the world.

Transgression is disobedience to the commands of God. Had these commands always been obeyed, there would have been no sin. The penalty of transgression is always death. Christ averted the immediate execution of the death sentence by giving His life for man. . . . Justice requires that men shall have light, and it also requires that he who refuses to walk in the Heaven-given light, the giving of which cost the death of the Son of God, must receive punishment. It is a principle of justice that the guilt of the sinner shall be proportionate to the knowledge given, but not used, or used in a wrong way. God expects human beings to walk in the light, to testify before angels and before men that they acknowledge Christ as the great propitiation for sin and that they respect His sacrifice as their greatest blessing. . . .

For time and for eternity the sacrifice of the Son of God to save the fallen race will have a binding claim on man. If God had failed to act His part, if He had not fully revealed His will, if He had given human beings any reason for neglecting the great salvation, man might plead ignorance as a valid excuse. But He has made the way plain. He would have all men to be saved. To some is given greater light than to others. Each will be judged by the light given him. . . . God designed that you should cherish as sacred the light given you.[37]

THE IMPRESS OF HEAVEN

See, saith he, that thou make all things according to the pattern shewed to thee in the mount. Heb. 8:5.

The Lord gave an important lesson to His people in all ages when to Moses on the mount He gave instruction regarding the building of the tabernacle. In that work He required perfection in every detail.[38]

As wickedness in the world becomes more pronounced and the teachings of evil are more fully developed and widely accepted, the teachings of Christ are to stand forth exemplified in the lives of converted men and women. . . .

Into all to which the Christian sets his hand should be woven the thought of the life eternal. If the work performed is agricultural or mechanical in its nature, it may still be after the pattern of the heavenly. . . . Through the grace of Christ every provision has been made for the perfecting of Christlike characters, and God is honored when His people in all their social and business dealings reveal the principles of heaven. . . .

The Lord demands uprightness in the smallest as well as the largest matters. Those who are accepted at last as members of the heavenly court will be men and women who here on earth have sought to carry out the Lord's will in every particular, who have sought to put the impress of heaven upon their earthly labors. In order that the earthly tabernacle might represent the heavenly, it must be perfect in all its parts, and it must be in the smallest detail like the pattern in the heavens. So it is with the characters of those who are finally accepted in the sight of Heaven.

The Son of God came down to earth that in Him men and women might have a representation of the perfect characters which alone God could accept. Through the grace of Christ every provision has been made for the salvation of the human family. It is possible for every transaction entered into by those who claim to be Christians to be as pure as were the deeds of Christ. And the soul who accepts the virtues of Christ's character and appropriates the merits of His life is as precious in the sight of God as was His own beloved Son.[38]

FILLED WITH HIS FULLNESS

And to know the love of Christ, which passeth knowledge, that ye might be filled with all the fulness of God. Eph. 3:19.

Only those will have a fitness for the mansions above who give to God full and implicit obedience. God knows that we would not appreciate His rarest gifts if we were not perfectly submissive to obey Him, and always keep His glory in view. . . .

Whatever your temperament may be, whatever your hereditary and cultivated tendencies may be, there is a character to be formed after the divine pattern. We have no excuse for retaining our own mold and superscription of nature, for Christ has died that we may have His mold and His superscription. We cannot retain our own self and be filled with the fullness of God. We must be emptied of self. If heaven is gained by us at last, it will be only through the renunciation of self and in receiving the mind, the spirit, and the will of Christ Jesus. . . .

Are we willing to pay the price for eternal life? Are we ready to sit down and count the cost, whether heaven is worth such a sacrifice as to die to self and let our will be bent and fashioned into perfect conformity with the will of God? Until this shall be, the transforming grace of God will not be experienced by us.

Just as soon as we present our emptied nature to the Lord Jesus and His cause, He will supply the vacuum by His Holy Spirit. We can then believe He will give us of His fullness. He does not want us to perish. We do not want more of God any more urgently than He wants all that there is of us to be consecrated to His service. . . .

Eternity is endless. Our life here is a short period at best, and what and whom are we living and working for? And what will be the outcome of it all?

The religion of Jesus Christ we need daily. Everything we do or say comes under the notice of God. We are a spectacle unto the world, to angels, and to men. . . . The church of Christ is to represent His character. . . . Though He had all the strength of passion of humanity, never did He yield to temptation to do one single act which was not pure and elevating and ennobling.[39]

WEIGHED IN HEAVEN'S BALANCES

The Lord is a God of knowledge, and by him actions are weighed. 1 Sam. 2:3.

The Lord is a God of knowledge. In His Word He is represented as weighing men, their development of character and all their motives, whether they be good or evil. . . .

It is for the eternal interest of everyone to search his own heart and to improve every God-given faculty. Let all remember that there is not a motive in the heart of any man that the Lord does not clearly see. The motives of each one are weighed as carefully as if the destiny of the human agent depended upon this one result. . . . God in heaven is true, and there is not a design, however intricate, or a motive, however carefully hidden, that He does not clearly understand. He reads the secret devisings of every heart.

Men may plan out crooked actions for the future, thinking that God does not understand; but in that great day when the books are opened, and every man is judged by the things written in the books, those actions will appear as they are. . . .

There are many who need now to consider the words, "TEKEL; Thou art weighed in the balances, and art found wanting" (Dan. 5: 27). God's holy, everlasting, immutable law is the standard by which man is to be tried. This law defines what we shall do and what we shall not do, saying, Thou shalt, and, Thou shalt not. This law is summed up in the two great principles, "Thou shalt love the Lord thy God with all thy heart, and with all thy soul, and with all thy strength, and with all thy mind; and thy neighbour as thyself" (Luke 10:27).

This means just what it says. O how few will be prepared to meet the law of God in the great day of judgment! . . . Man, weighed against God's holy law, is found wanting.

We are enlightened by the precepts of the law, but no man can by them be justified. Weighed and found wanting is our inscription by nature. But Christ is our mediator, and accepting Him as our Saviour, we may claim the promise, "Being justified by faith, we have peace with God through our Lord Jesus Christ" (Rom. 5:1).[40]

A DIVINE-HUMAN PARTNERSHIP

Thy hands have made me and fashioned me: give me under-standing, that I may learn thy commandments. Ps. 119:73.

The human organism is the handiwork of God. The organs employed in all the different functions of the body were made by Him. The Lord gives us food and drink, that the wants of the body may be supplied. He has given the earth different properties adapted to the growth of food for His children. He gives the sunshine and the showers, the early and the latter rain. He forms the clouds and sends the dew. All are His gifts. . . .

But all these blessings will not restore in us His moral image unless we cooperate with Him, making painstaking effort to know ourselves, to understand how to care for the delicate human machinery. Man must diligently help to keep himself in harmony with nature's laws. He who cooperates with God in the work of keeping this wonderful machinery in order, who consecrates all his powers to God, seeking intelligently to obey the laws of nature, stands in his God-given manhood, and is recorded in the books of heaven as *a man.*

God has given man land to be cultivated. But in order that the harvest may be reaped, there must be harmonious action between divine and human agencies. The plow and other implements of labor must be used at the right time. The seed must be sown in its season. Man is not to fail of doing his part. If he is careless and negligent, his unfaithfulness testifies against him. The harvest is proportionate to the energy he has expended.

So it is in spiritual things. . . . There is to be a copartnership, a divine relation between the Son of God and the repentant sinner. We are made sons and daughters of God. "As many as received him, to them gave he power to become the sons of God" (John 1:12). Christ provides the mercy and grace so abundantly given to all who believe in Him. He fulfills the terms upon which salvation rests. But we must act our part by accepting the blessing in faith. God works and man works. Resistance of temptation must come from man, who must draw his power from God. Thus he becomes a co-partner with Christ.[41]

157

BLESSINGS UNLIMITED

That ye might walk worthy of the Lord unto all pleasing, being fruitful in every good work, and increasing in the knowledge of God. Col. 1:10.

Let us study Paul's prayer for his Colossian brethren. "For this cause we also," he wrote, "since the day we heard it, do not cease to pray for you, and to desire that ye might be filled with the knowledge of his will in all wisdom and spiritual understanding; that ye might walk worthy of the Lord unto all pleasing, being fruitful in every good work, and increasing in the knowledge of God; strengthened with all might, according to his glorious power, unto all patience and longsuffering with joyfulness" (Col. 1:9-11).

How complete this prayer is! There is no limit to the blessings that it is our privilege to receive. We may be "filled with the knowledge of his will." The Holy Ghost would never have inspired Paul to offer this prayer in behalf of his brethren if it had not been possible for them to receive an answer from God in accordance with the request. . . .

To the church at Ephesus Paul wrote: "For this cause I bow my knees unto the Father of our Lord Jesus Christ, of whom the whole family in heaven and earth is named, that he would grant you, according to the riches of his glory, to be strengthened with might by his Spirit in the inner man; that Christ may dwell in your hearts by faith; that ye, being rooted and grounded in love, may be able to comprehend with all saints what is the breadth, and length, and depth, and height; and to know the love of Christ, which passeth knowledge, that ye might be filled with all the fulness of God. Now unto him that is able to do exceeding abundantly above all that we ask or think, according to the power that worketh in us, unto him be glory in the church by Christ Jesus throughout all ages, world without end" (Eph. 3:14-21).

Here are brought to view the possibilities of the Christian life. How far short of reaching this standard falls the church of today! . . . Self, self, self—all this is manifest. . . . When shall we awake? When shall we meet the expectations of Christ? [42]

BUILDING WITH GOD

For we are labourers together with God: ye are God's hus-bandry, ye are God's building. 1 Cor. 3:9.

This figure represents human character, which is to be wrought upon point by point. Each day God works on His building, stroke upon stroke, to perfect the structure, that it may become a holy temple for Him. Man is to cooperate with God, striving in His strength to make himself what God designs him to be, building his life with pure, noble deeds.[1]

Man works and God works. Man is called upon to strain every muscle and to exercise every faculty in the struggle for immortality, but it is God who supplies the efficiency. God has made amazing sacrifices for human beings. He has expended mighty energy to reclaim man from transgression and sin to loyalty and obedience, but He does nothing without the cooperation of humanity. . . . It is by unceasing endeavor that we maintain the victory over the temptations of Satan. . . .

No one is borne upward without stern, persevering effort in his own behalf. All must engage in the warfare for themselves. Individually we are responsible for the issue of the struggle; though Noah, Daniel, and Job were in the land, they could deliver neither son nor daughter by their righteousness. . . .

Often the training and education of a lifetime must be discarded, that one may become a learner in the school of Christ. Our hearts must be educated to become steadfast in God. We are to form habits of thought that will enable us to resist temptation. We must learn to look upward. The principles of the Word of God—principles that are as high as heaven and that compass eternity—we are to understand in their bearing on our daily life. Every act, every word, every thought, is to be in accord with these principles.

The precious graces of the Holy Spirit are not developed in a moment. Courage, fortitude, meekness, faith, unwavering trust in God's power to save, are acquired by the experience of years. By a life of holy endeavor and firm adherence to the right the children of God are to seal their destiny.[1]

159

THE BATTLE FOR A SPIRITUAL MIND

For to be carnally minded is death; but to be spiritually minded is life and peace. Because the carnal mind is enmity against God: for it is not subject to the law of God, neither indeed can be. Rom. 8:6, 7.

The natural mind leans toward pleasure and self-gratification. It is Satan's policy to manufacture an abundance of this. He seeks to fill the minds of men with a desire for worldly amusement, that they may have no time to ask themselves the question, How is it with my soul? The love of pleasure is infectious. Given up to this, the mind hurries from one point to another, ever seeking for some amusement. Obedience to the law of God counteracts this inclination and builds barriers against ungodliness. . . .

The ability to enjoy the riches of glory will be developed in proportion to the desire we have for these riches. How shall an appreciation of God and heavenly things be developed unless it is in this life? If the claims and cares of the world are allowed to engross all our time and attention, our spiritual powers weaken and die for lack of exercise. In a mind wholly given up to earthly things every inlet through which light from heaven may enter is closed. God's transforming grace cannot be felt on mind or character.[2]

We are living amid the perils of the last days, and we should guard every avenue by which Satan can approach us with his temptation. . . . A mere assent to the truth will never save a soul from death. We must be sanctified through the truth; every defect of character must be overcome, or it will overcome us and become a controlling power for evil. Commence without a moment's delay to root out every pernicious weed from the garden of the heart; and through the grace of Christ allow no plants to flourish there but such as will bear fruit unto eternal life.

Cultivate whatever in your character is in harmony with the character of Christ. Cherish those things that are true, honest, just, pure, lovely and of good report; but put away whatever is unlike our Redeemer. . . . Every soul that gains eternal life must be like Christ, "holy, harmless, undefiled, separate from sinners" (Heb. 7:26).[3]

WILL YOUR THOUGHTS BEAR INSPECTION?

The Lord searcheth all hearts, and understandeth all the imaginations of the thoughts: if thou seek him, he will be found of thee; but if thou forsake him, he will cast thee off for ever. 1 Chron. 28:9.

You must give an account to God of your thoughts, of your words, of your time, and of your actions. . . .

You can never enter heaven unless you enjoy the communion of God here below, for this is our fitting-up place for heaven. God should be the object of the soul's highest reverence, love, and fear. This world is the only school in which you can receive a preparation for the higher grade. Those who do not love to retain God in their thoughts in this world, those who consider it irksome to be in subjection to God in this life, will never have enjoyment with Christ in the future life. The very things they choose and love here in self-pleasing are educating their tastes so that heavenly discipline will be a restraint. Let your soul be brought under discipline to God. . . .

He who created man, who paid such a price for his redemption, is greatly dishonored when man chooses a low, earthly level, a life of frivolity and cheapness. . . . All who are content to turn away from that knowledge which will make them wise unto salvation in this life and the future, who accept of earthly, frivolous things, are feeding their souls upon brackish water when Jesus Christ invites them, "If any man thirst, let him come unto me, and drink" (John 7:37).[4]

Let your soul be absorbed in meditating upon the glorious truths contained in the Word of God, and you will have no constant craving for something which you have not. You will despise cheap, vain thoughts. You will be ever trying to meet the elevated standard of virtue and holiness which is kept before you in the gospel. You will seek for higher attainments in the divine life. Converse with God through the medium of His Word.[4] . . .

By contemplating the lofty ideal He has placed before you, you will be uplifted into a pure and holy atmosphere, even the presence of God. When you abide here, there goes forth from you a light which irradiates all who are connected with you.[5]

KEEPING THE HEART

Keep thy heart with all diligence; for out of it are the issues of life. Prov. 4:23.

Why are there so many . . . who are spiritual failures, who have unsymmetrical characters? It is because they did not, when they knew the truth, and do not now, begin to practice the truth as it is in Jesus. They do not let Him take away their faulty attributes of character. . . . He whose conversion is righteous carries righteous principles into all his life practices. He only is well grounded in the faith who lives by every word that proceedeth from the mouth of God.

There are many who testify daily, I am not changed in character, only in theory. . . . All may through faith gain a conqueror's crown, but many are not willing to engage in hand to hand warfare with their own imperfect dispositions. They retain attributes which make them offensive to God. Daily they are transgressing the principles of His holy law. If all would only learn the simple lesson that they must take and wear the yoke of Christ and learn of the Great Teacher His meekness and lowliness of heart, they would better fulfill their covenant to love God supremely and their neighbor as themselves. . . . They must begin at the very beginning. Christ says, Take My yoke of restraint and obedience upon you, and learn of Me. . . . The heart will then be made right with God, through the creative power of Christ. Partakers of the divine nature, they are transformed. . . .

The renovating, transforming work must begin in the heart, out of which flow the issues of life. Oh, how then can lip service be regarded as sufficient? . . . I entreat you, for Christ's sake, do not stop at any halfway place, but press on, press on. Advance to the perfection of Christian attainments. Leave nothing insecure. Watch thyself with all diligence. Remember that you are responsible not to misrepresent Christ in character. Let us not by our defects lead others to practice the same sins. . . .

Those who claim to have advanced light must reveal the influence of that light in their words, their deportment, their voice, their actions, at all times and in all places.[8]

CHRIST IN ALL OUR THOUGHTS

Search me, O God, and know my heart: try me, and know my thoughts: and see if there be any wicked way in me, and lead me in the way everlasting. Ps. 139:23, 24.

Few realize that it is a duty to exercise control over the thoughts and imaginations. It is difficult to keep the undisciplined mind fixed upon profitable subjects. But if the thoughts are not properly employed, religion cannot flourish in the soul. The mind must be preoccupied with sacred and eternal things, or it will cherish trifling and superficial thoughts. Both the intellectual and the moral powers must be disciplined, and they will . . . improve by exercise.

In order to understand this matter aright, we must remember that our hearts are naturally depraved, and we are unable of ourselves to pursue a right course. It is only by the grace of God, combined with the most earnest effort on our part, that we can gain the victory. The intellect, as well as the heart, must be consecrated to the service of God. He has claims upon all there is of us.[7]

Few believe that humanity has sunk so low as it has or that it is so thoroughly bad, so desperately opposed to God, as it is. . . . When the mind is not under the direct influence of the Spirit of God, Satan can mold it as he chooses. All the rational powers which he controls he will carnalize. He is directly opposed to God in his tastes, views, preferences, likes and dislikes, choice of things and pursuits; there is no relish for what God loves or approves, but a delight in those things which He despises. . . .

If Christ is abiding in the heart, He will be in all our thoughts. Our deepest thoughts will be of Him, His love, His purity. He will fill all the chambers of the mind. Our affections will center about Jesus. All our hopes and expectations will be associated with Him. To live the life we now live by faith in the Son of God, looking forward to and loving His appearing, will be the soul's highest joy. He will be the crown of our rejoicing.[8]

Those who have trained the mind to delight in spiritual exercises are the ones who can be translated and not be overwhelmed with the purity and transcendent glory of heaven.[9]

163

SECURITY IN RIGHT THINKING

Casting down imaginations, and every high thing that exalteth itself against the knowledge of God, and bringing into captivity every thought to the obedience of Christ. 2 Cor. 10:5.

Even the thoughts must be brought into subjection to the will of God, and the feelings under the control of reason and religion. Our imagination was not given us to be allowed to run riot and have its own way, without any effort at restraint and discipline. If the thoughts are wrong, the feelings will be wrong; and the thoughts and feelings combined make up the moral character.[10]

The power of right thought is more precious than the golden wedge of Ophir. . . . We need to place a high value upon the right control of our thoughts, for such control prepares the mind and soul to labor harmoniously for the Master. It is necessary for our peace and happiness in this life that our thoughts center in Christ. As a man thinketh, so is he. Our improvement in moral purity depends on right thinking and right acting. . . . Evil thoughts destroy the soul. The converting power of God changes the heart, refining and purifying the thoughts. Unless a determined effort is made to keep the thoughts centered on Christ, grace cannot reveal itself in the life. The mind must engage in the spiritual warfare. Every thought must be brought into captivity to the obedience of Christ. All the habits must be brought under God's control.

We need a constant sense of the ennobling power of pure thoughts and the damaging influence of evil thoughts. Let us place our thoughts upon holy things. Let them be pure and true, for the only security for any soul is right thinking. We are to use every means that God has placed within our reach for the government and cultivation of our thoughts. We are to bring our minds into harmony with His mind. His truth will sanctify us, body and soul and spirit, and we shall be enabled to rise above temptation.[11]

The control of the thoughts, in cooperation with the Holy Spirit, will give control of the words. This is true wisdom, and will ensure quietness of mind, contentment, and peace. There will be joy in the contemplation of the riches of the grace of God.[12]

IN HARMONY WITH GOD'S MIND

Draw nigh to God, and he will draw nigh to you. Cleanse your hands, ye sinners; and purify your hearts, ye double minded. James 4:8.

Angels of God are drawn toward all who in their thoughts and devoted service draw nigh to God. . . . It is a great misfortune to be double-minded. "A double minded man is unstable in all his ways" (James 1:8). . . . Let us use to a purpose the mind the Lord has given us. Ambition, covetousness, the mania to follow the fashions, the customs, and the practices of the world in order not to be thought singular, will soon obliterate all lines of distinction between the Christian's lines of pursuit and the practices of the world.

The love of pleasure is not to be cherished and indulged. When the human being, formed to do service for God, finds his time absorbed with plans that the Lord has nought to do with, he may well inquire, What end do I have in view? Whose service do I really enjoy? What does this eager strife for distinction amount to? [13]

As stewards over the Lord's property, we are to keep the temple of the soul cleansed from all the rubbish and defilement of the world. . . . All our talents are to be used, every thought is to be enlisted, every power to be put forth to bring us into harmony with the mind of God. We are to adorn ourselves with all the graces of the Spirit, emulating all that is upright and pure and elevating and ennobling, copying the excellencies, and embodying the perfections of the heavenly family, obtaining an education that will fit us to unite with the royal family in the courts of heaven.

We have the privilege of being trained under the inspiration of the Holy Spirit. All the attributes that are excellent are to strengthen our moral powers, that they may have no mist or tarnish upon them. We are weaving our threads in the web of humanity; not a thread of self-glory must be woven into the fabric. All heaven is imparting its help that we may surmount every obstacle. . . . We are to build characters of a goodly fabric, spiritual, heavenly, perfect. God bids us work for time and for eternity that we may grow after the divine likeness.[13]

165

LIKE CHRIST IN THOUGHT

Let this mind be in you which was also in Christ Jesus.
Phil. 2:5.

God expects those who bear the name of Christ to represent Him in thought, word, and deed. Their thoughts are to be pure and their words and deeds noble and uplifting, drawing those around them nearer to the Saviour.

In the life of the true Christian there is nothing of self. Self is dead. There was no selfishness in the life that Christ lived while on this earth. Bearing our nature, He lived a life wholly devoted to the service of others.

"Be ye therefore perfect" (Matt. 5:48) is God's word to us. And in order that we might obey this word, He sent His only-begotten Son to this earth to live in our behalf a perfect life. We have before us His example, and the strength by which He lived this life is at our disposal. In thought, word, and act Jesus was sinless. Perfection marked all that He did. He points us to the path that He trod, saying, "If any man will come after me, let him deny himself, and take up his cross, and follow me" (Matt. 16:24).[14]

We are to copy no human being. There is no human being wise enough to be our criterion. We are to look to the man Christ Jesus, who is complete in the perfection of righteousness and holiness. He is the author and finisher of our faith. He is the pattern man. His experience is the measure of the experience that we are to gain. His character is our model. Let us, then, take our minds off the perplexities and the difficulties of this life and fix them on Him, that by beholding we may be changed into His likeness. . . .

We are to have an intense interest in Christ Jesus, for He is our Saviour. He came to this world to be tempted in all points as we are, to prove to the universe that in this world of sin human beings can live lives that God will approve. . . . Let us seek for the blessings that Christ has placed within our reach, that we may be made capable of receiving more and still more of His grace, and that we may be filled with a living, active, growing faith—a faith that believes the promise, "Lo, I am with you alway, . . ." (Matt. 28:20).[15]

166

DARE TO BE DIFFERENT

Love not the world, neither the things that are in the world. If any man love the world, the love of the Father is not in him. 1 John 2:15.

Those who claim to know the truth and understand the great work to be done for this time are to consecrate themselves to God, soul, body, and spirit. In heart, in dress, in language, in every respect, they are to be separate from the fashions and practices of the world. They are to be a peculiar and holy people. It is not their dress that makes them peculiar; but because they are a peculiar and holy people, they cannot carry the marks of likeness to the world.

As a people we are to prepare the way of the Lord. Every iota of ability God has given us must be put to use in preparing the people after God's fashion, after His spiritual mold, to stand in this great day of God's preparation. . . . Many who suppose they are going to heaven are blindfolded by the world. Their ideas of what constitutes a religious education and religious discipline are vague, resting only upon possibilities. There are many who have no intelligent hope, and are running great risk in practicing the very things which Jesus has taught that they should not do, in eating, drinking, and dressing, binding themselves up with the world in a variety of ways. They have yet to learn the serious lesson so essential to growth in spirituality, to come out from the world and be separate.

The heart is divided, the carnal mind craves conformity, similarity to the world in so many ways, that the mark of distinction from the world is scarcely distinguishable. Money, God's money, is expended in order to make an appearance after the world's customs; the religious experience is contaminated with worldliness, and the evidence of discipleship—Christ's likeness in self-denial and cross bearing—is not discernible by the world or by the universe of heaven.[16]

The question to be settled is, "Are we willing to separate ourselves from the world, that we may become children of God?" This is not the work of a moment or of a day. . . . It is a lifelong work. Love to God must be a living principle, underlying every act and word and thought.[17]

167

NO PARTNERSHIP WITH THE WORLD

Know ye not that the friendship of the world is enmity with God? whosoever therefore will be a friend of the world is the enemy of God. James 4:4.

Christ and the world are not in partnership. The apostle says, "Know ye not that the friendship of the world is enmity with God?" . . . Conformity to the world will never be the means of converting the world to Christ. Christians must be entirely consecrated to God if the church is to be efficient in its influence for good upon unbelievers. The slightest diversion from Christ is so much influence, power, and efficiency given to the enemy.[18]

A Christian, as described by the Scriptures, is a person who is separated from the world in his aims and practices and is united with Christ—a possessor of the peace which Christ alone can bestow, finding that the joy of the Lord is his strength and that his joy is full. Christians will not leave the world to perish unwarned, and make no effort for the reclaiming of the lost. . . . Those who truly love Christ . . . watch for every opportunity to employ the means at their command in doing good and in patterning after the works of Christ. They will not yield to temptations to make alliances with the world. They will not unite with secret orders and bind themselves by intimacies with unbelievers. But those who are not wholly on the side of Christ are to a large degree controlled by the maxims and customs of the world. . . .

Satan is rich in this world's goods, and he is full of cunning to deceive, and his most effective agents are those whom he can lead to take a form of godliness while they deny the power of God by their un-Christlike characters. The children of God are to stand firmly for the right under all circumstances. They are not to be deceived by those who have the mind and spirit of the world. . . .

God has His faithful witnesses who are not attempting to do that which Christ has pronounced impossible—that is, seeking to serve God and Mammon at the same time. They are burning and shining lights amid the moral darkness of the world and amid the gross darkness that covers the people like the pall of death.[19]

SEVERED FROM EARTHLY THINGS

And have no fellowship with the unfruitful works of darkness, but rather reprove them. Eph. 5:11.

Many professed Christians are well represented by the vine that is trailing upon the ground and entwining its tendrils about the roots and rubbish that lie in its path. To all such the message comes, "Come out from among them, and be ye separate, saith the Lord, and touch not the unclean thing; and I will receive you, and will be a Father unto you, and ye shall be my sons and daughters, saith the Lord Almighty" (2 Cor. 6:17, 18).

There are conditions to meet if we would be blessed and honored by God. We are to separate from the world and refuse to touch those things that will separate our affections from God. God has the first and highest claims upon His people. Set your affections upon Him and upon heavenly things. Your tendrils must be severed from everything earthly. You are exhorted to touch not the unclean thing, for in touching this you will yourself become unclean. It is impossible for you to unite with those who are corrupt, and still remain pure. "What fellowship hath righteousness with unrighteousness? and what communion hath light with darkness? and what concord hath Christ with Belial?" (verses 14, 15). God and Christ and the heavenly host would have man know that if he unites with the corrupt, he will become corrupt. . . .

All our actions are affected by our religious experience. If our experience is founded in God; if we are daily tasting the power of the world to come, and have the fellowship of the Spirit; if each day we hold with a firmer grasp the higher life, principles that are holy and elevating will be inwrought in us, and it will be as natural for us to seek purity and holiness and separation from the world as it is for the angels of glory to execute the mission of love assigned them.[20]

Our consecration to God must be a living principle, interwoven with the life and leading to self-denial and self-sacrifice. It must underlie all our thoughts and be the spring of every action. This will elevate us above the world and separate us from its polluting influence.[20]

DISENTANGLED

No man that warreth entangleth himself with the affairs of this life; that he may please him who hath chosen him to be a soldier. 2 Tim. 2:4.

The Lord Jesus would have His purchased possession disentangle themselves from everything that would expose them to temptation. We are the Lord's by creation; we are His by redemption. All our senses are to be kept sharp and keen that we may place ourselves in right relation to God.

The company we choose will be a help or a hindrance to us. We are not to run any risk by placing ourselves where evil angels will surround us with their temptations and their snares. Satan . . . puts his alluring temptations before the soul. He appears as an angel of light and clothes his temptations with apparent goodness. Our first work is to disentangle ourselves from everything that is in any way calculated to tarnish the soul.

If the Bible is not made the rule of life, our hereditary and cultivated habits and tastes will ensnare the soul. . . . The soul is of value, and is regarded by God as more precious than gold, even the golden wedge of Ophir. Christ has given us the estimate He places upon the human soul. Look at His humiliation, His sufferings, His death. Had He studied His pleasure, His choice, His convenience, He would never have left the royal courts of heaven. . . .

After the human agent has spent his life in following his own impulses, placing his talents on the shrine of Satan, choosing his own interests, what has he gained? Cheap worldly applause. And what has he lost? An eternity of blessedness. . . .

God calls upon us, in the place of expending our powers, our talents, and the vigor of brain and muscle upon unimportant, frivolous things, merely to amuse and gratify self, to bring eternity to view and hold ourselves under the control of the Holy Spirit's guidance. Elevated, pure, ennobling themes are to be the subjects of contemplation. To us individually as His property God says, "Know ye not . . . ye are not your own? For ye are bought with a price: therefore glorify God in your body, and in your spirit, which are God's" (1 Cor. 6:19, 20).[21]

170

THE VITAL THREADS OF INFLUENCE

That thou mayest walk in the way of good men, and keep the paths of the righteous. **Prov. 2:20.**

It is generally the case that in school associations there are developed two classes of persons—those who seek to do the right and those who solicit others to enter into evil. . . .

In associating with the careless and reckless it is an easy matter to come to view things as they do and to lose all sense of what it means to be a follower of Jesus. Guard yourself on this one point in particular. Do not be influenced and led astray by those you have reason to know by their words and actions are not in connection with God. "By their fruits ye shall know them" (Matt. 7:20). . . .

Satan is seeking to imbue every soul that is not connected with Jesus Christ with his own spirit, and every soul who refuses to connect with Jesus Christ will be brought into connection with the enemy of Christ. There are threads of influence leading out from these souls to bind and draw other souls by human influence until they shall be placed under the control of Satan, and their feet be led into false paths. . . . This danger is common to all. You will be tempted to choose your own way and to have your own will, while disregarding the will of God. . . .

Let nothing draw you away from the work of character building, but do your work for time and for eternity. . . . Live a life of consistency, and fashion your character after the divine Pattern. If you live carelessly and do not watch unto prayer, you will surely fall a prey to the enemy and will yield to enticements to sin; thus you will lay upon the foundation stone, wood, hay, and stubble, which will be consumed in the last great day.[22]

Every heart is moved or drawn of Jesus Christ. As you become students of Scripture the Spirit of God takes the things of God and impresses them upon the soul. The golden threads that extend from the souls of those who make God their strength will fasten through the threads of influence to other souls and draw them to Christ. This is the work to be done by those who place on the foundation stone precious material, for they cooperate with Jesus Christ.[22]

A NETWORK OF VIRTUOUS INFLUENCES

I am a companion of all them that fear thee, and of them that keep thy precepts. Ps. 119:63.

Young people desire companionship, and just in proportion to the strength with which their feelings and affections fasten upon those with whom they associate, will be the power of those friends to be either a blessing or a curse to them. Then let parents beware. Let them guard every influence of association. "He that walketh with wise men shall be wise: but a companion of fools shall be destroyed" (Prov. 13:20). The youth will have associates and will feel their influence. . . .

Wax does not more certainly retain the figure of the seal than does the mind the impressions produced by intercourse and association. The influence is often silent and unconscious, nevertheless it is strong and impressive. If wise and good men and women are the chosen companions, then you put yourself in the direct way of becoming sound in thought, in ideas, and correct in principles. And such intimacies are of highest value in the formation of character. A network of virtuous influences will be woven around you, which the evil one will not be able to break with his seductive wiles. . . .

But let the youth choose the influence of, and become associated with, men and women of bad principles and practices, . . . and they are polluted. Silent and unconscious influences weave their sentiments into their lives, become a part of their very existence, and they walk on the very brink of a precipice and sense no danger. They learn to love the words of the smooth tongued, the honeyed words of the deceiver, and are restless, uneasy, and unhappy unless they are carried to the pinnacle of someone's flattery. . . . To walk in the counsel of the ungodly is the first step toward standing in the place of sinners and sitting in the seat of the scornful.[23]

The only safe course for the youth is to mingle with the pure, the holy, and thus natural tendencies to evil will be held in check. By choosing for their companions such as fear the Lord, they will seldom be found disbelieving God's Word, entertaining doubts and infidelity. The power of a truly consistent example is very great for good.[23]

THE GOLD OF CHRISTIAN CHARACTER

A good name is rather to be chosen than great riches, and loving favour rather than silver and gold. Prov. 22:1.

Men may aspire to renown. They may desire to possess a great name. With some the possession of houses and lands and plenty of money, that which will make them great according to the measure of the world, is the height of their ambition. They desire to reach the place where they can look down with a sense of superiority upon those who are poor. All such are building on the sand, and their house will fall suddenly. Superiority of position is not true greatness. That which does not increase the value of the soul is of no real value in itself. That which alone is worth obtaining is greatness of soul in the sight of Heaven. The true and exalted nature of your work you may never know. The value of your own being you can only measure by the value of that Life given to save all who will receive it.

Every man will have some estimate of his own worth when he becomes a laborer together with Christ, doing the work that Christ did, filling the world with Christ's righteousness, bearing a commission from the Most High. . . . The commission given to the disciples is given to all who are connected with Christ. They are to make any and every sacrifice for the joy of seeing souls saved who are perishing out of Christ. . . .

The highest honor that can be conferred upon human beings, be they young or old, rich or poor, is to be permitted to lift up the oppressed, to comfort the feeble-minded. The world is full of suffering. Go, and preach the gospel to the poor; heal the sick. This is the work to be connected with the gospel message. "The poor have the gospel preached to them" (Matt. 11:5). Colaborers with God are to fill the space they occupy in the world with the love of Jesus. . . . The love of Christ in the heart is expressed in the actions. If love for Christ is dull the love for those for whom Christ died will degenerate. . . .

True riches are genuine faith and genuine love. These make the character complete in Christ. If there were more faith, simple, trusting faith in Jesus, there would be love, pure love, which is the gold of Christian character.[24]

173

THE GIFT OF SPEECH

Keep thy tongue from evil, and thy lips from speaking guile.
Ps. 34:13.

Speech is one of the great gifts of God. It is the means by which the thoughts of the heart are communicated. It is with the tongue that we offer prayer and praise to God. With the tongue we convince and persuade. With the tongue we comfort and bless, soothing the bruised, wounded soul. With the tongue we may make known the wonders of the grace of God. With the tongue also we may utter perverse things, speaking words that sting like an adder.

The tongue is a little member, but the words it frames have great power. The Lord declares, "The tongue can no man tame" (James 3:8). It has set nation against nation and has caused war and bloodshed. Words have kindled fires that have been hard to quench. . . .

Satan puts into the mind thoughts which the Christian should never utter. The scornful retort, the bitter, passionate utterance, the cruel, suspicious charge, are from him. How many words are spoken that do only harm to those who utter them and to those who hear! Hard words beat upon the heart, awaking to life its worst passions. Those who do evil with their tongues . . . grieve the Holy Spirit; for they are working at cross purposes with God. . . .

Guard well the talent of speech, for it is a mighty power for evil as well as for good. You cannot be too careful of what you say; for the words you utter show what power is controlling the heart. If Christ rules there, your words will reveal the beauty, purity, and fragrance of a character molded and fashioned by His will. But if you are under the guidance of the enemy of all good, your words will echo his sentiments. . . .

Only through Christ can we gain the victory over the desire to speak hasty, un-Christlike words. When in His strength we refuse to give utterance to Satan's suggestions, the plant of bitterness in our hearts withers and dies. The Holy Spirit can make the tongue a savor of life unto life.[25]

God wants us to be a help and strength to one another. He wants us to speak words of hope and courage.[26]

EDUCATING THE TONGUE

Let no corrupt communication proceed out of your mouth, but that which is good to the use of edifying, that it may minister grace unto the hearers. Eph. 4:29.

The apostle, seeing the inclination to abuse the gift of speech, gives direction concerning its use. "Let no corrupt communication proceed out of your mouth," he says, "but that which is good to the use of edifying." The word "corrupt" means here any word that would make an impression detrimental to holy principles and undefiled religion, any communication that would eclipse the view of Christ, and blot from the mind true sympathy and love. It includes impure hints, which, unless instantly resisted, lead to great sin. Upon everyone is laid the duty of barring the way against corrupt communications.

It is God's purpose that the glory of Christ shall appear in His children. In all His teaching Christ presented pure, unadulterated principles. He did no sin, neither was guile found in His mouth. Constantly there flowed from His lips holy, ennobling truths. He spoke as never man spoke, with a pathos that touched the heart. . . . The truth never languished on His lips. With fearlessness He exposed the hypocrisy of priest and ruler, Pharisee and Sadducee. . . .

The great responsibility bound up in the use of the gift of speech is plainly made known in the Word of God. "By thy words thou shalt be justified, and by thy words thou shalt be condemned" (Matt. 12:37), Christ declared. And the psalmist asks, "Lord, who shall abide in thy tabernacle? who shall dwell in thy holy hill? He that walketh uprightly, and worketh righteousness, and speaketh the truth in his heart. He that backbiteth not with his tongue, nor doeth evil to his neighbour, nor taketh up a reproach against his neighbour" (Ps. 15:1-3).[27]

Cultivate a prayerful frame of mind and educate the tongue to speak right words, that will bless in the place of discouraging. . . . Talk of the goodness, the mercy, and the love of God. Put away all unbelieving words and all that is cheap and common. Let the words be sound words, that cannot be condemned, and the peace of God will surely come to the soul.[28]

DON'T RETALIATE!

Not rendering evil for evil, or railing for railing: but contrari-wise blessing; knowing that ye are thereunto called, that ye should inherit a blessing. 1 Peter 3:9.

Be determined not to please the enemy by allowing words of un-favorable criticism to lead you to retaliate or to depress you. Make the enemy's efforts a failure so far as you are concerned. Then the Lord will draw near to you and will give you a rich measure of love and peace and joy so deep and full that even in the midst of the trial of your faith you can bear triumphant witness to the truth of the word of promise. You will have a sense of the divine presence. The eyes of your understanding will be enlightened, and the truth that at times you have seen but dimly you will then see clearly. You will be able to tell the story of the cross with a deep appreciation of the Saviour's love, for this love will have melted your heart. You will bear about with you in the daily life the witness that Christ is formed within, the hope of glory.

Look constantly to Jesus. Take all your troubles to Him. He will never misunderstand you. He is the refuge of His people. Under the shadow of His protection they can pass unharmed. Believe in Him and trust in Him. He will not give you up to the spoiler.[29]

Let the atmosphere surrounding your soul be sweet and fragrant. If you will battle against selfish human nature, you will go steadily forward in the work of overcoming hereditary and cultivated tenden-cies to wrong. By patience, long-suffering, and forbearance you will accomplish much. Remember that you cannot be humiliated by the unwise speeches of someone else, but that when you speak unwisely you humiliate yourself and lose a victory that you might have gained. . . .

Keep yourselves where the three great powers of heaven—the Father, the Son, and the Holy Spirit—can be your efficiency. These powers work with the one who gives himself unreservedly to God. The strength of heaven is at the command of God's believing ones. The man who makes God his trust is barricaded by an impregnable wall.[30]

FRAGRANT IN WORD

But I say unto you, That every idle word that men shall speak, they shall give account thereof in the day of judgment. For by thy words thou shalt be justified, and by thy words thou shalt be condemned. Matt. 12:36, 37.

As the prophet Isaiah beheld the glory of the Lord, he was amazed, and overwhelmed with a sense of his own weakness and unworthiness, he cried, "Woe is me! for I am undone; because I am a man of unclean lips, and I dwell in the midst of a people of unclean lips: for mine eyes have seen the King, the Lord of hosts" (Isa. 6: 5). . . . Let every soul who claims to be a son or a daughter of God examine himself in the light of Heaven; let him consider the polluted lips that make him "undone." They are the medium of communication. . . . Then let them not be used in bringing from the treasure of the heart words that will dishonor God and discourage those around you, but use them for the praise and glory of God, who has formed them for this purpose. . . . When the love of Jesus is the theme of contemplation, the words coming from human lips will be full of praise and thanksgiving to God and to the Lamb.

How many words are spoken in lightness and foolishness, in jesting and joking! This would not be so did the followers of Christ realize the truth of the words, "Every idle word that men shall speak, they shall give account thereof in the day of judgment." . . .

The vision given to Isaiah represents the condition of God's people in the last days. . . . As they look by faith into the holy of holies, and see the work of Christ in the heavenly sanctuary, they perceive that they are a people of unclean lips—a people whose lips have often spoken vanity and whose talents have not been sanctified and employed to the glory of God. . . . If they will humble their souls before God, there is hope for them. The bow of promise is above the throne, and the work done for Isaiah will be performed in them.[31]

Be fragrant in your words. Remember that you are either a savor of life unto life or of death unto death. Let us be as fragrant flowers. Let the love of Christ pervade your lives. Let your words be such that they will be as apples of gold in pictures of silver.[32]

LOYAL TO ONE ANOTHER

Let all bitterness, and wrath, and anger, and clamour, and evil speaking, be put away from you, with all malice. Eph. 4:31.

There are those who think more highly of themselves than they ought to think. They speak evil of their brethren because after a thing is done they can look back and tell how differently they would have done it, but their forethought would not have been any better than that of their brethren had they been in their place. . . .

Keep yourselves off the judgment seat. All judgment is committed unto the Son of God. . . . Satan works zealously to cause men to offend on this point. Those whose tongues are so free to utter words of criticism, the adroit questioner who draws out expressions and opinions which have been put into minds by sowing seeds of alienation, are his missionaries. They may repeat the expressions they draw from others as originating with the ones they so slyly led on to forbidden ground. These persons seem always to see something to criticize and condemn. . . . Their tongues are ready to exaggerate everything evil. What a great matter a little fire kindleth! [33]

Never let your tongue and voice be employed in discovering and dilating upon the defects of your brethren, for the record of heaven identifies Christ's interests with those He has purchased with His own blood. "Inasmuch as ye have done it unto one of the least of these my brethren," He says, "ye have done it unto me" (Matt. 25: 40). We are to learn to be loyal to one another, to be true as steel in the defense of our brethren. Look to your own defects. You had better discover one of your own faults than ten of your brother's. Remember that Christ has prayed for these, His brethren, that they all might be one as He is one with the Father. Seek to the uttermost of your capabilities to be in harmony with your brethren to the extent of Christ's measurement, as He is one with the Father. . . .

"Love as brethren, be pitiful, be courteous" (1 Peter 3:8). True moral worth does not seek to have a place for itself by evil thinking and evil speaking, by demeriting others. All envy, all jealousy, all evil speaking, with all unbelief, must be put away from God's children. [33]

THE POWER OF TRUTHFULNESS

The lip of truth shall be established for ever: but a lying tongue is but for a moment. **Prov. 12:19.**

There are those who have so closely identified themselves with the truth that nothing, not even martyrdom and death, could sever them from it. Those who would evade the truth by silence, fearing to offend someone else, testify to a lie. Playing fast and loose with truth and dissembling to suit the opinions of someone else, means the shipwreck of faith. Let us despise falsifying. Let us never by a word or act or by silence testify to a lie. . . .

All who make untruthful statements . . . are serving him who has been a liar from the beginning. Let us be on our guard against untruthfulness, which grows upon him who practices it. I say to all, make truth your girdle. Be true to your faith. Put away all prevarication and exaggeration. Never make a false statement. For the sake of your own soul and the souls of others, be true in your utterances. Never speak or act a falsehood. The truth alone will bear to be repeated. A firm adherence to truth is essential to the formation of Christian character. "Stand therefore, having your loins girt about with truth, and having on the breastplate of righteousness" (Eph. 6:14).

He who utters untruths sells his soul in a cheap market. His falsehoods may seem to serve in emergencies. He may make business advancement because he gains by falsehood what he could not gain by fair dealing. But he finally reaches the place where he can trust no one. Himself a falsifier, he has no confidence in the word of others.[34]

There is absolutely no safeguard against evil but truth. No man can stand firm for right in whose heart the truth does not abide. There is only one power that can make and keep us steadfast—the power of God, imparted to us through the grace of Christ.[35]

Connected with Christ, human nature becomes true and pure. Christ supplies the efficiency, and man becomes a power for good. . . . Truthfulness and integrity are attributes of God, and he who possesses these qualities possesses a power that is invincible.[36]

179

GRACIOUS WORDS

Let your speech be alway with grace, seasoned with salt, that ye may know how ye ought to answer every man. Col. 4:6.

Courtesy is one of the graces of the Spirit. It is an attribute of Heaven. The angels never fly into a passion, never are envious or selfish. No harsh or unkind words escape their lips. If we are to be the companions of angels, we too must be refined and courteous.

The truth of God is designed to elevate the receiver, to refine his taste and sanctify his judgment. No man can be a Christian without having the spirit of Christ; and if he has the spirit of Christ, it will be manifested in a refined, courteous disposition. His character will be holy, his manners comely, his words without guile. He will cherish the love that is not easily provoked, that suffers long and is kind, that hopes all things and endures all things. . . .

Those who profess to be followers of Christ and are at the same time rough, unkind, and uncourteous in words and deportment have not learned of Jesus. . . . The conduct of some professing Christians is so lacking in kindness and courtesy that their good is evil spoken of. Their sincerity may not be doubted, their uprightness may not be questioned; but sincerity and uprightness will not atone for a lack of kindness and courtesy. The Christian is to be sympathetic as well as true, pitiful and courteous as well as upright and honest. . . .

True courtesy blended with truth and justice makes the life not only useful but beautiful and fragrant. Kind words, pleasant looks, a cheerful countenance, throw a charm about the Christian that makes his influence almost irresistible. In forgetfulness of self, in the light and peace and happiness that he is constantly bestowing on others, he finds true joy.

Let us be self-forgetful, ever on the watch to cheer others, to lighten their burdens by acts of tender kindness and deeds of unselfish love. Leave unspoken that unkind word; let that selfish disregard of the happiness of others give place to loving sympathy. These thoughtful courtesies, beginning in the home and extending far beyond the home circle, go far to make up the sum of life's happiness, and the neglect of them constitutes no small share of life's misery.[37]

KIND AND COURTEOUS WORDS

The Lord God hath given me the tongue of the learned, that I should know how to speak a word in season to him that is weary: he wakeneth morning by morning, he wakeneth mine ear to hear as the learned. Isa. 50:4.

What Christ was in His life on this earth, that every Christian is to be. He is our example, not only in His spotless purity, but in His patience, gentleness, and winsomeness of disposition. He was firm as a rock where truth and duty were concerned, but He was invariably kind and courteous. His life was a perfect illustration of true courtesy. . . . His presence brought a purer atmosphere into the home, and His life was as leaven working amid the elements of society. Harmless and undefiled, He walked among the thoughtless, the rude, the uncourteous; amid the unjust publicans, the unrighteous Samaritans, the heathen soldiers, the rough peasants, and the mixed multitude.

He spoke a word of sympathy here and a word there as He saw men weary and compelled to bear heavy burdens. He shared their burdens and repeated to them the lessons He had learned from nature, of the love, the kindness, the goodness of God. He sought to inspire with hope the most rough and unpromising, setting before them the assurance that they might become blameless and harmless, attaining such a character as would make them manifest as children of God. . . . Jesus sat an honored guest at the table of the publicans, by His sympathy and social kindliness showing that He recognized the dignity of humanity; and men longed to become worthy of His confidence. Upon their thirsty souls His words fell with blessed, life-giving power. New impulses were awakened, and the possibility of a new life opened to these outcasts of society.

The religion of Jesus softens whatever is hard and rough in the temper and smooths off whatever is rugged and sharp in the manners. It is this religion that makes the words gentle and the demeanor winning. Let us learn from Christ how to combine a high sense of purity and integrity with sunniness of disposition. A kind, courteous Christian is the most powerful argument that can be produced in favor of the gospel.[38]

181

NO SHARP OR HASTY WORDS

Wherefore laying aside all malice, and all guile, and hypocrisies, and envies, and all evil speakings, as newborn babes, desire the sincere milk of the word, that ye may grow thereby. 1 Peter 2:1, 2.

We should study this instruction. It is our privilege to grow "unto the measure of the stature of the fulness of Christ" (Eph. 4:13). We are not to be thoughtless or careless in speech, hurting one another by unkind words. . . .

Every human agency connected with the Lord's work needs to appreciate the work in which he is acting a part. The work in God's institutions is to be carried on without friction, without hasty speech, without dictatorial words. The workers are to be pure, clean, and holy in thought, in word, in act. They are to be Christ's witnesses, testifying that they are born again.[39]

There is to be no sharp speaking, no fretful scolding, for angels of God are walking up and down in every room. Christ loves to commend every faithful worker, and He will do it. Every good act is registered in the book. Little mistakes may be made, but words of censure arouse feelings of retaliation, and God is dishonored. . . . Any word spoken thoughtlessly or unadvisedly should be retracted on the spot. . . . We are to remember that as Christians professing to work in unity we must not act like sinners, whose sinful words and works, unless repented of, will condemn them. . . .

"Be watchful, and strengthen the things which remain, that are ready to die" (Rev. 3:2). This is our work. There are many ready to die spiritually, and the Lord calls upon us to strengthen them. God's people are to be firm to duty. They are to be bound together by the bonds of Christian fellowship and are to be strengthened in the faith by speaking often to one another about the precious truths entrusted to them. Never are they to quarrel and condemn. They are to unite upon the importance of obedience to God's law.[39]

In this life there is nothing of greater importance than preparation of character that we may at last enter with joy into the saints' abode on high. Why do we not improve our privilege of being saints here below? [39]

GROWING UP IN CHRIST

Therefore leaving the principles of the doctrine of Christ, let us go on unto perfection; not laying again the foundation of repentance from dead works, and of faith toward God. Heb. 6:1.

At the entrance gate of the path that leads to everlasting life God places faith, and He lines the whole way with the light and peace and joy of willing obedience. The traveler in this way keeps ever before him the mark of his high calling in Christ. The prize is ever in sight. To him God's commands are righteousness and joy and peace in the Holy Spirit. The things that first appeared to be crosses are found by experience to be crowns.

"Learn of me," is the Saviour's command. Yes, learn of Him how to live the Christ life—a life pure and holy, free from any taint of sin. . . .

Progression, not stagnation, is the law of heaven. Progression is the law of every faculty of mind and body. The things of nature obey this law. In the field there is seen first the blade, then the ear, then the full corn in the ear. In the spiritual life, as in the physical life, there is to be growth. Step by step we are to advance, ever receiving and imparting, ever gaining a more complete knowledge of Christ, daily approaching more closely the measure of the stature of the fullness of Christ.

The Christian is first a babe in Christ. Then he becomes a child. Constantly he is to make advancement proportionate to the opportunities and privileges granted him. Ever he is to remember that he is not his own, that he has been bought with a price, and that he must make the best possible use of the talents entrusted to him. Even in the infancy of his spiritual understanding, the Christian is to do his best, making steady advancement toward the higher, holier life. He is to realize that he is a laborer together with God. . . .

He is never to become self-sufficient, but is to count all things but loss for the excellency of the knowledge of Christ Jesus his Lord. He is to walk and work in the Saviour's companionship. As he does this, his faith will increase. Constantly beholding Christ, he will be changed into the same image from character to character.[40]

183

DON'T BE A RELIGIOUS DWARF

But grow in grace, and in the knowledge of our Lord and Saviour Jesus Christ. To him be glory both now and for ever. Amen. 2 Peter 3:18.

A genuine Christian experience unfolds day by day, bringing to its possessor new strength and earnestness and leading to constant growth in spiritual life. But the Christian world abounds with professors of religion who are merely religious dwarfs. Many seem to have graduated as soon as they learned the rudiments of the Christian faith. They do not grow in grace or in the knowledge of the truth. They do nothing, either with their means or their influence, to build up the cause of God. They are drones in the hive. This class will not long stand where they are. They will be converted and advance, or they will retrograde. . . .

To meet the claims of God, you will have to make personal effort; and in this work you will need the resources of an ever-growing Christian experience. Your faith must be strong, your consecration complete, your love pure and sincere, your zeal ardent, tireless, your courage unshaken, your patience unwearied, your hopes bright. Upon every one, old or young, rests a responsibility in this matter.[41]

The perils of the last days will test the genuineness of our faith. . . . The mighty surges of temptation will beat upon all, and unless they are riveted to the eternal Rock they will be borne away. Do not think that you can safely drift with the current. If you do, you will surely become the helpless prey of Satan's devices. By diligent searching of the Scriptures and earnest prayer for divine help prepare the soul to resist temptation. The Lord will hear the sincere prayer of the contrite soul and will lift up a standard for you against the enemy. But you will be tried; your faith, your love, your patience, your constancy will be tested. . . .

Our duty, our safety, our happiness and usefulness, and our salvation call upon us each to use the greatest diligence to secure the grace of Christ, to be so closely connected with God that we may discern spiritual things, and not be ignorant of Satan's devices. . . .

"This is the victory that overcometh the world, even our faith." [41]

"UNTO A PERFECT MAN"

Till we all come in the unity of the faith, and of the knowledge of the Son of God, unto a perfect man, unto the measure of the stature of the fulness of Christ. Eph. 4:13.

As we advance step by step in the path of obedience, we shall know how true is the promise that they who follow on to know the Lord shall know that His going forth is prepared as the morning. Clearer light is ready to shine upon all who follow Him who is the Light of the world. Every one who takes upon him the yoke of Christ, with full determination to obey the word of God, will have a healthy, symmetrical experience. He will enjoy the blessings that come to him as a result of the hiding of his life with Christ in God.

In business life he will work out the principles laid down in Christ's sermon on the mount. He will renounce the bag of deceitful weights and will despise the fraud of tricks in trade. . . . He has an abiding sense that he is a part of the heavenly firm and that it is his duty to trade upon the talents given him by God. He realizes that he is adopted into the family of God and that he must act toward all as Christ acted when He was upon this earth.

What a diligent, constant work is the work of a true Christian. Ever he wears the yoke of Christ. . . . He has genuine modesty, and does not talk of his qualifications and accomplishments. Self-admiration is not a part of his experience. There is much to learn in regard to what comprises true Christian character. It certainly is not self-inflation. . . . The glory and majesty of God should ever fill our souls with a holy awe, humbling us in the dust before Him. His condescension, His wide, deep compassion, His tenderness and love, are given us to strengthen our confidence and remove that fear which tendeth unto bondage. The Lord wants us to give Him all there is of us in a steady, evenly balanced Christian life. . . .

Let us not endure the thought of being religious dwarfs. . . . We must ever be growing unto the full stature of men and women in Christ Jesus, till we are complete in Him. Christ will come and abide with every soul who will say from the heart, Come in. He loves every one who has a desire to follow Him.[42]

PERFECT IN YOUR SPHERE

Be ye therefore perfect, even as your Father which is in heaven is perfect. Matt. 5:48.

In order for our character building to be pleasing to God, we must constantly advance in spirituality. We must regard as worthless anything that lessens faith and confidence in our Redeemer. The more light there is shining into our souls, the greater the demand upon us to reflect that light to others. God desires you to let your light shine forth to the world. He will be glorified in our individual reflection of His character. . . .

Resting in the love of Christ, trusting the Redeemer and Life-giver to work out for you the salvation of your soul, you will know, as you draw nearer and still nearer to Him, what it means to endure the seeing of Him who is invisible. God desires us to rest content in His love. The contentment that Christ bestows is a gift worth infinitely more than gold and silver and precious stones. . . .

Your perceptive faculties will increase in power and soundness if your whole being, body, soul, and spirit, is consecrated to the accomplishment of a holy work. Make every effort in and through the grace of Christ to attain to the high standard set before you. You can be perfect in your sphere as God is perfect in His sphere. Has not Christ declared, "Be ye therefore perfect, even as your Father which is in heaven is perfect"?

You are not to regard yourself as merely a passive recipient of the grace of our Lord Jesus Christ. God has entrusted to you precious talents, and He requires the improvement of these talents. Interest from the principal lent is His due. . . . Submitting your will to His will, you will improve in speech and in spiritual conceptions. . . .

You are carefully to guard the powers of the mind. Your thoughts are to be kept under the control of the Holy Spirit. . . . It is your work to advance toward perfection, making constant improvement, until at last you are pronounced worthy to receive immortal life. And even then the work of progression will not cease, but will continue throughout eternity.[43]

REVEALING CHRIST'S LIKENESS

The work of righteousness shall be peace; and the effect of righteousness quietness and assurance for ever. Isa. 32:17.

Christ will be to His people all that these words express if they will heed the invitation to come to Him. He will be to them life and power, strength and efficiency, wisdom and holiness. God calls upon us to live the Christ life, to reveal this life to the world.[44]

We can, *we can,* reveal the likeness of our divine Lord. We can know the science of spiritual life. We can honor our Maker. But do we do it? Oh, what an illustrious example we have in the life that Christ lived on this earth! He has shown us what we can accomplish through cooperation with divinity. We are to seek for the union of which He speaks when He says, "Abide in me, and I in you" (John 15:4). This union is deeper, stronger, truer, than any other union and is productive of all good. Those who are thus united to the Saviour are controlled by His will and are moved by His love to suffer with those who suffer, to rejoice with those who rejoice, to feel a deep sympathy for every one in weakness, sorrow, or distress.[44]

Wherever I go I shall urge the people to keep Christ uplifted. He is always the same, yesterday, today, and forever, always seeking to do us good, always encouraging and guiding us, leading us onward step by step. What He is today—a faithful high priest, touched with the feeling of our infirmities—He will be tomorrow and forevermore. He is our guide, our teacher, our counselor, our friend, ever bestowing His blessings upon us in response to our faith. He invites us to abide with Him. When we do this, when we make our home with Him, all friction, all ill temper, all irritation, will cease. . . .

I know that when I ask the Lord to be my helper He will not deny me, because it is my one desire to do His will and glorify His name. I am weak, but in depending wholly upon Him, I obtain strength. In laying my burden upon the Burden Bearer, I find comfort and strength and hope. This is my desire—to find abiding rest at His feet. While I keep firm hold of His hand, He leads me safely. The living God shall be the joy and rejoicing of my soul.[45]

CHRIST'S ABIDING PRESENCE

And, lo, I am with you alway, even unto the end of the world.
Matt. 28:20.

We have every encouragement that if we daily surrender our wills to God the promise will be fulfilled, "And of his fulness have all we received, and grace for grace" (John 1:16). Every revealing of the grace of Christ in our behalf is for us. We are to reveal His grace in our lives, in thought, word, and deed. . . . We are to represent the mercy, the love, and the power of Christ—the power that He has given us. . . .

Were it not for the power received through Christ we would have no strength. But Christ has all power. "Jesus came and spake unto them, saying, All power is given unto me in heaven and in earth. Go ye therefore, and teach all nations, . . . and, lo, I am with you alway, even unto the end of the world." Here is our power, our comfort. Of ourselves we have no strength. But He says, "I am with you alway," helping you to perform your duty, guiding, comforting, sanctifying, and sustaining you, giving you success in speaking words that will draw the attention of others to Christ and awaken in their minds the desire to understand the hope and meaning of the truth, turning them from darkness to light. . . .

It is a wonderful thought that human beings can speak the word of God, in simple words of comfort and encouragement. The humblest instruments will be used of God to sow the seeds of truth, which may spring up and bear fruit, because the one in whose heart they were sown needed help—a kind thought, a kind word, made effective by the One who has said, "Lo, I am with you alway." [46]

To us also the promise of Christ's abiding presence is given. The lapse of time has wrought no change in His parting promise. He is with us today as truly as He was with the disciples, and He will be with us "even unto the end." . . .

He finds His faithful ones, and holds communion with them, encouraging and strengthening them. And angels of God, that excel in strength, are sent forth by God to minister to His human workers who are speaking the truth to those who know it not. [47]

THE CHRISTIAN'S PLEDGE OF ALLEGIANCE

Ye shall be holy unto me: for I the Lord am holy, and have severed you from other people, that ye should be mine. Lev. 20:26.

The character of the one who comes to God in faith will bear witness that the Saviour has entered into his life, directing all, pervading all. Such a one is continually asking, "Is this thy will and way, O my Saviour?" Constantly he looks to Jesus. . . . He consults the will of his divine Friend in reference to all his actions, for he knows that in this confidence is his strength. He has made it a habit to lift up the heart to God in every perplexity, every uncertainty.

He who accepts God as his sovereign must take the oath of allegiance to Him. He must put on the Christian uniform and bear aloft the banner that shows to whose army he belongs. He must make an open avowal of his allegiance to Christ. Concealment is impossible. Christ's impress must appear on the life in sanctified works.

"I am the Lord your God, which have separated you from other people." "Ye shall be holy unto me: for I the Lord am holy, and have severed you from other people, that ye should be mine." "The very God of peace sanctify you wholly; and I pray God your whole spirit and soul and body be preserved blameless unto the coming of our Lord Jesus Christ." "This people have I formed for myself; they shall shew forth my praise." "Ye are a chosen generation, a royal priesthood, an holy nation, a peculiar people; that ye should shew forth the praises of him who hath called you out of darkness into his marvellous light" (Lev. 20:24, 26; 1 Thess. 5:23; Isa. 43:21; 1 Peter 2:9). . . .

Complete subjection through Christ to the will of God is our only safety. The selfish thoughts and impulses that sweep through the soul, producing discordant notes, can be separated from the life only as the whole being is under the control of Christ. The Saviour's words to all unruly elements is, "Peace, be still." Christ welcomes all who accept Him as their Saviour, and rules over them as their king. . . . Our zeal for the advancement of God's kingdom is to mark us as faithful subjects of the cross of Christ. God can trust as His representatives those who implicitly obey Him.[1]

TOTAL COMMITMENT TO GOD

The light of the body is the eye: if therefore thine eye be single, thy whole body shall be full of light. Matt. 6:22.

The work of the Spirit of God in a man is not a work that unfits him for the common duties of ordinary life. There is not to be one religion for business and another religion for the church. The work of the Spirit of God embraces the whole man, soul, body, and spirit.

If the Word of God is cherished as an abiding principle in the heart, and held fast under all and every circumstance, man is brought, with his entrusted capabilities, under [subjection] to the Lord Jesus Christ. His undivided powers, even his thoughts, are brought into captivity to Christ. This is true sanctification. All the parts of the experience blend in complete harmony. He is "wanting in nothing." He does not keep part to himself, to do with just as he pleases. . . .

"The light of the body is the eye: if therefore thine eye be single, the whole body shall be full of light." This says, "thine eye," not some other person's eye. The rich experience that it is our privilege to have, we lose when we expect someone else to do our seeing for us and guide us in our spiritual experience as if we were blind. We must have a single eye to God's glory, a single and persistent purpose to leave self and the preferences of others out of the question. . . .

He who truly loves and fears God, striving with a singleness of purpose to do His will, will place his body, his mind, his heart, his soul, his strength, under service to God. Thus it was with Enoch. He walked with God. His mind was not defiled by an impure, defective eyesight. Those who are determined to make the will of God their own must serve and please God in everything. Then the character will be harmonious and well balanced, consistent, cheerful, and true. . . .

You are each living your probationary time day by day, obtaining your experience as the days pass; but you can go over the ground only once. Then let every precious moment be employed as you will wish it had been when the judgment shall sit and the books shall be opened. Our Lord will judge us according to the opportunities that we have had.[2]

190

A TEMPLE FOR GOD

Know ye not that ye are the temple of God, and that the Spirit of God dwelleth in you? 1 Cor. 3:16.

From eternal ages it was God's purpose that every created being, from the bright and holy seraph to man, should be a temple for the indwelling of the Creator. Because of sin, humanity ceased to be a temple for God. . . .

God designed that the temple at Jerusalem should be a continual witness to the high destiny open to every soul. But the Jews had not understood the significance of the building they regarded with so much pride. . . . The courts of the temple at Jerusalem, filled with the tumult of unholy traffic, represented all too truly the temple of the heart, defiled by the presence of sensual passion and unholy thoughts. In cleansing the Temple from the world's buyers and sellers, Jesus announced His mission to cleanse the heart from the defilement of sin —from the earthly desires, the selfish lusts, the evil habits that corrupt the soul. . . . Only Christ can cleanse the soul temple. . . . His presence will cleanse and sanctify the soul, so that it may be a holy temple unto the Lord, and "an habitation of God through the Spirit" (Eph. 2:22).

By this beautiful and impressive figure God's Word shows the regard He places on our physical organism and the responsibility resting upon us to preserve it in the best condition. Our bodies are Christ's purchased possession, and we are not at liberty to do with them as we please. Man has done this. He has treated his body as if its laws had no penalty. Through perverted appetite its organs and powers have become enfeebled, diseased, crippled. . . .

When men and women are truly converted they will conscientiously regard the laws of life that God has established in their being, thus seeking to avoid physical, mental, and moral feebleness. Obedience to these laws must be made a matter of personal duty. We ourselves must suffer the ills of violated law. We must answer to God for our habits and practices. Therefore the question for us is not, "What will the world say?" but, "How shall I, claiming to be a Christian, treat the habitation God has given me?" [3]

191

CARING FOR THE BODY TEMPLE

I will praise thee; for I am fearfully and wonderfully made: marvellous are thy works; and that my soul knoweth right well. **Ps. 139:14.**

Said the psalmist, "I am fearfully and wonderfully made." God has given us faculties and powers of mind and body, which it is the duty of all to preserve in the best condition. If any weaken their powers through the indulgence of appetite, they decrease their power of influence, making themselves imperfect. Only by the expensive offering made upon the cross of Calvary can we understand the value of the human soul. We are placed on vantage ground by the redeeming power of Jesus Christ, to obtain freedom from the bondage of sin which was wrought by the fall of Adam.[4]

We are to make the most of the capabilities and talents lent us by God. All who are weakening and destroying the physical, mental, and moral powers by sinful eating, sinful dressing, and violation of the laws of health in any respect, will have to render an account to God for all the good they might have done had they observed the laws of health, rather than being self-indulgent, careless, and reckless of the house they live in. . . . God says, "Ye are not your own." You are God's property. Your ransom cost the life of the Son of God. . . . All are to consider the greatness of the sacrifice made. The Majesty of heaven, the King of glory, designs that men and women shall give to Him their wholehearted service.

In the words of the apostle Paul there is a depth of meaning: "I beseech you therefore, brethren, by the mercies of God, that ye present your bodies a living sacrifice, holy, acceptable unto God, which is your reasonable service. And be not conformed to this world: but be ye transformed by the renewing of your mind, that ye may prove what is that good, and acceptable, and perfect, will of God" (Rom. 12:1, 2). No one can bring honor to God if he pursues a course of action that will bring blemish upon the body or the soul. Our sacrifice is to be holy and without blame. This is the reasonable service of everyone. We are God's workmanship, God's building. . . .

God wants us to honor Him with all there is of us.[4]

"OUR REASONABLE SERVICE"

I beseech you therefore, brethren, by the mercies of God, that ye present your bodies a living sacrifice, holy, acceptable unto God, which is your reasonable service. Rom. 12:1.

The apostle entreats his brethren to consecrate their bodies to God. . . . When we pursue a course to lessen mental and physical vigor— in eating, drinking, or in any of our habits—we dishonor God, for we rob Him of the service He claims of us. When we indulge appetite at the expense of health, or when we indulge habits which lessen our vitality and mental vigor, we cannot have a high appreciation of the atonement and a right estimate of eternal things.

When our minds are beclouded and partially paralyzed by disease we are easily overcome by the temptations of Satan. Eating of unhealthful food to gratify the appetite has a direct tendency to unbalance the circulation of the blood, cause nervous debility, and as the result there is great lack of patience and true, elevated affection. Constitutional strength, as well as the tone of the morals and the mental faculties, is enfeebled through the indulgence of perverted appetite. . . .

All the treasures of the world sink into insignificance when compared to the value of the mental and moral powers. And the healthful action of these faculties is dependent upon the physical health. Then how important that we know how to preserve health, that our duty to God and man may be performed according to His commandments. The laws of God are plain and distinct. No uncertainty beclouds any of them. None of them need ever be misunderstood. Those who cannot discern them are benumbed by their own wrong habits enfeebling their intellect.

God designs to teach us the importance of temperance in all things. As intemperance caused the fall of our first parents from their holy and happy estate, by their transgressing the law of God, so temperance in all things will keep our faculties in as healthy a condition as possible, that no mist or uncertainty may becloud any of them, that intellect may guide to right actions in keeping His law. . . . We must work in harmony with natural laws if we would discern the binding claims of the law of God spoken from Sinai.[5]

THE TEST OF APPETITE

But I keep under my body, and bring it into subjection: lest that by any means, when I have preached to others, I myself should be a castaway. 1 Cor. 9:27.

After His baptism the Son of God entered the dreary wilderness, there to be tempted by the devil. For nearly six weeks He endured the agonies of hunger. . . . He realized the power of appetite upon man; and in behalf of sinful man, He bore the closest test possible upon that point. Here a victory was gained which few can appreciate. The controlling power of depraved appetite and the grievous sin of indulging it can only be understood by the length of the fast which our Saviour endured that He might break its power. . . .

Intemperance lies at the foundation of all the moral evils known to man. Christ began the work of redemption just where the ruin began. The fall of our first parents was caused by the indulgence of appetite. In redemption, the denial of appetite is the first work of Christ.[6]

The Son of God saw that man could not of himself overcome this powerful temptation. . . . He came to earth to unite His divine power with our human efforts, that through the strength and moral power which He imparts, we might overcome in our own behalf. Oh! what matchless condescension for the King of glory to come down to this world to endure the pangs of hunger and the fierce temptations of a wily foe, that He might gain an infinite victory for man. Here is love without a parallel. Yet this great condescension is but dimly comprehended by those for whom it was made.

It was not the gnawing pangs of hunger alone which made the sufferings of our Redeemer so inexpressibly severe. It was the sense of guilt which had resulted from the indulgence of appetite that had brought such terrible woe into the world, which pressed so heavily upon His divine soul. . . .

With man's nature, and the terrible weight of his sins pressing upon Him, our Redeemer withstood the power of Satan upon this great leading temptation, which imperils the souls of men. If man should overcome this temptation, he could conquer on every other point.[6]

THE BATTLE FOR PURITY

Keep thyself pure. 1 Tim. 5:22.

To know what constitutes purity of mind, soul, and body is an important part of education.[7]

When the character is lacking in purity, when sin has become a part of the character, it has a bewitching power that is equal to the intoxicating glass of liquor. The power of self-control and reason is overborne by practices that defile the whole being; and if these sinful practices are continued, the brain is enfeebled and diseased, and loses its balance. Such ones are a curse to themselves and to all who have any connection with them. . . .

Bad habits are more easily formed than good habits, and the bad habits are given up with more difficulty. The natural depravity of the heart accounts for this well-known fact—that it takes far less labor to demoralize the youth, to corrupt their ideas of moral and religious character, than to engraft upon their character the enduring, pure, and uncorrupted habits of righteousness and truth. Self-indulgence, love of pleasure, enmity, pride, self-esteem, envy, jealousy, will grow spontaneously, without example and teaching. In our present fallen state all that is needed is to give up the mind and character to its natural tendencies. In the natural world, give up a field to itself and you will see it covered with briers and thorns; but if it yields precious grain or beautiful flowers, care and unremitting labor must be applied.[8]

Now we present before you the necessity of constant resistance to evil. All heaven is interested in men and women whom God has valued so much as to give His beloved Son to die to redeem them. No other creature that God has made is capable of such improvement, such refinement, such nobility as man. Then when men become blunted by their own debasing passions, sunken in vice, what a specimen for God to look upon! Man cannot conceive what he may be and what he may become. Through the grace of Christ he is capable of constant mental progress. Let the light of truth shine into his mind and the love of God be shed abroad in his heart and he may, through the grace Christ has died to impart to him, be a man of power—a child of earth but an heir of immortality.[8]

DANGER AT EVERY STEP

Flee also youthful lusts: but follow righteousness, faith, charity, peace, with them that call on the Lord out of a pure heart. 2 Tim. 2:22.

The moral dangers to which all, both old and young, are exposed are daily increasing. Moral derangement, which we call depravity, finds ample room to work, and an influence is exerted by men, women, and youth professing to be Christians that is low, sensual, devilish. . . .

Those who have learned the truth and do not have works corresponding with their profession of faith are subject to Satan's temptations. They encounter danger at every step they advance. They are brought into contact with evil, they see sights, they hear sounds, that will awaken their unsubdued passions; they are subjected to influences that lead them to choose the evil rather than the good, because they are not sound at heart. Just at the time when the power of the will is to be exercised, when firmness is required to resist the first approach of temptation, you find them easy subjects of Satan's devices, a mere plaything of the devil. Every temptation is now at work to lead those who claim to keep God's commandments, to break them. . . .

All must learn the lesson of what power there is in a good character. There is no training we need so much now as the preparing of young men and women to have moral rectitude and to cleanse their souls of every spot and stain of moral defilement. The standard of morality and holiness is trailing in the dust. . . .

We are near the close of probation, when every case is to pass in review before God. Now, in probation, is the time God has given us for the formation of pure and holy characters. If this time is not improved, if the thoughts are impure, if the heart is not sanctified, if unholy practices are indulged, be sure that the portion of such will be with the unholy, the debased, the abominable.

It is now, in probationary time, that every soul must make his choice. This choice will be seen in the family, will be seen in the association with the church. Virtue and true, unselfish principles will bring their own reward, for they will be reproduced in others. . . . "By their fruits ye shall know them" (Matt. 7:20).

SAFEGUARDING THE MORAL POWERS

Dearly beloved, I beseech you as strangers and pilgrims, abstain from fleshly lusts, which war against the soul. 1 **Peter** 2:11.

There is an alarming commonness in conversation at the present day, which shows a low state of thoughts and morals. True dignity of character is very rare. True modesty and reserve are seldom seen. There are but few who are pure and undefiled. . . . God looks upon these things with displeasure. . . .

Polluted thoughts harbored become habit, and the soul is scarred and defiled. Once do a wrong action and a blot is made which nothing can heal but the blood of Christ; and if the habit is not turned from with firm determination, the soul is corrupted and the streams flowing from this defiling fountain corrupt others.[10]

There are men and women who invite temptation; they place themselves in positions where they will be tempted, where they cannot but be tempted, when they place themselves in society that is objectionable. The best way to keep safe from sin is to move with due consideration at all times and under all circumstances, never to move or act from impulse. Move with the fear of God ever before you and you will be sure to act right; then leave your reputation with God. Slander cannot then sully your character one particle. No one can degrade our character but ourselves, by our own course of action. . . .

The mind must be kept meditating upon pure and holy subjects. An impure suggestion must be dismissed at once, and pure, elevating thoughts, holy contemplation, be entertained, thus obtaining more and more knowledge of God, by training the mind in the contemplation of heavenly things. God has simple means open to every individual case, sufficient to secure the great end, the salvation of the soul.

Resolve to reach a high and holy standard; make your mark high; act with earnest purpose, as did Daniel, steadily, perseveringly, and nothing that the enemy can do will hinder your improvement. Notwithstanding inconveniences, changes, perplexities, you may constantly advance in mental vigor and moral power.[10]

CRUCIFYING THE FLESH

And they that are Christ's have crucified the flesh with the affections and lusts. Gal. 5:24.

We are not our own. We have been "bought with a price" (1 Cor. 6:20), not "with corruptible things, as silver and gold, . . . but with the precious blood of Christ" (1 Peter 1:18, 19); "that they which live should not henceforth live unto themselves, but unto him which died for them, and rose again" (2 Cor. 5:15).

All men have been bought with this infinite price. By pouring the whole treasury of heaven into this world, by giving us in Christ all heaven, God has purchased the will, the affections, the mind, the soul, of every human being. . . . All men are the Lord's property.[11]

This expression, "bought with a price," means everything to us. In consideration of the price paid for us, shall we not yield our bodies and souls up to Him who has bought us with His blood? Shall not that which He has redeemed be kept in as wholesome and pure and holy a condition as possible? . . . Our very flesh He has saved at an infinite cost, giving His own flesh for the life of the world.

The lower passions have their seat in the body, and work through it. The words "flesh" or "fleshly" or "carnal lusts" embrace the lower, corrupt nature; the flesh of itself cannot act contrary to the will of God. We are commanded to crucify the flesh, with the affections and lusts. How shall we do it? Shall we inflict pain on the body? No; but put to death the temptation to sin. The corrupt thought is to be expelled. . . . All animal propensities are to be subjected to the higher powers of the soul. The love of God must reign supreme; Christ must occupy an undivided throne. Our bodies are to be regarded as His purchased possession. The members of the body are to become the instruments of righteousness.[12]

Jesus will be the helper of all who put their trust in Him. Those who are connected with Christ have happiness at their command. They follow the path where their Saviour leads, for His sake crucifying the flesh, with its affections and lusts. They have built their hopes on Christ, and the storms of earth are powerless to sweep them from the sure foundation.[13]

A FIRM, DECISIVE "NO"

How then can I do this great wickedness, and sin against God?
Gen. 39:9.

There are always those of pliant, accommodating dispositions who can with difficulty pronounce the word NO squarely, who are ready to be led away from God by a stronger, determined will. These have no interior strength to rely upon, no firm principle to save them from accepting evil suggestions and forming wrong habits. . . .

The moral dangers to which all, both old and young, are exposed are daily increasing. . . . Satan is making masterly efforts to involve married men and women and children and youth in impure practices. His temptations find acceptance in many hearts, because they have not been elevated, purified, refined, and ennobled by the sacred truth which they claim to believe. Not a few have been low and vile in thought and common in talk and deportment, so that when Satan's temptations come they have no moral power to resist them and fall an easy prey. . . .

We have need to be alarmed if we have not the fear of God constantly before us. We have need to fear if there is any departing from the living God, for He alone is our strength and fortress, into which we may run and be safe when the enemy makes a charge upon us with his temptations.

It is a subject of interest to every soul of us, how we shall keep our vessels unto honor in the sight of a holy God. . . . There is no safety for us when we lie down, when we rise up, when we go out, and when we come in. Satan and evil angels have conspired with evil men and evil women, and the whole energies of the powers of darkness will gather themselves together to lead astray and destroy every soul that is not garrisoned with firm principles of eternal truths. . . .

The principles of righteousness must be implanted in the soul. Faith must grasp the power of Jesus Christ, else there is no safety. Licentious practices are getting to be as common as in the days before the Flood. . . . The weak moral powers of men and women in this age who claim to be commandment keepers alarm me. Everyone needs to arouse and lift up the standard of purity.[14]

JULY 12

COMPLETE SANCTIFICATION

And the very God of peace sanctify you wholly; and I pray God your whole spirit and soul and body be preserved blameless unto the coming of our Lord Jesus Christ. 1 Thess. 5:23.

Sanctification—how many understand its full meaning? The mind is befogged by sensual malaria. The thoughts need purifying. What might not men and women have been had they realized that the treatment of the body has everything to do with the vigor and purity of mind and heart! . . . Men and women have been bought with a price, and what a price! Even the life of the Son of God. What a terrible thing it is for them to place themselves in a position where their physical, mental, and moral powers are corrupted, where they lose their vigor and purity. Such men and women cannot offer an acceptable sacrifice to God.[15]

The true Christian obtains an experience which brings holiness. He is without a spot of guilt upon the conscience or a taint of corruption upon the soul. The spirituality of the law of God, with its limiting principles, is brought into his life. The light of truth irradiates his understanding. A glow of perfect love for the Redeemer clears away the miasma which has interposed between his soul and God. The will of God has become his will, pure, elevated, refined, and sanctified. His countenance reveals the light of heaven. His body is a fit temple for the Holy Spirit. Holiness adorns his character. God can commune with him, for soul and body are in harmony with God.[15]

There are many who, though striving to obey God's commandments, have little peace or joy. This lack in their experience is the result of a failure to exercise faith. They walk, as it were, in a salt land, a parched wilderness. They claim little, when they might claim much; for there is no limit to the promises of God. Such ones do not correctly represent the sanctification that comes through obedience to the truth. The Lord would have all His sons and daughters happy, peaceful, and obedient. Through the exercise of faith the believer comes into possession of these blessings. Through faith, every deficiency of character may be supplied, every defilement cleansed, every fault corrected, every excellence developed.[16]

OUR SUPREME OBLIGATION

But the God of all grace, who hath called us unto his eternal glory by Christ Jesus, after that ye have suffered a while, make you perfect, stablish, strengthen, settle you. 1 Peter 5:10.

So perfect is the character represented which men must have in order to be Christ's disciples that the infidel has said that it is not possible for any human being to attain unto it. But no less a standard must be presented by all who claim to be children of God. Infidels know not that celestial aid is provided for all who seek for it by faith. Every provision has been made in behalf of every soul who shall seek to be a partaker of the divine nature and be complete in Jesus Christ. Every defect is to be discerned and cut away from the character with an unsparing decision.

The people of God are to turn every action into devotion. They are to partake of every meal as if they knew it was a token of the love of the infinite God expressed to them. The termination of one duty is to be the commencement of the next that presents itself. Then the Christian character will be manifest in a life of continuous obedience and service to Jesus Christ.

Whatever business engagements men may yoke up with, if Christians, they must wear the yoke of duty to Christ. This is their allegiance. They are to consider themselves bound by superior obligations. The Master, Jesus Christ, has placed His yoke upon the neck of every disciple. The life service is pledged to Him in accepting His yoke. Anything that will mar or hinder his perfect service to God is to be broken off, whatever its nature or character may be. . . .

The Lord has united His nature with humanity expressly that He might become a more distinguishable and definite object for our contemplation and love. He invites us to draw near and contemplate the great light, the invisible God invested in robes of humanity, emitting a glory so softened and subdued that our eyes can endure the sight. Christ is the light of heaven. In His face we shall see God. Bear in mind the prayer of Christ, that His people may be one with Him as He is one with the Father, that they may be with Him where He is and behold His glory.[17]

201

MARRIAGE A SACRED INSTITUTION

Whoso findeth a wife findeth a good thing, and obtaineth favour of the Lord. Prov. 18:22.

Marriage has received Christ's sanction and blessing and is to be regarded as a sacred institution. True religion does not counterwork the Lord's plans. God ordained that woman should be united with man in holy wedlock, to raise up families that would be crowned with honor who would be symbols of the family in heaven. . . . Marriage, when joined with purity and holiness, truth and righteousness, is one of the greatest blessings ever given to the human family. . . .

The divine love emanating from Christ never destroys human love, but includes human love, refined and purified. By it human love is elevated and ennobled. Human love can never bear its precious fruit until it is united with the divine nature and trained to grow heavenward. Jesus wants to see happy marriages, happy firesides. The warmth of true friendship and the love that binds the hearts of husband and wife are a foretaste of heaven. God has ordained that there should be perfect love and perfect harmony between those who enter into the marriage relation. Let bride and bridegroom in the presence of the heavenly universe pledge themselves to love one another as God has ordained they should. . . .

God made from the man a woman, to be a companion and helpmeet for him, to be one with him, to cheer, encourage, and bless him, he in turn to be her strong helper. All who enter into matrimonial relations with a holy purpose—the husband to obtain the pure affections of a woman's heart, the wife to soften and improve her husband's character and give it completeness—fulfill God's purpose for them.

Christ came not to destroy this institution, but to restore it to its original sanctity and elevation. He came to restore the moral image of God in man, and He began His work by sanctioning the marriage relation. He who made the first holy pair and who created for them a paradise, has put His seal upon the marriage institution, first celebrated in Eden, when the morning stars sang together and all the sons of God shouted for joy.[18]

202

THE BONDS OF WEDLOCK

And the Lord God said, It is not good that the man should be alone; I will make him an help meet for him. Gen. 2:18.

I have often read these words: "Marriage is a lottery." Some act as if they believed the statement, and their married life testifies that it is such to them. But true marriage is not a lottery. Marriage was instituted in Eden. After the creation of Adam, the Lord said, "It is not good that the man should be alone; I will make him an help meet"—suitable—"for him." When the Lord presented Eve to Adam, angels of God were witnesses to the ceremony. But there are few couples who are completely united when the marriage ceremony is performed. The form of words spoken over the two who take the marriage vow does not make them a unit. In their future life is to be the blending of the two in wedlock. It may be made a really happy union, if each will give to the other true heart affection.

But time strips marriage of the romance with which imagination had clothed it, and then the thought finds entrance into the mind through Satan's suggestions, "We do not love each other as we supposed." Expel it from the mind. Do not linger over it. Let each, forgetful of self, refuse to entertain the ideas that Satan would be glad to have you cherish. He will work to make you suspicious, jealous of every little thing that shall furnish the least occasion, in order to alienate your affections from each other. . . . When the romance is gone, let each think, not after a sentimental order, how he or she can make the married life what God would be pleased to have it.

Life is a precious gift of God and is not to be wasted in selfish regrets or more open indifference and dislike. Let the husband and wife talk things all over together. Renew the early attentions to each other, acknowledge your faults to each other, but in this work be very careful that the husband does not take it upon himself to confess his wife's faults or the wife her husband's. Be determined that you will be all that it is possible for you to be to each other, and the bonds of wedlock will be the most desirable of ties.[19]

Your home may be a symbol of heaven.[20]

COUNSEL TO A BRIDE AND GROOM

Therefore shall a man leave his father and his mother, and shall cleave unto his wife: and they shall be one flesh. Gen. 2:24.

You, my children,* have given your hearts to one another; unitedly give them wholly, unreservedly to God. In your married life seek to elevate one another. Do not come down to common, cheap talk and actions. Show the high and elevating principles of your holy faith in your everyday conversations and in the most private walks of life. Be ever careful and tender of the feelings of one another. Do not, either of you, for even the first time, allow a playful, bantering, joking censuring of one another. These things are dangerous. They wound. The wound may be concealed, nevertheless the wound exists and peace is being sacrificed and happiness endangered. . . .

My son, guard yourself and in no case manifest the least disposition savoring of a dictatorial, overbearing spirit. It will pay to watch your words before speaking. This is easier than to take them back or efface their impression afterward. . . . Ever speak kindly; do not throw into the tones of your voice that which will be taken by others as irritability. Modulate even the tones of your voice. Let only love, gentleness, and mildness be expressed in your countenance and in your voice. Make it a business to shed rays of sunlight, but never leave a cloud. Emma will be all to you you can desire if you are watchful and give her no occasion to feel distressed and troubled and to doubt the genuineness of your love. You yourselves can make your happiness or lose it. You can by seeking to conform your life to the Word of God be true, noble, elevated, and smooth the pathway of life for each other. . . .

Yield to each other. Edson, yield your judgment sometimes. Do not be persistent, even if your course appears just right to yourself. You must be yielding, forbearing, kind, tenderhearted, pitiful, courteous, ever keeping fresh the little courtesies of life, the tender acts, the tender, cheerful, encouraging words. And may the best of heaven's blessings rest upon you both, my dear children, is the prayer of your mother.[21]

---

* From a letter by Ellen White to her son Edson and wife, soon after their marriage.

TAKE MARRIAGE PROBLEMS TO GOD

But from the beginning of the creation God made them male and female. For this cause shall a man leave his father and mother, and cleave to his wife. Mark 10:6, 7.

Too often the marriage relation is entered into without proper consideration. None should marry in uncertainty. But if they have not been properly considerate in this matter, and after marriage find themselves dissimilar in character, and liable to reap unhappiness in the place of joy, let them not breathe into another's mind the fact that their marriage was unwise. . . . The evil is always increased when either the wife or the husband, finding some one who appears to be a congenial spirit, ventures to whisper to this trusted one the secrets of the married life. The very act of making known the secret confirms the existence of a condition of things that would not be at all necessary if the husband and wife loved God supremely. . . .

In many cases where these difficulties are thought to exist, the cause is imaginary. . . . If the husband and wife would freely talk over the matter with each other in the spirit of Christ, the difficulty would be healed. . . . If they loved God supremely, their hearts would be so filled, so satisfied, with His love, that they would not be consumed with longing for affection to be manifested in acts toward themselves.

Many have mistaken the true duty of the wife to the husband and the husband to the wife. Self becomes all absorbing, and Satan . . . has his net all ready to draw about the human soul, to get it so entangled by human imaginations that it seems impossible for human wisdom to disentangle the meshes of his finely woven snares.

But what human wisdom cannot do the wisdom of God can do through the surrender of the will, the mind, the soul, the strength, the entire being, to God. His providence can unite hearts in bonds that are of heavenly origin. But the result will not be a mere external interchange of affection in soft and flattering words. There will be a new experience; the loom of heaven weaves with warp and woof finer, yet more firm, than those of earth. The material is not a mere tissue fabric, but a texture that will bear the wear and test of trial; heart is bound firmly to heart in the golden chain of a love that is genuine.[22]

KEEPING LOVE ALIVE

Wives, submit yourselves unto your own husbands, as it is fit in the Lord. Husbands, love your wives, and be not bitter against them. Col. 3:18, 19.

How much trouble and what a tide of woe and unhappiness would be saved if men, and women also, would continue to cultivate the regard, attention, and kind words of appreciation and little courtesies of life which kept love alive and which they felt were necessary in gaining the companions of their choice. If the husband and wife would only continue to cultivate these attentions which nourish love, they would be happy in each other's society and would have a sanctifying influence upon their families. They would have in themselves a little world of happiness and would not desire to go outside this world for new attractions and new objects of love. . . .

Many women pine for words of love and kindness and the common attentions and courtesies due them from their husbands who have selected them as their life companions. . . . It is these little attentions and courtesies which make up the sum of life's happiness. . . .

If the hearts were kept tender in our families, if there were a noble, generous deference to each other's tastes and opinions, if the wife were seeking opportunities to express her love by actions in her courtesies to her husband, and the husband were manifesting the same consideration and kindly regard for the wife, the children would partake of the same spirit. The influence would pervade the household, and what a tide of misery would be saved in families! . . .

Every couple who unite their life interest should seek to make the life of each as happy as possible. That which we prize we seek to preserve and make more valuable if we can. In the marriage contract men and women have made a trade, an investment for life, and they should do their utmost to control their words of impatience and fretfulness, even more carefully than they did before their marriage, for now their destinies are united for life as husband and wife, and each is valued in exact proportion to the amount of painstaking effort put forth to retain and keep fresh the love so eagerly sought for and prized before marriage.[23]

THE WIDENING CIRCLE OF LOVE

Let the husband render unto the wife due benevolence: and likewise also the wife unto the husband. 1 Cor. 7:3.

Husbands and wives should feel it their privilege and their duty to reserve for the privacy of each other's society the interchange of love tokens between themselves. For while the manifestation of love for each other is right in its place, it may be made productive of harm to both the married and the unmarried. There are persons of an entirely different cast of mind and character, and of different education and training, who love each other just as devotedly and healthfully as do those who have educated themselves to manifest their affection freely; and there is danger that by contrast these persons who are more reserved will be misjudged, and placed at a disadvantage. While the wife should lean on her husband with respect and deference, she can, in a wholesome, healthful way, manifest her strong affection for and confidence in the man she has chosen as her life companion. . . .

It is the high privilege and the solemn duty of Christians to make each other happy in their married life; but there is positive danger in making self all absorbing, pouring out all the wealth of affection upon each other, and being too well satisfied with such a life. All this savors of selfishness.

Instead of shutting up their love and sympathy to themselves, they should seize every opportunity of contributing to the good of others, distributing the abundance of affection in a chaste and sanctified love for souls that in the sight of God are just as precious as themselves, being purchased by the infinite sacrifice of His only-begotten Son. Kind words, looks of sympathy, expressions of appreciation, would be to many a struggling and lonely one as the cup of cold water to a thirsty soul. A word of sympathy, an act of kindness, would lift burdens that are resting heavily upon some shoulders. And words of counsel, admonitions, warnings from a heart sanctified by love, are just as essential as an effusion of loving sentiments and expressions of appreciation. Every word or deed of unselfish kindness to souls with whom we are brought in connection is an expression of the love that Jesus has manifested for the whole human family.[24]

207

A MESSAGE TO PARENTS

And these words, which I command thee this day, shall be in thine heart: and thou shalt teach them diligently unto thy children, and shalt talk of them when thou sittest in thine house, and when thou walkest by the way, and when thou liest down, and when thou risest up. Deut. 6:6, 7.

Parents should be united in their faith, that they may be united in their efforts to bring their children up in the belief of the truth. Upon the mother in a special sense rests the work of molding the minds of the young children. . . . Business matters often keep the father much from home and prevent him from taking an equal share in the training of the children, but whenever he can, he should unite with the mother in this work. Let parents work unitedly, instilling into their children's hearts the principles of righteousness.[25]

There has been too little definite work done in preparing our children for the tests that all must meet in their contact with the world and its influences. They have not been helped as they should to form characters strong enough to resist temptation and stand firm for the principles of right, in the terrible issues before all who remain faithful to the commandments of God and the testimony of Jesus Christ.

Parents need to understand the temptations that the youth must daily meet, that they may teach them how to overcome them. There are influences in the school and in the world that parents need to guard against. God wants us to turn our eyes from the vanities and pleasures and ambitions of the world, and set them on the glorious and immortal reward of those who run with patience the race set before them in the gospel. He wants us to educate our children to avoid the influences that would draw them away from Christ. The Lord is soon coming, and we must prepare for this solemn event. . . . Let your daily life in the home reveal the living principles of the Word of God. Heavenly agencies will cooperate with you as you seek to reach the standard of perfection and as you seek to teach your children how to conform their lives to the principles of righteousness. Christ and heavenly agencies are waiting to quicken your spiritual sensibilities, to renew your activities, and to teach you of the deep things of God.[25]

THE HOME A SCHOOL

Train up a child in the way he should go: and when he is old, he will not depart from it. **Prov. 22:6.**

The home is to be a school in which children are to be trained for the higher school. The father and mother should make the decision, "I will behave myself wisely in a perfect way. . . . I will walk within my house with a perfect heart" (Ps. 101:2). . . . Parents are the first teachers of their children, and by the lessons that they give, they, as well as their children, are being educated. As parents consecrate themselves, body, soul, and spirit, to the doing of their God-given work, the Lord will teach them precious lessons, giving them wise words to speak and helping them to show patience and forbearance under provocation. . . .

We need homes that are surrounded by a sanctified atmosphere. Unconverted families are Satan's strongest allies. The members of them work counter to God. Some parents are harsh, denunciatory, overbearing, while others are careless and overindulgent, letting their children follow the course of disobedience until they do very wicked things. . . . Such parents need to feel the converting power of God. By giving way to anger and by selfish indifference they unfit their children for this world and the next. . . .

I am writing this to the parents among us because I greatly desire them to learn, and to teach to their children, the beautiful lessons that we must learn on earth before we can enter heaven. In everything you do ask yourselves, "How will this help my children to prepare for the mansions that Christ has gone to prepare for those who love Him?" When the work in the home school is done as it should be, families will bring into the church such a noble unselfishness that heavenly angels will love to linger there. . . . Hearts will be refined and purified, made fit for the indwelling of the Lord Jesus.

Keep Christ before your children by singing songs to His glory, by seeking Him in prayer, and by reading from His Word, so that He will seem to them an ever-present Guest. Then they will love Him, and will be brought so closely into unison with Him that they will breathe out His Spirit. They will feel a new relationship to one another in Christ.[26]

209

TRAINING OUR CHILDREN FOR CHRIST

And all thy children shall be taught of the Lord; and great shall be the peace of thy children. Isa. 54:13.

Children and youth are to be taught that their capabilities were given them for the honor and glory of God. To this end they must learn the lesson of obedience, for only by lives of willing obedience can they render to God the service He requires. . . .

Parents who truly love Christ will bear witness to this in a love for their children that will not indulge, but will work wisely for their highest good. These children have been bought with a price. Christ sacrificed His life that He might redeem them from wrongdoing. Parents who appreciate the sacrifice Christ and the Father have made in behalf of the race will cooperate with them, lending every sanctified energy and ability to the work of saving their children. Instead of treating them as playthings, they will regard them as the purchase of Christ, and will teach them that they are to become the children of God. Instead of allowing them to indulge evil temper and selfish desires, they will teach them lessons of self-restraint.

As parents and children cooperate in seeking to reach God's ideal for them, strength and blessing will come into their lives; and joy and satisfaction will fill the hearts of parents when they see, as the fruit of their labors, their children growing up in the love of the truth and endeavoring to reach the fullness of God's purpose for them.[27]

He desires to see gathered out from the homes of our people a large company of youth who, because of the godly influences of their homes, have surrendered their hearts to Him and go forth to give Him the highest service of their lives. Directed and trained by the godly instruction of the home, the influence of the morning and evening season of worship, the consistent example of parents who love and fear God, they have learned to submit to God as their teacher and leader, and they are prepared to render Him acceptable service. . . . Such youth are prepared to represent to the world the grace and power of Christ. . . .

Would you help other families to use their God-given talents to His glory? Then reveal in your own lives conformity to the image of Christ.[27]

PREPARING FOR HEAVEN'S SCHOOL

That our sons may be as plants grown up in their youth; that our daughters may be as corner stones, polished after the similitude of a palace. Ps. 144:12.

Let not parents forget the great mission field that lies before them in the home. In the children committed to her, every mother has a sacred charge from God. "Take this son, this daughter," God says, "and train it for Me. Give it a character polished after the similitude of a palace, that it may shine in the courts of the Lord forever." [28]

Let the determination of each member of the family be, I will be a Christian, for in the school here below I must form a character that will give me entrance into the higher grade, even the school above. I must do unto others as I desire them to do to me.

Make the home life as nearly as possible like heaven. Let the members of the family forget not, as they gather round the family altar, to pray for the men in positions of responsibility in God's work. The physicians in our sanitariums, the ministers of the gospel, those in charge of our publishing houses and schools, need your prayers. They are tempted and tried. As you plead with God to bless them, your own hearts will be subdued and softened by His grace. We are living amid the perils of the last days, and we are to cleanse ourselves from all defilement and put on the robe of Christ's righteousness. [29]

My brother, my sister, I urge you to prepare for the coming of Christ in the clouds of heaven. Day by day cast the love of the world out of your hearts. Understand by experience what it means to have fellowship with Christ. Prepare for the judgment, that when Christ shall come, to be admired in all them that believe, you may be among those who will meet Him in peace. In that day the redeemed will shine forth in the glory of the Father and the Son. The angels, touching their golden harps, will welcome the King and His trophies of victory —those who have been washed and made white in the blood of the Lamb. A song of triumph will peal forth, filling all heaven. Christ has conquered. He enters the heavenly courts, accompanied by His redeemed ones, the witnesses that His mission of suffering and sacrifice has not been in vain. [30]

INFLUENCE OF GODLY PARENTS

Only take heed to thyself, and keep thy soul diligently, lest thou forget the things which thine eyes have seen, and lest they depart from thy heart all the days of thy life: but teach them thy sons, and thy sons' sons. Deut. 4:9.

To all parents who profess to believe in the soon return of Christ there is given a solemn work of preparation, that they and their children may be ready to meet the Lord at His coming. God desires to see parents take their position wholeheartedly for Him, that there may be no perverting of the work He has given them to do and that our children and youth may understand clearly the will of God concerning them. They are to learn to resist evil and choose righteousness, to turn from sin and become the faithful servants of God, prepared to give Him their life's highest service.

There are few parents who realize how important it is to give to their children the influence of a godly example. Yet this is far more potent than precept. No other means is so effective in training them in right lines. The children and youth must have a true copy in right-doing if they succeed in overcoming sin and perfecting a Christian character. This copy they should find in the lives of their parents. If they enter the city of God, . . . someone must show them the way. By living before their children godly, consistent lives, parents may make the work before them clear and plain.

It is God's desire that parents should be to their children the embodiment of the principles laid down in His Word. . . . To keep the feet of their children in the narrow path will call for faithful effort and constant prayer, but it is possible to train the children and youth to love and serve God. . . . It is possible to inculcate the principles of righteousness, line upon line, precept upon precept, here a little, and there a little, until the desires and inclinations of the heart are in harmony with the mind and will of God.

When fathers and mothers realize the responsibility resting upon them, and respond to the appeals of God's Spirit in behalf of this neglected work, there will be seen in the homes of the people transformations that will cause the angels to rejoice.[31]

THE FAMILY ALTAR

And there he builded an altar unto the Lord, and called upon the name of the Lord. **Gen. 12:8.**

Abraham, the friend of God, set us a worthy example. His was a life of prayer and humble obedience, and he was as a light in the world. Wherever he pitched his tent, close beside it was set up his altar, calling for the morning and evening sacrifice of each member of his family. . . . From Christian homes a similar light should shine forth. Love should be revealed in action. It should flow out in all home intercourse, showing itself in thoughtful kindness, in gentle, unselfish courtesy. There are homes where these principles are carried out— homes where God is worshiped and truest love reigns. From these homes morning and evening prayer comes up before God as sweet incense, and His mercies and blessings descend upon the suppliants like the morning dew.

We must have more religion. We need the strength and grace that are born of earnest prayer. This means of grace should be diligently used in order to gain spiritual muscle. Prayer does not bring God down to us, but brings us up to Him. It makes us realize more and more our great needs, and hence our obligation to God and our dependence upon Him. It leads us to feel our own nothingness and the weakness of our judgment. God has made earnest prayer the condition of the bestowal of His richest blessings. . . .

This is a daily matter. Each morning consecrate yourself and your family to God for that day. Make no calculation for months or years, for they are not yours. One brief day is given you, and that one day work for yourself and your family as though it were your last. Surrender all your plans to God, to be carried out or given up, as His providence shall indicate. In this manner you may day by day be giving your life with its plans and purposes into the hands of God, accepting His plans instead of your own, no matter how much they may interfere with your arrangements nor how many pleasant projects may have to be abandoned. Thus the life will be molded more and more after the divine Model; and "the peace of God, which passeth all understanding, shall keep your hearts and minds through Christ Jesus." [32]

213

PATTERN FOR CHILDREN AND YOUTH

And Jesus increased in wisdom and stature, and in favour with God and man. Luke 2:52.

While on earth Christ lived in the home of a peasant. He wore the best garments His parents could provide, but they were the humble garments of the peasants. He walked the rough paths of Nazareth and climbed the steeps of its hillsides and mountains. In His home He was a constant worker, and left on record a life filled with useful deeds. Had Christ passed His life among the grand and the rich, the world of toilers would have been deprived of the inspiration that the Lord intended they should have.

But Christ knew that His work must begin in consecrating the humble trade of the craftsmen who toil for their daily bread. He learned the trade of a carpenter that He might stamp honest labor as honorable and ennobling to all who work with an eye single to the glory of God. And angels were His attendants, for Christ was just as truly doing His Father's business when toiling at the carpenter's bench as when working miracles for the multitude. He held His commission and authority from the highest power, the Sovereign of heaven.

Christ descended to poverty that He might teach how closely in our daily life we may walk with God. . . . He could engage in toil, bear His part in sustaining the family in their necessity, become accustomed to weariness, and yet show no impatience. His spirit was never so full of worldly cares as to leave no time nor thought for heavenly things. He often held communion with heaven in song. The men of Nazareth often heard His voice raised in prayer and thanksgiving to God. . . . A fragrant influence was diffused to those around Him, and they were blessed. His praises seemed to drive away the evil angels and fill the place with sweet fragrance. . . .

His life was in conformity to the life and character of God. His childhood and manhood ennobled and sanctified every phase of practical life. . . . He was a perfect pattern in every place. . . . He passed through the experience of infancy, childhood, and manhood without a stain upon His character.[33]

214

CHILDREN THE OBJECTS OF GOD'S SPECIAL CARE

I will contend with him that contendeth with thee, and I will save thy children. Isa. 49:25.

The vows of David recorded in Psalm 101 should be the vows of all upon whom rest the responsibilities of guarding the influences of the home. David declared: "I will behave myself wisely in a perfect way. . . . I will walk within my house with a perfect heart. I will set no wicked thing before mine eyes" (Ps. 101:2, 3).[34]

The enemy of souls will invent many things to lead the minds of our youth from firm faith in God to the idolatrous practices of the world. Let the cautions given to ancient Israel be carefully studied. Satan's efforts to spoil the thoughts and confuse the judgment are unceasing, and we must be on our guard. We must be careful to maintain our allegiance to God as His peculiar people. . . .

We should endeavor to keep out of our homes every influence that is not productive of good. In this matter some parents have much to learn. To those who feel free to read story magazines and novels, I say: You are sowing seed, the harvest of which you will not care to gather. There is no spiritual strength to be gained from such reading. Rather it destroys the love for the pure truth of the Word. Through the agency of novels and story magazines Satan is working to fill with unreal and trivial thoughts the minds that should be diligently studying the Word of God. Thus he is robbing thousands upon thousands of the time and energy and self-discipline demanded by the stern problems of life.

Let the youth be taught to give close study to the Word of God. Received into the soul, it will prove a mighty barricade against temptation. "Thy word," the psalmist declares, "have I hid in mine heart, that I might not sin against thee." "By the word of thy lips I have kept me from the paths of the destroyer" (Ps. 119:11; 17:4).[35]

If the counsels of the Word of God are faithfully followed, the saving grace of Christ will be brought to our youth; for the children who are trained to love and obey God, and who yield themselves to the molding power of His Word, are the objects of God's special care and blessing.[35]

215

A MESSAGE TO CHILDREN

Children, obey your parents in the Lord: for this is right. Honour thy father and mother, which is the first commandment with promise. Eph. 6:1, 2.

Children are admonished by the apostle to obey their parents in the Lord, to be helpful and submissive. Those who truly love God will not strive for their own way and thus bring unhappiness to themselves and to others. They will strive to represent Christ in character. How precious is the thought that the youth who strive against sin, who believe, and wait and watch for Christ's appearing, who submit to parental authority, and who love the Lord Jesus, will be among those who love His appearing and who meet Him in peace.

These will stand without spot or wrinkle before the throne of God and enjoy His favor forever. They have formed lovely characters; they have guarded their speech; they have not spoken falsely; they have guarded their actions that they should not do any evil thing, and they are crowned with everlasting life.[36]

It is the privilege of parents to take their children with them to the gates of the city of God, saying, I have tried to instruct my children to love the Lord, to do His will, and to glorify Him. To such the gates will be thrown open, and parents and children will enter in. . . .

Every family that finds entrance to the city of God will have been faithful workers in their earthly homes, fulfilling the responsibilities that Christ has laid on them. There Christ, the heavenly Teacher, will lead His people to the tree of life, and He will explain to them the truths they could not in this life understand. In that future life His people will gain the higher education in its completeness.

Those who enter the city of God will have the golden crown placed upon their heads. That will be a joyful scene, which none of us can afford to miss. We shall cast our crowns at the feet of Jesus, and again and again we will give Him the glory, and praise His holy name. Angels will unite in the songs of triumph. Touching their golden harps, they will fill all heaven with rich music and songs to the Lamb.[37]

Eternal life in the city of God is the reward of obedience in the home life.[37]

A MESSAGE TO YOUTH

I have written unto you, young men, because ye are strong, and the word of God abideth in you, and ye have overcome the wicked one. 1 John 2:14.

The children and youth, with their fresh talent, energy, and courage, their quick susceptibilities, are loved of God, and He desires to bring them into harmony with divine agencies. . . .

Our children stand, as it were, at the parting of the ways. On every hand the world's enticements to self-seeking and self-indulgence call them away from the path cast up for the ransomed of the Lord. Whether their lives shall be a blessing or a curse depends upon the choice they make. . . . They belong to Christ. They are the purchase of His blood, the claim of His love. They live because He keeps them by His power. Their time, their strength, their capabilities, are His, to be developed, to be trained, to be used for Him. . . .

Young men and young women, gather a stock of knowledge. . . . Keep reaching higher and still higher. It is the ability to put to the tax the powers of mind and body, ever keeping eternal realities in view, that is of value now. Seek the Lord most earnestly, that you may become more and more refined, more spiritually cultured. Then you will have the very best diploma that any one can have—the endorsement of God.

However large, however small, your talents, remember that what you have is yours only in trust. Thus God is testing you, giving you opportunity to prove yourself true. . . . To Him belong your powers of body, mind, and soul, and for Him these powers are to be used. Your time, your influence, your capabilities, your skill—all must be accounted for to Him who gives all. . . .

With such an army of workers as our youth rightly trained might furnish, how soon the message of a crucified, risen, and soon-coming Saviour might be carried to the whole world! How soon might the end come—the end of suffering and sorrow and sin! How soon, in place of a possession here, with its blight of sin and pain, our children might receive their inheritance where "the righteous shall inherit the land, and dwell therein for ever" (Ps. 37:29).[38]

ON GUARD AGAINST SATAN

Let no man despise thy youth; but be thou an example of the believers, in word, in conversation, in charity, in spirit, in faith, in purity. 1 Tim. 4:12.

Those who decide to be on the Lord's side, and have made up their minds understandingly, have commenced a good work. Yet the work has but just begun. They have just enlisted in the army. The conflicts and battles are before them.[39]

I have been shown in regard to the temptations of the young. Satan is ever on their track seeking to lead their inexperienced feet astray, and the youth seem ignorant of his devices. They do not guard themselves against the snares of the devil as they should. This foe is ever watchful, ever vigilant, and when the young cease watching their own hearts, cease guarding themselves, then Satan controls them and employs his arts against them. Secret prayer is the strength of the Christian. He cannot live and flourish in the Lord without constant watchfulness and earnest prayer. . . .

Jesus should be the object of our affections, but Satan will try to tear the affections from heavenly things and place them upon objects that are undeserving of our affection and love. . . . The best affections of a great share of the world are bestowed upon worthless objects.

The minds of the young left unrestrained are directed in a channel to suit their own corrupt nature. They relax their vigilance and watchfulness and bestow their affections upon each other, have special friends, special confidants, and when these friends are together, Jesus is not so much as named among them. Their conversation is not upon Christian experience, upon Christ, upon heaven, but upon frivolous things. . . . They are unacquainted with the wiles of the devil, and at twelve, fourteen, fifteen, and sixteen think themselves young men and women and able to choose their own course and conduct themselves with propriety and caution.[40]

Jesus loves the youth. He died to save them. . . . Oh, if they could only know how God loves them! He wants to make them good and pure, noble and kind and courteous, that they may ever live with the pure, holy angels throughout eternity.[41]

"IS MY FAMILY PREPARED TO MEET THE LORD?"

For so an entrance shall be ministered unto you abundantly into the everlasting kingdom of our Lord and Saviour Jesus Christ. 2 Peter 1:11.

Let parents study the first chapter of the Second Epistle of Peter. Here is represented the exalted excellence of Bible truth. It teaches that the Christian's experience is to be one of steady growth, of constant gain in graces and virtues that will give strength to the character and fit the soul for eternal life. . . .

It is the privilege of parents and children to grow together in the grace of Christ. Those who comply with the conditions laid down in the Word will find full provision for their spiritual needs and for power to overcome. . . . The Lord expects parents to make earnest united efforts in the training of their children for Him. In the home they are to cultivate the graces of the Spirit, in all their ways acknowledging Him who through the sanctification of the Spirit has promised to make us perfect in every good work. . . .

Shall the people who have a solemn message to bear for the enlightenment and salvation of the world, make little or no effort for the members of their own family who are unconverted to the truth? Will parents allow their minds to be engrossed with trifling matters to the neglect of the all-important question, "Is my family prepared to meet the Lord?" Will they assent to the great truths that are present truth for these last days, and be interested to see this message going to other peoples and lands, while they allow their children, their most precious possession, to go on unwarned of their danger and unprepared for the future? Shall those who, from the Word of God and through the witness of His Spirit, have had clear light concerning their duty allow the years to pass without making definite efforts to save their children?

Christ is waiting for the cooperation of human agencies, that He may impress the hearts of our children and youth. With intense desire heavenly beings long to see parents making that preparation which is essential if they and their children stand loyal to God in the coming conflict, and enter in through the gates to the city of God.[42]

WE ARE GOD'S PROPERTY

Know ye that the Lord he is God: it is he that hath made us, and not we ourselves; we are his people, and the sheep of his pasture. **Ps. 100:3.**

God has created man and given him all his faculties of body, soul, and spirit. The Lord Jesus has bought him with a price so full, so ample, that there could be no competition. What can man offer to God that is not already the Lord's own? God gave the faculties, and every working of these faculties belongs to God. This means that your experience from first to last is to be yoked up with Christ. Learning the lessons of meekness and lowliness of heart makes you a partaker of Christ's sufferings and appreciative of the virtues of the life of Christ.

There will be a constant prayer, Keep me by Thy power; let not my feet slide; let not my heart be filled with ambitious plans to exalt myself. . . . Teach me how to practice the art of self-emptying in order to be supplied with the grace of Christ and have that love Christ prayed that I might have, "as I have loved you" (John 13:34). I must receive grace that I may supply others with that grace. Oh, give my soul much nearness to God, that I may receive His disposition and love my brethren. Help me, O Lord, to realize that I am of myself unable to do anything in its true, pure bearings. Self, self, will be continually active for recognition, even in the very holiest of exercises. . . .

Our work individually is to copy the character of Christ, who gave His life to make it possible for us to do this. Shall we evidence to the world that we are children of God, bought with a price, and that we are bearing fruit in speech, in tone of voice, and in kindness of redeeming love, showing what it means to keep the commandments of God? . . .

The grace given cost Heaven a price it is impossible for us to measure. That grace is our choicest treasure, and Christ means that it shall be communicated through us. It is sacred, in the name of Jesus, to the saving of the soul. It is the revealing of the honor of God, an unfolding of His glory. And shall any man or woman professing godliness misinterpret the gift, ignore the Giver, and present a substitute? [1]

220

ALL WE POSSESS COMES FROM GOD

But who am I, and what is my people, that we should be able to offer so willingly after this sort? for all things come of thee, and of thine own have we given thee. 1 Chron. 29:14.

Those who live on this earth should unite with the heavenly host in ascribing all praise and glory to the Creator. No man has the least cause for boasting or self-exaltation. . . .

Constantly God is laboring to make up man's deficiencies. Even repentance is brought about through the application of grace. The natural heart feels no need of repentance. The tears that fall from the eyes of man because of sorrow for his sinfulness and because of sympathy for other sinners, start unbidden. They are as dew from eyes that belong to God. . . . The reformed life is but the better employment of a life that has been ransomed by the sacrifice of His Son Jesus. No credit should we take to ourselves for anything that we may do. . . .

Faith, too, is the gift of God. Faith is the assent of man's understanding to God's words, that binds the heart to God's service. And whose is man's understanding if it be not God's? Whose the heart if it be not God's? To have faith is to render to God the intellect, the energy, that we have received from Him; therefore those who exercise faith do not themselves deserve any credit. Those who believe so firmly in a heavenly Father that they can trust Him with unlimited confidence; those who by faith can reach beyond the grave to the eternal realities beyond, must pour forth to their Maker the confession, "All things come of thee, and of thine own have we given thee." . . .

Heavenly bestowed capabilities should not be made to serve selfish ends. Every energy, every endowment, is a talent that should contribute to God's glory by being used in His service. . . .

Let no one seek to exalt himself by talking of his deeds, extolling his abilities, displaying his knowledge, and cultivating self-conceit. . . . Christ was never self-confident or conceited.[2]

He to whom God has entrusted unusual gifts should return to the Lord's storehouse that which he has received, by freely giving to others the benefit of his blessings. Thus God will be honored and glorified.[2]

THE DEBT WE OWE

How much owest thou unto my lord? Luke 16:5.

"Know ye not that . . . ye are not your own? For ye are bought with a price" (1 Cor. 6:19, 20). What a price has been paid for us! Behold the cross, and the Victim uplifted upon it. Look at those hands, pierced with the cruel nails. Look at His feet, fastened with spikes to the tree. Christ bore our sins in His own body. That suffering, that agony, is the price of your redemption. . . .

The wonderful love of God, manifest in Christ, is the science and the song of all the heavenly universe. Should it not call forth from us gratitude and praise? . . . When the blessed light of the Sun of Righteousness shines into our hearts, and we rest in peace and joy in the Lord, then let us praise the Lord. . . . Let us praise Him not in words only but by the consecration to Him of all that we are and all that we have.

How much owest thou unto my Lord? Compute this you cannot. Is there any part of your being that He has not redeemed? or anything in your possession that is not already His? When He calls for it, will you selfishly grasp it as your own? Will you keep it back, and apply it to some other purpose than the salvation of souls? It is in this way that thousands of souls are lost. How can we better show that we appreciate God's sacrifice, His great donation to our world, than by sending forth gifts and offerings, with praise and thanksgiving from our lips, because of the great love wherewith He has loved us . . . ?

Looking up to heaven in supplication, present yourself to God as His servants, and all that you have as His, saying, Lord, of thine own we freely give thee. Standing in view of the cross of Calvary and the Son of the infinite God crucified for you, realizing that matchless love, that wonderful display of grace, let your earnest inquiry be, Lord, what wilt thou have me to do? He has told you. "Go ye into all the world, and preach the gospel to every creature" (Mark 16:15). When you see souls in the kingdom of God saved through your gifts and your service, you will rejoice that you had the privilege of doing this work. . . . The same power that the apostles had is now for those who will do God's service.[3]

A TIME FOR HEART SEARCHING

Examine yourselves, whether ye be in the faith; prove your own selves. **2 Cor. 13:5.**

One's claim to manhood is determined by the use he makes of the powers that God has given him. The members of the human family are entitled to the name of men and women only as they employ their talents for the good of others. It is when ministering to others that man is most closely allied to God. He who is true to his God-given manhood will not only promote the happiness of his fellow beings in this life but will aid them to secure the reward of the life to come. . . .

Man is required to love God supremely, with his might, mind, and strength, and his neighbor as himself. This he cannot possibly do unless he denies himself. To deny self means to rule the spirit when passion is striving for the mastery; to resist the temptation to censure and to speak words of faultfinding; to have patience with the child that is dull, and whose conduct is grievous and trying; to stand at the post of duty even though others may fail; to lift responsibilities wherever and whenever duty requires, not to gain applause, not for policy, but for the sake of the Master, who has given each of His followers a work that is to be done with unwavering fidelity. To deny self means to do good when inclination would lead us to serve and please ourselves. It means to work patiently and cheerfully for the good of others, even though our efforts may not seem to be appreciated. . . .

Fellow Christians, search carefully to see whether the Word of God is indeed the rule of your life. Do you take Christ with you when you leave the place of prayer? Does your religion stand guard at the door of your lips? Is your heart drawn out in interest and sympathy for those in need of help? Are you seeking earnestly for a clearer understanding of God's will, that you may let the light shine forth to others? Is your speech seasoned with grace? Does your demeanor show Christian nobility? . . .

Remember that you need to be braced by constant watchfulness and prayer. So long as you look to Christ you are safe, but the moment you trust in yourself you are in great peril. He who is in harmony with God will continually depend upon Him for help.[4]

USING OUR TALENTS FOR GOD

For the kingdom of heaven is as a man travelling into a far country, who called his own servants, and delivered unto them his goods. And unto one he gave five talents, to another two, and to another one; to every man according to his several ability; and straightway took his journey. Matt. 25:14, 15.

The parable of the Talents ... has a personal and individual application to every man, woman, and child possessed of the powers of reason. ... When the master of the house called his servants he gave to every man *his* work. The whole family of God are included in the responsibility of using their Lord's goods. Every individual, from the lowliest and most obscure to the greatest and most exalted, is a moral agent endowed with abilities for which he is accountable to God. ... The spiritual, mental, and physical ability, the influence, station, possessions, affections, sympathies, all are precious talents to be used in the cause of the Master for the salvation of souls for whom Christ died.

How few appreciate these blessings! How few seek to improve their talent and increase their usefulness in the world! The Master has given to every man his work. He has given to every man according to his ability, and his trust is in proportion to his capacity. ... Let the businessman do his business in a way that will glorify his Master because of his fidelity. Let him carry his religion into everything that is done and reveal to men the spirit of Christ. Let the mechanic be a diligent and faithful representative of Him who toiled in the lowly walks of life in the cities of Judea. ...

Those who have been blessed with superior talents should not depreciate the value of the services of those who are less gifted than themselves. The smallest trust is a trust from God. With the blessing of God, the one talent through diligent use will be doubled, and the two used in the service of Christ will be increased to four; and thus the humblest instrument may grow in power and usefulness.

The earnest purpose, the self-denying efforts, are all seen, appreciated, and accepted by the God of heaven. ... Use your gift in meekness, in humility, in trusting faith, and wait till the day of reckoning, and you will have no cause for grief or shame.[5]

THE PATHWAY OF SACRIFICE

And he said to them all, If any man will come after me, let him deny himself, and take up his cross daily, and follow me. Luke 9:23.

Christ declares that as He lived so we are to live. . . . His footsteps lead along the pathway of sacrifice. As we pass through life there come to us many opportunities for service. All around us there are open doors for ministry. By the right use of the talent of speech we may do much for the Master. Words are a power for good when they are weighted with the tenderness and sympathy of Christ. Money, influence, tact, time, and strength—all these are gifts entrusted to us to make us more helpful to those around us and more of an honor to our Creator.

Many feel that it would be a privilege to visit the scenes of Christ's life on earth, to walk where He trod, to look upon the lake where He loved to teach, and the valleys and hills where His eyes so often rested; but we need not go to Palestine in order to walk in the steps of Jesus. We shall find His footprints beside the sickbed, in the hovels of poverty, in the crowded alleys of the great city, and in every place where there are human hearts in need of consolation.[6]

Just as we trace the pathway of a stream of water by the line of living green it produces, so Christ could be seen in the deeds of mercy that marked His path at every step. Wherever He went, health sprang up, and happiness followed wherever He passed. The blind and deaf rejoiced in His presence. The face of Christ was the first that many eyes had ever looked upon; His words the first that had ever fallen upon their ears. . . . His words to the ignorant opened to them a fountain of life. He dispensed His blessings abundantly and continuously. They were the garnered treasures of eternity, the Lord's rich gift to man.[7]

Millions upon millions of souls ready to perish, bound in chains of ignorance and sin, have never so much as heard of Christ's love for them. Were our conditions and theirs reversed, what would we desire them to do for us? All this, as far as lies in our power, we are under the most solemn obligation to do for them. Christ's rule of life, by which every one must stand or fall in the judgment, is, "Whatsoever ye would that men should do to you, do ye even so to them." [8]

THE VOICE OF DUTY

Whatsoever thy hand findeth to do, do it with thy might.
Eccl. 9:10.

The voice of duty is the voice of God—an inborn, heaven-sent guide. Whether it be pleasing or unpleasing, we are to do the duty that lies directly in our pathway. If the Lord would have us bear a message to Nineveh, it will not be pleasing to Him for us to go to Joppa or Capernaum. God has reasons for sending us to the place to which our feet are directed. . . .

It is the little foxes that spoil the vines; the little neglects, the little deficiencies, the little dishonesties, the little departures from principle, that blind the soul and separate it from God.

It is the little things of life that develop the spirit and determine the character. Those who neglect the little things will not be prepared to endure severe tests when they are brought to bear upon them. Remember that the character building is not finished till life ends. Every day a good or bad brick is placed in the structure. You are either building crookedly or with the exactness and correctness that will make a beautiful temple for God. Therefore, in looking for great things to do, neglect not the little opportunities that come to you day by day. He who neglects the little things, and yet flatters himself that he is ready to do wonderful things for the Master, is in danger of failing altogether. Life is made up, not of great sacrifices and of wonderful achievements, but of little things.[9]

Whatever your hands find to do, do it with your might. Make your work pleasant with songs of praise. If you would have a clean record in the books of heaven, never fret or scold. Let your daily prayer be, "Lord, help me to do my best. . . . Give me energy and cheerfulness. Help me to bring into my service the loving ministry of the Saviour."

Look upon every duty, however humble, as sacred because it is part of God's service. Do not allow anything to make you forgetful of God. Bring Christ into all that you do. Then your lives will be filled with brightness and thanksgiving. You will do your best, moving forward cheerfully in the service of the Lord, your hearts filled with His joy.[10]

ONE DAY AT A TIME

The Lord knoweth the days of the upright: and their inherit-ance shall be for ever. **Ps. 37:18.**

The talent of time is precious. Every day it is given to us in trust, and we shall be called upon to give an account of it to God.[11]

Day by day we are all to be trained, disciplined, and educated for usefulness in this life. Only one day at a time—think of this. One day is mine. I will in this one day do my best. I will use my talent of speech to be a blessing to some other one, a helper, a comforter, an example which the Lord my Saviour shall approve. I will exercise myself in patience, kindness, forbearance, that the Christian virtues may be developed in me today.[12]

If you are right with God today, you are ready if Christ should come today. What we need is Christ formed within, the hope of glory. We want that you should have a deep and earnest longing for the righteousness of Jesus Christ. Your old, tattered garments of self-righteousness will not give you an entrance into the kingdom of God, but that garment that is woven in the loom of heaven—the righteousness of Jesus Christ—will. It will give you an inheritance among the sanctified. That is what we want. It is worth more than all worldly gain; it is worth more than all your farms; it is worth more than all the honor that finite beings can bestow upon you. . . .

Are you individually daily preparing that you can unite with the family of heaven? Are you quarrelsome here? Are you finding fault with your household here? If you are, you will find fault with them in heaven. Your character is being tested and proved in this life, whether you will make a peaceable subject of God's kingdom in heaven.[13]

The Lord requires us to perform the duties of today and to endure its trials. We are today to watch that we offend not in word or deed. We must today praise and honor God. By the exercise of living faith today, we are to conquer the enemy. We must today seek God and be determined that we will not rest satisfied without His presence. We should watch and work and pray as though this were the last day that would be granted us. How intensely earnest, then, would be our life. How closely would we follow Jesus in all our words and deeds.[14]

EACH IN HIS PLACE

With good will doing service, as to the Lord, and not to men.
Eph. 6:7.

The Lord is acquainted with us individually. Every one born into the world is given his or her work to do for the purpose of making the world better. . . . Each one has his sphere, and if the human agent makes God his counselor then there will be no working at cross purposes with God. He allots to every one a place and a work, and if we individually submit ourselves to be worked by the Lord, however confused and tangled life may seem to our eyes, God has a purpose in it all, and the human machinery, obedient under the hand of divine wisdom, will accomplish the purposes of God. As in a well-disciplined army every soldier has his allotted position and is required to act his part in contributing to the strength and perfection of the whole, so the worker for God must do his allotted part in the great work of God.

Life as it now appears is not what God designed it should be, and this is why there is so much that is perplexing; there is much wear and friction. The man or woman who leaves the place God has given him or her, in order to please inclination and act on his own devised plan, meets with disappointment, because he has chosen his way instead of God's way.

There are those who accept positions of responsibility but fail to sense the responsibility, and thus do haphazard work without at all understanding its character. Others accept a work for which they have no fitness. . . . Other individuals study to have their own way and work out their own plans, and God erects His barriers and does not allow them to do as they would. . . .

Our heavenly Father is our ruler, and we must submit to His discipline. We are members of His family. He has a right to our service; and if one of the members of His family would persist in having his own way, persist in doing just that which he pleases, that spirit would bring about a disordered and perplexing state of things. We must not study to have our own way, but God's way and God's will. . . .

Let God speak, and we will say, "Not my will, but Thy will, O God, be done." [15]

228

JOY IN SERVICE

Whosoever will be great among you, shall be your minister: and whosoever of you will be the chiefest, shall be servant of all. Mark 10:43, 44.

It is in a life of service only that true happiness is found. He who lives a useless, selfish life is miserable. He is dissatisfied with himself and with everyone else. The Lord disciplines His workers that they may be prepared to fill the places appointed them. Thus He desires to fit them to do more acceptable service. . . .

There are many who are not satisfied to serve God cheerfully in the place that He has marked out for them or to do uncomplainingly the work that He has placed in their hands. It is right for us to be dissatisfied with the way in which we perform duty, but we are not to be dissatisfied with the duty itself, because we would rather do something else. In His providence God places before human beings service that will be as medicine to their diseased minds. Thus He seeks to lead them to put aside the selfish preference, which if cherished would disqualify them for the work He has for them.[16]

There are those who desire to be a ruling power and who need the sanctification of submission. God brings about a change in their lives. Perhaps He places before them duties that they would not choose. If they are willing to be guided by Him, He will give them grace and strength to perform these duties in a spirit of submission and helpfulness. Thus they are being qualified to fill places where their disciplined abilities will make them of great service.

Some, God trains by bringing to them disappointment and apparent failure. It is His purpose that they shall learn to master difficulty. He inspires them with a determination to make every apparent failure prove a success.

Often men pray and weep because of the perplexities and obstacles that confront them. But if they will hold the beginning of their confidence steadfast unto the end He will make their way clear. Success will come to them as they struggle against apparently insurmountable difficulties, and with success will come the greatest joy.[16]

DEMONSTRATING CHRIST'S LOVE

Be kindly affectioned one to another with brotherly love; in honour preferring one another. Rom. 12:10.

We must not allow ourselves to become self-absorbed and so forget the claims of God and humanity upon us. . . . God would have us more kind, more loving and lovable, less critical and suspicious. O that we all might have the Spirit of Christ, and know how to deal with our brethren and neighbors! . . .

We must forget self in loving service for others. . . . We may not remember some act of kindness which we do, it may fade from our memory; but eternity will bring out in all its brightness every act done for the salvation of souls, every word spoken for the comfort of God's children; and these deeds done for Christ's sake will be a part of our joy through all eternity.

When we pursue toward our brethren any course save that of kindness and courtesy, we pursue an unchristian course. We should manifest courtesy at home, in the church, and in our intercourse with all men. But especially we should manifest compassion and respect for those who are giving their lives to the cause of God. We should exercise that precious love that suffereth long and is kind; that envieth not, that vaunteth not itself, is not puffed up, doth not behave itself unseemly, seeketh not its own, is not easily provoked, thinketh no evil. . . . Where Jesus reigns in the heart, there will be sweet love, and we shall be tender and true to one another. . . .

You should give no occasion for faultfinding. A moment's petulance, a single gruff answer, the want of Christian politeness and courtesy in some small matter, may result in the loss of friends, in the loss of influence. God would have you appear at your best under all circumstances—in the presence of those who are inferior to you as well as in the presence of equals and superiors. We are to be followers of Christ at all times, seeking His honor, seeking to rightly represent Him in every way. . . .

Let self drop out of sight, and let Jesus appear as the One altogether lovely. We should seek to live for His glory alone, not that men may praise us.[17]

DEVELOPING SELF-CONTROL

He that is slow to anger is better than the mighty; and he that ruleth his spirit than he that taketh a city. **Prov. 16:32.**

It is by faithfulness in little things that we become trustworthy sentinels. Guard carefully against the little irritations, not allowing them to harass your soul, and you will gain many victories. And when greater troubles come you will be prepared to resist the enemy manfully and nobly. . . . Each soul inherits certain un-Christlike traits of character. It is the grand and noble work of a lifetime to keep under control these tendencies to wrong. It is the little things that cross our path that are likely to cause us to lose our power of self-control.[18]

So long as we are in the world, we shall meet with adverse influences. There will be provocations to test the temper; and it is by meeting these in the right spirit that the Christian graces are developed. If Christ dwells in us, we shall be patient, kind, and forbearing, cheerful amid frets and irritations. Day by day and year by year we shall conquer self, and grow into a noble heroism. This is our allotted task; but it cannot be accomplished without help from Jesus, resolute decision, unwavering purpose, continual watchfulness, and unceasing prayer. Each one has a personal battle to fight. Not even God can make our characters noble or our lives useful, unless we become co-workers with Him. Those who decline the struggle lose the strength and joy of victory.

We need not keep our own record of trials and difficulties, griefs and sorrows. All these things are written in the books, and heaven will take care of them.[19]

God will understand you as you open your heart to Him. He knows what discipline each one needs. If you ask Him, He will surely give you power to resist evil. Your faith will be increased, and you will give evidence to others of the keeping power of God.

Your strength and growth in grace come only from one Source. If when you are tempted and tried you stand bravely for the right, victory is yours. You are one step nearer to perfection of Christian character. A holy light from heaven fills the chambers of your soul, and you are surrounded by a pure, fragrant atmosphere.[20]

OVERCOMING SELFISHNESS

Even as I please all men in all things, not seeking mine own profit, but the profit of many, that they may be saved. 1 Cor. 10:33.

There exists in the hearts of many an element of selfishness which clings to them like the leprosy. They have so long consulted their own wishes, their own pleasure and convenience, that they do not feel that others have claims upon them. Their thoughts, plans, and efforts are for themselves. They live for self, and do not cultivate disinterested benevolence, which if exercised, would increase and strengthen until it would be their delight to live for others' good. This selfishness must be seen and overcome, for it is a grievous sin in the sight of God. They need to exercise a more special interest for humanity; and in thus doing, they would bring their souls into closer connection with Christ, and would be imbued with His Spirit, so that they would cleave to Him with so firm a tenacity that nothing could separate them from His love.[21]

The man whose experience is least to be envied is the one who shuts up his sympathies within his own heart. Those who get the most good out of life, who feel the truest satisfaction, are those who receive to give. Those who live for self are always in want, for they are never satisfied. There is no Christianity in shutting our sympathies up in our own selfish hearts. We are to bring brightness and blessing into the lives of others. The Lord has chosen us as channels through which to communicate His blessings.[22]

The time is coming when the earth shall reel to and fro and shall be removed like a cottage. But the thoughts, the purposes, the acts of God's workers, although now unseen, will appear at the great day of final retribution and reward. Things now forgotten will then appear as witnesses, either to approve or to condemn.

Love, courtesy, self-sacrifice—these are never lost. When God's chosen ones are changed from mortality to immortality, their words and deeds of goodness will be made manifest, and will be preserved through the eternal ages. No act of unselfish service, however small or simple, is ever lost. Through the merits of Christ's imputed righteousness, the fragrance of such words and deeds is forever preserved.[23]

LIVING FOR OTHERS

Even as the Son of man came not to be ministered unto, but to minister, and to give his life a ransom for many. Matt. 20:28.

We are not to live for ourselves. Christ came to this world to live for others—not to be ministered unto, but to minister. If you strive to live as He lived you are saying to the world, "Behold the Man of Calvary." By precept and example you are leading others in the way of righteousness.[24]

The sin which is indulged to the greatest extent, and which separates us from God and produces so many contagious spiritual disorders, is selfishness. There can be no returning to the Lord except by self-denial. Of ourselves we can do nothing; but through God strengthening us we can live to do good to others, and in this way shun the evil of selfishness. We need not go to heathen lands to manifest our desire to devote all to God in a useful, unselfish life. We should do this in the home circle, in the church, among those with whom we associate and with whom we do business. Right in the common walks of life is where self is to be denied and kept in subordination.

Paul could say: "I die daily" (1 Cor. 15:31). It is the daily dying to self in the little transactions of life that makes us overcomers. We should forget self in the desire to do good to others. With many there is a decided lack of love for others. Instead of faithfully performing their duty, they seek rather their own pleasure.

God positively enjoins upon all His followers a duty to bless others with their influence and means. . . . In doing for others, a sweet satisfaction will be experienced, an inward peace which will be a sufficient reward. When actuated by a high and noble desire to do others good, they will find true happiness in a faithful discharge of life's manifold duties. This will bring more than an earthly reward; for every faithful, unselfish performance of duty is noticed by the angels and shines in the life record. In heaven none will think of self, nor seek their own pleasure; but all, from pure, genuine love, will seek the happiness of the heavenly beings around them. If we wish to enjoy heavenly society in the earth made new, we must be governed by heavenly principles here.[25]

LOVE THE IMPELLING MOTIVE

For the love of Christ constraineth us. 2 Cor. 5:14.

"But now abideth faith, hope, love, these three; and the greatest of these is love" (1 Cor. 13:13). In the life of Christ this love found perfect expression. He loved us in our sin and degradation. He reached to the very depths of woe to uplift the erring sons and daughters of earth. There was no wearying of His patience, no lessening of His zeal. The waves of mercy, beaten back by proud, impenitent, unthankful hearts, ever returned in a stronger tide of love.

He who is constrained by the love of Christ goes forth among his fellow men to help the helpless and encourage the desponding, to point sinners to God's ideal for His children, and to lead them to Him who alone can enable them to reach this ideal. . . .

Never are we to be cold and unsympathetic, especially when dealing with the poor. Courtesy, sympathy, and compassion are to be shown to all. Partiality for the wealthy is displeasing to God. Jesus is slighted when His needy children are slighted. They are not rich in this world's goods, but they are dear to His heart of love. God recognizes no distinction of rank. With Him there is no caste. In His sight men are simply men, good or bad. In the day of final reckoning, position, rank, or wealth will not alter by a hairbreadth the case of any one. By the all-seeing God, men will be judged by what they are in purity, in nobility, in love for Christ. . . .

Christ declared that the gospel is to be preached to the poor. Never does God's truth put on an aspect of greater loveliness than when brought to the needy and destitute. Then it is that the light of the gospel shines forth in its most radiant clearness, lighting up the hut of the peasant and the rude cottage of the laborer. Angels of God are there, and their presence makes the crust of bread and the cup of water a banquet. Those who have been neglected and abandoned by the world are raised to be sons and daughters of the Most High. Lifted above any position that earth can give, they sit in heavenly places in Christ Jesus. They may have no earthly treasure, but they have found the pearl of great price.[26]

SELF HIDDEN IN CHRIST

My soul shall make her boast in the Lord: the humble shall hear thereof, and be glad. **Ps. 34:2.**

Dr. John Cheyne, while he rose to a high point in his profession, did not forget his obligations to God. He once wrote to a friend, "You may wish to know the condition of my mind. I am humbled in the dust by the thought that there is not one action of my busy life which will bear the eye of a holy God. But when I reflect on the invitation of the Redeemer, 'Come unto me,' and that I have accepted this invitation; and, moreover, that my conscience testifies that I earnestly desire to have my will in all things conformed to the will of God, I have peace; I have the promised rest, promised by Him in whom was found no guile."

Before his death this eminent physician ordered a column to be erected near the spot where his body was to lie, on which were to be inscribed these texts, as voices from eternity: "God so loved the world, that he gave his only begotten Son, that whosoever believeth in him should not perish, but have everlasting life" (John 3:16). "Come unto me, all ye that labor and are heavy laden, and I will give you rest" (Matt. 11:28). "Follow peace with all men, and holiness, without which no man shall see the Lord" (Heb. 12:14).

And while Dr. Cheyne thus strove, even from the tomb, to beckon sinners to the Saviour and to glory, he concealed his own name, withholding it from the column entirely. He was not less careful to say, as speaking to the passer-by, "The name and profession and age of him whose body lies beneath are of little consequence, but it may be of great importance to you to know that by the grace of God he was brought to look to the Lord Jesus as the only Saviour of sinners, and that this looking unto Jesus gave peace to his soul." "Pray to God, pray to God," it says, "that you may be instructed in the gospel; and be assured that God will give the Holy Spirit, the only teacher of true wisdom, to them that ask Him."

This memorial was designed to turn the attention of all to God, and cause them to lose sight of the man. This man brought no reproach upon the cause of Christ.[27]

235

THE PRECIOUS ATTRIBUTE OF MEEKNESS

Blessed are the meek: for they shall inherit the earth. Matt. 5:5.

Meekness is a precious, Christian attribute. The meekness and low-liness of Christ are only learned by wearing Christ's yoke. . . . That yoke signifies entire submission.

The heavenly universe looks upon an absence of meekness and lowliness of heart. The self-exaltation, the feeling of swelling importance, makes the human agent so large in his own estimation that he feels that he has no need of a Saviour, no need to wear Christ's yoke. But the invitation to each soul is, "Take my yoke upon you, and learn of me; for I am meek and lowly in heart: and ye shall find rest unto your souls" (Matt. 11:29).

The power of God awaits our demand upon it. . . . Pure spiritual power is fresh every morning and new every evening. It lifts men above worldly ambition and expels all selfishness from the soul. . . .

Selfishness and covetousness have spoiled many lives. . . . Those who behold Jesus lose sight of self. By the eye of faith they behold Him who is invisible. They see the King in His beauty and the land that is very far off. They practice economy, and reveal justice and righteousness, mortifying self in the place of exalting self. . . .

The submission which Christ demands, the self-surrender of the will which admits truth in its sanctifying power, which trembles at the word of the Lord, are brought about by the work of the Holy Spirit. There must be a transformation of the entire being, heart, soul, and character. . . . Only at the altar of sacrifice, and from the hand of God, can the selfish, grasping man receive the celestial torch which reveals his own incompetence and leads him to submit to Christ's yoke, to learn His meekness and lowliness.

As learners we need to meet with God at the appointed place. Then Christ puts us under the guidance of the Spirit, who leads us into all truth, placing our self-importance in submission to Christ. He takes the things of Christ as they fall from His lips and conveys them with living power to the obedient soul. Thus we may take a perfect impress of the Author of truth.[28]

THE MEASURE OF A MAN'S WORTH

He hath shewed thee, O man, what is good; and what doth the Lord require of thee, but to do justly, and to love mercy, and to walk humbly with thy God? Micah 6:8.

What a man is has greater influence than what he says. The quiet, consistent, godly life is a living epistle, known and read of all men. Holiness is not shaped from without or put on; it radiates from within. If goodness, purity, meekness, lowliness, and integrity dwell in the heart, they will shine forth in the character; and such a character is full of power. Not the instrument, but the great Worker in whose hand the instrument is used, receives the glory. The heart filled with the Saviour's love, daily receives grace to impart. The life reveals the redeeming power of the truth.

The witness borne concerning Jesus was, "Never man spake like this man" (John 7:46). The reason that Christ spoke as no other man spoke was that He lived as no other man lived. If He had not lived as He did, He could not have spoken as He did. His words bore with them convincing power, because they came from a heart pure and holy, burdened with love and sympathy, beneficence and truth. . . .

While the shepherds were watching their flocks on the hills of Bethlehem, angels from heaven visited them. So today, while the humble worker for God is following his employment, angels stand by his side, listening to his words, noting the manner in which he does his work. . . . If he trusts constantly in God, these angel watchers will not allow his work to deteriorate. They will not permit it to be warped into lines that will imperil the cause of God. The Lord is looking upon the work that comes from the hands of His people. He will judge every piece of work, to see of what sort it is.

Pure and undefiled religion speaks for itself. It transforms the characters of all who receive it, improving their usefulness and beautifying all with which it is brought in contact. . . . A man's worth is not measured by the position of responsibility that he occupies but by the Christlike spirit that he reveals. When the Saviour abides in the heart the work bears the impress of the divine touch. Self does not appear. Christ is revealed as the One altogether lovely.[29]

237

MERCY FOR THE MERCIFUL

Be ye therefore merciful, as your Father also is merciful.
Luke 6:36.

Mercy is an attribute that the human agent may share with God. As did Christ, so man may lay hold on the divine arm and be in communication with divine power. To us has been given a service of mercy to perform for our fellow man. In performing this service, we are laboring together with God. We do well, then, to be merciful, even as our Father in heaven is merciful.

"I will have mercy," God says, "and not sacrifice" (Matt. 9:13). Mercy is kind, pitiful. Mercy and the love of God purify the soul, beautify the heart, and cleanse the life from selfishness. Mercy is a manifestation of divine love and is shown by those who, identified with God, serve Him by reflecting the light of heaven upon the pathway of their fellow creatures. The condition of many persons calls for the exercise of genuine mercy. Christians, in their dealing with one another, are to be controlled by principles of mercy and love. They are to improve every opportunity for helping fellow beings in distress. . . .

Let those who desire to perfect a Christlike character ever keep in view the cross on which Christ died a cruel death in order to redeem mankind. Let them ever cherish the same merciful spirit that led the Saviour to make an infinite sacrifice for our redemption. . . .

The merciful "shall obtain mercy" (Matt. 5:7). "The liberal soul shall be made fat: and he that watereth shall be watered also himself" (Prov. 11:25). There is sweet peace for the compassionate spirit, a blessed satisfaction in the life of self-forgetful service for the good of others.

He who has given his life to God in ministry to His children is linked with Him who has all the resources of the universe at His command. By the golden chain of the immutable promises his life is bound up with the life of God. The Lord will not fail him in the hour of suffering and need. "My God shall supply all your need according to his riches in glory by Christ Jesus" (Phil. 4:19). And in the hour of final need the merciful shall find refuge in the mercy of the compassionate Saviour and by Him shall be received into everlasting habitations.[30]

WAVES OF BLESSING

Ye are the salt of the earth: but if the salt have lost his savour,
wherewith shall it be salted? it is thenceforth good for nothing,
but to be cast out, and to be trodden under foot of men. Matt. 5:13.

These words were spoken to a few poor, humble fishermen. Priests and rabbis were in that congregation of hearers, but these were not the ones addressed. . . . By these words of Christ we gain some idea of what constitutes the value of human influence. It is to work with the influence of Christ, to lift where Christ lifts, to impart correct principles, and stay the progress of the world's corruption. It is to diffuse the grace which Christ alone can impart. It is to uplift, to sweeten, the lives and characters of others by the power of a pure example united with earnest faith and love. God's people are to exercise a reforming, preserving power in the world. They are to counterwork the destroying, corrupting influence of evil.[31]

As you go through life, you will meet with those whose lot is far from easy. Toil and deprivation, with no hope for better things in the future, make their burden very heavy. . . . Careworn and oppressed, they know not where to turn for relief. Put your whole heart into the work of helping them. It is not God's purpose that His children shall shut themselves up to themselves. Remember that for them, as well as for you, Christ died. Hold out to them a helping hand. . . . Make it a rule never to utter one word of doubt or discouragement. You can do much to brighten the lives of others . . . by words of holy cheer.[32]

The humblest and poorest of the disciples of Jesus can be a blessing to others. They may not realize that they are doing any special good, but by their unconscious influence they may start waves of blessings that will widen and deepen, and the blessed results they may never know till the day of final reward. They are not required to weary themselves with anxiety about success. They have only to go forward quietly, doing faithfully the work God's providence assigns, and their life will not be in vain. Their own souls will be growing more and more into the likeness of Christ; they are workers together with God in this life and are thus fitting for the higher work and the unshadowed joy of the life to come.[32]

239

STREAMS IN THE DESERT

The righteous shall flourish like the palm tree: he shall grow like a cedar in Lebanon. **Ps. 92:12.**

See the weary traveler toiling over the hot sand of the desert, with no shelter to protect him from the rays of the tropical sun. His water supply fails, and he has nothing with which to slake his burning thirst. His tongue becomes swollen; he staggers like a drunken man. Visions of home and friends pass before his mind as he believes himself ready to perish. Suddenly he sees in the distance, rising out of the dreary sandy waste, a palm tree, green and flourishing. Hope quickens his pulses; he presses on, knowing that that which gives vigor and freshness to the palm tree will cool his fevered blood and give him renewed life.

As is the palm tree in the desert—a guide and consolation to the fainting traveler—so the Christian is to be in the world. He is to guide weary souls, full of unrest, and ready to perish in the desert of sin, to the living water. He is to point his fellow men to Him who gives to all the invitation, "If any man thirst, let him come unto me, and drink."

The sky may be as brass, the burning sand may beat about the palm tree's roots and pile itself about its trunk; yet the tree lives on, fresh and vigorous. Remove the sand, and you discover the secret of its life; its roots strike down deep into waters hidden in the earth.

Thus it is with the Christian. His life is hid with Christ in God. Jesus is to him a well of water, springing up unto everlasting life. His faith, like the rootlets of the palm tree, penetrates beneath the things that are seen, drawing life from the Fountain of life. And amid all the corruption of the world he is true and loyal to God. The sweet influence of Christ's righteousness surrounds him. . . .

The faces of men and women who walk and work with God express the peace of heaven. They are surrounded with the atmosphere of heaven. For these souls the kingdom of God has begun. They have Christ's joy, the joy of being a blessing to humanity. They have the honor of being accepted for the Master's use; they are trusted to do His work in His name.[33]

GOD HONORS THE HUMBLE

For whosoever exalteth himself shall be abased; and he that humbleth himself shall be exalted. Luke 14:11.

God honors those who humble themselves before Him. Moses, disheartened by the discontent and murmuring of the people he was leading into the land of promise, pleaded with God for the assurance of His presence. . . . And the Lord said, "My presence shall go with thee, and I will give thee rest" (Ex. 33:14).

Encouraged by the assurance of God's presence, Moses drew still nearer, and ventured to ask for still further blessings. "I beseech thee," he said, "shew me thy glory" (verse 18). Think you that God reproved Moses for his presumption? No, indeed. Moses did not make this request from idle curiosity. He had an object in view. He saw that in his own strength he could not do the work of God acceptably. He knew that if he could obtain a clear view of the glory of God, he would be enabled to go forward in his important mission, not in his own strength, but in the strength of the Lord God Almighty. His whole soul was drawn out after God; he longed to know more of Him, that he might feel the divine presence near in every emergency or perplexity. It was not selfishness that led Moses to ask for a sight of the glory of God. His only object was a desire better to honor his Maker.

God knows the thoughts and intents of the heart, and He understood the motives that prompted the request of His faithful servant. . . . "And the Lord passed by before him, and proclaimed, The Lord, The Lord God, merciful and gracious, longsuffering, and abundant in goodness and truth" (Ex. 34:6).

Moses had genuine humility, and the Lord honored him by showing him His glory. Even so will He honor all who will serve Him, as did Moses, with a perfect heart. He does not require His servants to work in their own strength. He will impart His wisdom to those who have a humble and contrite spirit. The righteousness of Christ will go before them, and the glory of the Lord will be their rereward. Nothing in this world can harm those who are thus honored by a close connection with God. The earth may shake, the pillars of the world may tremble under them, but they need not fear.[34]

FAITHFUL IN LITTLE THINGS

*These were the potters, and those that dwelt among plants and
hedges: there they dwelt with the king for his work.* 1 Chron. 4:23.

The Lord designs that the mind of the youthful Christian should
be trained and developed, that the young soldier may be capable of
the highest effort; but this can be done only as you cooperate with the
heavenly intelligences, appropriating to yourself every opportunity
and privilege for your training and culture. The Lord desires that you
should be faithful in little things, that you do the everyday duties
which appear small and unimportant, thoroughly, and to the best of
your ability. You are in danger the moment you are satisfied in doing
carelessly the work committed to your hands. Remember that what is
worth doing at all is worth doing well.

Satan is ever near to tempt him who would be a worker for God,
suggesting to him that it will matter little if the work is slighted, for
no one will know that it has been done negligently. Let none of you
be deceived with this suggestion; for you will know yourself that you
have not done your duty, and will lose respect for yourself and confidence in yourself. You will know that you are not doing your best for
God, and you will realize that God understands all your neglect. Do
not be slack, for the habit will grow upon you and be made manifest
not only in your outward affairs but in your spiritual life. In doing
superficial work you will receive a training that will wholly unfit you for
the duties of this life or the enjoyment of the next.[35]

In the plan that God has for every Christian there are no non-
essentials. There are lessons for each one to learn in the daily experience. Be patient, and perform faithfully the work given you, however
humble it may be. Go about your work calmly, relying upon God for
strength. Look not anxiously into the morrow. Today employ your
time to the very best account. Today let your light shine for Christ,
even in the performance of little duties. . . . The faithful performance
of today's duties will prepare you to take hold of tomorrow's work
with fresh courage, saying, "Hitherto hath the Lord helped me" (1 Sam.
7:12)! Ever stand as minutemen before God.[36]

UNBENDING INTEGRITY

And as for me, thou upholdest me in mine integrity, and settest me before thy face for ever. **Ps.** 41:12.

In every action of life the true Christian is just what he desires those around him to think he is. He is guided by truth and uprightness. He does not scheme; therefore he has nothing to gloss over. He may be criticized, he may be tested; but through all, his unbending integrity shines out like pure gold. He is a friend and benefactor to all connected with him, and his fellow men place confidence in him, for he is trustworthy. Does he employ laborers to gather in his harvest? He does not keep back their hard-earned money. Has he means for which he has no immediate use? He relieves the necessities of his less-fortunate brother. He does not seek to enlarge his possessions by taking advantage of the untoward circumstances of his neighbor. He accepts only a fair price for that which he sells. If there are defects in the articles sold, he frankly tells the buyer, even though by so doing he may seem to work against his own pecuniary interests. . . .

Satan knows full well what a power for good is the life of a man of unbending integrity, and he puts forth zealous efforts to prevent men from living such lives. He comes to them with alluring temptations, promising them wealth, position, worldly honor, if they will but yield the principles of righteousness. And he has much success. . . . From the sad history of many who have failed we learn the danger of prosperity. It is not those who have lost their property who are in greatest danger, but those who have obtained a fortune. . . . Prayer is often requested for men and women in affliction, and this is right. But those in prosperity are more in need of the prayers of God's servants, for they are in greater danger of losing salvation. In the valley of humiliation men walk securely while they reverence God and make Him their trust. On the lofty pinnacle, where praise is heard they need the help of special power from above. . . .

True religion is not an experiment. It is an actual imitation of Christ. God keeps a personal account with every man, testing him by the practical results of his work. Soon will be heard the call, "Give an account of thy stewardship." [37]

243

GRACES TO CHERISH

But the fruit of the Spirit is love, joy, peace, longsuffering, gentleness, goodness, faith, meekness, temperance: against such there is no law. Gal. 5:22, 23.

Here is held out the very thing for which we are to labor: "But the fruit of the Spirit is love." If we have the love of Christ in our souls it will be a natural consequence for us to have all the other graces—joy, peace, long-suffering, gentleness, goodness, faith, meekness, temperance; and "against such there is no law." The law of God does not condemn and hold in bondage those who have these graces, because they are obeying the requirements of the law of God. They are law keepers, and . . . are not under the bondage of the law. . . .

We are to have love, and connected with this are joy, peace, long-suffering, patience. We see the restlessness of the world, their dissatisfied condition. They want something they have not. They want something to keep up an excitement or something for amusement. But for the Christian there is joy, there is peace, there is long-suffering, gentleness, meekness, forbearance, and patience; and to these things we want to open the door of our heart, cherishing the heavenly graces of the Spirit of God. . . . One cannot do it for another. *You* may set to work and obtain the graces of the Spirit, but that will not answer for me. . . . Each one individually must do the work, and determine through personal efforts to have the grace of God in the heart. I cannot form a character for you nor can you for me. It is a burden that rests upon every one individually, young or old.[38]

Christ says: "I will make a man more precious than fine gold; even a man than the golden wedge of Ophir" (Isa. 13:12). How? By the cultivation of the graces of the Spirit—love, joy, peace, long-suffering, gentleness, goodness, meekness, faith. We want the living faith that will grasp the strong arm of Jehovah. . . . We all need the graces of the Spirit of God in the heart.[39]

When the love of Christ is enshrined in the heart, like sweet fragrance it cannot be hidden. The holy influence it reflects through the character will be manifest to all. Christ will be formed within, "the hope of glory."[40]

244

CHEERFULNESS WITHOUT LEVITY

The blessing of the Lord, it maketh rich, and he addeth no sorrow with it. **Prov. 10:22.**

The cheerfulness of the Christian is created by the consideration of the great blessings we enjoy because we are children of God. . . . The cheerful enlightenment of the mind and the soul temple by the assurance that we have reconciliation with God, the hope we have of everlasting life through Christ, and the pleasure of blessing others are joys which bring no sorrow with them.

Those who indulge in chaffing, mirth, levity, and vanity of spirit, which arise from a superficial, cheap experience, have no real, solid foundation for hope and joy in the love of God and belief of the truth. The giddy, the heedless, the gay, the jovial spirit is not the joy which Paul is anxious that Christ's followers shall have. This class spend their time in frivolity and excessive levity. Time is passing, the end is near; yet they have not laid up for themselves a good foundation against the time to come that they may lay hold on everlasting life. We need not encourage that mirth which dissipates reflection, leaves no time for consideration, and establishes habits of lightness and cheap talk which grieve the Holy Spirit of God and unfit us for the contemplation of heaven and heavenly things. This is the class that will have cause to mourn and lament because they are not prepared for the elevated joys of heaven. They are banished from the presence of God.[41]

It is not what is around us, but what is in us; not what we have, but what we are, that makes us really happy. We want a cheerful fire on the altar of our own hearts; then we shall view everything in a happy, cheerful light. We may have the peace of Christ. . . . If we will be obedient, trustful in God, as a child in its simplicity trusts its earthly parents, we shall have peace—not the peace that the world gives, but that peace which Jesus gives. . . . Life, this life, has much brightness in it if we will gather the flowers and let the briers and thistles alone.[42]

Bring the joy of heaven into your lives. The light of heaven, reflected in its beauteous charm from those who are preparing for translation, brings joy to the heavenly family.[43]

245

"LONGSUFFERING WITH JOYFULNESS"

Strengthened with all might, according to his glorious power, unto all patience and longsuffering with joyfulness. Col. 1:11.

"Strengthened with all might." This is not might to speak hasty words, which hurt and bruise others and which injure us more than anyone else, making us ashamed when we think afterward of what we have said.

"Longsuffering with joyfulness." Wherever you are, you may be tantalized, and reproach may come upon you. If I were to undertake to hunt up a thousandth part of what has been said against me, I should have no time to do anything else. I have said, "God knows all about this, and I will let Him take care of it." I am not at all troubled by what other people say concerning me. . . . If I lose my self-control, and flash out in anger, I would in so doing give people some reason to say that the representation of my accusers is correct. . . .

Never should we lose control over ourselves. Let us ever keep before us the perfect Pattern. It is a sin to speak impatiently and fretfully or to feel angry—even though we do not speak. We are to walk worthy, giving a right representation of Christ. The speaking of an angry word is like flint striking flint: it at once kindles wrathful feelings. Never be like a chestnut bur. . . .

When others are impatient, fretful, and complaining, because self is not subdued, begin to sing some of the songs of Zion. While Christ was working at the carpenter's bench others would sometimes surround Him, trying to cause Him to be impatient; but He would begin singing some of the beautiful psalms, and before they realized what they were doing they had joined with Him in singing, influenced, as it were, by the power of the Holy Spirit, which was there.

God desires us to be patient in tribulation and affliction, content to rest in His great arms of infinite love, believing that He is working for us all the time. It is our privilege to be joyful in the Lord. Let us praise Him more. By our joyfulness we reveal that our life is hid with Christ in God, that in Him we find the most blessed companionship, and that through His grace we have a living connection with heaven.[44]

NO PLACE FOR DISCOURAGEMENT

Giving thanks unto the Father, which hath made us meet to be partakers of the inheritance of the saints in light: who hath delivered us from the power of darkness, and hath translated us into the kingdom of his dear Son. Col. 1:12, 13.

How full is this language! If you attempted to measure it, you would find that in these words are measureless depths of meaning. We are now being fitted up to dwell in the mansions which Christ has gone to prepare for those who love Him.

"Who hath delivered us from the power of darkness." If this is true, what excuse then have we for talking discouragement and unbelief and doubt—drawing darkness around us as a mantle? . . .

If I should look at the dark clouds—the troubles and perplexities that come to me in my work—I should have time to do nothing else. But I know that there is light and glory beyond the clouds. By faith I reach through the darkness to the glory. At times I am called to pass through financial perplexities. But I do not worry about money. God takes care of my affairs. I do all that I can, and when the Lord sees that it is best for me to have money, He sends it to me.

The more you talk faith, the more faith you will have. The more you dwell upon discouragement, talking to others about your trials and enlarging upon them, to enlist the sympathy which you crave, the more discouragements and trials you will have. Why mourn over that which you cannot avoid? . . .

We are preparing for promotion from the school in this world, in which we are forming characters for the future, immortal life, to the higher grade, the school of heaven. But man is not to depend upon his own finite strength to wrestle with difficulty. In faith he is to look to God, believing that all the resources of heaven are at his command to help him overcome. Thousands upon thousands and ten thousand times ten thousand of heavenly angels are ministering unto those who shall be heirs of salvation.[45]

God is inviting us to close the windows of the soul earthward and open them heavenward, that He may flood our hearts with the glory which is shining across the threshold of heaven.[45]

OUR GLORIOUS WORK

Sing unto the Lord, bless his name; shew forth his salvation from day to day. Declare his glory among the heathen, his wonders among all people. Ps. 96:2, 3.

The great and glorious work committed to us in acting a part in the plan of salvation is wonderfully high and exalted. We cannot weigh its merits. We are to walk by faith; and as we strive to appreciate the possibilities, and realize the immensity of the plan of salvation, it is our privilege to pray with the apostle Paul that we may be able to "comprehend with all saints what is the breadth, and length, and depth, and height; and to know the love of Christ, which passeth knowledge" (Eph. 3:18). Lift Him up, the Man of Calvary. Let the mind dwell upon the beauties of His character until by beholding you become changed into the same image. A life of prayer and faith will lead us to speak of His praise and tell of His power. . . .

Genuine conversion will unite our hearts in faith and love. It will teach us to hold fast our confidence in Him who is our only hope. By conversion we join our weakness to God's strength, our ignorance to His wisdom, our unworthiness to His merits, our poverty to His boundless riches, our helplessness to His enduring might.[46]

We must search the Word of God, making it a part of ourselves. A spirit of humility, the spirit of Christ, will help us to know Him who has called us to glory and virtue.

If we brought the truth into the daily life as we should we would advance higher and still higher, gaining a clearer and still clearer understanding of the revelation of God. We would lift Him up in songs of praise. Through the psalmist Christ declared, "In the midst of the congregation will I praise thee" (Ps. 22:22). His voice was the keynote of the universe. His unconfined power, His unsearchable understanding, His wonderful sacrifice for the human race, help us to comprehend the love of God. We need individually to have Christ abiding in the soul. We need to open our minds and hearts to the indwelling of the Spirit of truth. We need to appreciate our privileges as the possessors of sacred, elevating truth. Think of what this means to us—heirs of God and joint heirs with Christ! [46]

248

CHRIST'S LEGACY OF PEACE

Peace I leave with you, my peace I give unto you: not as the world giveth, give I unto you. Let not your heart be troubled, neither let it be afraid. John 14:27.

Before our Lord went to His agony on the cross He made His will. He had no silver or gold or houses to leave His disciples. He was a poor man, as far as earthly possessions were concerned. Few in Jerusalem were so poor as He. But He left His disciples a richer gift than any earthly monarch could bestow on his subjects. "Peace I leave with you, my peace I give unto you," He said. . . . He left them the peace which had been His during His life on the earth, which had been with Him amid poverty, buffeting, and persecution, and which was to be with Him during His agony in Gethsemane and on the cruel cross.

The Saviour's life on this earth, though lived in the midst of conflict, was a life of peace. . . . No storm of satanic wrath could disturb the calm of that perfect communion with God. And He says to us, "My peace I give unto you."

Those who take Christ at His word and surrender their souls to His keeping, their lives to His ordering, will find peace and quietude. Nothing of the world can make them sad when Jesus makes them glad by His presence. In perfect acquiescence there is perfect rest. The Lord says, "Thou wilt keep him in perfect peace, whose mind is stayed on thee: because he trusteth in thee" (Isa. 26:3).

It is the love of self that destroys our peace. While self is alive we stand ready continually to guard it from mortification and insult; but when self is dead, and our life hid with Christ in God, we shall not take neglects or slights to heart. . . .

When we receive Christ into the soul as an abiding guest, the peace of God, which passeth all understanding, will keep our hearts and minds. There is no other ground of peace than this. The grace of Christ, received into the heart, subdues enmity; it allays strife and fills the soul with love. He who is at peace with God and his fellow men cannot be made miserable. . . . The heart that is in harmony with God is a partaker of the peace of heaven and will diffuse its blessed influence all around.[47]

249

PREPARING TO MEET JESUS

And now, little children, abide in him; that, when he shall appear, we may have confidence, and not be ashamed before him at his coming. 1 John 2:28.

Only by knowing God here can we prepare to meet Him at His coming. . . . In His lessons and His mighty works Christ is a perfect revelation of God. This Christ declares through the inspired evangelist. "No man hath seen God at any time," He says; "the only begotten Son, which is in the bosom of the Father, he hath declared him" (John 1:18). "No man knoweth the Son, but the Father; neither knoweth any man the Father, save the Son, and he to whomsoever the Son will reveal him." These words show the importance of studying Christ's character. Only by knowing Christ can we know God.

As our representative, Christ stands on the highest possible ground. When He came to the world as God's messenger, He held the salvation of God in His hand. All mankind was delivered to Him, for in Him was the fullness of the Godhead. . . . So fully did Christ reveal the Father that the messengers sent by the Pharisees to take Him were charmed by His presence. . . . As they beheld the soft light of the glory of God that enshrouded His person, as they heard the gracious words that fell from His lips, they loved Him. And when . . . they were asked by the Pharisees, "Why have ye not brought him?" they answered, "Never man spake like this man" (John 7:45, 46).

As we behold Christ we shall be changed into His image and made fit to meet Him at His coming. Now is the time to prepare for the coming of our Lord. Readiness to meet Him cannot be attained in a moment's time. Preparatory to that solemn scene there must be vigilant waiting combined with earnest work. The union of these two makes us complete in Christ. The active and devotional must be combined as were the human and divine in Christ. So God's children glorify Him. Amid the busy scenes of life their voices will be heard speaking words of encouragement, hope, and faith. The will and the affections will be consecrated to Christ. Thus they prepare to meet their Lord; and when He comes, they will say, with joy: "This is our God; we have waited for him, and he will save us." [48]

THE "WHY" OF TEMPTATION

There hath no temptation taken you but such as is common to man: but God is faithful, who will not suffer you to be tempted above that ye are able; but will with the temptation also make a way to escape, that ye may be able to bear it. 1 Cor. 10:13.

What is temptation? It is the means by which those who claim to be the children of God are tested and tried. We read that God tempted Abraham, that He tempted the children of Israel. This means that He permitted circumstances to occur to test their faith and lead them to look to Him for help. God permits temptation to come to His people today that they may realize that He is their helper. If they draw nigh to Him when they are tempted, He strengthens them to meet the temptation. . . .

Temptations will pour in upon us, for by them we are to be tried during our probation. This is the proving of God, the revelation of our own hearts. There is no sin in having temptation, but sin comes in when temptation is yielded to. . . .

Abraham certified his obedience to God when, with Isaac by his side, he journeyed on his way in response to the command, "Take now thy son, thine only son Isaac, whom thou lovest, and get thee into the land of Moriah; and offer him there for a burnt offering . . ." (Gen. 22:2). Job was permitted to suffer; he was severely tempted; but he would not speak one word against God. During Christ's life on earth the scribes and Pharisees, instigated by Satan, tempted Him in every possible way. But He never allowed these temptations to lead Him from the path of obedience. . . .

Christ's example shows us that our only hope of victory is in continual resistance of Satan's attacks. He who triumphed over the adversary of souls in the conflict with temptation understands Satan's power over the race, and has conquered in our behalf. As an overcomer, He has given us the advantage of His victory, that in our efforts to resist the temptations of Satan we may unite our weakness to His strength, our worthlessness to His merits. And sustained by His enduring might, under strong temptation, we may resist in His all-powerful name and overcome as He overcame.[1]

251

CHRIST THE MIGHTY CONQUEROR

For we have not an high priest which cannot be touched with the feeling of our infirmities; but was in all points tempted like as we are, yet without sin. Heb. 4:15.

When Jesus was led into the wilderness to be tempted, He was led by the Spirit of God. By going into the wilderness, He did not invite temptation. But Satan knew that the Saviour had gone there, and he thought it the best time to approach Him. Christ went to the wilderness to be alone, to contemplate His mission and work. He had taken the steps which every sinner must take, in conversion, repentance, and baptism. He Himself had no sins of which to repent, and therefore He had no sins to wash away. But He was our example in all things, and therefore He must do that which He would have us do.

Christ fasted and prayed, bracing Himself for the blood-stained path which He must travel. He was the Son of the eternal God, but as man's surety He must meet and resist every temptation with which man is assailed. . . . With the terrible weight of the sins of the world upon Him, He withstood the fearful test upon appetite, upon the love of the world, and upon that love of display that leads to presumption. . . .

If Christ's soldiers look faithfully to their Captain for their orders, success will attend their warfare against the enemy. No matter how they may be beset, in the end they will be triumphant. Their infirmities may be many, their sins great, their ignorance seemingly insurmountable; but if they realize their weakness, and look to Christ for aid, He will be their efficiency. . . . If they avail themselves of His power, their characters will be transformed; they will be surrounded with an atmosphere of light and holiness. Through His merits and imparted power they will be "more than conquerors." Supernatural help will be given them, enabling them in their weakness to do the deeds of omnipotence. . . .

By faith they are to look calmly upon every foe, exclaiming: "We fight the good fight of faith, under the command of an omnipotent Power. Because He lives, we shall live also. Through Jesus . . . we may withstand all the fiery darts of the enemy." [2]

AN UNSEEN BATTLE OVER EVERY SOUL

For we wrestle not against flesh and blood, but against princi-palities, against powers, against the rulers of the darkness of this world, against spiritual wickedness in high places. Eph. 6:12.

We do not understand as we should the great conflict going on between invisible agencies, the controversy between loyal and disloyal angels. Over every man, good and evil angels strive. This is no make-believe conflict. It is not mimic battles in which we are engaged. We have to meet most powerful adversaries, and it rests with us to determine which shall win.[3]

Could human beings know the number of the evil angels, could they know their devices and their activity, there would be far less pride and frivolity. Satan is the prince of demons. The evil angels over whom he rules do his bidding. Through them he multiplies his agencies. . . . He instigates all the evil that exists in our world.[4]

If Satan sees that he is in danger of losing one soul, he will exert himself to the utmost to keep that one. And when the individual is aroused to his danger, and, with distress and fervor, looks to Jesus for strength, Satan fears that he will lose a captive, and he calls a reinforcement of his angels to hedge in the poor soul, and form a wall of darkness around him, that heaven's light may not reach him.

But if the one in danger perseveres, and in his helplessness casts himself upon the merits of the blood of Christ, our Saviour listens to the earnest prayer of faith, and sends a reinforcement of those angels that excel in strength to deliver him. Satan cannot endure to have his powerful rival appealed to, for he fears and trembles before His strength and majesty. At the sound of fervent prayer, Satan's whole host trembles. . . . And when angels, all-powerful, clothed with the armory of heaven, come to the help of the fainting, pursued soul, Satan and his host fall back. . . . The great Commander in heaven and earth has limited Satan's power.[5]

Around every tempted soul there are angels of God, ready to lift up the standard of righteousness, if the tempted one will only show a spirit of resistance to evil. Each may be an overcomer. Christ has in our behalf withstood the fiercest temptations of the enemy.[6]

253

KEEP OFF SATANIC GROUND

My son, if sinners entice thee, consent thou not. Prov. 1:10.

We must not put ourselves on the enemy's ground. We are only here as probationers. We must not act as though there were no tempting devil. There are temptations that come to us, and we cannot accept them and give them a place in the mind unless we peril our souls. We want to know that our feet are in safe paths.

You who associate with the disobedient and worldly-minded, heed the injunction: "Wherefore come out from among them, and be ye separate, saith the Lord, and touch not the unclean thing; and I will receive you, and will be a Father unto you, and ye shall be my sons and daughters, saith the Lord Almighty" (2 Cor. 6:17, 18). Is this not encouragement enough for us—to have living connection with the God of heaven?

When you go where sin is, and place yourself on the enemy's ground, you place yourself where the angels of God do not preserve you from evil influence. We are to know that Christ is constantly by our side. We are to put all our trust in Christ. . . . What dependence can you place in human nature that is not under the control of the influence of God? The world knows Him not today. The line of demarcation is plain and distinct between those who keep His commandments and those who do not. We cannot serve the world and please God. . . .

Many seem to be sad because of their religion. We should not go about begging pardon of the world because we are Christians. I beg pardon of Jesus Christ only, because I am not complete in Him. . . . If we love Jesus we shall become heirs of God, and the Father will love us as He loves His Son Jesus Christ. We are members of the royal family, children of the heavenly King. . . .

It was the highest exaltation of Christ to obey His Father and keep His law as the apple of His eye. Let it have this effect upon our characters. . . . Let us exalt Jesus. Let us give Him our hearts' best service, and He will say, I will confess you before My Father, and before His angels.[7]

254

NEVER ACCEPT SATAN'S DARE

Jesus said unto him, It is written again, Thou shalt not tempt the Lord thy God. Matt. 4:7.

Let all remember how adroitly and cunningly did Satan command Christ to cast Himself from the Temple, quoting scripture to show Him that it was the very thing for Him to do, for in this way He could give evidence to all the people that He was what He claimed to be. "If thou be the Son of God, cast thyself down: for it is written, He shall give his angels charge concerning thee: and in their hands they shall bear thee up, lest at any time thou dash thy foot against a stone" (verse 6).

In quoting the scripture Satan left out a very important point, . . . "to keep thee *in all thy ways*" (Ps. 91:11). In consenting to do Satan's bidding, Christ would be venturing into Satan's ways, not in ways that God had devised for His Son. That was a dare, and Satan's agents are full of presumptuous dares to get a chance to work his will with those who will accept his dare. But Christ would not accept the dare of Satan. Christ would not enter into controversy with the arch deceiver and tempter. He said, "It is written again, Thou shalt not tempt the Lord thy God." . . .

Angels, as ministering spirits, are in the path where duty calls the heirs of salvation to travel, and God will protect them from all evil. But when Satan marked out a path of his own, . . . Christ had no right to walk in that way. He was to keep His feet in the path which the Lord had marked out. Thus Christ in His humanity gave an example of what man should do when tempted by Satan's suggestions.

We are . . . never to accept a dare to prove the truth to men who are inspired by Satan to make proposals that God has not originated; for in this way Satan would lead us to step out of the path of God's providence and place ourselves in a position where we might be worsted by the enemy, and be overcome to our own hurt and to the injury of the cause of God.[8]

Our only safety every day and every hour is to be on watch. We cannot become indolent and careless. I tell you that God would have His people to be ever on guard.[8]

VICTORY IN THE MIGHTY NAME OF JESUS

The name of the Lord is a strong tower: the righteous runneth into it, and is safe. Prov. 18:10.

It was in the time of greatest weakness that Christ was assailed by the fiercest temptations. Thus Satan thought to prevail. By this policy he had gained the victory over man. When strength failed, and the will power weakened, and faith ceased to repose in God, then those who had stood long and valiantly for the right were overcome. Moses was wearied with the forty years' wandering of Israel, when for the moment his faith let go its hold upon infinite power. He failed just upon the borders of the Promised Land. So with Elijah, who had stood undaunted before King Ahab, who had faced the whole nation of Israel with the four hundred and fifty prophets of Baal at their head. After that terrible day upon Carmel, when the false prophets had been slain and the people had declared their allegiance to God, Elijah fled for his life before the threats of idolatrous Jezebel. Thus Satan had taken advantage of the weakness of humanity. . . .

Whenever one is encompassed with clouds, perplexed by circumstances, or afflicted by poverty or distress, Satan is at hand to tempt and annoy. He attacks our weak points of character. He seeks to shake our confidence in God, who suffers such a condition of things to exist. We are tempted to distrust God, to question His love. Often the tempter comes to us as he came to Christ, arraying before us our weakness and infirmities. He hopes to discourage the soul and to break our hold upon God. Then he is sure of his prey. If we would meet him as Jesus did, we should escape many a defeat. By parleying with the enemy we give him an advantage. . . .

Jesus gained the victory through submission and faith in God, and by the apostle He says to us, "Submit yourselves therefore to God. Resist the devil, and he will flee from you" (James 4:7). We cannot save ourselves from the tempter's power; he has conquered humanity, and when we try to stand in our own strength, we shall become a prey to his devices; but "the name of the Lord is a strong tower: the righteous runneth into it, and is safe." Satan trembles and flees before the weakest soul who finds refuge in that mighty name.[9]

256

NO ONE FREE FROM TEMPTATION

Who are kept by the power of God through faith unto salvation ready to be revealed in the last time. Wherein ye greatly rejoice, though now for a season, if need be, ye are in heaviness through manifold temptations. 1 Peter 1:5, 6.

Do not think that the Christian life is free from temptation. Temptations will come to every Christian. Both the Christian and the one who does not accept Christ as his leader will have trials. The difference is that the latter is serving a tyrant, doing his mean drudgery, while the Christian is serving the One who died to give him eternal life. Do not look upon trial as something strange, but as the means by which we are to be purified and strengthened. "Count it all joy when ye fall into divers temptations," James admonishes; "knowing this, that the trying of your faith worketh patience" (James 1:2, 3).

In the future life we shall understand things that here greatly perplex us. We shall realize how strong a helper we had and how angels of God were commissioned to guard us as we followed the counsel of the Word of God.

To all who receive Him, Christ will give power to become the sons of God. He is a present help in every time of need. Let us be ashamed of our wavering faith. Those who are overcome have only themselves to blame for their failure to resist the enemy. All who choose can come to Christ and find the help they need.

There stands among you the mighty Counselor of the ages, inviting you to place your confidence in Him. Shall we turn away from Him to uncertain human beings, who are as wholly dependent on God as we ourselves are? Have we fallen so far below our privileges? Have we not been guilty of expecting so little that we have not asked for what God is longing to give?

"I will mention the lovingkindnesses of the Lord, and the praises of the Lord, according to all that the Lord hath bestowed on us, and the great goodness toward the house of Israel. . . . For he said, Surely they are my people, children that will not lie: so he was their Saviour. In all their affliction he was afflicted, and the angel of his presence saved them" (Isa. 63:7-9).[10]

PERILS ON LIFE'S PATHWAY

Hold up my goings in thy paths, that my footsteps slip not.
Ps. 17:5.

At this time above all others the paths of life are beset with perils that I cannot find language to describe. In a single departure from the path of sanctified principle Satan obtains an advantage, and he leads on and on, farther and farther from right and truth. . . .

Not for any soul living, be he young or old, is there security from the temptations of Satan, and those who choose to bind up with unholy men will imbibe their spirit and bear similar fruit. The only safety for any one of us is in walking humbly with God, in going where the Master leads the way. . . .

We need to pray without ceasing. Let the heart long after God. Let the heart go out in daily, hourly prayer, believing, trusting, holding on to the promise, saying as did Jacob, "I will not let thee go, except thou bless me" (Gen. 32:26). "Hold up my goings in thy paths," O God, "that my footsteps slip not" into the pitfalls which men have dug for my feet.

The removal of one safeguard from the conscience, the failure to do the very thing that the Lord has marked out, one step in the path of wrong principle, often leads to an entire change of the life and action. . . . We are safe only in following where Christ leads the way. The path will grow clearer, brighter and brighter, unto the perfect day.

Man's business is to work in cooperation with God. Alone, his feet will slip, in apparently the safest path. We cannot walk one step safely in mere human wisdom. If we would walk without fear, we must know that the hand of Jesus Christ holds our own firmly. And we can only know this by searching the Word of the living God. . . .

God desires that men shall feel their dependence upon Him and trust to that Hand that can save to the uttermost, that Heart that throbs in response to the appeals of suffering humanity. We must not trust in man or make flesh our arm. Our trust must be placed in a Hand that is warm with life and a Heart that throbs with love for the helpless.[11]

ARMED FOR THE CONFLICT

Wherefore take unto you the whole armour of God, that ye may be able to withstand in the evil day, and having done all, to stand. Eph. 6:13.

There are many who do not understand the conflict that is going on between Christ and Satan over the souls of men. They do not realize that if they would stand under the blood-stained banner of Prince Emmanuel they must be willing to be partakers of His conflicts and wage a determined war against the powers of darkness.

When thinking on the conflict, Paul writes to his Ephesian brethren exhorting them to "be strong," not feeble, not wavering, tossed to and fro like the waves of the sea. But in what are they to be strong? In their own might? No. "Be strong in the Lord, and in the power of his might." He says, "Put on the whole armour of God, that ye may be able to stand against the wiles of the devil. For we wrestle not against flesh and blood, but against principalities, against powers, against the rulers of the darkness of this world, against spiritual wickedness in high places . . ." (verses 10-13).

The gaining of eternal life will ever involve a struggle, a conflict. We are continually to be found fighting the good fight of faith. We are soldiers of Christ; and those who enlist in His army are expected to do difficult work, work which will tax their energies to the utmost. We must understand that a soldier's life is one of aggressive warfare, of perseverance and endurance. For Christ's sake we are to endure trials.

Victories are not gained by ceremonies or display but by simple obedience to the highest General, the Lord God of heaven. He who trusts in this Leader will never know defeat. Obedience to God is liberty from the thraldom of sin, deliverance from human passion and impulse. Man may stand conqueror of himself, conqueror of his own inclinations, conqueror of principalities and powers, and of the "rulers of the darkness of this world," and of "spiritual wickedness in high places." . . .

"Wherefore take unto you the whole armour of God, that ye may be able to withstand in the evil day, and having done all, to stand." [12]

259

RESOLUTE WILL ESSENTIAL FOR VICTORY

Ye have not yet resisted unto blood, striving against sin. Heb. 12:4.

In every age since the fall of Adam the opposition of evil agencies has made the lives of those who would be loyal and true to God's commandments a continual warfare. Those who would at last be victorious must meet and conquer the forces of Satan, who with fierce determination opposes every step of advance. They must meet a vigilant foe, a crafty enemy who never sleeps and who tries untiringly to undermine the faith of God's servants. . . .

Good and evil never harmonize. Between light and darkness there can be no compromise. Truth is light revealed; error is darkness. Light has no fellowship with darkness, righteousness no fellowship with unrighteousness. . . .

I wish that I could trace words which would present this matter as it is. God expects His soldiers to be ever on duty. Never are they to yield to temptation, never to be unjust. They are neither to yield nor flee. Relying on the strength of God, they are to maintain their integrity. With a firmness that will not yield an inch, they are to hold fast to the word, "It is written."

Bear in mind that we are placed on vantage ground because Christ has overcome in our behalf. He has made every provision for us to overcome. Divine power stands behind every will resolutely set to do the right. God has provided the armor and the weapons with which each one is to fight. Let the soldiers of Christ put on the whole armor of God and flinch not at Satan's attacks. . . . Success in the Christian warfare means watchfulness and a daily crucifixion of self.

He who is guided by clean, holy principles will be quick to discern the slightest taint of evil, because he keeps Christ before him as his pattern. His deep regret at the discovery of a wrong act means the prompt correction of every step wherein he has diverged from truth. It means a constant, earnest striving for higher and still higher attainments in the Christian life. It means helping others to climb heavenward. It means taking hold of Christ by living faith and resisting evil if need be unto blood, striving against sin.[13]

260

AS STEADFAST AS DANIEL

For the Lord God will help me; therefore shall I not be con-founded: therefore have I set my face like a flint, and I know that I shall not be ashamed. Isa. 50:7.

The youth have an example in Daniel, and if they are true to principle and to duty they will be instructed as Daniel was. As the wisdom of the world viewed the matter, he and his three companions had every advantage secured to them. But here their first test was to come. Their principles must come into collision with the regulations and appointments of the king. They were to eat the food placed upon his table and drink his wine. . . . Daniel "purposed in his heart that he would not defile himself with the portion of the king's meat, nor with the wine which he drank: therefore he requested of the prince of the eunuchs that he might not defile himself" (Dan. 1:8).

This request was not preferred in a defiant spirit, but was solicited as a great favor. . . . Daniel and his companions . . . were courteous, kind, respectful, possessing the grace of meekness and modesty. And now as Daniel and his fellows were brought to the test, they placed themselves fully on the side of righteousness and truth. They did not move capriciously, but intelligently. They decided that as flesh meat had not composed their diet in the past, neither should it come into their diet in the future. And as the use of wine had been prohibited to all those who should engage in the service of God, they determined that they would not partake of it. . . .

Daniel and his companions knew not what would be the result of their decision. They knew not but that it would cost them their lives, but they determined to keep the straight path of strict temperance, even in the courts of licentious Babylon. . . . The good behavior of these youth obtained for them favor. They rested their case in the hands of God, following a discipline of self-denial and temperance in all things. And the Lord cooperated with Daniel and his fellows. . . .

These particulars were placed on record in the history of the children of Israel as a warning to all youth to avoid all approach to customs and practices and indulgences that would dishonor God in any way.[14]

261

NONE NEED BE OVERCOME

Blessed is the man that endureth temptation: for when he is tried, he shall receive the crown of life, which the Lord hath promised to them that love him. James 1:12.

When trials come into our lives, when clouds darken the horizon, how ready we are to forget that Jesus is our Saviour, that behind the clouds the Sun of Righteousness is shining, that angels are close beside us, preserving us from harm. I would say to the despairing, Look and live. Hope thou in God, for on Calvary's cross a complete sacrifice was offered for you. Jesus is the sinner's Friend, the sinner's Redeemer. Eternal joy—a life of undimmed happiness—awaits the one who surrenders all to Christ. Look away from yourself to Jesus, who is pleading before the throne of God in your behalf. Listen to His words, "Come unto me, . . . and I will give you rest." "Him that cometh to me I will in no wise cast out" (Matt. 11:28; John 6:37). With the hand of faith grasp the promises of God. Appropriate these blessings to yourself, not at some future time, but today.

The strongest temptation cannot excuse sin. However great the pressure brought to bear upon the soul, transgression is our own act. It is not in the power of earth or hell to compel anyone to do evil. Satan attacks us at our weakest points, but we need not be overcome. However severe or unexpected the attack, God has provided help for us, and in His strength we may conquer. In the hour of greatest need, when discouragement overwhelms the soul, then it is that Jesus comes very near. The hour of man's necessity is God's opportunity. He sees our danger and provides help for us. . . .

Do not think that when you walk with Jesus you must walk in the shadow. The happiest people in the world are those who trust in Jesus and gladly do His bidding. He is the light of life. From the lives of those who follow Him unrest and discontent are banished. With a full heart they echo the words of the wise man, Wisdom's "ways are ways of pleasantness, and all her paths are peace" (Prov. 3:17). Though they meet with trials and difficulties, their lives are full of joy; for Christ walks beside them, and His presence makes the pathway bright.[15]

PRESSING AGAINST THE CURRENT

Then said one unto him, Lord, are there few that be saved?
And he said unto them, Strive to enter in at the strait gate: for
many, I say unto you, will seek to enter in, and shall not be able.
Luke 13:23, 24.

When we read that many will seek to enter in and shall not be able, then we want to understand what we shall do in order to succeed. This to us is a mournful statement, that there are those who will fail to enter in at the strait gate because they only seek to enter in, and do not *strive.* . . .

We are in a world where sin and iniquity prevail, and we want to know what we shall do in order to inherit life. We cannot any of us afford to miss the great reward that is presented before the overcomer. We want to know that the steps that we are taking are heavenward instead of earthward. . . .

A great and solemn responsibility rests upon us who profess to obey God's commandments, to show to the world around us that we are bending our steps heavenward. And as we press against the current that is bearing all down, then we should know for what we should strive. We are to press toward the mark of the prize of our high calling in Christ Jesus. We cannot remain in listless resistance and yet gain the prize. . . .

We are to grow up to the full stature of men and women in Christ Jesus, and we are thus growing up a precious temple unto the Lord. He says, "I will dwell in them, and walk in them; and I will be their God, and they shall be my people" (2 Cor. 6:16). . . . What we want is the Spirit of God in our souls. We want our faces set constantly heavenward. And when we see that sin in us is striving for the mastery, then we must strive. . . .

The pitying Saviour stands right by your side to help you. He would send every angel out of glory while you are struggling to overcome sin, so that Satan cannot have the victory over you. Christ . . . took man's human nature upon Him that He might come right down to man in the temptation wherewith man is beset. The pitiful Redeemer knows just how to help us in every one of our strivings.[16]

JESUS OUR ADVOCATE

My little children, these things write I unto you, that ye sin not. And if any man sin, we have an advocate with the Father, Jesus Christ the righteous. 1 John 2:1.

When tempted to sin let us remember that Jesus is pleading for us in the heavenly sanctuary. When we put away our sins and come to Him in faith, He takes our names on His lips and presents them to His Father, saying, "I have graven them upon the palms of my hands; I know them by name." And the command goes forth to the angels to protect them. Then in the day of fierce trial He will say, "Come, my people, enter thou into thy chambers, and shut thy doors about thee: hide thyself as it were for a little moment, until the indignation be overpast" (Isa. 26:20). What are the chambers in which they are to hide? They are the protection of Christ and holy angels. The people of God are not at this time all in one place. They are in different companies and in all parts of the earth, and they will be tried singly, not in groups. Everyone must stand the test for himself.

There has never been a time when the people of God have had greater need to claim His promises than now. Let the hand of faith pass through the darkness and grasp the arm of infinite power. While we speak of the necessity of separating from sin, remember that Christ came to our world to save sinners, and that "he is able also to save them to the uttermost that come unto God by him" (Heb. 7:25). It is our privilege to believe that His blood is able to cleanse us from every spot and stain of sin. We must not limit the power of the Holy One of Israel. He wants us to come to Him just as we are, sinful and polluted. His blood is efficacious. . . . If you fall under temptation do not become discouraged. This promise comes ringing down along the line to our time: "If any man sin, we have an advocate with the Father, Jesus Christ the righteous." I feel that for this one promise a continual song of thanksgiving ought to go forth. . . .

Let us gather up these precious jewels of promise, and when Satan accuses us of our great sinfulness and tempts us to doubt the power of God to save, let us repeat the words of Christ, "Him that cometh to me I will in no wise cast out" (John 6:37).[17]

264

UNDER GOD'S DISCIPLINE

Behold, happy is the man whom God correcteth: therefore despise not thou the chastening of the Almighty: for he maketh sore, and bindeth up: he woundeth, and his hands make whole. Job 5:17, 18.

Our heavenly Father does not willingly afflict or grieve the children of men. He has His purpose in the whirlwind and in the storm, in the fire and in the flood. The Lord permits calamities to come to His people to save them from greater dangers. He desires everyone to examine his own heart closely and carefully, and then draw near to God, that God may draw near to him.

Our life is in the hands of God. He sees dangers threatening us that we cannot see. He is the giver of all our blessings; the provider of all our mercies; the orderer of all our experiences. He sees the perils that we cannot see. He may permit to come upon His people that which fills their hearts with sadness, because He sees that they need to make straight paths for their feet, lest the lame be turned out of the way. He knows our frame, and remembers that we are dust. Even the very hairs of our head are numbered. He works through natural causes to lead His people to remember that He has not forgotten them, but that He desires them to forsake the way which, if they were permitted to follow unchecked and unreproved, would lead them into great peril. Trials come to us all to lead us to investigate our hearts, to see if they are purified from all that defiles. Constantly the Lord is working to our present and eternal good. . . .

Every soul that is saved must be a partaker with Christ of His sufferings, that he may be a partaker with Him of His glory. How few understand why God subjects them to trial. It is by the trial of our faith that we gain spiritual strength. The Lord seeks to educate His people to lean wholly upon Him. . . .

Let everyone examine his own course of action. Let everyone ask himself whether he is meeting the standard that God has placed before him. Can we say from the heart, I lay aside my own will? "I delight to do thy will, O my God: yea, thy law is within my heart"? Do we ask daily, "Lord, what is thy will concerning me?" [18]

265

TESTS ALL ALONG THE WAY

My son, despise not the chastening of the Lord; neither be weary of his correction: for whom the Lord loveth he correcteth; even as a father the son in whom he delighteth. Prov. 3:11, 12.

God brings men into trying places to see if they will trust in a power out of and above themselves. He sees not as man sees. He often has to break up human connections and change the order which man has mapped out, which is perfect in his estimation. What man thinks is for his spiritual and temporal interests may be altogether at variance with the experience he must have in order to be a follower of Christ. His idea of his own value may be far out of the way.

Tests are placed all along the way from earth to heaven. It is because of this that the road to heaven is called the narrow way. Character must be tested, else there would be many spurious Christians who would keep up a fair semblance of religion until their inclinations, their desire to have their own way, their pride and ambition, were crossed. When by the Lord's permission sharp trials come to them, their lack of genuine religion, of the meekness and lowliness of Christ, shows them to be in need of the work of the Holy Spirit.

Christ's command, "If any man will come after me, let him deny himself, and take up his cross daily, and follow me" (Luke 9:23), is the touchstone that discovers the quality of the experience. When a man's inclinations or ambitious hopes are crossed he reveals the spirit that governs him. . . .

He [Christ] invites all to wear His yoke and learn His meekness and lowliness. He knows that it is positively necessary for them to do this. But no human being can wear the yoke of submission and obedience who does not learn daily in the school of Christ. . . . No one, whatever his supposed abilities, can bear the test of trial unless he is a student in the school of Christ. . . .

The true Christian keeps his eyes fixed on Him who searches the heart and tries the reins, who requires truth in the inward parts. His constant prayer is, "Search me, O God, and know my heart: try me, and know my thoughts: and see if there be any wicked way in me, and lead me in the way everlasting" (Ps. 139:23, 24).[19]

266

THE POLISHING PROCESS

Beloved, think it not strange concerning the fiery trial which is to try you, as though some strange thing happened unto you: but rejoice, inasmuch as ye are partakers of Christ's sufferings; that, when his glory shall be revealed, ye may be glad also with exceeding joy. 1 Peter 4:12, 13.

Not without a purpose does God send trial to His children. He never leads them otherwise than they would choose to be led if they could see the end from the beginning, and discern the glory of the purpose which they are fulfilling as workers together with Him. He subjects them to discipline to humble them, to lead them, through trial and affliction, to see their weakness and draw near to Him. . . .

Christians are Christ's jewels. They are to shine brightly for Him, shedding forth the light of His loveliness. Their luster depends on the polishing they receive. They may choose to be polished or to remain unpolished. But everyone who is pronounced worthy of a place in the Lord's temple must submit to the polishing process. Without the polishing that the Lord gives, they can reflect no more light than a common pebble. Christ says to man, You are mine. I have bought you. You are now only a rough stone; but if you will place yourself in My hands, I will polish you, and the luster with which you shall shine will bring honor to My name. No man shall pluck you out of My hand. I will make you My peculiar treasure. On My coronation day, you will be a jewel in My crown of rejoicing.

The Divine Worker spends little time on worthless material. Only the precious jewels does He polish after the similitude of a palace, cutting away all rough edges. This process is severe and trying; it hurts human pride. Christ cuts deep into the experience that man in his self-sufficiency has regarded as complete and takes away self-uplifting from the character. He cuts away the surplus surface, and putting the stone to the polishing wheel, presses it close, that all roughness may be worn away. Then, holding the jewel up to the light, the Master sees in it a reflection of Himself, and He pronounces it worthy of a place in His casket. Blessed be the experience, however severe, that gives new value to the stone.[20]

267

NO EXEMPTION FROM SORROW

Therefore I take pleasure in infirmities, in reproaches, in necessities, in persecutions, in distresses for Christ's sake: for when I am weak, then am I strong. 2 Cor. 12:10.

Christianity promises no exemption from sorrow. "We must through much tribulation enter into the kingdom of God" (Acts 14: 22). Faith is needed, strong, trusting faith, which believes that God will bring His children into no temptation greater than they are able to bear. What such faith has power to do is told by Paul in his letter to the Hebrews. Speaking of those who in the face of persecution and death had maintained an unshaken trust in God, he says:

"Who through faith subdued kingdoms, wrought righteousness, obtained promises, stopped the mouths of lions, quenched the violence of fire, escaped the edge of the sword, out of weakness were made strong, waxed valiant in fight, turned to flight the armies of the aliens. Women received their dead raised to life again: and others were tortured, not accepting deliverance; that they might obtain a better resurrection: and others had trial of cruel mockings and scourgings, yea, moreover of bonds and imprisonment: they were stoned, they were sawn asunder, were tempted, were slain with the sword: they wandered about in sheepskins and goatskins; being destitute, afflicted, tormented" (Heb. 11:33-37).

In this world these heroes of faith were counted unworthy of life; but in heaven they are enrolled as sons of God, worthy of the highest honor. "They shall walk with me in white," Christ declares: "for they are worthy" (Rev. 3:4). In the courts of heaven there awaits them an "eternal weight of glory." "Wherefore seeing we also are compassed about with so great a cloud of witnesses, let us lay aside every weight, and the sin which doth so easily beset us, and let us run with patience the race that is set before us, looking unto Jesus the author and finisher of our faith" (Heb. 12:1). "Our light affliction, which is but for a moment, worketh for us a far more exceeding and eternal weight of glory; while we look not at the things which are seen, but at the things which are not seen: for the things which are seen are temporal; but the things which are not seen are eternal" (2 Cor. 4:17, 18).[21]

STRENGTH FOR TODAY

And I will bring the third part through the fire, and will refine them as silver is refined, and will try them as gold is tried: they shall call on my name, and I will hear them: I will say, It is my people: and they shall say, The Lord is my God. Zech. 13:9.

By trial the Lord proves the strength of His children. Is the heart strong to bear? Is the conscience void of offense? Does the Spirit bear witness with our spirit that we are the children of God? This the Lord ascertains by trying us. In the furnace of affliction He purifies us from all dross. He sends us trials, not to cause needless pain, but to lead us to look to Him, to strengthen our endurance, to teach us that if we do not rebel, but put our trust in Him, we shall see of His salvation. . . .

Christ's love for His children is as strong as it is tender. It is a love stronger than death, for He died for us. It is a love more true than that of a mother for her children. The mother's love may change, but Christ's love is changeless. "I am persuaded," Paul says, "that neither death, nor life, nor angels, nor principalities, nor powers, nor things present, nor things to come, nor height, nor depth, nor any other creature, shall be able to separate us from the love of God, which is in Christ Jesus our Lord" (Rom. 8:38, 39).

In every trial we have strong consolation. Is not our Saviour touched with the feeling of our infirmities? Has He not been tempted in all points like as we are? And has He not invited us to take every trial and perplexity to Him? Then let us not make ourselves miserable over tomorrow's burdens. Bravely and cheerfully carry the burdens of today. Today's trust and faith we must have. But we are not asked to live more than a day at a time. He who gives strength for today will give strength for tomorrow. . . .

Nothing wounds the soul like the sharp darts of unbelief. When trial comes, as it will, do not worry or complain. Silence in the soul makes more distinct the voice of God. "Then are they glad because they be quiet" (Ps. 107:30). Remember that underneath you are the everlasting arms. "Rest in the Lord, and wait patiently for him" (Ps. 37:7). He is guiding you into a harbor of gracious experience.[22]

269

WHEN FAITH IS TRIED

That the trial of your faith, being much more precious than of gold that perisheth, though it be tried with fire, might be found unto praise and honour and glory at the appearing of Jesus Christ. 1 Peter 1:7.

When we are brought into adverse circumstances, when our natural feelings are stirred, and we want to give vent to them, then our faith is tried; then we are to manifest the meekness and gentleness of Christ. Not by one word are we to give expression to the feelings of the natural heart. "If any man offend not in word, the same is a perfect man, and able also to bridle the whole body" (James 3:2)—the whole man. What we want is to be under the control of Jesus. We do not want our own way. I have heard some plead as an excuse for their wrong course, "You know that it is my temperament, it is my disposition, transmitted to me from my parents." Yes; and they have cultivated it and educated themselves in it and thus excused all their wrongdoing. Instead of yielding to temptation, they should lay hold upon the arm of Infinite Power, saying, "I will come to God just as I am, and plead with Christ to give me the victory. I shall be more than conqueror through Him that loved me."

In order to understand how great the love of Jesus is for you, look to Calvary. You can then know something of the depth, the breadth, and the height of that love, and you can see something of the condescension of God and the Lord Jesus Christ, as step by step the Saviour descended into the valley of humiliation. He did not stoop to sin, to defilement, but He stood on this atom of a world to battle with Satan and his host, and here to win for us an immortal inheritance, an inheritance which . . . fadeth not away.

When He ascended on high, and led captivity captive, and gave gifts unto men, He left the battle in our hands, but we are not to fight in our own strength; we should certainly fail if we attempted it. Christ is there present with the Father to bring to our help the unseen intelligences. . . . What we need is the simplicity of faith, the meekness and humility of Christ. Then we shall trust wholly in the Lord of heaven, and He will be at our right hand to help us.[23]

HEAVEN'S HONOR ROLL

But he knoweth the way that I take: when he hath tried me, I shall come forth as gold. Job 23:10.

The Christian who loves his heavenly Father may not discern by outward providences or visible signs any heavenly favor above that given those with little or no consecration. Often he is sorely afflicted, distressed, perplexed, and hedged in on every side. Appearances seem to be against him. . . .

Joseph was virtuous and his character was marked for true goodness and strength of purpose, yet he was maligned, persecuted, and dealt with as a criminal; but God had signal victories for Joseph, even as he appeared to suffer because of his rightdoing.

Daniel was cast into the lions' den because of his firm adherence to principle and his loyalty to God, but he triumphed in the end, and God was glorified through His servant whom He permitted to be humbled. Job was stripped of his earthly treasures, bereaved of his children, and made a spectacle of loathing to his friends, but in God's time He showed He had not forsaken His servant. . . .

A true and faithful Stephen was stoned to death by the enemies of Christ. Surely it did not appear that God was strengthening His cause in the earth by thus permitting wicked men to triumph, but from this very circumstance Paul was converted to the faith, and through his word thousands were brought to the light of the gospel.

A precious, affectionate John was an exile on the lonely Isle of Patmos, but here Jesus met with him and revealed to him events . . . stretching over the ages to the coming of Christ, and making known the counsel of the Lord for future ages. . . . He was permitted to look upon the throne of God and to behold the white-robed redeemed ones who had come out of great tribulation and washed their robes and made them white in the blood of the Lamb.[24]

If you are called to go through the fiery furnace for His sake, Jesus will be by your side even as He was with the faithful three in Babylon. Those who love their Redeemer will rejoice at every opportunity of sharing with Him humiliation and reproach. The love they bear their Lord makes suffering for His sake sweet.[25]

271

IN THE HOUR OF GRIEF

But though he cause grief, yet will he have compassion accord-ing to the multitude of his mercies. For he doth not afflict will-ingly nor grieve the children of men. Lam. 3:32, 33.

* We have drunk at the same cup of sorrow, but it was mingled with joy and rest and peace in Jesus. He doeth all things well. Our heavenly Father doth not willingly afflict and grieve the children of men. . . .

This world is the scene of our trials, our griefs, our sorrows. We are here to bear the test of God. The fire of the furnace is to kindle till our dross is consumed and we come forth as gold purified in the furnace of affliction. . . . Light will come out of this darkness which to you at times seems incomprehensible. "The Lord gave, and the Lord hath taken away; blessed be the name of the Lord" (Job 1:21). Let this be the language of your heart. The cloud of mercy is hovering over your head even in the darkest hour. God's benefits to us are as numerous as the drops of rain falling from the clouds upon the parched earth to water and refresh it. The mercy of God is over you.

Mary, dear precious child, is at rest. She was the companion of your sorrows and disappointed hopes. She will no more have grief or want or distress. Through faith's discerning eye you may anticipate, amid your sorrows and griefs and perplexities, your Mary with her mother and other members of your family answering the call of the Life-giver and coming forth from their prison house triumphing over death and the grave. Your faith may see the loved and the lost ones re-united among the redeemed of earth. You with them erelong, if faith-ful, will be walking in the streets of the New Jerusalem, singing the song of Moses and the Lamb, wearing the jeweled crown. . . .

"All things work together for good to them that love God" (Rom. 8:28). Could your eyes be opened, you would see your heav-enly Father bending over you in love; and could you hear His voice it would be in tones of compassion to you who are prostrate with suffer-ing and affliction. Stand fast in His strength; there is rest *for you.*[26]

---

* From a letter of comfort to one bereaved of his only daughter.

SWEETNESS THROUGH AFFLICTION

Who comforteth us in all our tribulation, that we may be able to comfort them which are in any trouble, by the comfort wherewith we ourselves are comforted of God. 2 Cor. 1:4.

Those who have borne the greatest sorrows are frequently the ones who carry the greatest comfort to others, bringing sunshine wherever they go. Such ones have been chastened and sweetened by their afflictions; they did not lose confidence in God when trouble assailed them, but clung closer to His protecting love. Such ones are living proof of the tender care of God, who makes the darkness as well as the light and chastens us for our good. Christ is the light of the world; in Him is no darkness. Precious light! Let us live in that light! Bid adieu to sadness and repining. Rejoice in the Lord always.[27]

It is selfish to devote our precious time to mourning over disappointed hopes, indulging in useless grief that clouds the family circle. We should be cheerful, if only for the benefit of those who depend more or less upon us for happiness. . . . It is our duty to make the best of everything, and to cultivate a habit of looking at the bright side of things. Let the cloud that shadows us pass over, while we wait patiently till the clear blue sky again appears and the blessed sunshine is revealed. . . . Let us all forget self as much as possible, cultivate cheerfulness, seek to brighten the lives of others, and we shall then have less desire to complain of our own lot.

The afflicted may take courage, the desponding may hope, for they have a sympathizing friend in Jesus. All our troubles and griefs we may pour into His sympathizing ears. When we associate together let it not be to talk darkness and unbelief, to recount the gloomy chapters in our life experience. Let us talk of the love of God that has been manifested to us, that is seen in nature, in the firmament of the heavens, in all the wise arrangements of Providence. Let us search out the rays of sunshine that have brightened our pathway, and linger over their memory with grateful hearts. Let us dwell upon the matchless love of Christ, for in Him we have a constant theme of rejoicing. In Him is no darkness. He is the Light of life, the Chief among ten thousand, and the One altogether lovely.[28]

CLOUDS WILL PASS

A merry heart maketh a cheerful countenance: but by sorrow of heart the spirit is broken. **Prov. 15:13.**

Sorrow comes and goes; it is the lot of man; we should not seek to magnify it, but rather dwell upon that which is bright and pleasant. When winter spreads its icy covering over the earth, we do not let our gladness freeze up with the flowers and brooks and continually mourn because of the dismal days and the chilling winds. On the other hand, we reach forward in imagination to the coming summer, with its warmth and life and beauty. Meanwhile we enjoy all the sunshine that comes to us, and find much comfort, in spite of the cold and snow, while we are waiting for nature to put on her fresh, bright garments of rejoicing.

Just now a cloud has shut from our sight the bright rays of the sun, and we are left in the shadow. Should we fret and repine because of this, and forget everything else that is bright and lovely around us? No; we should forget the *cloud* and remember that the sun is not blotted out, but has only veiled its face for a moment, to shine forth again in greater apparent brightness and to be prized and enjoyed more highly than if it had never been hidden.

God is not pleased to have us pass our lives in despondency and gloom, magnifying every trouble that visits us. By so doing we not only make ourselves miserable but cloud the happiness of those around us. We should not search out and linger over the dark shadows in our life experience, but rather open our eyes and arouse our senses to see and appreciate the many blessings surrounding us, which should make us not only grateful but very happy.

It is God's will that we should be cheerful. He would have us open our hearts to the sunbeams of heaven; He would have our spirits mellowed by His love and goodness, apparent in our own lives and in the things of nature surrounding us. Those who are brought in contact with us are affected for good or evil by our words and actions. We are unconsciously diffusing the fragrance of our character upon the moral atmosphere surrounding us or we are poisoning that atmosphere by thoughts, words, and deeds which have a deleterious influence.[20]

JESUS LIGHTS THE WAY

Casting all your care upon him; for he careth for you.
1 Peter 5:7.

Do not take your troubles to human beings. Take them to the Lord. You may think that others ought to sympathize with you in your trials, but you will sometimes be disappointed. Jesus never disappoints the one who comes to Him for help. He is saying to you today, "Come unto me, . . . and I will give you rest" (Matt. 11:28). He will give you *rest* in Him. No one who comes to Him goes away unhelped. Take your burdens to the divine Burden Bearer and leave them with Him, knowing that He will carry them for you. . . .

Act your part in helping yourselves, as all must do who would be blessed. Do not dwell upon the hardships of the Christian life. Do not talk of your trials. . . . Do not utter one despondent word, for such words please Satan. Talk of Christ's goodness and tell of His power. Words of hope and trust and courage are as easily spoken as words of complaint. . . .

When the enemy tells you that the Lord has forsaken you, tell him that you know He has not; for He declares, "I will never leave thee, nor forsake thee" (Heb. 13:5). Dismiss the enemy. Tell him you will not dishonor the Lord by doubting His love. . . .

There is no limit to the help that the Saviour is willing to bestow on us. He asks us to bring into our lives the grace that will keep us from sin. From the cross of Calvary there comes to us liberty, hope, and strength. Do not dishonor your Redeemer by doubting His power. Trust Him all the time. Take hold of the riches of His grace, saying, "I will believe; I do believe that Jesus died for me." The way before you may seem dark, but Jesus can make it light.

Be joyful in God. Christ is light and in Him is no darkness at all. Look toward the light. Accustom yourselves to speak the praise of God. Make others happy. This is your first work. It will strengthen the best traits of character. Throw the windows of the soul wide open heavenward and let the sunshine of Christ's righteousness in. Morning, noon, and night your hearts may be filled with the bright rays of heaven's light.[30]

275

I PRESS TOWARD THE MARK

Brethren, I count not myself to have apprehended: but this one thing I do, forgetting those things which are behind, and reaching forth unto those things which are before, I press toward the mark for the prize of the high calling of God in Christ Jesus. Phil. 3:13, 14.

In the heavenly race we can all run and all receive the prize. There is no uncertainty, no risk, in the matter. We must put on the heavenly graces, and with the eye directed upward to the crown of immortality, keep the Pattern ever before us. . . . The humble, self-denying life of our divine Lord we are to keep constantly in view. And then as we seek to imitate Him, keeping our eye upon the mark of the prize, we can run this race with certainty, knowing that if we do the very best we can we shall certainly secure the prize. . . .

When we have this great inducement before us cannot we "run with patience the race that is set before us, looking unto Jesus the author and finisher of our faith" (Heb. 12:1, 2)? He has pointed out the way for us, and marked it all along by His own footsteps.[31]

In order to fight successfully the battle against sin, you must keep close to Jesus. Do not talk unbelief; you have no excuse for doing this. Christ has made a complete sacrifice for you, that you might stand before God complete in Him. God is not pleased with our lack of faith. Unbelief always separates the soul from Christ.

It is not praiseworthy to talk of our weakness and discouragement. Let each one say, "I am grieved that I yield to temptation, that my prayers are so feeble, my faith so weak. I have no excuse to plead for being dwarfed in my religious life. But I am seeking to obtain completeness of character in Christ. I have sinned, and yet I love Jesus. I have fallen many times, and yet He has reached out His hand to save me. I have told Him all about my mistakes. I have confessed with shame and sorrow that I have dishonored Him. I have looked to the cross, and have said, All this He suffered for me. The Holy Spirit has shown me my ingratitude, my sin, in putting Christ to open shame. He who knows no sin has forgiven me. He calls me to a higher, nobler life, and I press on to the things that are before."[32]

"BE STRONG"

Watch ye, stand fast in the faith, quit you like men, be strong.
1 Cor. 16:13.

Let all bear in mind that the Christian ministration is not a work for drones. God calls for men who will do and dare danger. Hold no parleying with Satan, but meet him with "It is written." "Quit you like men, be strong." Faith alone, unfeigned, can be the basis of our actions and prove by a clean, pure example that it is possible to be active, "Not slothful in business; fervent in spirit; serving the Lord" (Rom. 12:11), and then all commercial enterprises will be conducted on Bible principles. . . .

We wish to repeat over and over again, until it is indelibly imprinted upon the heart, the blessed invitation, Abide in Me. Read the Word, and in the light of a "Thus saith the Lord," meditate upon it. Pray until the lesson and meaning of *abiding in* is fully learned, accompanied with its claims and its promises. The Holy Spirit, Christ's representative, is now in our world to bring all things to our remembrance, that His claims shall not be forgotten or neglected. Read the Word and pray. Meditate on the Scriptures until the understanding, the gate to the door to the heart, is opened to comprehend its requirements and our dependence. Those who will wait to hear what the Spirit saith unto them shall not hear in vain. Fix the eye upon Christ alone in quiet waiting upon Him to hear His voice saying, "Abide in me, and I in you." . . .

There are many who come to the Saviour in a feeble way. They receive baptism and yet there is no apparent change in their character. We would invite all to come, all to abide in Christ, to advance daily in the perfection of character by abiding in Christ. As they do this, they find that rest that can come only through perfect obedience.

But I warn you, be careful how you settle down in the middle walk between spirituality and worldliness. "Ye cannot serve God and mammon" (Matt. 6:24). You will be wholly on one side or the other. . . . Christ draws to His side; Satan hangs out every attraction to draw on his side. Whom will you choose? Under whose banner will you stand? [33]

OVERCOMING POWER

And they overcame him by the blood of the Lamb, and by the word of their testimony; and they loved not their lives unto the death. Rev. 12:11.

The Saviour watches with a deep interest over the human family. When He ascended to the Father, He did not leave His followers without help. In His earthly life He overcame in their behalf, and they are to overcome in His strength. All have trials to meet. There are the old natural temperaments to contend with; but these temperaments are to be brought into subjection to Jesus Christ, that we may stand on vantage ground with God. . . .

The crown of glory will be placed on the brow of all who have overcome temptation by the blood of the Lamb and the word of their testimony. This word of our testimony means a great deal. It is before all the heavenly universe and before the world. The soul who dishonors God by his words and works, who does not acknowledge Christ as his Saviour, places himself on the losing side. . . .

Jesus is your helper. No one understands so well as He your peculiarities of character. He is watching over you, and if you are willing to be taught, He will throw around you influences for good that will enable you to accomplish all His will for you. We are preparing for the future eternal life. Soon there is to be a grand review, in which every soul who is seeking to perfect a Christian character must bear the test of God's searching questions: Have you set an example that others are safe in following? Have you watched for souls as they that must give an account? The heavenly host are . . . intensely anxious that you should bear the test. . . .

The Lord looks with deepest interest upon each striving soul. He loves each one. Did He not, He never would have given His only-begotten Son to die for us. . . .

The Lord will help all who will do their best, walking humbly with God. Let us be encouraged in believing that we have a mighty arm to lean upon, and that so long as we rely upon Christ's strength we cannot dishonor God. We are on trial now, but under every test let us make it manifest to all around us that we are on the Lord's side.[34]

278

WE MAY TRIUMPH GLORIOUSLY

These things I have spoken unto you, that in me ye might have peace. In the world ye shall have tribulation: but be of good cheer; I have overcome the world. John 16:33.

"These things have I spoken unto you," the Saviour said, "that my joy might remain in you, and that your joy might be full" (John 15: 11). The work of overcoming is not a joyless work; no, indeed. It means communication with Heaven. You can go to God in prayer; you can ask, and receive; you can believe, hanging your helpless soul on Christ. It means that humanity can work the will and ways of God. Humanity and divinity are combined for this very purpose.[35]

God sends trials to prove who will stand faithful under temptation. He brings us into trying positions to see if we will trust in a power out of and above ourselves. Everyone has undiscovered traits of character that must come to light through trial. God allows those who are self-sufficient to be sorely tempted that they may understand their helplessness. He suffers the deep waters of affliction to go over our souls, in order that we may know Him and Jesus Christ whom He has sent, in order that we may have deep heart longings to be cleansed from defilement, and may come forth from the trial purer, holier, happier. Often we enter the furnace of affliction with our souls darkened with selfishness; but if patient under the crucial test, we shall come forth reflecting the divine character. When His purpose in the affliction is accomplished "he shall bring forth thy righteousness as the light, and thy judgment as the noonday" (Ps. 37:6).

"Watch ye and pray, lest ye enter into temptation" (Mark 14:38). Watch against the stealthy approach of the enemy, watch against old habits and natural inclinations, lest they assert themselves; force them back, and watch. Watch the thoughts, watch the plans, lest they become self-centered. Watch over the souls that Christ has purchased with His own blood. Watch for opportunities to do them good.[36]

A great crisis is just before us. To meet its trials and temptations and to perform its duties will require persevering faith. But we may triumph gloriously; not one watching, praying, believing soul will be ensnared by the enemy.[38]

279

THE OVERCOMER'S REWARD

*He that overcometh shall inherit all things; and I will be his
God, and he shall be my son.* Rev. 21:7.

We do not realize how near is the end of all things. We do not
sense as we should the need of being daily overcomers and of securing
the eternal reward. It is those who overcome the temptations that are
in the world through lust who are partakers of the divine nature. The
sacrifice has been made for us. Will we accept it? . . . .

It requires prayer, it requires faith, it requires understanding, to
become a partaker of the divine nature. But as we obtain this experience we are not benefiting ourselves alone; we are giving to all around
us an evidence that all may be partakers of the divine nature, all may
be overcomers.

Let us determine to be victorious. Let us seek for a large measure
of divine grace. . . . Let us not be swayed by the elements of the
world, but let us show that we are determined to become overcomers
day by day and hour by hour. . . . Let us represent Christ and the truth
wherever we go, that we may . . . glorify God. My brethren and sisters,
Jesus loves to make intercession for you. Cling to Jesus. Strive to be
overcomers, that the Saviour may welcome you to the city of God,
where you can sing the triumphs of redeeming grace.

O what a scene of rejoicing it will be when the Lamb of God shall
place upon the heads of the redeemed the victor's crown! Never,
never more will you be led into temptation and sin. You will see the
King in His beauty. And those whom you have helped heavenward
will meet you there. They will throw their arms about you and acknowledge what you have done for them. "You watched over me,"
they will say; "you prayed for me; you helped me to gain heaven." . . .

Let us go forward in the strength of the Mighty One, considering
the joy that is set before us of seeing His face in the kingdom of God
and of going out no more forever. Let us remember that we are to
be partakers of the divine nature, and that angels of God are right
around us, that we need not be overcome by sin. Let us send our petitions to the throne of God in time of temptation, and in faith lay
hold of His divine power.[37]

GOD'S CHURCH ON EARTH

Ye also, as lively stones, are built up a spiritual house, an holy priesthood, to offer up spiritual sacrifices, acceptable to God by Jesus Christ. 1 **Peter** 2:5.

The church on earth is God's temple, and it is to assume divine proportions before the world. This building is to be the light of the world. It is to be composed of living stones laid close together, stone fitting to stone, making a solid building. All these stones are not of the same shape or dimension. Some are large and some are small, but each one has its own place to fill. In the whole building there is not to be one misshapen stone. Each one is perfect. And each stone is a living stone, a stone that emits light. The value of the stones is determined by the light they reflect to the world.

Now is the time for the stones to be taken from the quarry of the world and brought into God's workshop, to be hewed, squared, and polished, that they may shine. This is God's plan, and He desires all who profess to believe the truth to fill their respective places in the great, grand work for this time.[1]

The angelic architect has brought his golden measuring rod from heaven, that every stone may be hewed and squared by the divine measurement, and polished to shine as an emblem of heaven, radiating in all directions the bright, clear beams of the Sun of Righteousness.[2]

In this world we are to shine in good works. The Lord requires His people . . . to reflect the light of God's character, God's love, as Christ reflected it. As we look unto Jesus, all our lives will be aglow with that wondrous light. Every part of us is to be light; then whichever way we turn, light will be reflected from us to others. Christ is the way, the truth, and the life. In Him is no darkness at all; therefore, if we are in Christ, there will be no darkness in us.[3]

The church on earth is to become the court of holy love. . . . Christian fellowship is one means by which character is formed. Thus selfishness is purged from the life, and men and women are drawn to Christ, the great center. Thus is answered His prayer that His followers may be one as He is one with the Father.[4]

MEMBERS OF GOD'S HOUSEHOLD

Now therefore ye are no more strangers and foreigners, but fellowcitizens with the saints, and of the household of God; and are built upon the foundation of the apostles and prophets, Jesus Christ himself being the chief corner stone. Eph. 2:19, 20.

The Lord Jesus is making experiments on human hearts through the exhibition of His mercy and abundant grace. He is effecting transformations so amazing that Satan . . . stands viewing them as a fortress impregnable to his sophistries and delusions. They are to him an incomprehensible mystery. The angels of God . . . look on with astonishment and joy, that fallen men, once children of wrath, are through the training of Christ developing characters after the divine similitude, to be sons and daughters of God, to act an important part in the occupations and pleasures of heaven.[5]

The Lord has provided His church with capabilities and blessings, that they may present to the world an image of His own sufficiency, and that His church may be complete in Him, a continual representation of another, even the eternal world, of laws that are higher than earthly laws. His church is to be a temple built after the divine similitude. . . .

To His church, Christ has given ample facilities, that He may receive a large revenue of glory from His redeemed, purchased possession. The church, being endowed with the righteousness of Christ, is His depository, in which the wealth of His mercy, His love, His grace, is to appear in full and final display. The declaration in His intercessory prayer, that the Father's love is as great toward us as toward Himself, the only-begotten Son, and that we shall be with Him where He is, forever one with Christ and the Father, is a marvel to the heavenly host, and it is their great joy. The gift of His Holy Spirit, rich, full, and abundant, is to be to His church as an encompassing wall of fire, which the powers of hell shall not prevail against. In their untainted purity and spotless perfection, Christ looks upon His people as the reward of all His suffering, His humiliation, and His love, and the supplement of His glory—Christ, the great center from which radiates all glory.[6]

OBJECT OF GOD'S TENDEREST CARE

In whom all the building fitly framed together groweth unto an holy temple in the Lord: in whom ye also are builded together for an habitation of God through the Spirit. Eph. 2:21, 22.

The living church of God is individually a habitation of God through the Spirit, that man may become a well-built temple for the indwelling of the Holy Spirit of God, that the Lord Jesus Christ may dwell in his innermost being, ennobling and sanctifying his human nature by His divine attributes.[7]

The church of Christ is to be in the world but not of the world. In calling His people together in church capacity, God designs that they shall form one Christian family and daily be fitting for membership in the family above.

God thus forms the believers in His Word in one body, that their influence may be a blessing to one another and to the world. Each member converted reveals a transformation of character, and he is strengthened and sustained by the courage and faith of the whole. The weakest saint, if he believes in Christ, is a member of Christ's body; and if he lives in humble dependence upon God, he will become strong; for he has a right to all the privileges of a child of God.[8]

The church is the object of God's tenderest love and care. If the members will allow Him, He will reveal His character through them. He says to them, "Ye are the light of the world." Those who walk and talk with God practice the gentleness of Christ. In their lives, forbearance, meekness, and self-restraint are united with holy earnestness and diligence. As they advance heavenward, the sharp, rough edges of character are worn off, and godliness is seen. The Holy Spirit, full of grace and power, works upon mind and heart.[9]

Christ has made provision that His church shall be a transformed body illumined with the light of heaven, possessing the glory of Immanuel. It is His purpose that every Christian shall be surrounded with a spiritual atmosphere of light and peace.

There is no limit to the usefulness of the one who, putting self aside, makes room for the working of the Holy Spirit upon the heart and lives a life wholly consecrated to God.[10]

"THE APPLE OF HIS EYE"

For thus saith the Lord of hosts; After the glory hath he sent me unto the nations which spoiled you: for he that toucheth you toucheth the apple of his eye. Zech. 2:8.

The church of Christ, enfeebled and defective as it may be, is the only object on earth on which He bestows His supreme regard. . . . The Lord has a people, a chosen people, His church, to be His own, His own fortress, which He holds in a sin-stricken, revolted world.[11]

The church is the property of God, and God constantly remembers her as she stands in the world, subject to the temptations of Satan. Christ has never forgotten the days of His humiliation. In passing from the scenes of His humiliation, Jesus has lost none of His humanity. He has the same tender, pitying love, and is ever touched with human woe. He ever bears in mind that He was a Man of Sorrows and acquainted with grief. He forgets not His representative people who are striving to uphold His downtrodden law. He knows that the world that hated Him, hates them. Although Jesus Christ has passed into the heavens, there is still a living chain binding His believing ones to His own heart of infinite love. The most lowly and weak are bound by a chain of sympathy closely to His heart. He never forgets that He is our representative, that He bears our nature.

Jesus sees His true church on the earth, whose greatest ambition is to cooperate with Him in the grand work of saving souls. He hears their prayers, presented in contrition and power, and Omnipotence cannot resist their plea for the salvation of any tried, tempted member of Christ's body. . . . Jesus ever liveth to make intercession for us. Through our Redeemer what blessings may not the true believer receive? The church, soon to enter upon her most severe conflict, will be the object most dear to God upon earth.

The confederacy of evil will be stirred with power from beneath, and Satan will cast all the reproach possible upon the chosen ones whom he cannot deceive and delude with his satanic inventions and falsehoods. But exalted "to be a Prince and a Saviour, . . ." (Acts 5:31), will Christ, our representative and head, close His heart, or withdraw His hand, or falsify His promise? No; never, never.[12]

FITTING UP FOR HEAVEN'S MANSIONS

That he might present it to himself a glorious church, not having spot, or wrinkle, or any such thing; but that it should be holy and without blemish. **Eph. 5:27.**

Christ is soon coming in the clouds of heaven, and we must be prepared to meet Him, not having spot or wrinkle or any such thing. . . . The converting power of God must be upon our hearts. We must study the life of Christ, and imitate the divine Pattern. We must dwell upon the perfection of His character, and be changed into His image. No one will enter the kingdom of God unless his will is brought into captivity to the will of Christ.[13]

Professed Christians keep altogether too near the lowlands of earth. Their eyes are trained to see only commonplace things, and their minds dwell upon the things their eyes behold. Their religious experience is often shallow and unsatisfying, and their words are light and valueless. How can such reflect the image of Christ? How can they send forth the bright beams of the Sun of Righteousness? . . .

Heaven is free from all sin, from all defilement and impurity; and if we would live in its atmosphere, if we would behold the glory of Christ, we must be pure in heart, perfect in character through His grace and righteousness. We must not be taken up with pleasure and amusement, but be fitting up for the glorious mansions Christ has gone to prepare for us. . . .

Christ is soon coming in glory; and when His majesty is revealed, the world will wish that they had His favor. At that time we shall all desire a place in the mansions of heaven; but those who do not confess Christ now in word, in life, in character, cannot expect that He will confess them then before His Father and the holy angels. . . .

Oh, how happy will those be who have made themselves ready for the marriage supper of the Lamb, who are robed in the righteousness of Christ, and reflect His lovely image! They will have on the pure white linen which is the righteousness of the saints, and Christ will lead them by the side of living waters; God will wipe away all tears from their eyes, and they will have the life that runs parallel with the life of God.[13]

LOYAL TO THE FAMILY NAME

For as many of you as have been baptized into Christ have put on Christ. Gal. 3:27.

Those who take the name of Christian pledge themselves to be true to God. They are bound up with Him and the heavenly angels in family relation. . . . Their actions in every respect are to be such as become saints. All that is unbecoming is to be discarded. They are to live a new and holy life. . . .

Like a brave soldier you are to obey your Captain's orders, even if in so doing you sacrifice your life. . . . Mind and body are now to be treated with the greatest respect, for they are Christ's. Day by day they are to be improved, that to the earnest gaze of the heavenly angels they may reveal that Christ has not died for you in vain.

When you took the name of Christian you promised in this life to prepare for the higher life in the kingdom of God. To be a Christian means to be Christlike. Not a satanic feature is to remain on mind or body, which are to reveal comeliness, purity, integrity, and dignity. Take the Christlife as your pattern. Keep eternity before your view. Then you will in some degree approach Christ's appreciation of the heritage which cost Him so much.

Let those who work for Christ keep their principles pure. Let the life be untainted by any polluting practice. All heaven is interested in the restoration of the moral image of God in man. All heaven is working to this end. God and the holy angels have an intense desire that human beings shall reach the standard of perfection which Christ died to make it possible for them to reach. It is His desire that we shall be one with Christ, complete in Christ, that we shall be heirs of heaven; but we are left free to choose. God calls upon us to make our choice on the right side, to connect with heavenly agencies, to adopt principles which have a reviving, restoring influence, which will restore in us the moral image lost through disobedience. As by faith we adopt the principles which characterize the life of Christ, they are in the soul as a well of water, springing up unto everlasting life. The soul overflows with the riches of the grace of Christ, and this overflow refreshes other souls.[14]

A RELATIONSHIP OF INTERDEPENDENCE

And whether one member suffer, all the members suffer with it; or one member be honoured, all the members rejoice with it. Now ye are the body of Christ, and members in particular. 1 Cor. 12:26, 27.

In the Lord's plan human beings have been made necessary to one another. To every one God has entrusted talents, to be used in helping others to walk in the path of right. It is by unselfish service for others that we improve and increase our talents.

Like the different parts of a machine, all are closely related to one another, and all dependent upon one great Center. There is to be unity in diversity. No member of the Lord's firm can work successfully in independence. Each is to work under the supervision of God; all are to use their entrusted capabilities in His service, that each may minister to the perfection of the whole. . . .

He who claims to be a Christian should examine himself and see if he is as kind and considerate of his fellow beings as he desires his fellow beings to be of him. . . . Christ taught that rank or wealth should make no difference in our treatment of one another and that in the light of heaven all are brethren. Earthly possessions or worldly honor do not count in God's valuation of man. He created all men equal; He is no respecter of persons. He values a man according to the virtue of his character.

To possess true godliness means to love one another, to help one another, to make apparent the religion of Jesus in our lives. We are to be consecrated channels through which the love of Christ flows to those who need help. . . . He who approaches nearest to obedience to the divine law will be of the most service to God. He who follows Christ, reaching out after His goodness, His compassion, His love for the human family, will be accepted by God as a worker together with Him. . . .

When the Lord's people are filled with meekness and tenderness for one another, they will realize that His banner over them is love and His fruit will be sweet to their taste. Heaven will begin on earth. They will make a heaven below in which to prepare for heaven above.[15]

ONE BROTHERHOOD

Who shall not fear thee, O Lord, and glorify thy name? for thou only art holy: for all nations shall come and worship before thee; for thy judgments are made manifest. Rev. 15:4.

Christ would have us realize that our interests are one. A divine Saviour died for all, that all might find in Him their divine source. In Christ Jesus we are one. By the utterance of one name, "Our Father," we are lifted to the same rank. We become members of the royal family, children of the heavenly King. His principles of truth bind heart to heart, be they rich or poor, high or low.

When the Holy Spirit moves upon human minds all petty complaints and accusations between man and his fellow man will be put away. The bright beams of the Sun of Righteousness will shine into the chambers of the mind and heart. In our worship of God there will be no distinction between rich and poor, white and black. All prejudice will be melted away. When we approach God it will be as one brotherhood. We are pilgrims and strangers, bound for a better country, even a heavenly. There all pride, all accusation, all self-deception, will forever have an end. Every mask will be laid aside, and we shall "see him as he is." [16]

Our house of worship may be very humble, but it is none the less acknowledged by God. If we worship in spirit and in truth and in the beauty of holiness, it will be to us the very gate of heaven. As lessons of the wondrous works of God are repeated, and as the heart's gratitude is expressed in prayer and song, angels from heaven take up the strain and unite in praise and thanksgiving to God. These exercises drive back the power of Satan. They expel murmurings and complainings, and Satan loses ground.

God teaches us that we should assemble in His house to cultivate the attributes of perfect love. This will fit the dwellers of earth for the mansions Christ has gone to prepare for those who love Him, where, from Sabbath to Sabbath, from one new moon to another, they will assemble in the sanctuary to unite in loftier strains of song, in thanksgiving and praise to Him that sitteth upon the throne and to the Lamb forever and ever. [16]

HELPING ONE ANOTHER

But speaking the truth in love, may grow up into him in all things, which is the head, even Christ. Eph. 4:15.

I wish we could have a pledge in our hearts that we would not utter one word against a brother or a sister. Remember that they also are tempted, it may be more strongly than you. . . . Those who are really the most erring are in greatest need of your help. Do not gossip about them and make remarks about their character, but go to them in the love of Jesus and the love of the truth and try to help them. . . .

When you are troubled with doubts, and darkness compasses your own soul, the very best course you can pursue to get out of this darkness is to help someone else who is discouraged. As you try to lift others up, behold, you lift up yourself into close connection with God. As you show kindness to others you will help yourself, for the same will be reflected back upon you. The man who has the most of Christ in the soul will manifest the tenderest sympathy for the souls who need help. . . .

You will always have erring ones among you, and here is where you can show a Christian character. Do not push them away from you, but if you have light seek to let it shine upon them, and in this way you can help them toward heaven. Every soul that has the spirit of Christ will work the works of Christ. And if any see one wandering away from Christ, he will feel as Christ did about the lost sheep. There were ninety and nine in the fold, but He went out after the one that had strayed away. This is the spirit we should manifest. As children of God we should walk in the light, and as we follow in the light we shall lighten the path for others. Let us cultivate gratitude to God and then we shall not get our eyes upon little difficulties. And although our brethren and sisters may err, shall we err? We have faults, as well as they, and we want compassion, as well as they; we should have compassion for one another.

"Let the word of Christ dwell in you richly in all wisdom; teaching and admonishing one another in psalms and hymns and spiritual songs, singing with grace in your hearts to the Lord" (Col. 3:16). Here is the privilege of the Christian.[17]

LIVING BY THE GOLDEN RULE

Judge not, and ye shall not be judged: condemn not, and ye shall not be condemned: forgive, and ye shall be forgiven. Luke 6:37.

The duty of every Christian is plainly outlined in the words: "Judge not, and ye shall not be judged: condemn not, and ye shall not be condemned: forgive, and ye shall be forgiven: give, and it shall be given unto you; good measure, pressed down, and shaken together, and running over." "As ye would that men should do to you, do ye also to them likewise" (verses 37, 38, 31). These are the principles that we shall do well to cherish. . . .

Let not those who themselves have sinned against God refuse to forgive a repentant sinner. Just as they deal with a fellow being who in spirit or in action has done wrong and has afterward repented, so God will deal with them for their defects of character. He who does not show mercy to his fellow men cannot expect to be shielded by the mercy of God. He himself is dependent on the mercy that God has enjoined him to exercise in seeking to restore every unsaved soul brought within the sphere of his influence. If he refuses to cultivate this divine grace, he himself will suffer the result of his neglect. . . .

We should remember that all make mistakes; even men and women who have had years of experience sometimes err. But God does not cast them off because of their errors; to every erring son and daughter of Adam He gives the privilege of another trial. The true follower of Jesus manifests a Christlike spirit toward his erring brother. Instead of speaking in condemnation, he remembers the words, "He which converteth the sinner from the error of his way shall save a soul from death, and shall hide a multitude of sins" (James 5:20).

In the church militant men will be ever in need of restoration from the results of sin. The one who in some respects is superior to another is in other respects inferior to him. Every human being is subject to temptation and in need of brotherly interest and sympathy. The exercise of mercy in our daily relations with one another is one of the most effective means of attaining perfection of character, for only those who walk with Christ can be truly merciful.[18]

HELP FOR THE ERRING

Brethren, if a man be overtaken in a fault, ye which are spiritual, restore such an one in the spirit of meekness; considering thyself, lest thou also be tempted. Gal. 6:1.

God is love, God is life. It is the prerogative of God to redeem, reconstruct, and restore. Before the foundation of the world the Son of God was given to die, and redemption is the mystery that was "kept in silence through time eternal" (Rom. 16:25, R.V.). Yet sin is unexplainable, and no reason can be found for its existence. No soul knows what God is until he sees himself a sinner in the light from the cross of Calvary; but when in his great need he cries out for a sin-pardoning Saviour, God is revealed to him as gracious and merciful, long-suffering, and abundant in goodness and truth. The work of Christ is to redeem, to restore, to seek and to save that which was lost. If we are connected with Christ, we also are partakers of the divine nature and are to be laborers together with God. We are to bind up the bruised and wounded soul; and if a brother or a sister has erred, we are not to join with the enemy in destroying and ruining, but to work with Christ to restore such a one in the spirit of meekness.

The foundation of our hope in Christ is the fact that we recognize ourselves as sinners in need of restoration and redemption. It is because we are sinners that we have courage to claim Him as our Saviour. Then let us take heed lest we deal with the erring in a way that would say to others that we have no need of redemption. Let us not denounce, condemn, and destroy as though we were faultless. It is the work of Christ to mend, to heal, to restore. God is love. . . . He . . . gives Satan no occasion for triumphing by making the worst appear or by exposing our weaknesses to our enemies.[19]

Christ came to bring salvation within the reach of all. . . . The most erring, the most sinful, were not passed by; His labors were especially for those who most needed the salvation He came to bring. The greater their need of reform, the deeper was His interest, the greater His sympathy, and the more earnest His labors. His great heart of love was stirred to its depths for the ones whose condition was most hopeless and who most needed His transforming grace.[20]

DEALING WITH EVIL REPORTS

Moreover if thy brother shall trespass against thee, go and tell him his fault between thee and him alone: if he shall hear thee, thou hast gained thy brother. Matt. 18:15.

"Above all things," the apostle writes, "have fervent charity among yourselves" (1 Peter 4:8). Do not listen to reports against a brother or a sister. Be very cautious how you take up a reproach against your neighbor. Ask the one who brings the accusation if he has obeyed the word of God in regard to this matter. Christ has left explicit directions as to what should be done. Go to your brother and tell him his fault between him and you alone. Do not excuse yourself from this, saying, There is no personal grievance between the one who is accused and myself. The rules given by Christ are so definite, so explicit, that this excuse is not valid.

Whether or not the grievance is between you and the one accused, the injunction of Christ is the same. Your brother needs help. Tell him, not someone else, that reports are being circulated about him. Give him opportunity to explain. It is possible that the reports are false and that the difficulties may be adjusted by some simple explanation. This treatment is due every one supposed to be in error.[21]

Paul says, "If a man be overtaken in a fault, ye which are spiritual, restore such an one in the spirit of meekness; considering thyself, lest thou also be tempted" (Gal. 6:1). . . . These words are the injunction of Heaven, and they are to be brought into the daily practice. If one is at fault, instead of telling someone else of this, go to the one you think to be in error, and tenderly and respectfully, as you would wish to be treated were you in his place, tell him of his mistake. If he is not told of his fault, but instead there are surmisings among others, and no effort is made to save the erring one by telling him of his danger, how will God look upon those who do this cruel work?

God declares, "There is none righteous, no, not one" (Rom 3:10). All have the same sinful nature. All are liable to make mistakes. No one is perfect. The Lord Jesus died for the erring that they might be forgiven. It is not our work to condemn. Christ did not come to condemn, but to save.[21]

"HAVE FERVENT CHARITY"

*And above all things have fervent charity among yourselves:
for charity shall cover the multitude of sins.* 1 **Peter** 4:8.

Followers of Christ will not exhibit characteristics that are cheap
and selfish, but in word, spirit, and action they will reveal the tenderness of Christ. . . . A domineering, overbearing spirit is not of God
and should not be exercised toward believers or unbelievers, however
lowly may be their station. Christians are required to represent Christ
in all their dealings with those for whom He has given His precious
life. . . .

He who continually beholds Christ will make it manifest in his
spirit, in his words, in his course of action. He will not crowd anyone,
will not push tried souls into stronger temptation or indifferently leave
them on Satan's battleground. He will reach out a hand to help and
seek to draw souls upward and heavenward. As a laborer together
with God he will see to it that the feet of the tempted ones are firmly
planted on the Rock of Ages. . . .

There is no limit to the forgiving love of Christ. . . . We should
let those who are in danger understand that we appreciate them, that
we are not willing to give them up. Speak to them, pray with them,
and exhort them in love. . . .

The religion of the Bible is to guide the conduct of everyone
who sincerely believes in Christ. The Bible must guide us in our dealings in daily life. We may make a profession of being followers of
Christ, and yet if we are not doers of His Word we shall be like the
counterfeit coin. We shall not have the right ring. Everyone of us is
a member of the human family. We owe it to God to love Him, to
manifest affection for Him in our ways and words. We owe it to every
member of the human family, whether black or white, high or low,
to treat him with kindness and to manifest interest for his soul. As
members of one family we are all brethren. . . .

Children of God are citizens of heaven. They are the purchase of
the Son of God, His blood-bought family. Every soul is precious in His
sight, more precious than fine gold, even the golden wedge of Ophir.[22]

293

STRENGTH FOR THE WEAK

Be watchful, and strengthen the things which remain, that are ready to die: for I have not found thy works perfect before God. Rev. 3:2.

There are many ready to die spiritually, and the Lord calls upon us to strengthen them. God's people are to be firmly united in the bonds of Christian fellowship and are to be strengthened in the faith by speaking often to one another about the precious truths entrusted to them. . . .

There is spiritual power for all who will seek for it with intensity of purpose. These will become partakers of the divine nature, for they have cooperated with God. Influence will be given them, to be increased by a right use. They will be given an enlargement of power proportionate to their desire to do the will of God. . . .

Jesus declares that the Father is more willing to give the Holy Spirit to those who ask Him than parents are to give good gifts to their children. The Holy Spirit understands man's every necessity. He will bestow upon the earnest seeker that for which he hungers and thirsts. The blessings that God has to bestow are unlimited. We cannot comprehend their height and depth and breadth. All heaven is at the command of those who, realizing their lack of wisdom, come directly to the source of wisdom. To such ones God gives liberally and upbraids not. But let them ask in faith, nothing wavering. . . . The one who receives wisdom from on high is the one who holds fast to the promise, the one who feels his need, and will not be turned aside. . . .

"Thou hast a few names even in Sardis which have not defiled their garments; and they shall walk with me in white: for they are worthy" (verse 4). Because of their faith this honor is bestowed on them. In this life they did not boast, nor lift up their souls unto vanity. With intensity of desire, with a pure, holy faith, they grasped the promise of eternal riches. Their one desire was to be like Christ. Ever they kept the standard of righteousness uplifted. To them is given an eternal weight of glory, because on the earth they walked with God, keeping themselves unspotted from the world, revealing to their fellow beings the righteousness of Christ.[23]

A HELPING HAND FOR THE DESPAIRING

Brethren, if any of you do err from the truth, and one convert him; let him know, that he which converteth the sinner from the error of his way, shall save a soul from death, and shall hide a multitude of sins. James 5:19, 20.

There are many who err and who feel their shame and folly. They look upon their mistakes and errors until they are driven almost to desperation. These souls we are not to neglect. When one has to swim against the stream, there is all the force of the current driving him back. Let a helping hand then be held out to him as was the Elder Brother's hand to the sinking Peter. Speak to him hopeful words. . . .

Thy brother, sick in spirit, needs thee as thou thyself has needed a brother's love. He needs the experience of one who has been as weak as he, one who can sympathize with him and help him. The knowledge of our own weakness should help us to help another in his need. Never should we pass by one suffering soul without seeking to impart to him the comfort wherewith we ourselves are comforted of God.

It is fellowship with Christ, personal contact with a living Saviour, that enables the mind and heart and soul to triumph over the lower nature. Tell the wanderer of an almighty Hand that will hold him up, of an infinite humanity in Christ that pities him. It is not enough for him to believe in law and force, things that have no pity and never hear the call for help. He needs to clasp a hand that is warm, to trust in a heart full of tenderness. Keep his mind stayed on the thought of a divine presence ever beside him, ever looking upon him with pitying love. Bid him think of a Father's heart that ever grieves over sin, of a Father's hand stretched out still, of a Father's voice saying, "Let him take hold of my strength, and make peace with me . . ." (Isa. 27:5).

As you engage in this work you have companions unseen by human eyes. Angels of heaven were beside the Samaritan who cared for the wounded stranger. Angels from the heavenly courts stand by the side of all who do God's service in ministering to their fellow men. And you have the cooperation of Christ Himself. He is the restorer, and as you work under His supervision you will see great results.[24]

COURTESY TOWARD ALL

Finally, be ye all of one mind, having compassion one of another, love as brethren, be pitiful, be courteous. 1 Peter 3:8.

"Be courteous," is a Bible injunction. We all have our peculiar temperaments. Some have very quick tempers; some are inclined to be morose, some stubborn, and others coarse and rough, unkind in words. Therefore we need to cultivate our tempers, take ourselves in hand. . . . Soften whatever is harsh in your temper and burnish off the rough edges of your character.

Never be sour and harsh at any time. Abstain from frowns and contempt, however much you may feel them. You should win respect by being respectful and courteous. Treat every one with civility; they are the purchase of the blood of Christ. If you seek to imitate Christ in your character, the impression upon the people will not be made by you, but by the angels of God that stand right by your side; they will touch the hearts of those to whom you speak.[25]

Those who hope to be the companions of holy angels should possess refined manners. If the principles of the Christian religion are carried out in the daily life, there will be a kind thoughtfulness for others, for this was characteristic of Christ. Then, although a man may be poor, he will have true dignity, for he is God's nobleman.

Christianity will make a man a gentleman. We are the purchase of Christ's blood, and we are to represent Him, to pattern after Him. And He was courteous, even to His persecutors. The true follower of Jesus manifests the same mild, self-sacrificing spirit that marked the life of his Master. Look at Paul when brought before rulers. His speech before Agrippa is a model of dignified courtesy as well as persuasive eloquence. I would not encourage the formal politeness current with the world, which is destitute of the true spirit of courtesy, but the politeness that springs from real kindness of feeling.[26]

In Christ a greater example has been given us than that of either patriarch or apostle. Here we have genuine courtesy illustrated. This virtue ran parallel with His life, clothing it with a softened and refined beauty, and shedding its luster over every action.[27]

DELIVERANCE FOR THE OPPRESSED

As an eagle stirreth up her nest, fluttereth over her young, spreadeth abroad her wings, taketh them, beareth them on her wings: so the Lord alone did lead him, and there was no strange god with him. Deut. 32:11, 12.

The Captain of our salvation strengthens His followers, not with scientific falsehoods, but with genuine faith in the word of a personal God. This word is repeated over and over and over again with deeper affirmative power. Satan brings all his powers to the assault in the last close conflict, and the endurance of the follower of Christ is taxed to the utmost. At times it seems that he must yield. But a word of prayer to the Lord Jesus goes like an arrow to the throne of God, and angels of God are sent to the field of battle. The tide is turned. The wondrous light that shines in the face of Jesus Christ has stopped the mouth of the caviling opponents. Under the power of the spell that is upon them their lips are closed, and the oppressed are delivered. The believing, harassed souls are borne up as on eagles' wings, and the victory is gained.

God calls upon His people to prepare themselves for scenes of severe conflict. Take up your duties in a meek and lowly spirit. Ever face your enemies in the strength of Jesus. Discharge with faithfulness every duty. Realize that you must now obtain by daily conversion and humility an unquestioning trust in the One who has all power and who will not leave you to be destroyed. You may know Christ by personal experience. . . . In the trials of these last days Christ will be made unto His people wisdom and righteousness and sanctification and redemption. . . . They are to develop an experience that will be a convincing power in the world. . . .

What wonderful lessons we shall learn as the result of depending constantly on the sufficiency of Christ. He who is learning these lessons need not depend on another's experience. He has the witness in himself, and his experience is the actual knowledge that Christ is all-sufficient, faithful, and powerful. He has the realization of the promise, "My grace is sufficient for thee" (2 Cor. 12:9). "God is faithful, who will not suffer you to be tempted above that ye are able" (1 Cor. 10:13).[28]

297

FOLLOWERS OF THE LAMB

These are they which follow the Lamb whithersoever he goeth. These were redeemed from among men, being the firstfruits unto God and to the Lamb. And in their mouth was found no guile: for they are without fault before the throne of God. Rev. 14:4, 5.

The Lord has a people on the earth, who follow the Lamb whithersoever He goeth. He has His thousands who have not bowed the knee to Baal. Such will stand with Him on Mount Zion. But they must stand on this earth, girded with the whole armor, ready to engage in the work of saving those who are ready to perish. . . .

We need not wait till we are translated to follow Christ. God's people may do this here below. We shall follow the Lamb of God in the courts above only if we follow Him here. . . . We are not to follow Christ fitfully or capriciously, only when it is for our advantage. We must choose to follow Him. In daily life we must follow His example, as a flock trustfully follows its shepherd. We are to follow Him by suffering for His sake, saying at every step, "Though he slay me, yet will I trust in him" (Job 13:15). His life practice must be our life practice. And as we thus seek to be like Him and to bring our wills into conformity to His will we shall reveal Him.[29]

We are not in a dreamland of inaction. We are soldiers of Christ, enlisted in the work of showing our loyalty to Him who has redeemed us. What we are in the heavenly home, when saved, eternally saved, will be the reflection of what we now are in character and holy service. Shall we not show our loyalty by keeping God's commandments here, in this our place of probation? . . .

Are we following Christ with unswerving loyalty, keeping His life of perfect obedience, of purity and self-sacrifice, ever before us that by beholding we may become changed into His image? Do we strive to imitate His fidelity? If we educate ourselves to say, Be Thou my Pattern; if by the eye of faith we see Him as a living Saviour, we shall be strengthened to follow Him. Then with the undefiled we shall follow Him in the future life. As eye- and heart-witnesses we can bear testimony to His majesty, for by faith we have been with Him in the holy mount.[29]

EVER REMEMBER YOUR HIGH CALLING

Wherefore I will not be negligent to put you always in remembrance of these things, though ye know them, and be established in the present truth. **2 Peter 1:12.**

No matter how long we may have been traveling in the way of life eternal we need often to recount the mercies of our heavenly Father toward us and gather hope and courage from the promises of His Word. . . . Peter realized the value of constant vigilance in the Christian life, and he felt impelled by the Holy Spirit to urge upon the believers the importance of exercising great carefulness in the daily life. . . .

"Always in remembrance." Oh, if only we were to keep before our minds those things that pertain to our eternal welfare, we should not engage in any foolishness or idle speaking! Our lifework is before us. It is for us to give diligence to make our calling and election sure, by giving heed to the plain instruction contained in God's Holy Word. . . .

There are many wrong things which we allow to pass by unnoticed, when by our godly conversation we might set an example of rightdoing that would be a standing rebuke to the evildoers. We cannot afford by our example to seem to sanction wrongdoing. There is a heaven to win and a hell to shun. In large churches of believers . . . there is special danger of lowering the standard. Where many are gathered together some are more liable to grow careless and indifferent than they would be if isolated and made to stand alone. But even under adverse circumstances we may watch unto prayer and set an example in godly conversation that will be a powerful testimony for the right. . . . We cannot afford to speak words that would discourage our fellow pilgrims in the Christian pathway. Christ has given His life in order that we might live with Him in glory. Throughout eternity He will bear in His hands the prints of the cruel nails by which He was transfixed to the cross of Calvary. . . .

We are now fitting up for the future, eternal life; and soon, if faithful, we shall see the gates of the city of our God swing back on their glittering hinges that the nations who have kept the truth may enter in to their eternal inheritance.[30]

299

CHRISTLIKE THROUGH SELF-DENIAL

Then said Jesus unto his disciples, If any man will come after me, let him deny himself, and take up his cross, and follow me. Matt. 16:24.

The most difficult sermon to preach and the hardest to practice is self-denial. The greedy sinner, self, closes the door to the good which might be done but which is not done because shillings and pounds* are invested in selfish purposes. We may never have opportunity to do great things; we may never be required to make sublime sacrifices. But the greatest victory we can gain is to follow Jesus. . . . Every day that Christ lived in our world was for Him a day of self-denial. If we would follow Him over the rugged path of self-denial . . . this denial must be carried into the everyday occurrences and actions of our life. . . .

The world's policy is to acquire money and advantages in any way that they can be obtained. An accumulation of this world's treasure is the ambition of worldlings. The aim and object of the followers of our Lord Jesus Christ is to become Christlike by self-denial and self-sacrifice. They keep their eyes on the eternal riches which they can obtain by renouncing earthly treasure for heavenly treasure. Here are the conditions: He that will be My disciple, let him forsake all, and follow Me. Keep Christ in view, following where He leads the way. . . .

"It is more blessed to give than to receive" (Acts 20:35). . . . Self-denial will bring into the treasury of God the means necessary to advance His work. Thus we may act in copartnership with Christ. Christ's followers consider that in giving back to the Lord His own they are receiving a blessing; for they are accumulating heavenly treasure, which will be given to them when they shall hear the "Well done, good and faithful servant; . . . enter thou into the joy of thy Lord" (Matt. 25:23). What is that joy? "Who for the joy that was set before him endured the cross, despising the shame, and is set down at the right hand of the throne of God" (Heb. 12:2). The joy of seeing souls redeemed, souls eternally saved, is the privilege of those who have overcome obstacles in order to put their feet in the footprints of Him who said, "Follow me." [31]

---

* Written in Australia when these were standard monetary units.

THE PERIL OF RICHES

Jesus answereth again, and saith unto them, Children, how hard is it for them that trust in riches to enter into the kingdom of God! It is easier for a camel to go through the eye of a needle, than for a rich man to enter into the kingdom of God. Mark 10:24, 25.

It is God's plan that riches should be used properly, distributed to bless the needy and to advance the work of God. If men love their riches better than they love their fellow men, better than they love God or the truths of His Word, if their hearts are on their riches, they cannot have eternal life. . . . Here souls are proved; and like the rich young man, many go away sorrowful because they cannot have their riches and a treasure in heaven too. . . .

"With God all things are possible" (verse 27). . . . Truth, sent home to the heart by the Spirit of God, will crowd out the love of riches. The love of Jesus and the love of money cannot dwell in the same heart. The love of God so far surpasses the love of money that the possessor breaks away from his riches and transfers his affections to God. Through love he is then led to minister to the wants of the needy and to assist the cause of God. It is his highest pleasure to make a right disposition of his Lord's goods. He holds all that he has as not his own, and faithfully discharges his duty as God's steward. . . . In this way it is possible for a rich man to enter the kingdom of God. . . .

Some give of their abundance, yet feel no lack. They do not practice self-denial for the cause of Christ. They give liberally and heartily, but they still have all that heart can wish. God regards it. The action and motive are strictly marked by Him, and they will not lose their reward.

But those who have less means must not excuse themselves because they cannot do as much as some others. Do what you can. Deny yourself of some article you can do without and sacrifice for the cause of God. Like the poor widow, cast in your two mites. You will actually give more than all those who give of their abundance; and you will know how sweet it is to deny self, to give to the needy, to sacrifice for the truth, and to lay up treasure in heaven.[32]

GOD'S PRIOR CLAIMS

And thou say in thine heart, My power and the might of mine hand hath gotten me this wealth. But thou shalt remember the Lord thy God: for it is he that giveth thee power to get wealth. Deut. 8:17, 18.

Those who love God supremely will realize that they are rich beyond computation in the wealth that God gives them. . . . Man possesses nothing to which he has an exclusive right. He does not even own himself; for he has been bought with a price, even the blood of the Son of God. Christ has a claim on all the property in our world. He can set in operation a train of circumstances which will sweep away the accumulated gain of years. He can also call in needed help for His children. . . .

It is God who gives man the breath of life. We cannot originate; we can only collect that which God has originated. He is our guardian, our counsellor; and more than this, from His liberal supply we derive all the skill, tact, and ability that we possess. . . . All you possess is His gift, for you had nothing with which to create or purchase it. It is given you, not to become a wedge to separate you from Him, but to help you in doing His service.

The moment a man loses sight of the fact that his capabilities and possessions are the Lord's, that moment he is embezzling his Lord's goods. He is acting the part of an unjust steward, provoking the Lord to transfer His goods to more faithful hands. God calls upon those to whom He has entrusted His goods to handle them faithfully, to show to the world that they are laboring for the salvation of sinners. He calls upon those who profess to be under His supervision not to misrepresent Him in character. . . . He daily loadeth us with benefits. . . . Let us glorify Him by imparting to others the abundance He has bestowed upon us.

O for love, sacred, holy, unselfish love! Let us, as the Lord's representatives, realize what a terrible thing it is to misrepresent the Saviour by revealing selfishness. God calls upon His sons and daughters to show to the world that He is not selfish, but full of liberal, unselfish plans. He is waiting for channels through which to communicate the wealth of His love.[33]

GOD'S PLAN FOR SUPPORT OF HIS WORK

The liberal soul shall be made fat: and he that watereth shall be watered also himself. Prov. 11:25.

The Lord has made the proclamation of the gospel dependent on the consecrated ability and the voluntary gifts and offerings of His people. While He has called men to preach the Word, He has made it the privilege of the whole church to share in the work by contributing of their means to its support. And He has bidden them also to care for the poor, as representatives of Himself. A tithe of all our income the Lord claims as His own, to be devoted solely to the support of those who give themselves to the preaching of the gospel. And besides this He asks of us gifts and offerings for His cause and also to supply the needs of the poor. . . .

The Lord is ever bestowing His blessings and mercies upon men. Should He withdraw these gifts we should perish. Every moment He has His human family in view. "He maketh his sun to rise on the evil and on the good, and sendeth rain on the just and on the unjust" (Matt. 5:45). He gives us "fruitful seasons, filling our hearts with food and gladness" (Acts 14:17). It is God who gives men power to get wealth. The quick, sharp thought, the ability to plan and execute, are from Him. It is He who blesses us with health and opens ways for us to acquire means by diligent use of our powers. And He says to us, "A portion of the money I have enabled you to gain is Mine. Put it into the treasury in tithes, in gifts and offerings, that there may be meat in Mine house—that there may be something to sustain those who carry the gospel of My grace to the world." [34]

God might have carried forward His work in the world, and have provided for the poor, without the cooperation of man. He asks for our service and our gifts, not only that we may thus manifest our love for Him and our fellow men but because the service and sacrifice for the good of others will strengthen the spirit of beneficence in the giver's heart, allying us more closely to Him who was rich, yet for our sakes became poor, that we through His poverty might be rich. And it is only as we thus imitate the Saviour's example that our characters will be developed in His likeness. [34]

THE BIBLE RULES FOR GIVING

Every man shall give as he is able, according to the blessing of the Lord thy God which he hath given thee. Deut. 16:17.

A beautiful illustration of that spirit of love and self-sacrifice which the grace of Christ implants in the heart is given in the experience of the Macedonian Christians. The apostle Paul writes of them: "In a great trial of affliction the abundance of their joy and their deep poverty abounded unto the riches of their liberality. . . . Praying us with much intreaty that we would receive the gift, and take upon us the fellowship of the ministering to the saints. And this they did, not as we hoped, but first gave their own selves to the Lord, and unto us by the will of God" (2 Cor. 8:2-5). And wherever the Spirit of Christ abides the same fruits will be manifested.[35]

In the Bible system of tithes and offerings the amounts paid by different persons will of course vary greatly, since they are proportioned to the income. With the poor man the tithe will be a comparatively small sum, and his gifts will be according to his ability. But it is not the greatness of the gift that makes the offering acceptable to God; it is the purpose of the heart, the spirit of gratitude and love that it expresses. Let not the poor feel that their gifts are so small as to be unworthy of notice. Let them give according to their ability, feeling that they are servants of God, and that He will accept their offering.

The one to whom God has entrusted a large capital will not, if he loves and fears God, find it a burden to meet the demands of an enlightened conscience according to the claims of God. The rich will be tempted to indulge in selfishness and avarice, and to withhold from the Lord His own, but he who is true to God will, when tempted, answer to Satan, "It is written," "Will a man rob God?" . . .

Those who keep eternal realities in view, who love the Lord with all the heart and soul and strength, and their neighbor as themselves, will conscientiously do their whole duty, as if the curtain were rolled back and they could see that they were working in view of the heavenly universe. . . . All who possess . . . the spirit of Christ will with cheerful alacrity press their gifts into the Lord's treasury.[36]

SETTLE YOUR ACCOUNTS WITH HEAVEN

Freely ye have received, freely give. Matt. 10:8.

Jesus gave His life for you. Like a child who has full confidence in his parents, and who is not troubled for fear of being taken advantage of and misused, you may rest in God with perfect confidence that He will be to you a friend and a helper. . . .

It is not for you to expect every blessing of God and return nothing. Through Christ we possess all things; without Christ we should have had nothing but poverty, misery, and despair. Shall we respond to this love which Jesus has bestowed upon us? To be sons of God is to possess all things. What more can you want? If the Christian is not content with such an inheritance, nothing can give him contentment. We are indebted to the Lord for all we possess. Then let us return to the Giver all that He claims as His own. Let us not commit robbery toward God. . . .

He who so loved man that He came from the realms of bliss, from His royal throne, and humiliated Himself to clothe His divinity with humanity, has given us unmistakable tokens of His love and the value He places upon man. He who has made for us this infinite sacrifice summons us to estimate the value of the soul, to strike the balance between earthly gain and heavenly loss, between temporal success and everlasting failure. . . .

Christ points you away from the earthly to the heavenly. He invites you to lay up your treasures above. . . . Will you say as you present your offering to God, Of Thine own, O Lord, we freely give Thee? . . . All the means you may give will not buy for you salvation. You must give yourself. In surrendering yourself to the claims and influences of the Saviour your life may be as a fruitful branch in a beautiful vine. The fruits of the Spirit may adorn it. Clusters of rich graces will appear, such as love, joy, peace, gentleness, goodness, and meekness, which will make it attractive. . . .

I entreat of you to send your treasure before you into heaven by using the Lord's goods to advance His cause in the earth. . . . Settle your accounts with high heaven.[37]

"A MEMORIAL BEFORE GOD"

Thy prayers and thine alms are come up for a memorial before God. Acts 10:4.

It is a wonderful favor for any man in this life to be commended of God as was Cornelius. And what was the ground of this approval? "Thy prayers and thine alms are come up for a memorial before God."

Neither prayer nor almsgiving has any virtue in itself to recommend the sinner to God; the grace of Christ, through His atoning sacrifice, can alone renew the heart and make our service acceptable to God. This grace had moved upon the heart of Cornelius. The Spirit of Christ had spoken to his soul; Jesus had drawn him, and he had yielded to the drawing. His prayer and alms were not urged or extorted from him; they were not a price he was seeking to pay in order to secure heaven, but they were the fruit of love and gratitude to God.

Such prayer from a sincere heart ascends as incense before the Lord; and offerings to His cause and gifts to the needy and suffering are a sacrifice well pleasing to Him. Thus the gifts of the Philippian brethren, who ministered to the needs of the apostle Paul while a prisoner at Rome, are said to be "an odour of a sweet smell, a sacrifice acceptable, wellpleasing to God" (Phil. 4:18).

Prayer and almsgiving are closely linked together—the expression of love to God and to our fellow men. They are the outworking of the two great principles of the divine law, "Thou shalt love the Lord thy God with all thy heart, and with all thy soul, and with all thy mind, and with all thy strength": and "Thou shalt love thy neighbour as thyself" (Mark 12:30, 31). Thus while our gifts cannot recommend us to God or earn His favor, they are an evidence that we have received the grace of Christ. They are a test of the sincerity of our profession of love.[38]

The offerings that are the fruit of self-denial prompted by love are represented by the words spoken by God to Cornelius [Acts 10:4 quoted]. . . . Who does not desire such memorials—deeds which are before God as a voice speaking in behalf of the human agent, keeping our names fresh and fragrant in the heavenly sanctuary?[39]

WHERE ARE YOUR AFFECTIONS?

If ye then be risen with Christ, seek those things which are above, where Christ sitteth on the right hand of God. Set your affection on things above, not on things on the earth. Col. 3:1, 2.

We may have high anticipations in regard to the things of this life, but we shall meet with disappointment. We shall find that they fade away. But here is "an inheritance incorruptible, and undefiled, and that fadeth not away, reserved in heaven for you" (1 Peter 1:4). We want our thoughts to be fixed on the things that will abide, not upon those that pass away with the using. . . .

When Christ came into this world He saw that men had left the future, eternal life out of their reckoning. He came to present that life before us, that by beholding it we might be led to change our relation to the things of this life, that our affections might be placed upon the things above, and not upon the things of the earth, so soon to pass away. The shadow that Satan has caused to intervene between our souls and God Christ seeks to roll back, that the view of God and eternity may become clear. While He does not despise this world, He places it in its proper position of subordination. And then He places the things of eternity in their relative importance before us, that we may fix the eye of faith upon the unseen. The things of temporal interest have power to engross the thoughts and affections, and it is important that we should be constantly educating and training our minds to dwell upon things of eternal interest. Will this make us unhappy? Will it cause us to have a hard time here? No, indeed. . . . The more of the Spirit of God, the more of His grace, is brought into our daily experience, the less friction there will be, the more happiness we shall have, and the more we shall impart to others.[40]

God does not design that eternity shall overwhelm us and unfit us for the duties of this life, and it will never do this if we accustom our minds to dwell upon the themes of eternity and mingle them with our life duties. The contemplation of eternal realities will not disqualify us for the duties of this life. All the useful pursuits and activities of life are to stand revealed to us as encircled with the hallowed rainbow of promise.[41]

LIVING ABOVE THE WORLD

While we look not at the things which are seen, but at the things which are not seen: for the things which are seen are temporal; but the things which are not seen are eternal. 2 Cor. 4:18.

In His teaching, Christ sought to adjust the claims of heaven and earth. . . . He saw that men are in danger of cherishing an inordinate love for the world. The love of God is supplanted by a love for the world. Nothing but the power of the omnipotent God can dislodge this love. The things which are earthly and temporal lead men away from God, although the advantages to be gained are but an atom in comparison with eternal realities. . . . Turning away from heavenly attractions, from imperishable wealth, from peace, from nobility of soul, man pours out his affections on unworthy, unsatisfying things; and by constantly beholding this world, he becomes conformed to it. His mind, capable of elevation and privileged to grasp the eternal blessedness of the saints, turns away from an eternity of greatness and allows its powers to be chained like a slave to an atom of a world. It is humiliated and dwarfed by allegiance to worldly things.

Jesus came to change this order of things, to correct this widespread evil. He lifts up His voice as the voice of God in warnings, reproofs, and entreaties, seeking to break the spell which infatuates, enslaves, and ensnares men. He . . . says, "For what is a man profited, if he shall gain the whole world, and lose his own soul?" (Matt. 16:26).

God would have us lift ourselves above the world. Jesus, the world's Redeemer, presents before us the eternal inheritance, the immortal riches. . . . He takes the world from its position of boasted supremacy, placing it where it should be, subject to the spiritual and eternal world. . . .

Christ gave Himself a sacrifice for the world. He cheerfully gave His own life as a ransom for an apostate world, and He does not design that selfishness and worldliness shall exist in the hearts of His followers. Conformity to the world is expressly forbidden by the Word of God. . . . God's chosen ones are to be just what He meant they should be, and what the apostle declares they are—"a spectacle unto the world, and to angels, and to men" (2 Cor. 4:9).[42]

THE CHURCH AND THE WORLD

For all that is in the world, the lust of the flesh, and the lust of the eyes, and the pride of life, is not of the Father, but is of the world. And the world passeth away, and the lust thereof: but he that doeth the will of God abideth for ever. 1 John 2:16, 17.

Many who profess to believe the Word of God do not seem to understand the deceptive working of the enemy. They do not realize that the end of time is near, but Satan knows it, and while men sleep he works. The lust of the flesh, the lust of the eye, and the pride of life are controlling men and women. Satan is at work even among the people of God, to cause disunion. Selfishness, corruption, and evil of every kind are taking a firm hold upon hearts. With many the precious Word of God is neglected. A novel or a storybook engages the attention. . . . That which excites the imagination is eagerly devoured, while the Word of God is set aside.[43]

The world is the chief enemy of religion; for satanic forces are continually at work through the world, and it is the object of Satan to bring the church and the world into such close fellowship that their aims, their spirit, their principles, shall harmonize, and that it will be impossible to distinguish between him who professes to serve God and him who serveth Him not. The enemy works continually to push the world to the front.[44]

The command is given, "Come out from among them, and be ye separate." But it is not for you to say, I have nothing to do with my neighbor. He is buried in the world; I am not his keeper. For this very reason you should have something to say to him. The light given you, you are not to hide under a bushel. . . . It may be understood that you believe the seventh day is the Sabbath, that you believe in the Lord's soon return, but what good will this do your neighbor unless you carry your belief into your daily life? . . . A pure example will do more to enlighten the world than all your profession. . . .

How many there are as weak as water who might have a never-failing source of strength. Heaven is ready to impart to us that we may be mighty in God and attain to the full stature of men and women in Christ Jesus.[45]

"BE NOT CONFORMED"

And be not conformed to this world: but be ye transformed by the renewing of your mind, that ye may prove what is that good, and acceptable, and perfect, will of God. Rom. 12:2.

Christ never leads His followers to take upon themselves vows that will unite them with those who have no connection with God. . . .

Between the worldly man and the one who is faithfully serving God there is a great gulf fixed. Upon the most momentous subjects —God and truth and eternity—their thoughts and sympathies and feelings are not in harmony. One class is ripening as wheat for the garner of God, the other as tares for the fires of destruction. How can there be unity of purpose or action between them? . . .

We are to beware of indulging a spirit of bigotry and intolerance. We are not to stand aside from others in a spirit that seems to say, "Come not near to me, for I am holier than thou." We are not to shut ourselves away from our fellow human beings, but are to seek to impart to them the precious truth that has blessed our own hearts. . . . But if we are Christians, having the spirit of Him who died to save men from their sins, we shall love the souls of our fellow men too well to countenance their sinful pleasures by our presence and our influence. . . . Such a course, so far from benefiting them, would only cause them to doubt the reality of our religion. . . . We should be firmly rooted in the conviction that whatever in any sense turns aside from truth and justice in our association and partnership with men, cannot benefit us and greatly dishonors God.

The work of God for the salvation of the human family is the one work of supreme importance to be carried forward in our world. When men are willing to count all things but loss that they may win Christ, their eyes will be open to see things as they really are. Then they will turn away from the earthly attractions to the heavenly. . . .

"They shall be mine, saith the Lord of hosts," of the obedient, "in that day when I make up my jewels; and I will spare them, as a man spareth his own son that serveth him. Then shall ye return, and discern between the righteous and the wicked, between him that serveth God and him that serveth him not" (Mal. 3:17, 18).[46]

KEPT FROM THE EVIL

I pray not that thou shouldest take them out of the world, but that thou shouldest keep them from the evil. John 17:15.

Those whose business makes it necessary for them to come in contact with worldly men should stand constantly on guard, keeping strict watch over themselves and praying always, lest the enemy take them unawares. To those of His followers who are of necessity compelled to deal with worldlings, God gives grace according to their need. If they stand ever on guard, special wisdom will be given them when they are obliged to be in the company of those who do not respect the Lord Jesus Christ. Their every transaction is to reveal the fact that they are Christians. They are to be kind and courteous in all that they say and do, showing that they are under the control and discipline of God, that they are serving the Lord Jesus Christ.

The followers of Christ are to be separate from the world in principles and interests, but they are not to isolate themselves from the world. "As thou hast sent me into the world," Christ said, "even so have I also sent them into the world" (verse 18). . . . We are not to withdraw ourselves from the world in order to escape persecution. We are to abide among men, that the savor of divine love may be as salt to preserve the world from corruption.

Hearts that respond to the influence of the Holy Spirit are the channels through which God's blessings flow. Were those who serve God removed from the earth, and His Spirit withdrawn from among men, this earth would be left to desolation and destruction. Though the wicked know it not, they owe even the blessings of this life to the presence in this world of God's people, whom they despise and oppress. . . . Following the instruction of Christ brings the sanctification of the Holy Spirit, and this enables men and women to reveal . . . the fragrance and the saving grace of the truth. . . .

Those who study the Word of God and day by day receive instruction from Christ bear the stamp of heaven's principles. A high, holy influence goes forth from them. A helpful atmosphere surrounds their souls. The pure, holy, elevated principles that they follow enable them to bear a living testimony to the power of divine grace.[47]

311

OUR MISSION TO THE WORLD

As thou hast sent me into the world, even so have I also sent them into the world. John 17:18.

Will separation from the world, in obedience to the divine command, unfit us for the work the Lord has left us? Will it hinder us from doing good to those around us? No; the firmer hold we have on heaven, the greater will be our power for usefulness. We should study the Pattern, that the spirit which dwelt in Christ may dwell in us. The Saviour was not found among the exalted and honorable of the world. He did not spend His time among those who were seeking their ease and pleasure. He worked to help those who needed help, to save the lost and perishing, to lift up the bowed down, to break the yoke of oppression from those in bondage, to heal the afflicted, and to speak words of sympathy and consolation to the distressed and sorrowing. We are required to follow this example. The more we partake of the spirit of Christ, the more we shall seek to do for our fellow men. We shall bless the needy and comfort the distressed. . . .

Probation is about to close. . . . Soon the last prayer for sinners will have been offered, the last tear shed, the last warning given, the last entreaty made, and the sweet voice of mercy will be heard no more. This is why Satan is making such mighty efforts to secure men and women in his snare. . . . The enemy is playing the game of life for every soul. He is working to remove from us everything of a spiritual nature, and in the place of the precious graces of Christ to crowd our hearts with the evil traits of the carnal nature—hatred, evil surmising, jealousy, love of the world, love of self, love of pleasure, and the pride of life. We need to be fortified against the incoming foe, . . . for unless we are watchful and prayerful these evils will enter the heart and crowd out all that is good.[1]

How great is the responsibility placed upon the disciple of Christ. How imperative the duty to reflect the light of heaven upon a world enshrouded in darkness. The deeper the surrounding gloom, the brighter should shine out the light of Christian faith and Christian example.[2]

BATTLING MORAL DARKNESS

For, behold, the darkness shall cover the earth, and gross darkness the people: but the Lord shall arise upon thee, and his glory shall be seen upon thee. Isa. 60:2.

This age presents a sad picture to those whose eyes have been opened to discern the evils that prevail on every hand. The fear and love of God have almost left the world. This is the time prophesied of by Isaiah, when "darkness shall cover the earth, and gross darkness the people." Multitudes are led away by the delusions of a faithless generation and are living in the darkness of error. . . .

The baleful spirit of unbelief is found in every land and is permeating all ranks of society. It is taught freely in many of the universities, colleges, and high schools, and it comes even into the lessons taught in the common schools and the nurseries. Thousands who profess to be Christians give heed to lying spirits. . . .

The world today is in crying need of a revelation of Christ Jesus in the person of His saints. God desires that His people shall stand before the world a holy people. Why? Because there is a world to be saved by the light of gospel truth; and as the message of truth that is to call men out of darkness into God's marvelous light is given by the church, the lives of its members, sanctified by the Spirit of truth, are to bear witness to the verity of the messages proclaimed. . . .

The world is in need of a demonstration of practical Christianity. In view of the fact that those who claim to be followers of Christ are a spectacle to an unbelieving world, it behooves them to make sure that they are in right relation to God. . . . In order to stand as lights in the world, they need to have the clear light of the Sun of Righteousness constantly shining upon them. . . .

When God's people so fully separate themselves from evil that He can let the light of heaven rest upon them in rich measure, and shine forth from them to the world, then there will be fulfilled more fully than it has ever been fulfilled in the past the prophecy of Isaiah, . . . "The Gentiles shall come to thy light, and kings to the brightness of thy rising. . . . The abundance of the sea shall be converted unto thee, and the force of the Gentiles shall come unto thee" (Isa. 60:3-5).[3]

"ARISE, SHINE"

Arise, shine; for thy light is come, and the glory of the Lord is risen upon thee. Isa. 60:1.

In a special sense Seventh-day Adventists have been set in the world as watchmen and light bearers. To them has been entrusted the last message of mercy for a perishing world. On them is shining wonderful light from the Word of God. What manner of persons, then, ought they to be? . . .

It is the purpose of God to glorify Himself in His people before the world. He longs to make them channels through which He can pour His boundless love and mercy. . . . Let us come up to the help of the Lord, to the help of the Lord against the mighty powers of darkness. Satan is working with intensity of purpose to enslave and destroy souls. Let us take a firm stand against him. He who is fully consecrated to the service of God will be made strong for the battle. He will be strengthened with "all might." He who feels his weakness, and wrestles with God as did Jacob, saying, "I will not let thee go, except thou bless me" (Gen. 32:26), will go forth with the fresh anointing of the Holy Spirit. The atmosphere of heaven will surround him. He will go about doing good. His influence will be a positive force in favor of the religion of Christ.

God calls for light bearers, who will fill the world with the light and peace and joy that come from Christ. He calls for humble men, men who cherish a sense of their weakness and who remember what the service of God demands of them—the propriety of speech and action which shows the power of the grace of Christ. . . .

Time is precious. The destiny of souls is in the balance. God is holding back His judgments, waiting for the message to be sounded to all. There are many who have not yet heard the testing message of truth for this time. The last call of mercy is to be proclaimed throughout the earth. Heavenly angels have long been waiting for human agents . . . to cooperate with them in the great work to be done. They are waiting for you. So vast is the field, so comprehensive the design, that every sanctified heart will be pressed into service as an agent of divine power.[4]

314

LIGHT REVEALED IN THE LIFE

Let your light so shine before men, that they may see your good works, and glorify your Father which is in heaven. Matt. 5:16.

In bearing a light on a dark night, to direct the footsteps of others, frequently the light bearer becomes careless, permitting his own body to come between the light and those whom he is guiding. Thus those who follow lose the benefit of the light. This is the case with some who hold up the light of truth to others. They reveal their own selfish interests, their lack of consecration, their errors, their defects of character, all of which affect their actions and make their dark bodies conspicuous but benefit no one by the truth which they professedly believe.

The light of truth should be allowed to shine so that men, by seeing the righteous course of those who know the truth, will acknowledge that there is power in the truth, because it has accomplished so great a work for those who have received it. They will fall in love with the principles of holiness that shine forth in the lives of the representatives of truth, and they will accept the truth and glorify God by consecrating themselves to Him to become lights to the world in their turn.[5]

As Abraham and other holy men of old were a light in their generation, so must God's people be a light in the world. The beams of heaven's attractive loveliness are to shine forth from us, showing the only good and right way, and ever showing the superiority of God's law above every human enactment. Bible religion is not to be hidden away in the dark. It delights to be examined. Every additional ray of light that shines upon our pathway is in God's plan a fresh element of strength, an added power by which to draw the world to God.[6]

Christ declares, "Ye are the light of the world." Christ is the source of light and power for His church. If the heart is pure and right, if godliness is dwelling there, it will be revealed in the life. It will pervade the conversation and all the relations of man to his fellow man. He will be a doer of the words of Christ. . . . His every action will shine with a holy luster. He will be invested with power, for the divine presence is with him.[7]

LIGHT BEARERS ON THE WAY TO HEAVEN

That ye may be blameless and harmless, the sons of God, without rebuke, in the midst of a crooked and perverse nation, among whom ye shine as lights in the world. Phil. 2:15.

In all ages the "Spirit of Christ which was in them" has made God's true children the light of the people of their generation. Joseph was a light bearer in Egypt. In his purity and benevolence and filial love he represented Christ in the midst of a nation of idolaters. While the Israelites were on their way from Egypt to the promised land the truehearted among them were a light to the surrounding nations. Through them God was revealed to the world. From Daniel and his companions in Babylon, and from Mordecai in Persia, bright beams of light shone out amid the darkness of the kingly courts.

In like manner the disciples of Christ are set as light bearers on the way to heaven; through them the Father's mercy and goodness are made manifest to a world enshrouded in the darkness of misapprehension of God. By seeing their good works, others are led to glorify the Father, who is above; for it is made manifest that there is a God on the throne of the universe whose character is worthy of praise and imitation. The divine love glowing in the heart, the Christlike harmony manifested in the life, are as a glimpse of heaven granted to men of the world. . . . The world watches to see what fruit is borne by professed Christians. It has a right to look for self-denial and self-sacrifice from those who claim to believe advanced truth. . . .

God has ordained that His work shall be presented to the world in distinct, holy lines. He desires His people to show by their lives the advantage of Christianity over worldliness. By His grace every provision has been made for us in all our transaction of business to demonstrate the superiority of heaven's principles over the principles of the world. We are to show that we are working upon a higher plane than that of worldliness. In all things we are to manifest purity of character, to show that the truth received and obeyed makes the receivers sons and daughters of God, children of the heavenly King, and that as such they are honest in their dealings, faithful, true, and upright in the small as well as the great things of life.[8]

SOWING THE WORLD WITH TRUTH

Go ye therefore, and teach all nations, baptizing them in the name of the Father, and of the Son, and of the Holy Ghost: teaching them to observe all things whatsoever I have commanded you. Matt. 28:19, 20.

Christ's last act before leaving the earth was to commission His ambassadors to go to the world with His truth. His last words were spoken to impress the disciples with the thought that they held in trust the message of heaven for the world. . . .

If we but realized how earnestly Jesus worked to sow the world with the gospel seed, we, living at the very close of probation, would labor untiringly to give the bread of life to perishing souls. . . .

God calls upon every church member to enter His service. Truth that is not lived, that is not imparted to others, loses its life-giving power, its healing virtue. Everyone must learn to work and to stand in his lot and place as a burden bearer. Every addition to the church should be one more agency for the carrying on of the great plan of redemption. The entire church, acting as one, blending in perfect union, is to be a living, active, missionary agency.[9]

It is a law of heaven that as we receive we are to impart. The Christian is to be a benefit to others; thus he himself is benefited. "He that watereth shall be watered also himself" (Prov. 11:25). This is not merely a promise. It is a law of God's divine administration, a law by which He designs that the streams of beneficence shall be kept, like the waters of the great deep, in constant circulation, perpetually flowing back to their source. In the fulfilling of this law is the power of Christian missions. . . .

We have only a little longer time in which to prepare for eternity. . . . The whole body of believers needs to be vitalized by the Holy Spirit of God. We should study, plan, economize, and set in operation every means possible whereby we may reach and bless suffering and ignorant humanity. The light which God has given to us as a people is not given that we may treasure it among ourselves. We are to act in harmony with the great commission given to every disciple of Christ, to carry to all the world the light of truth.[10]

THE MOST POWERFUL ARGUMENT

I, even I, am the Lord; and beside me there is no saviour. . . .
Therefore ye are my witnesses, saith the Lord, that I am God.
Isa. 43:11, 12.

Of His true followers the Lord says, "This people have I formed for myself; they shall shew forth my praise" (verse 21). They are My witnesses, My chosen representatives, in an apostate world. . . .

God calls for our cooperation. His requirements are just and reasonable. . . . When we take the name of Christ we pledge ourselves to represent Him. In order for us to be true to our pledge, Christ must be formed within, the hope of glory. The daily life must become more and more like the Christ life. We must be Christians in deed and in truth. Christ will have nothing to do with pretense. He will welcome to the heavenly courts those only whose Christianity is genuine. The lives of professed Christians who do not live the life of Christ are a mockery to religion.[11]

God does not ask us to purchase His favor by any costly sacrifice. He asks only for the service of a humble, contrite heart, which has gladly and thankfully accepted His free gift. The one who receives Christ as his personal Saviour has in his possession the salvation provided by Christ. And he is never to forget that as he has freely received, so he is freely to impart.[12]

Do you realize your value in the sight of God? He says, Ye are laborers together with Me. Are you letting your light shine in clear rays to a fallen world? Are you seeking to exercise every faculty and every power which God has given you? You may not be a minister, but you can be a witness. You may not be an eloquent speaker, but you can be eloquent in living Christ, you can be eloquent in letting your light shine before men.[13]

A true, lovable Christian is the most powerful argument that can be advanced in favor of Bible truth. Such a man is Christ's representative. His life is the most convincing evidence that can be borne to the power of divine grace. When God's people bring the righteousness of Christ into the daily life, sinners will be converted and victories over the enemy will be gained.[14]

NO BOUNDARY LINES

Then spake Jesus again unto them, saying, I am the light of the world: he that followeth me shall not walk in darkness, but shall have the light of life. John 8:12.

Those who follow Jesus will be laborers together with God. They will not walk in darkness, but will find the true path where Jesus, the Light of the world, leads the way; and as they bend their steps Zionward, moving on in faith, they will attain unto a bright experience in the things of God. The mission of Christ, so dimly understood, so faintly comprehended, that called Him from the throne of God to the mystery of the altar of the cross of Calvary, will more and more unfold to the mind, and it will be seen that in the sacrifice of Christ are found the spring and principle of every other mission of love. . . .

Jesus taught His followers that they were debtors both to the Jews and the Greeks, to the wise and the unwise, and gave them to understand that race distinction, caste, and lines of division made by man were not approved of Heaven and were to have no influence in the work of disseminating the gospel. The disciples of Christ were not to make distinctions between their neighbors and their enemies, but they were to regard every man as a neighbor who needed help, and they were to look upon the world as their field of labor, seeking to save the lost. Jesus has given to every man his work, taking him from the narrow circle which his selfishness has prescribed, annihilating territorial lines and all artificial distinctions of society; He marks off no limited boundary for missionary zeal, but bids His followers extend their labors to the uttermost parts of the earth. . . .

The Lord Jesus is our efficiency in all things; His Spirit is to be our inspiration; and as we place ourselves in His hands to be channels of light, our means of doing good will never be exhausted, for the resources of the power of Jesus Christ are to be at our command. We may draw upon His fullness and receive of that grace which has no limit. The Captain of our salvation at every step would teach us that almighty power is at the demand of living faith. He says, "Without me ye can do nothing;" but again declares that "greater works than these shall ye do; because I go unto my Father." [15]

319

EVERY MAN OUR NEIGHBOR

Unto me, who am less than the least of all saints, is this grace given, that I should preach among the Gentiles the unsearchable riches of Christ. Eph. 3:8.

In the hearts of the majority of men there is little respect for truth and righteousness. Unbelief in God and His Word is everywhere manifest. . . . While such conditions prevail in the world, we are not to shut ourselves in our homes and think that assent to truth is all that is required of us. Christ gave Himself a sacrifice for the sins of the world. . . . If you have the riches of the grace of Christ in your heart, you will not keep them to yourselves while the salvation of souls depends upon a knowledge of the way of salvation that you can give. These may not come to you and tell you their heart longings, but many are hungry, unsatisfied, and Christ died that they might have the riches of His grace. What are you going to do that these souls may share the blessings that you enjoy? [16]

Are you seeking to become acquainted with those who need your help? Are you using your opportunities and advantages and means in winning souls to Christ? You may say, I am not a minister and therefore cannot preach the truth. You may not be a minister in the generally accepted sense of the word. You may never be called to stand in the desk. Nevertheless you can be a minister for Christ. If you will watch for the opportunities that present themselves for speaking a word to this soul and to that, God will speak through you to win hearts to Him. . . . Drop a word here and a word there that will lift up the Saviour before men and lead them to higher and holier purposes.[16]

Growth in grace is shown in an increasing ability to work for God. He who learns in the school of Christ will know how to pray and how to speak for the Master. Realizing that he lacks wisdom and experience, he will place himself under the training of the Great Teacher, knowing that only thus he can obtain perfection in God's service. And daily he becomes better able to comprehend spiritual things. Every day of diligent labor finds him at its close better fitted to help others. Abiding in Christ, he bears much fruit.[17]

BEFORE THE HEAVENLY UNIVERSE

For we are made a spectacle unto the world, and to angels, and to men. 1 Cor. 4:9.

God desires His children to show the world what it means to sit together in heavenly places in Christ, "that in the ages to come he might shew the exceeding riches of his grace in his kindness toward us through Christ Jesus" (Eph. 3:7). This kindness He expects us to bring into our dealings with one another. . . .

The Lord desires His children to esteem one another as the purchase of the blood of Christ. When they do this they will know what it means to sit together in heavenly places in Christ. Our lips need to be sanctified with a live coal from the altar of God. Then we shall speak words that are elevating, refining, ennobling, words that are filled with the fragrance of Christ's righteousness, words that are a savor of life unto life.

Christ wants His followers to be like Him, because He desires to be correctly represented in the family circle, in the church, and in the world. He wants us to attend to ourselves. When we do this we shall find that we have enough to keep us busy. We are to accept Christ as our efficiency, our strength, that we may reveal His character to the world. This is the work resting upon us as Christians. We are to witness to the power of heavenly grace.

But are there not many who are . . . like a chestnut bur, hurting those with whom they come in contact? . . . Those who represent Christ will not speak harshly. Their words will be pleasant and helpful. "Speaking the truth in love," we "grow up into him in all things, which is the head, even Christ . . ." (Eph. 4:15).

God wants His sons and daughters to reveal before the synagogue of Satan, before the heavenly universe, before the world, the power of His grace, that men and angels may know that Christ has not died in vain. Let us show the world that we have power from on high. . . . May God help His people to get out of the rut into which they have fallen, and come to the place where they can walk and talk with God. Then, as they reflect the light and joy of heaven, God Himself will rejoice over them with singing.[18]

SEEKERS FOR TRUTH

For the eyes of the Lord run to and fro throughout the whole earth, to shew himself strong in the behalf of them whose heart is perfect toward him. 2 Chron. 16:9.

In every place, in regions afar as well as nearer home, there are God-fearing men and women searching for truth. They know that there is a God; they offer their prayers to Him; they trust Him; they act just as Christians act. From the story of Cornelius [Acts 10] we learn that God will lead every one who is willing to be led. He led Cornelius. He drew out His servant's heart in prayer. He prepared him to receive the light of His truth, and He chose to enlighten the mind of Cornelius through the agency of one who had already received light from above. . . . The Lord noticed every act of Cornelius. All heaven observed the giving of alms and the praying of this devout centurion. . . .

Thus it is today. The Lord has His eye upon every soul that is seeking Him. He is interested in every soul needing help, and He will not leave one in the darkness of error, but step by step will lead him into the full light of the truth that is shining from every page of the Scriptures. . . . The Lord sees our every act. He knows just what progress we have made in the Christian pathway. How kind, how tender, our Great Shepherd is! With intense interest He looks down from His exalted throne upon the sheep of His pasture, and gives them grace and strength. . . .

Constantly the heavenly agencies are communicating with men and women on the earth. We cannot see personally the angels of God round about us; nevertheless they are with us, guiding and directing. We are to be so fully under the influence of the Spirit of God that we shall be susceptible to His leadings.

Whenever we are impressed to say or do something to help a fellow being, we should be ready to respond at once to the promptings of the Holy Spirit. We can be ready to do this only when we are living in close relation with God. The giving of alms, the earnest prayers offered, are but indications that we are doing the works of a Christian, and that we are submitting our minds to the molding influence of God's Spirit.[19]

A WORK FOR EVERYONE

How think ye? if a man have an hundred sheep, and one of them be gone astray, doth he not leave the ninety and nine, and goeth into the mountains, and seeketh that which is gone astray? Matt. 18:12.

The parables of the Lost Piece of Silver and the Lost Sheep teach most precious lessons. They deal with the subject of man lost and man recovered. Many, many more would be recovered if they were labored for as represented in these parables. . . .

Church members, ask God to give you a burden to open the Scriptures to others and to do missionary work for those who need help. Some will be rescued in one way and some in another, but the work must always be done as the Lord shall lead. . . . Let the publications containing Bible truth be scattered like the leaves of autumn. Lift Him up, the Saviour of souls, lift Him up higher and still higher. . . .

Catch the spirit of the great Master Worker. Learn from the Friend of sinners how to minister to sin-sick souls. Remember that in the lives of His followers must be seen the same devotion, the same subjection to God's work of every social claim, every earthly affection, that was seen in His life. God's claims must always be made paramount. Christ's example is to inspire us to put forth unceasing effort for the good of others.[20]

You have neighbors. Will you give them the message? You may never have had the hands of ordination laid upon you, but you can humbly carry the message. You can testify that . . . all for whom Christ died shall have everlasting life if they believe on Him.[21]

Let no one remain in idleness because he cannot do the same class of work that the most experienced servants of God are doing. . . . It is not alone by men in high places of responsibility in the ministry, not alone by men holding positions on boards or committees, not alone by the managers of our sanitariums and publishing houses, that the work is to be done which will cause the earth to be filled with the knowledge of the Lord as the waters cover the sea. This work can be accomplished only by the whole church acting their part under guidance and in the power of God.[22]

OUR OBLIGATIONS TO THE POOR

For I was an hungred, and ye gave me meat: I was thirsty, and ye gave me drink: I was a stranger, and ye took me in: naked, and ye clothed me: I was sick, and ye visited me: I was in prison, and ye came unto me. Matt. 25:35, 36.

While the world needs sympathy, while it needs the prayers and assistance of God's people, while it needs to see Christ in the lives of His followers, the people of God are equally in need of opportunities that draw out their sympathies, give efficiency to their prayers, and develop in them a character like that of the divine pattern.

It is to provide these opportunities that God has placed among us the poor, the unfortunate, the sick, and the suffering. They are Christ's legacy to His church, and they are to be cared for as He would care for them. In this way God takes away the dross and purifies the gold, giving us that culture of heart and character which we need.

The Lord could carry forward His work without our cooperation. He is not dependent on us for our money, our time, or our labor. But the church is very precious in His sight. It is the case which contains His jewels, the fold which encloses His flock, and He longs to see it without spot or blemish or any such thing. He yearns after it with unspeakable love. This is why He has given us opportunities to work for Him, and He accepts our labors as tokens of our love and loyalty.

In placing among us the poor and the suffering, the Lord is testing us to reveal to us what is in our hearts. . . . The culture of the mind and heart is more easily accomplished when we feel such tender sympathy for others that we bestow our benefits and privileges to relieve their necessities. . . .

Good works cost us a sacrifice, but it is in this very sacrifice that they provide discipline. These obligations bring us into conflict with natural feelings and propensities, and in fulfilling them we gain victory after victory over the objectionable traits of our characters.[23]

The world will be convinced not so much by what the pulpit teaches as by what the church lives. The preacher announces the theory of the gospel, but the practical piety of the church demonstrates its power.[23]

"UNTO ONE OF THE LEAST OF THESE"

And the King shall answer and say unto them, Verily I say unto you, Inasmuch as ye have done it unto one of the least of these my brethren, ye have done it unto me. Matt. 25:40.

Christ makes the necessities of His children His own personal interest. He regards any slight or neglect of His brethren as a slight to Himself, and a benefit conferred upon the humblest of them as if it were conferred upon Himself. He says, "I was an hungred, and ye gave me meat: I was thirsty, and ye gave me drink: I was a stranger, and ye took me in. . . . Inasmuch as ye have done it unto one of the least of these my brethren, ye have done it unto me" (verses 35-40).

He whom Providence has blest with plenty but who padlocks the door of his heart to keep back all generous impulses that would find expression in deeds of charity and kindness, will hear from the lips of the Master the solemn words, "Inasmuch as ye did it not to one of the least of these, ye did it not to me" (verse 45). Love of Christ cannot exist in the heart without a corresponding love for our fellow men. . . .

The physical and the spiritual health suffer from inaction. The idler in the vineyard, he who lives for self alone, is ever dissatisfied with himself and with others; the gloom and chill of discontent are mirrored upon his countenance. But he who is drawn out of and away from self, who, like his Master, identifies himself with suffering humanity, will be softened and refined by the exercise of sympathy for others. Courtesy, patience, and gentleness will characterize such a one and will make his presence a continual joy and blessing. His countenance will shine with the luster of true benevolence.

Those who labor hardest to secure their own happiness are miserable. Those who forget self in their interest for others have reflected back upon their own hearts the light and blessings they dispense to them. . . . All that we have is given us on trust. Yet when He rewards us with His approval it is as though the merit were our own: "Well done, good and faithful servant." It is not the greatness of the work which we do, but the love and fidelity with which we do it, that wins the approval of the Saviour.[24]

325

TO THE GLORY OF GOD

That the name of our Lord Jesus Christ may be glorified in you, and ye in him, according to the grace of our God and the Lord Jesus Christ. 2 Thess. 1:12.

It is our duty to be very jealous of the glory of God, and bring no evil report even by the sadness of the countenance or by the ill advised words, as though the requirements of God were a restriction upon our liberty. The whole person is privileged to bear a decided testimony in every line—in features, in temper, in words, in character—that the service of the Lord is good. . . .

God loves His commandment-keeping people, because through their obedience they give honor to His holy name, testifying of their love for God. . . . Our faith and intensity of zeal should be proportionate to the great light which shines upon our pathway. Faith, humble, trusting faith in God—in our homes, in our neighborhood, in our churches—will reveal itself. The Holy Spirit's working will not, cannot be hindered. God delights to reveal Himself to His people as a Father, as a God in whom they can trust implicitly. . . .

When the farmers seek to recommend or exhibit their products, they do not gather up the poorest but the best specimens. The women possess a zeal to bring the very best golden lumps of butter, molded and prettily stamped. The men bring the best yield of vegetables of every kind. The very best and most attractive fruit is brought, and their appearance does the skillful workers credit. The variety of fruits—the apples, peaches, apricots, oranges, lemons, and plums— all these are very attractive. . . . No one would bring the most dwarfed specimens, but the very choicest which the land can produce.

And why should not Christians living in these last days reveal the most attractive fruit in unselfish actions? Why should not the fruit of the commandment-keeping people of God appear in the very best representation of good works? Their words, their deportment, their dress should bear fruit of the very best quality. By their fruits, Christ said, ye shall know them. . . . Let the church members have the precious traits of the character of Christ.[25]

UNDAUNTED COURAGE

Be of good courage, and he shall strengthen your heart, all ye that hope in the Lord. Ps. 31:24.

Heaven's resources are limitless, and they are all at our command. . . . Are there not presented before Christ's followers the highest virtues to be cultivated, the greatest honors to be gained? God calls upon them to enter a race in which everyone may win. He calls upon them to enlist in a warfare in which everyone may be a conqueror. A robe of righteousness and a crown of everlasting life—this is the reward held out before the overcomer.

The inhabitants of the heavenly universe expect the followers of Christ to shine as lights in the world. They are to show forth the power of the grace that Christ died to give to men. God expects those who profess to be Christians to reveal in their lives the highest development of Christianity. They are the recognized representatives of Christ. Their work is to show that Christianity is a reality. They are to be men of faith, men of constant growth, . . . whole-souled men, who without questioning trust in God and His promises.

God calls for men of undaunted courage, men full of hope and faith and trust, who rejoice in the thought of the final triumph, refusing to be hindered by obstacles. He who steadfastly adheres to the principles of truth has the assurance that his weakest points of character may become his strongest points. Heavenly angels are close by him who strives to bring his life into harmony with God and His holy law. God is with him as he declares, "I must overcome the temptations that surround me, else they will drive Christ from my heart." He combats all temptation and braves all opposition. By the strength obtained from on high, he holds in control the passions and tendencies which, uncontrolled, would lead him to defeat. . . .

Why, then, should not those who are fighting against the powers of darkness move forward with faith and courage? God and Christ and the Holy Spirit are on their side. . . . Let not those who stand under the blood-stained banner of Prince Emmanuel do anything that will dishonor the cause for which they are fighting. Christ expects His soldiers to be brave and loyal and true.[26]

THE GRACIOUS INVITATION

Seek the Lord and his strength, seek his face continually.
1 Chron. 16:11.

Those who become children of God are under obligation to Him to do all in their power to seek and to save the lost. . . . The gracious invitation first given by Christ is to be taken up by human voices and sounded throughout the world: "The Spirit and the bride say, Come. And let him that heareth say, Come. And let him that is athirst come. And whosoever will, let him take the water of life freely" (Rev. 22:17). The church is to say, Come. Every power in the church is to be actively engaged on the side of truth. The followers of Christ are to combine in a strong effort to call the attention of the world to the fast-fulfilling prophecies of the Word of God.

Oh, how solemn and important is the work entrusted to us! How far reaching this work is in its results! How are we to obtain strength and wisdom necessary for its successful accomplishment? As Daniel sought the Lord, so we are to seek Him. Daniel declares, "I set my face unto the Lord God, to seek by prayer and supplications, with fasting, and sackcloth, and ashes" (Dan. 9:3). We are to seek the Lord in humility and contrition, confessing our own sins and coming into close unity with one another. . . .

As surely as we seek the Lord earnestly, He will make the way plain before us. All around us are doors open for service. Let us prayerfully study the work to be done, and then enter upon it with full assurance of faith. We are to labor in quietness and humility, in the meekness and lowliness of Christ, realizing that there is a trying time before us and that we shall always need heavenly grace in order to understand how to deal with minds. It is the patient, humble, god-like worker who will have something to show for his labors. As a people and as individuals our success depends, not on numbers, on standing, nor on intellectual attainments, but on walking and working with Christ.[27]

It is time now to gather strength from the Source of all strength, to cry aloud and spare not, to press back the clouds of darkness, that the light of heaven may be revealed.[27]

HOPE FOR LOST SINNERS

Jesus answering said unto them, They that are whole need not a physician; but they that are sick. I came not to call the righteous, but sinners to repentance. Luke 5:31, 32.

Sinners were the special objects of the mission of Christ—sinners of every race and clime. . . . All are dear to Him because they are the purchase of His blood. The home missions are to receive decided attention. Let every sinner within our households and within our own neighborhoods be sought for. Let personal efforts be bestowed upon them. The cases that seem the most hopeless are to be labored for the most earnestly, in faith and hope and earnest prayer. . . .

Those upon whom Satan exercises his power the most decidedly are the ones who awaken the sympathy of the Saviour's great heart of love. He is ever having the ones gathered into the fold to go out into the wilderness to seek and rescue the lost sheep. He feels the tenderest love for those who are entrapped through the deceiving power of Satan. And when the lost sheep are indeed found by Jesus, what joy and rejoicing there is in the whole universe of heaven. . . .

His voice is heard in tones of yearning tenderness, entreaty, and love! "Seek ye the Lord while he may be found, call ye upon him while he is near: let the wicked forsake his way, and the unrighteous man his thoughts: and let him return unto the Lord, and he will have mercy upon him; and to our God, for he will abundantly pardon" (Isa. 55:6, 7). . . .

Mortal man cannot read the heart of man, and is often misled by outward shallow appearances. But He who can read the hearts of men as an open book never misjudges. . . . He knows the atmosphere surrounding each soul. He knows how many and fierce are the struggles of the human soul to overcome the natural hereditary tendencies and the sins which have become common through habit of repetition.

He says, He is mine; I have bought him with human agony and blood. Long have I borne with his manners, his uncourteous, ungrateful behavior toward Me, yet I forbear to cut him down, hoping, through my living colaborers, to bring him to repentance, that I might heal him, and wash and cleanse him in My own blood.[28]

329

WHERE GOD LEADS

Wherefore we receiving a kingdom which cannot be moved, let us have grace, whereby we may serve God acceptably with reverence and godly fear. Heb. 12:28.

A life of monotony is not the most conducive to spiritual growth. Some can reach the highest standard of spirituality only through a change in the regular order of things. When in His providence God sees that changes are essential for the success of the character building, He disturbs the smooth current of the life. . . .

God sees that a worker needs to be more closely associated with Him; and to bring this about, He separates him from friends and acquaintances. When He was preparing Elijah for translation He moved him from place to place that he might not settle down at ease and thus fail of obtaining spiritual power. And it was God's design that Elijah's influence should be a power to help many. . . .

Let those who are not permitted to rest in quietude, who must be continually on the move, pitching their tent tonight in one place and tomorrow night in another place, remember that the Lord is leading them and that this is His way of helping them to form perfect characters. In all the changes that we are required to make, God is to be recognized as our companion, our guide, our dependence. . . .

Many are ignorant of how to work for God, not because they need to be ignorant, but because they are unwilling to submit to His training. Moab is spoken of as a failure because, the prophet declares, "Moab hath been at ease from his youth, . . . and hath not been emptied from vessel to vessel, neither hath he gone into captivity: therefore his taste remained in him, and his scent is not changed" (Jer. 48:11). Thus it is with those whose hereditary and cultivated tendencies to wrong are not purged from them. . . .

The Christian is to be prepared for the doing of a work that reveals kindness, forbearance, long-suffering, gentleness, patience. The cultivation of these precious gifts is to come into the life of the Christian, that, when called into service by the Master, he may be ready to use his highest powers in helping and blessing those around him.[29]

GOD GIVES THE INCREASE

He that goeth forth and weepeth, bearing precious seed, shall doubtless come again with rejoicing, bringing his sheaves with him. **Ps. 126:6.**

If our neighbors were perishing for bread, we would be thought very uncharitable if we did not supply their wants. There are those among us who have never had the Word of God brought to their minds or understanding; they are perishing for want of the Bread of Life, and is it not in us an expression of great selfishness when we keep these sacred truths to ourselves . . . ?

Our heavenly Father gives the rain, the dew, and the sunshine from heaven to refresh the flowers and to cause vegetation to spring up and flourish. But man has a part to act, to prepare the soil and to put the seeds into the ground in order to have a harvest. If he had folded his arms and said, "I will let things take their course. . . . God will give the harvest. He will give the sunshine and the rain from heaven, and I will take my ease," what kind of harvest would come? Man must cooperate with God and act his part in preparing the soil and in sowing the seed, and God will give the increase.

Our heavenly Father has not sent angels from heaven to preach salvation to men. He has opened to us the precious truths of His Word and implanted the truth in our hearts that we may give it to those who are in darkness. If we have indeed tasted of the precious gifts of God in His promises, we are to impart this knowledge to others. . . .

We are individually to work as though a great responsibility rested upon us. We are to manifest untiring energy and tact and zeal in this work and take the burden, feeling the peril in which our neighbors and friends are placed. We are to work as Christ worked. We are to present the truth as it is in Jesus, that the blood of souls shall not be upon our garments. At the same time we are to feel entire dependence and trust in God, for we know we cannot do anything without His grace and power to help. A Paul may plant, and an Apollos water, but God alone can give the increase. Then we are indeed to go forward to the work, weeping, sowing the precious seeds of truth and trusting in God to give the increase.[30]

"WHAT MANNER OF PERSONS?"

Seeing then that all these things shall be dissolved, what manner of persons ought ye to be in all holy conversation and godliness, looking for and hasting unto the coming of the day of God? 2 Peter 3:11, 12.

God expects those who bear the name of Christ to represent Him in thought, word, and deed. Their thoughts are to be pure and their words and deeds noble and uplifting, drawing those around them nearer to the Saviour. . . . In a special sense Seventh-day Adventists have been set in this world as watchmen and light bearers. To them has been entrusted the last message of mercy for a perishing world. On them is shining wonderful light from the Word of God. What manner of persons, then, ought they to be?

Our lives should show steady spiritual growth. But I have seen that which makes me tremble—men and women dwarfed in character, possessing the Word of God, which tells them what they must do in order to be saved, yet unsanctified and unholy. . . .

There needs to be a deeper work of grace in the hearts of God's people. Less of self, and more of Christ, must be seen. Tests, close and sharp, are coming to all. The religion of the Bible must be interwoven with all that we do and say. Every business transaction must be fragrant with the presence of God. . . .

My brother, my sister, I urge you to prepare for the coming of Christ in the clouds of heaven. Day by day cast the love of the world out of your hearts. Understand by experience what it means to have fellowship with Christ. Prepare for the judgment, that when Christ shall come, to be admired in all them that believe, you may be among those who will meet Him in peace. In that day the redeemed will shine forth in the glory of the Father and the Son. The angels, touching their golden harps, will welcome the King and His trophies of victory—those who have been washed and made white in the blood of the Lamb. A song of triumph will peal forth, filling all heaven. Christ has conquered. He enters the heavenly courts, accompanied by His redeemed ones, the witnesses that His mission of suffering and sacrifice has not been in vain.[81]

THE OUTPOURING OF THE SPIRIT

But ye shall receive power, after that the Holy Ghost is come upon you: and ye shall be witnesses unto me both in Jerusalem, and in all Judaea, and in Samaria, and unto the uttermost part of the earth. Acts 1:8.

The Christian church began its existence by praying for the Holy Spirit. It was in its infancy, without the personal presence of Christ. Just before His ascension Christ had commissioned the disciples to preach the gospel to the world. . . .

In obedience to the word of their Master the disciples returned to Jerusalem, and for ten days they prayed for the fulfillment of God's promise. These ten days were days of deep heart searching. The disciples put away all difference that had existed among them, and drew close together in Christian fellowship. . . . At the end of the ten days the Lord fulfilled His promise by a wonderful outpouring of His Spirit. When they were "all with one accord in one place" in prayer and supplication, the promised blessing came. . . .

What was the result of the outpouring of the Spirit on the day of Pentecost? The glad tidings of a risen Saviour were carried to the utmost bounds of the inhabited world. The hearts of the disciples were surcharged with a benevolence so full, so deep, so far reaching, that it impelled them to go to the ends of the earth.[32]

By the grace of Christ the apostles were made what they were. It was sincere devotion and humble, earnest prayer that brought them into close communion with Him. They sat together with Him in heavenly places. They realized the greatness of their debt to Him. By earnest, persevering prayer they obtained the endowment of the Holy Spirit, and then they went forth, weighted with the burden of saving souls, filled with zeal to extend the triumphs of the cross. . . .

Shall we be less earnest than were the apostles? Shall we not by living faith claim the promises that moved them to the depths of their being to call upon the Lord Jesus for the fulfillment of His word: "Ask, and ye shall receive" (John 16:24)? Is not the Spirit of God to come today in answer to earnest, persevering prayer, and fill men with power? [33]

333

THE PROMISE IS FOR US

If ye then, being evil, know how to give good gifts unto your children: how much more shall your heavenly Father give the Holy Spirit to them that ask him? Luke 11:13.

We should pray as earnestly for the descent of the Holy Spirit as the disciples prayed on the day of Pentecost. If they needed the Spirit's power at that time, we need it more today. All manner of false doctrines, heresies, and deceptions are misleading the minds of men; and without the Spirit's aid, our efforts to present divine truth will be in vain.[34]

God desires to refresh His people by the gift of the Holy Spirit, baptizing them anew in His love. There is no need for a dearth of the Spirit in the church. After Christ's ascension the Holy Spirit came upon the waiting, praying, believing disciples with a fullness and power that reached every heart. In the future, the earth is to be lightened with the glory of God. A holy influence is to go forth to the world from those who are sanctified through the truth. The earth is to be encircled with an atmosphere of grace. The Holy Spirit is to work on human hearts, taking the things of God and showing them to men.[35]

Christ declared that the divine influence of the Spirit was to be with His followers to the end of time. But the promise is not appreciated as it should be, and therefore its fulfillment is not seen as it might be. . . . Minor matters occupy the attention, and the divine power which is necessary for the growth and prosperity of the church, and which would bring all other blessings in its train, is lacking, though offered in its infinite plenitude. . . .

My brethren and sisters, plead for the Holy Spirit. God stands back of every promise He has made. With your Bibles in your hands say, "I have done as Thou hast said. I present Thy promise, 'Ask, and it shall be given you; seek, and ye shall find; knock, and it shall be opened unto you'" (Matt. 7:7). Christ declares, "What things soever ye desire, when ye pray, believe that ye receive them, and ye shall have them" (Mark 11:24). "Whatsoever ye shall ask in my name, that will I do . . . " (John 14:13).[36]

DEEP MOVING OF THE SPIRIT

And I will pray the Father, and he shall give you another Comforter, that he may abide with you for ever; even the Spirit of truth; whom the world cannot receive, because it seeth him not, neither knoweth him: but ye know him; for he dwelleth with you, and shall be in you. John 14:16, 17.

God's people seem to be incapable of comprehending and appropriating this promise. They seem to think that only the scantiest showers of grace are to fall on the thirsty soul. . . . They have not felt the need of reaching for the exalted privileges provided for them at infinite cost. . . .

It is not because of any restriction on God's part that the riches of His grace do not flow to men. . . . If all were willing to receive, all would be filled with the Spirit. By resting content with small blessings, we disqualify ourselves for receiving the Spirit in its unlimited fullness. We are too easily satisfied with a ripple on the surface, when it is our privilege to expect the deep moving of the Spirit of God. Expecting little, we receive little.

The necessity of the Holy Spirit's working should be realized by all. Unless this Spirit is accepted and cherished as the representative of Christ, whose work it is to renew and sanctify the entire being, the momentous truths that have been entrusted to human beings will lose their power on the mind. It is not enough for us to have a knowledge of the truth. We are to walk and work in love, conforming our will to the will of God. Of those who do this the Lord declares, "I will put my laws into their mind, and write them in their hearts" (Heb. 8:10). . . . Thus divine relationship is renewed between God and man. " 'I will be to them a God,' " He says, " 'and they shall be to me a people.' There is no attribute of My nature that I will not freely give in order that man may reveal My image." . . .

Are we seeking for His fullness, ever pressing toward the mark set before us—the perfection of His character? When the Lord's people reach this mark, they will be sealed in their foreheads. Filled with the Spirit, they will be complete in Christ, and the recording angel will declare, "It is finished." [37]

335

THE GIFT ALL MAY POSSESS

But the Comforter, which is the Holy Ghost, whom the Father will send in my name, he shall teach you all things, and bring all things to your remembrance, whatsoever I have said unto you. John 14:26.

The Comforter that Christ promised to send after He ascended to heaven is the Spirit in all the fullness of the Godhead, making manifest the power of divine grace to all who receive and believe in Christ as a personal Saviour. There are three living persons of the heavenly trio; in the name of these three great powers—the Father, the Son, and the Holy Spirit—those who receive Christ by living faith are baptized and these powers will cooperate with the obedient.[38]

Those who have been privileged to hear the truth, and have been impressed by the Holy Spirit to receive the Holy Scriptures as the voice of God, have no excuse for becoming dwarfs in the religious life. By exercising the ability which God has given, they are to be daily learning and daily receiving spiritual fervor and power. . . .

If we would be growing plants in the Lord's garden, we must have a constant supply of spiritual life and earnestness. Growth will then be seen in the faith and knowledge of our Lord Jesus Christ. There is no halfway house where we may throw off responsibility and rest by the way. We are to keep advancing heavenward, developing a solid religious character. The measure of the Holy Spirit we receive will be proportioned to the measure of our desire and the faith exercised for it. . . .

Christ says, "Every one that asketh receiveth, and he that seeketh findeth" (Matt. 7:8). He who truly seeks for the precious grace of Christ will be sure not to be disappointed. This promise has been given to us by Him who will not deceive us. It is not stated as a maxim or a theory, but as a fact, as a law of the divine government. We can be assured that we shall receive the Holy Spirit if we individually try the experiment of testing God's word. God is true; His order is perfect. . . . Light and truth will shine forth according to the desire of the soul. O that all would hunger and thirst after righteousness, that they might be filled! [39]

CHRIST ACCESSIBLE THROUGH HIS SPIRIT

Nevertheless I tell you the truth; It is expedient for you that I go away: for if I go not away, the Comforter will not come unto you; but if I depart, I will send him unto you. John 16:7.

Christ said, "It is expedient for you that I go away." No one could then have any preference because of his location or personal contact with Christ. The Saviour would be accessible to all alike, spiritually, and in this sense He would be nearer to us all than if He had not ascended on high. Now all may be equally favored by beholding Him and reflecting His character. The eye of faith sees Him ever present, in all His goodness, grace, forbearance, courtesy, and love. . . . And as we behold, we are changed into His likeness.[40]

It is impossible for any of us by our own power or our own efforts to work this change in ourselves. It is the Holy Spirit, the Comforter, which Jesus said He would send into the world, that changes our character into the image of Christ; and when this is accomplished, we reflect as in a mirror the glory of the Lord. That is, the character of the one who thus beholds Christ is so like His that one looking at him sees Christ's own character shining out as from a mirror. Imperceptibly to ourselves, we are changed day by day from our ways and will into the ways and will of Christ, into the loveliness of His character. Thus we grow up into Christ, and unconsciously reflect His image. . . .

Enoch kept the Lord ever before him, and the Inspired Word says that he "walked with God." He made Christ his constant companion. He was in the world, and performed his duties to the world; but he was ever under the influence of Jesus. He reflected Christ's character, exhibiting the same qualities in goodness, mercy, tender compassion, sympathy, forbearance, meekness, humility, and love. His association with Christ day by day transformed him into the image of Him with whom he was so intimately connected. Day by day he was growing away from his own way into Christ's way, the heavenly, the divine, in his thoughts and feelings. . . . His was a constant growth and he had fellowship with the Father and the Son. This is genuine sanctification.[40]

337

THE LATTER RAIN

Ask ye of the Lord rain in the time of the latter rain; so the Lord shall make bright clouds, and give them showers of rain, to every one grass in the field. Zech. 10:1.

Our heavenly Father claims not at our hands that which we cannot perform. He desires His people to labor earnestly to carry out His purpose for them. They are to pray for power, expect power, and receive power, that they may grow up into the full stature of men and women in Christ Jesus.

Not all members of the church are cultivating personal piety; therefore they do not understand their personal responsibility. They do not realize that it is their privilege and duty to reach the high standard of Christian perfection. . . . Are we looking forward to the latter rain, confidently hoping for a better day, when the church shall be endued with power from on high and thus fitted for work? The latter rain will never refresh and invigorate the indolent, who do not use the powers God has given them.[41]

We are in great need of the pure, life-giving atmosphere that nurtures and invigorates the spiritual life. We need greater earnestness. The solemn message given us to give to the world is to be proclaimed with greater fervency, even with an intensity that will impress unbelievers, leading them to see that the Most High is working with us, that He is the source of our efficiency and strength. . . .

God has given us talents to be used in the upbuilding of His kingdom. . . . Do we ask ourselves the question, How am I using the talents my Lord has given me? Have you given . . . to God only a feeble, diseased service? . . .

Are you using all your powers in an effort to bring the lost sheep back to the fold? There are thousands upon thousands in ignorance who might be warned. Pray as you have never prayed before for the power of Christ. Pray for the inspiration of His Spirit, that you may be filled with a desire to save those who are perishing. Let the prayer ascend to heaven, "God be merciful unto us, and bless us; and cause his face to shine upon us; that thy way may be known upon earth, thy saving health among all nations" (Ps. 67:1, 2).[41]

ECHO THE MESSAGE

And the Spirit and the bride say, Come. And let him that heareth say, Come. And let him that is athirst come. And whosoever will, let him take the water of life freely. Rev. 22:17.

A short time before His ascension to His heavenly throne Christ commissioned His disciples to go into all the world as teachers of righteousness. . . . Among the believers to whom the commission was given, were many from the humbler walks of life—men and women who had learned to love their Lord and who had determined to follow His example of self-denying service. To these lowly ones of but limited talent, as well as to the disciples who had been with the Saviour during the years of His earthly ministry, was the commission given to go "into all the world, and preach the gospel to every creature" (Mark 16:15). . . .

To the members of the early Christian church was given a sacred trust. They were to be executors of the will in which Christ had bequeathed to the world the treasure of life eternal. . . . In the trust given to the first disciples believers in every age have shared. God desires that every believer shall be an executor of the Saviour's will. . . . The unselfish labor of God's people in ages past is to His servants today an object lesson and an inspiration. Today God's chosen people are to be zealous of good works, separating from all worldly ambition and walking humbly in the footsteps of the lowly Nazarene. . . .

"The Spirit and the bride say, Come. And let him that heareth say, Come." This commission to bid others come, embraces the entire church, and applies to every one who has accepted Christ as his personal Saviour. . . . Every soul who has heard the divine invitation is to echo the message . . . , saying to those with whom he comes in contact, "Come." From the moment of conversion those who receive Christ are to become the light of the world. . . .

The Holy Spirit, Christ's representative, arms the weakest with might to press forward to victory. . . . The work that some are able to do may appear to be restricted by circumstances; but wherever it is, if performed with faith and diligence, it will be felt to the uttermost parts of the earth.[42]

339

A WORLD TO BE WARNED

And this gospel of the kingdom shall be preached in all the world for a witness unto all nations; and then shall the end come. Matt: 24:14.

As the rays of the sun penetrate to the remotest corners of the globe, so God designs that the light of the gospel shall extend to every soul upon the earth. . . . At this time, when the enemy is working as never before to engross the minds of men and women, we should be laboring with increasing activity. Diligently, disinterestedly, we are to proclaim the last message of mercy in the cities—in the highways and byways. All classes are to be reached. As we labor we shall meet with different nationalities. None are to be passed by unwarned. The Lord Jesus was the gift of God to the entire world— not to the higher classes alone, and not to one nationality, to the exclusion of others. His saving grace encircles the world. Whosoever will, may drink of the water of life. A world is waiting to hear the message of present truth. . . .

The kingdom of grace is now being established as day by day hearts that have been full of sin and rebellion yield to the sovereignty of His love. But the full establishment of the kingdom of His glory will not take place till the second coming of Christ to this world. "The kingdom and dominion, and the greatness of the kingdom under the whole heaven" is to "be given to the people of the saints of the most High" (Dan. 7:27). . . .

The heavenly gates are again to be lifted up, and with ten thousand times ten thousand and thousands of thousands of holy ones, our Saviour will come forth as "King of kings, and Lord of lords" (1 Tim. 6:15). Jehovah Immanuel "shall be king over all the earth: in that day shall there be one Lord, and his name one" (Zech. 14: 9). "The tabernacle of God is with men, and he shall dwell with them, . . . and be their God" (Rev. 21:3).

But before that coming, Jesus said, "This gospel of the kingdom shall be preached in all the world for a witness unto all nations." His kingdom will not come until the good tidings of His grace shall have been carried to all the earth.[43]

340

DAY OF TRIUMPH

Behold, I come quickly: blessed is he that keepeth the sayings of the prophecy of this book. Rev. 22:7.

We are rapidly approaching the end of this earth's history; and as we realize that Jesus is indeed coming soon, we shall be aroused to labor as never before. . . . We are to raise the banner on which is inscribed, "The commandments of God, and the faith of Jesus." Obedience to God's law is the great issue. Let it not be put out of sight. . . .

The Lord desires to see the work of proclaiming the third angel's message carried forward with increasing efficiency. As He has worked in all ages to give victories to His people, so in this age He longs to carry to a triumphant fulfillment His purposes for His church. He bids His believing saints to advance unitedly, going from strength to greater strength, from faith to increased assurance and confidence in the truth and righteousness of His cause.

We are to stand firm as a rock to the principles of the Word of God, remembering that God is with us to give us strength to meet each new experience. Let us ever maintain in our lives the principles of righteousness. . . . We are to hold as very sacred the faith that has been substantiated by the instruction and approval of the Spirit of God from our earliest experience until the present time. We are to cherish as very precious the work that the Lord has been carrying forward through His commandment-keeping people, and which, through the power of His grace, will grow stronger and more efficient as time advances. The enemy is seeking to becloud the discernment of God's people and to weaken their efficiency, but if they will labor as the Spirit of God shall direct, He will open doors of opportunity before them for the work of building up the old waste places. Their experience will be one of constant growth, until the Lord shall descend from heaven with power and great glory to set His seal of final triumph upon His faithful ones.

The work that lies before us is one that will put to the stretch every power of the human being. . . . Jesus will be with you; . . . and He will be your helper in every emergency.[44]

From Mrs. White's last message to a General Conference Session, 1913.

CRISIS OF THE AGES

Blow ye the trumpet in Zion, and sound an alarm in my holy mountain: let all the inhabitants of the land tremble: for the day of the Lord cometh, for it is nigh at hand. Joel 2:1.

Troublous times are right upon us. The fulfilling of the signs of the times gives evidence that the day of the Lord is near at hand. The daily papers are full of indications of a terrible conflict in the future. Bold robberies are of frequent occurrence. Strikes are common. Thefts and murders are committed on every hand. Men possessed of demons are taking the lives of men and women and little children. All these things testify that the coming of Christ is near at hand. . . .

In accidents and calamities by land and by sea, in great conflagrations, in fierce tornadoes and terrific hailstorms, in tempests, floods, cyclones, tidal waves, and earthquakes, in every place and in a thousand forms, Satan is exercising his power. . . .

The crisis is stealing gradually upon us. The sun shines in the heavens, passing over its usual round, and the heavens still declare the glory of God. Men are still eating and drinking, planting and building, marrying and giving in marriage. Merchants are still buying and selling. . . . Pleasure lovers are still crowding to theaters, horse races, gambling hells. The highest excitement prevails, yet probation's hour is fast closing, and every case is about to be eternally decided. Satan sees that his time is short. He has set all his agents to work, that men may be deceived, deluded, occupied, and entranced, until the day of probation shall be ended and the door of mercy be forever shut. The time is right upon us when there will be sorrow that no human balm can heal. Sentinel angels are now restraining the four winds, that they shall not blow till the servants of God are sealed in their foreheads; but when God shall bid His angels loose the winds, there will be a scene of strife such as no pen can picture. . . .

"Our God shall come, and shall not keep silence. . . . He shall call to the heavens from above, and to the earth, that he may judge his people. Gather my saints together unto me; those that have made a covenant with me by sacrifice" (Ps. 50:3-5).[1]

342

WARNING MESSAGES

And as it was in the days of Noe, so shall it be also in the days of the Son of man. They did eat, they drank, they married wives, they were given in marriage, until the day that Noe entered into the ark, and the flood came, and destroyed them all. Luke 17:26, 27.

The Lord God of Israel is jealous for His honor. How then, I inquire, does He regard the inhabitants of this world, who live in His house and from His liberal treasury are provided by Him with food and clothing but who never so much as say, Thank You, to Him? They are unmindful of His goodness. They are like the inhabitants of the antediluvian world, who were destroyed because they worked continually in opposition to their Creator.

Of the antediluvians we read, "God saw that the wickedness of man was great in the earth, and that every imagination of the thoughts of his heart was only evil continually. . . . And God said unto Noah, The end of all flesh is come before me; for the earth is filled with violence through them; and, behold, I will destroy them with the earth" (Gen. 6:5, 13).

God warned the inhabitants of the old world of what He purposed to do in cleansing the earth of its impurity. But they laughed to scorn what they regarded as a superstitious prediction. They mocked at Noah's warning of a coming flood. When Christ was upon the earth He gave warning of what was coming upon Jerusalem because the people had rejected truth, despising the messages that God had sent. But His warning was unheeded.

The Lord has sent us, by His ambassadors, messages of warning, declaring that the end of all things is at hand. Some will listen to these warnings, but by the vast majority they will be disregarded.

Thus will it be when Christ comes. Farmers, merchants, lawyers, tradesmen, will be wholly engrossed in business, and upon them the day of the Lord will come as a snare.

"Watch ye therefore: for ye know not when the master of the house cometh, at even, or at midnight, or at the cockcrowing, or in the morning: lest coming suddenly he find you sleeping. And what I say unto you I say unto all, Watch" (Mark 13:35-37).[2]

A TIME OF TROUBLE

Therefore rejoice, ye heavens, and ye that dwell in them. Woe to the inhabiters of the earth and of the sea! for the devil is come down unto you, having great wrath, because he knoweth that he hath but a short time. Rev. 12:12.

As we approach the perils of the last days, the temptations of the enemy become stronger and more determined. Satan has come down in great power, knowing that his time is short; and he is working "with all deceivableness of unrighteousness in them that perish" (2 Thess. 2:10). The warning comes to us through God's Word that, if it were possible, he would deceive the very elect.

Wonderful events are soon to open before the world. The end of all things is at hand. The time of trouble is about to come upon the people of God. Then it is that the decree will go forth forbidding those who keep the Sabbath of the Lord to buy or sell, and threatening them with punishment, and 'even death, if they do not observe the first day of the week as the Sabbath.

"And at that time shall Michael stand up, the great prince which standeth for the children of thy people: and there shall be a time of trouble, such as never was since there was a nation even to that same time: and at that time thy people shall be delivered, every one that shall be found written in the book" (Dan. 12:1). By this we see the importance of having our names written in the book of life. All whose names are registered there will be delivered from Satan's power, and Christ will command that their filthy garments be removed, and that they be clothed with His righteousness. "And they shall be mine, saith the Lord of hosts, in that day when I make up my jewels . . ." (Mal. 3:17).

In the time of trouble Satan stirs up the wicked, and they encircle the people of God to destroy them. But he does not know that "pardon" has been written opposite their names in the books of heaven. He does not know that the command has been given, "Take away the filthy garments" from them, clothe them with "change of raiment," and set "a fair miter" upon their heads (Zech. 3:4, 5). . . .

How precious in the sight of God are His people! [3]

344

"WHILE HE MAY BE FOUND"

Seek ye the Lord while he may be found, call ye upon him while he is near. Isa. 55:6.

There is coming, rapidly and surely, an almost universal guilt upon the inhabitants of the great cities because of the steady increase of determined wickedness. God has given life to man, in order that through a knowledge of the Word and by practicing its principles, the human agent may become one with God, obedient to the divine will. But Satan has been working constantly by many devisings to bring man into disfavor with God. In the antediluvian world, human agencies brought in all manner of devisings and ingenious practices to make of no effect the law of Jehovah. They cast aside His authority, because it interfered with their schemes. As in the days before the Flood, so now the time is right upon us when the Lord God must reveal His omnipotent power. . . .

For years Satan has been gaining control of human minds through subtle sophistries that he has devised to take the place of the truth. In this time of peril, rightdoers, in the fear of God, will glorify His name by repeating the words of David, "It is time for thee, Lord, to work: for they have made void thy law." [4]

Our God is a God of compassion. With long-suffering and tender mercy He deals with the transgressors of His law. And yet in this our day, when men and women have so many opportunities for becoming familiar with the divine law as revealed in Holy Writ, the great Ruler of the universe cannot behold with any satisfaction the wicked cities, where reign violence and crime. . . .

The forbearance of God has been very great, so great that when we consider the continuous insult to His holy commandments we marvel. The Omnipotent One has been exerting a restraining power over His own attributes. But He will certainly arise to punish the wicked, who so boldly defy the just claims of the decalogue. [5]

Now is a time when there should be a humbling of the heart before God. Let us seek Him while He is to be found on the pardoning side, and not on the judgment side. Wake up, my brethren and sisters. . . . Call upon the Lord while He may be found. [6]

P.ROBATION'S CLOSING HOUR

For he saith, I have heard thee in a time accepted, and in the day of salvation have I succoured thee: behold, now is the accepted time; behold, now is the day of salvation. 2 Cor. 6:2.

Now, just now, is our time of probation, wherein we are to prepare for heaven. Christ gave His life that we might have this probation. But so long as time shall last, Satan will strive for the mastery over us. He works with power to lead men to become absorbed in money getting. He invents many kinds of amusement, so that their minds may be engrossed with worldly pleasure. He would have them forget all about the inward adorning—the adorning of a meek and quiet spirit—which in the sight of God is of great price. He is determined that every moment shall be filled with efforts to carry out ambitious projects or to amuse and gratify self. . . .

Satan uses his influence to drown the voice of God and the voice of conscience, and the world acts as if under his control. Men have chosen him as their leader. . . . Infatuated with schemes for pleasure and amusement, they are striving for that which will perish with the using. . . .

The fast-fulfilling signs of the times declare that the great day of the Lord is right upon us. In that day shall it be said of any of us: "This man was called by God, but he would not hear, he would not give heed. Again and again the Spirit moved upon his heart, but he said, 'Go thy way for this time; when I have a convenient season, I will call for thee.' This man saw the Saviour's sacrifice in a beautiful light, but some matter of minor importance came in, and his heart was captivated. . . . Every gracious, heavenly influence was dismissed." [7]

Christ is ready to set us free from sin, but He does not force the will, and if by persistent transgression the will itself is wholly bent on evil, and we do not *desire* to be set free, if we *will* not accept His grace, what more can He do? We have destroyed ourselves by our determined rejection of His love. "Behold, now is the accepted time; behold, now is the day of salvation." "To day if ye will hear his voice, harden not your hearts" (2 Cor. 6:2; Heb. 3:7, 8).[8]

A WORK OF PREPARATION

Being confident of this very thing, that he which hath begun a good work in you will perform it until the day of Jesus Christ. Phil. 1:6.

There is an earnest work of preparation to be done by Seventh-day Adventists if they would stand firm in the trying experiences just before them. If they remain true to God in the confusion and temptation of the last days, they must seek the Lord in humility of heart for wisdom to resist the deceptions of the enemy. . . .

Ever are we to keep in mind the solemn thought of the Lord's soon return, and in view of this to recognize the individual work to be done. Through the aid of the Holy Spirit we are to resist natural inclinations and tendencies to wrong, and weed out of the life every un-Christlike element. Thus we shall prepare our hearts for the reception of God's blessing, which will impart to us grace and bring us into harmony with the faith of Jesus. For this work of preparation great advantages have been granted to this people in light bestowed, in messages of warning and instruction, sent through the agency of the Spirit of God.

Because of the increasing power of Satan's temptations, the times in which we live are full of peril for the children of God, and we need to learn constantly of the Great Teacher, that we may take every step in surety and righteousness. Wonderful scenes are opening before us, and at this time a living testimony is to be borne in the lives of God's professing people, so that the world may see that in this age when evil reigns on every side, there is yet a people who are laying aside their will and are seeking to do God's will—a people in whose hearts and lives the law of God is written. There are strong temptations before us, sharp tests. The commandment-keeping people of God are to prepare for this time of trial by obtaining a deeper experience in the things of God and a practical knowledge of the righteousness of Christ. . . . Not to unbelievers only, but to church members the words are spoken, "Seek ye the Lord while he may be found, call ye upon him while he is near" (Isa. 55:6). . . .

Let your daily lives witness to the faith you profess.[9]

347

OUR SURE DEFENSE

Because thou hast kept the word of my patience, I also will keep thee from the hour of temptation, which shall come upon all the world, to try them that dwell upon the earth. Rev. 3:10.

Satan is now more earnestly engaged in playing the game of life for souls than at any previous time; and unless we are constantly on our guard, he will establish in our hearts, pride, love of self, love of the world, and many other evil traits. He will also use every possible device to unsettle our faith in God and in the truths of His Word. If we have not a deep experience in the things of God, if we have not a thorough knowledge of His Word, we shall be beguiled to our ruin by the errors and sophistries of the enemy. False doctrines will sap the foundations of man, because they have not learned to discern truth from error. Our only safeguard against the wiles of Satan is to study the Scriptures diligently, to have an intelligent understanding of the reasons of our faith, and faithfully to perform every known duty. The indulgence of one known sin will cause weakness and darkness and subject us to fierce temptation. . . .

Are our supplications ascending to God in living faith? Are we opening the door of the heart to Jesus and closing every means of entrance to Satan? Are we daily obtaining clearer light and greater strength, that we may stand in Christ's righteousness? Are we emptying our hearts of all selfishness, and cleansing them, preparatory to receiving the latter rain from heaven?

Now is the time when we are to confess and forsake our sins, that they may go beforehand to judgment and be blotted out. Now is the time to "cleanse ourselves from all filthiness of the flesh and spirit, perfecting holiness in the fear of God" (2 Cor. 7:1). It is dangerous to delay this work. Satan is even now seeking by disasters upon sea and land to seal the fate of as many as possible. What is the defense of the people of God at this time? It is a living connection with heaven. If we would dwell in safety from the noisome pestilence, if we would be preserved from dangers seen and unseen, we must hide in God; we must secure the protecting care of Jesus and holy angels.[10]

BEWARE OF SATAN'S DELUSIONS

Beware lest any man spoil you through philosophy and vain deceit, after the tradition of men, after the rudiments of the world, and not after Christ. Col. 2:8.

We need a firm reliance upon God if we would be saved from the power of satanic agencies. If we will keep close to the teachings of the Word, the truths of that Word will be our safeguard, saving us from the delusions of these last days. We need the truth. We need to believe in it. Its principles are adapted to all the circumstances of life. They prepare the soul for duty and brace it for trial. They bear the stamp of the divine Author. . . .

The natural stubbornness of the human heart resists the light of truth. Its natural pride of opinion leads to independence of judgment and a clinging to human ideas and philosophy. There is with some a constant danger of becoming unsettled in the faith by the desire for originality. They wish to find some new and strange truth to present, to have a new message to bring to the people; but such a desire is a snare of the enemy to captivate the mind and lead away from the truth. . . . The Lord would have those who understand the reasons for their faith rest in their belief of that which they have been convinced is truth, and not be turned from the faith by the presentation of human sophistries. . . . In these last days we need a large and increasing faith. We need to be established in the faith by a knowledge and wisdom not derived from any human source, but which is found only in the riches of the wisdom of God. . . .

Those who have accepted the truth of the third angel's message are to hold it fast by faith, and it will hold them from drifting into superstitions and theories that would separate them from one another and from God. Our reception of the truth we hold as Seventh-day Adventists was not a chance experience. It was reached by earnest prayer and careful research of the Inspired Word. The Lord would have us walk and work in perfect unity. His name, Christ Jesus, is to be our watchword, His example our badge of distinction, the principles of His Word the foundation of our piety. In unity of spirit and action will be our strength.[11]

TRUTH OUR SAFEGUARD

Then if any man shall say unto you, Lo, here is Christ, or there; believe it not. For there shall arise false Christs, and false prophets, and shall shew great signs and wonders; insomuch that, if it were possible, they shall deceive the very elect. Matt. 24:23, 24.

In the wilderness of temptation Satan came to Christ as an angel from the courts of God. It was by his words, not by his appearance, that the Saviour recognized the enemy.[12]

The time is coming when Satan will work miracles right in your sight, claiming that he is Christ; and if your feet are not firmly established upon the truth of God, then you will be led away from your foundation. The only safety for you is to search for the truth as for hid treasures. Dig for the truth as you would for treasures in the earth, and present the Word of God, the Bible, before your heavenly Father, and say, Enlighten me; teach me what is truth. And when His Holy Spirit shall come into your hearts, to impress the truth into your souls, you will not let it go easily. You have gained such an experience in searching the Scriptures that every point is established.[13]

Without the enlightenment of the Spirit of God we shall not be able to discern truth from error and shall fall under the masterful temptations and deceptions that Satan will bring upon the world. We are near the close of the controversy between the Prince of light and the prince of darkness, and soon the delusions of the enemy will try our faith, of what sort it is.[14]

If ever there was a time when we needed faith and spiritual enlightenment, it is now. Those who are watching unto prayer and are searching the Scriptures daily with an earnest desire to know and do the will of God, will not be led astray by any of the deceptions of Satan. . . . We want the truth on every point. We want it unadulterated with error and unpolluted by the maxims, customs, and opinions of the world. We want the truth with all its inconvenience. The acceptance of truth ever involves a cross. But Jesus gave His life as a sacrifice for us, and shall we not give Him our best affections, our holiest aspirations, our fullest service?[15]

A MOMENT OF RESPITE

Ye that love the Lord, hate evil: he preserveth the souls of his saints; he delivereth them out of the hand of the wicked.
Ps. 97:10.

The Lord is soon to come. Wickedness and rebellion, violence and crime, are filling the world. The cries of the suffering and the oppressed rise to Him for justice. In the place of being softened by the patience and forbearance of God, the wicked are growing stronger in stubborn rebellion. The time in which we live is one of marked depravity. Religious restraint is thrown off, and men reject the law of God. . . . A more than common contempt is placed upon this holy law.

A moment of respite has been graciously given us of God. Every power lent us of Heaven is to be used in doing the work assigned us by the Lord for those who are perishing in ignorance. The warning message is to be sounded in all parts of the world. There must be no delay. The truth must be proclaimed in the dark places of the earth. Obstacles must be met and surmounted. A great work is to be done, and this work is entrusted to those who know the truth for this time.

Now is the time to lay hold of the arm of our strength. The prayer of David should be the prayer of pastors and laymen: "It is time for thee, Lord, to work: for they have made void thy law" (Ps. 119:126). Let the servants of God weep between the porch and the altar, crying, "Spare thy people, O Lord, and give not thine heritage to reproach" (Joel 2:17).

God has always wrought in behalf of His truth. The designs of wicked men, the enemies of the church, are subject to His power and His overruling providence. He can move upon the hearts of statesmen; the wrath of the haters of His truth and His people can be turned aside, even as the waters of a river could be turned, if thus He ordered it. Prayer moves the arm of Omnipotence. He who marshals the stars in order in the heavens, whose word controls the waves of the great deep—the same infinite Creator will work in behalf of His people, if they will call upon Him in faith. He will restrain all the forces of darkness until the warning is given to the world and all who will heed it are prepared for His coming.[16]

351

THE BLESSED HOPE

Looking for that blessed hope, and the glorious appearing of the great God and our Saviour Jesus Christ. Titus 2:13.

Jesus said He would go away and prepare mansions for us, that where He is there we may be also. We shall ever dwell with and enjoy the light of His precious countenance. My heart leaps with joy at the cheering prospect. We are almost home. Heaven, sweet heaven! It is our eternal home. I am glad every moment that Jesus lives, and because He lives we shall live also. My soul says, Praise the Lord. There is a fullness in Jesus, a supply for each, for all, and why should we die for bread or starve in foreign lands?

I hunger, I thirst for salvation, for entire conformity to the will of God. We have a good hope through Jesus. It is sure and steadfast and entereth into that within the veil. It yields us consolation in affliction, it gives us joy amid anguish, disperses the gloom around us, and causes us to look through it all to immortality and eternal life. . . . Earthly treasures are no inducement to us, for while we have this hope it reaches clear above the treasures of earth that are passing away and takes hold of the immortal inheritance, the treasures that are durable, incorruptible, undefiled, and that fade not away. . . .

Our mortal bodies may die and be laid away in the grave. Yet the blessed hope lives on until the resurrection, when the voice of Jesus calls forth the sleeping dust. We shall then enjoy the fullness of the blessed, glorious hope. We know in whom we have believed. We have not run in vain, neither labored in vain. A rich, a glorious reward is before us; it is the prize for which we run, and if we persevere with courage we shall surely obtain it. . . .

There is salvation for us, and why do we stay away from the fountain? Why not come and drink that our souls may be refreshed, invigorated, and may flourish in God? Why do we cling so closely to earth? There is something better than earth for us to talk about and think of. We can be in a heavenly frame of mind. Oh, let us dwell upon Jesus' lovely, spotless character, and by beholding we shall become changed to the same image. Be of good courage. Have faith in God.[17]

VICTORY OVER DEATH

So when this corruptible shall have put on incorruption, and this mortal shall have put on immortality, then shall be brought to pass the saying that is written, Death is swallowed up in victory. 1 Cor. 15:54.

"And as they thus spake, Jesus himself stood in the midst of them, and saith unto them, Peace be unto you" (Luke 24:36). . . . Here we have before us the precious evidence that Christ is a living Saviour. A little while before, He was enclosed in Joseph's new tomb, but He had burst the bands of death and walked forth a triumphant conqueror. . . . The angel of God said, He is risen. Wonderful testimony! The hope of the world! Christ had risen and their Saviour was a risen Saviour! . . . Christ had obtained the victory, and although man had fallen and was condemned to death, yet he could live again. Those who sleep in Jesus will be called from their prison house . . . to a glorious immortality. . . . He has risen, dear friends, and in your despondency you may know . . . that Jesus is by your side to give you peace.

I know what I am talking about. I have seen the time when I thought the waves were going over my head; in that time I felt my Saviour precious to me. When my eldest son was taken from me I felt my grief was very great, but Jesus came to my side and I felt His peace in my soul. The cup of consolation was placed to my lips.

And then he who had stood by my side for thirty-six years . . . was taken. We had labored together side by side in the ministry, but we had to fold the hands of the warrior and lay him down to rest in the silent grave. Again my grief seemed very great, but after all came the cup of consolation. Jesus is precious to me. He walked by my side . . . and He will walk by your side. When our friends go into the grave they are beautiful to us. It may be our father or mother that we lay away: when they come forth those wrinkles are all gone but the figure is there, and we know them. . . .

We want to be prepared to meet these dear friends as they come forth in the resurrection morning. . . . Shall we lay hold upon the hope set before us in the gospel that we shall be like Him, for we shall see Him as He is?[18]

CHILDREN OF THE HEAVENLY KING

In my Father's house are many mansions: if it were not so, I would have told you. I go to prepare a place for you. And if I go and prepare a place for you, I will come again, and receive you unto myself; that where I am, there ye may be also. John 14:2, 3.

The invitation is, "Come out from among them, and be ye separate, ... and I will receive you, and will be a Father unto you, and ye shall be my sons and daughters, saith the Lord Almighty" (2 Cor. 6:17, 18). Oh, what an exaltation is this—to be members of the royal family, children of the heavenly King! To have the Saviour of the universe, the King over all kings, know us by name, and to be heirs of God to the immortal inheritance, the eternal substance! This is our privilege; will we have the prize? Will we fight the battles of the Lord? Will we press the battle to the gate? Will we be victorious? I have decided that I must have heaven, and I want you to have it. . . .

Search the Bible, for it tells you of Jesus. I want you to read the Bible and see the matchless charms of Jesus. I want you to fall in love with the Man of Calvary, so that at every step you can say to the world, His "ways are ways of pleasantness, and all" His "paths are peace" (Prov. 3:17). You want to represent Christ to the world. You want to show to the world you have a hope big with immortality. You want to drink of the waters of salvation. You want the heavenly angels to be in your dwelling. You want Christ to abide there. . . .

Praise the Lord, oh, my soul! He says He has gone to prepare mansions for me: "Let not your heart be troubled: ye believe in God, believe also in me. In my Father's house are many mansions: if it were not so, I would have told you. I go to prepare a place for you. And if I go and prepare a place for you, I will come again, and receive you unto myself; that where I am, there ye may be also" (John 14:1-3).

Thank God! It is these mansions that I am looking to. It is not the earthly mansions here, for they are to be shaken down by the mighty earthquake erelong; but it is those heavenly mansions that Christ has gone to prepare for the faithful. We have no home here. We are only pilgrims and strangers here, passing to a better country, even an heavenly. . . . May God help us to win the boon of eternal life.[19]

354

IF CHRIST SHOULD COME TODAY

Watch ye therefore, and pray always, that ye may be accounted worthy to escape all these things that shall come to pass, and to stand before the Son of man. Luke 21:36.

Christ bids us watch, that we may be accounted worthy to escape the things that are coming on the earth. It is of the greatest importance that we heed this warning. The enemy of all righteousness is on our track, seeking to lead us to forget God.

We should be filled with joy at the thought of Christ's soon appearing. To those that love His appearing He will come without sin unto salvation. But if our minds are filled with thoughts of earthly things, we cannot look forward with joy to His appearing.

"If I knew that Christ were coming in a few years," one says, "I should live very differently." But if we believe that He is coming at all, we should live just as faithfully as if we knew that He would appear in a few years. We cannot see the end from the beginning, but Christ has provided sufficient help for every day in the year.

All we have to do with is this one day. Today we must be faithful to our trust. Today we must love God with all the heart and our neighbor as ourselves. Today we must resist the temptations of the enemy, and through the grace of Christ gain the victory. Thus we shall watch and wait for Christ's coming. Each day we should live as if we knew that this would be our last day on this earth. If we knew that Christ would come tomorrow, would we not crowd into today all the kind words, all the unselfish deeds, that we could? We should be patient and gentle, and intensely in earnest, doing all in our power to win souls to Christ. . . .

I urge you to turn your thoughts from worldly things and center them on the things of eternity. Christ has placed everlasting life within your reach, and He has promised to give you help in every time of need. . . . We should never rest satisfied with present attainments. If we put mind and heart into the work of reaching God's ideal for us, if we go to Christ, the mighty helper, for aid, He will give us the very assistance that we need. He will bestow on us the very power that will enable us to be victorious in the struggle against evil.[20]

WOULD YOU BE READY?

Therefore be ye also ready: for in such an hour as ye think not the Son of man cometh. Matt. 24:44.

Suppose that today Christ should appear in the clouds of heaven, who . . . would be ready to meet Him? Suppose we should be translated into the kingdom of heaven just as we are. Would we be prepared to unite with the saints of God, to live in harmony with the royal family, the children of the heavenly King? What preparation have you made for the judgment? Have you made your peace with God? . . . Are you seeking to help those around you, those in your home, those in your neighborhood, those with whom you come in contact that are not keeping the commandments of God? . . . Remember that profession is worthless without a practice that enters into the daily life. God knows whether we are keeping His law in truth. He knows just what we are doing, just what we are thinking and saying. Are we getting ready to meet the King? When He comes in the clouds of heaven with power and great glory, will you be able to say, "Lo, this is our God; we have waited for him, and he will save us" (Isa. 25:9)? To those who can say this Christ will say, "Come up higher. Upon this earth you have loved Me. You have loved to do My will. You can now enter the Holy City and receive the crown of everlasting life."

If it were possible for us to be admitted into heaven as we are, how many of us would be able to look upon God? How many of us have on the wedding garment? How many of us are without spot or wrinkle or any such thing? . . .

This is our washing and ironing time—the time when we are to cleanse our robes of character in the blood of the Lamb. John says, "Behold the Lamb of God, which taketh away the sin of the world" (John 1:29). . . . Shall we not let our sins go? . . .

I entreat you, brethren and sisters, to labor earnestly to secure the crown of everlasting life. The reward will be worth the conflict, worth the effort. . . . In the race in which we are running, everyone may receive the reward offered—a crown of everlasting life. I want this crown; I mean by God's help to have it. I mean to hold fast to the truth, that I may see the King in His beauty.[21]

356

A CROWN OF THORNS—A CROWN OF GLORY

And then shall appear the sign of the Son of man in heaven: and then shall all the tribes of the earth mourn, and they shall see the Son of man coming in the clouds of heaven with power and great glory. Matt. 24:30.

Christ is coming in the clouds of heaven with power and great glory. Who . . . will meet Him in peace? Who will be among that number to whom the words apply, "He shall come to be glorified in his saints, and to be admired in all them that believe"?

It is called the glorious appearing of the great God and our Saviour Jesus Christ. His coming surpasses in glory all that the eye has ever seen. Far exceeding anything the imagination has conceived will be His personal revelation in the clouds of heaven. Then there will be a perfect contrast to the humility which attended His first advent. Then He came as the Son of the infinite God, but His glory was concealed by the garb of humanity. Then He came without any worldly distinction of royalty, without any visible manifestation of glory; but at His second appearing He comes with His own glory and the glory of the Father and attended by the angelic host of heaven. In the place of that crown of thorns which marred His brow, He wears a crown within a crown. No longer is He clad with the garments of humility, with the old kingly robe placed upon Him by His mockers. No: He comes clad in a robe whiter than the whitest white. Upon His vesture and thigh a name is inscribed, "King of kings, and Lord of lords."

As the representative of God, Christ appeared in human flesh. Though in the form of a man, He was the Son of God, and the world was given an opportunity to see how it would treat God. Christ declared, "He that hath seen me hath seen the Father" (John 14:9). But when He comes the second time, divinity is no longer concealed. He comes as One equal with God, as His own beloved Son, Prince of heaven and earth. He is also the Redeemer of His people, the Life-giver. The glory of the Father and the Son are seen to be one. . . . Then shall He shine forth "before his ancients gloriously" (Isa. 24:23).[22]

357

GLORY INDESCRIBABLE

Wherefore God also hath highly exalted him, and given him a name which is above every name: that at the name of Jesus every knee should bow, of things in heaven, and things in earth, and things under the earth; and that every tongue should confess that Jesus Christ is Lord, to the glory of God the Father. **Phil. 2:9-11.**

The Father's wisdom and glory shine forth in His [Christ's] majesty. He is exalted and precious to all who believe. But His own personal glory, who can describe it? He comes with His divine nature plainly revealed—He who was denied and rejected by man, who stood at the bar of Pilate as a criminal. . . .

Christ is now acknowledged as the King of Glory. "Blessed is he that cometh in the name of the Lord" (Matt. 21:9). The question of His divinity is forever settled. Where are those who held the Saviour bound at Pilate's bar, who smote Him in the face, who scourged Him, who drove the nails through His hands and feet? those who mocked Him, saying, "He saved others; himself he cannot save. . . ." (Matt. 27:42)? Where is the puny arm that will be lifted against Him now? The scene is changed. At the name of Jesus every knee shall bow, and every tongue shall confess that Jesus is Christ, Lord of heaven and earth. . . .

The glory of Christ's humanity did not appear when He was upon the earth. He was regarded as a man of sorrows, and acquainted with grief. We hid as it were our faces from Him. But He was pursuing the path the plan of God had devised. That same humanity now appears as He descends from heaven, robed in glory, triumphant, exalted. . . . His believing people have made their calling and election sure. They come forth at the first resurrection, and the song is sung by innumerable voices, "Behold, the tabernacle of God is with men, and he will dwell with them, and they shall be his people, and God himself shall be with them, and be their God. And God shall wipe away all tears from their eyes; and there shall be no more death, neither sorrow, nor crying, neither shall there be any more pain: for the former things are passed away" (Rev. 21:3, 4).[23]

JUDGE OF THE WHOLE WORLD

When the Son of man shall come in his glory, and all the holy angels with him, then shall he sit upon the throne of his glory: and before him shall be gathered all nations. Matt. 25:31, 32.

In His teachings Christ sought to impress men with the certainty of the coming judgment and with its publicity. This is not the judgment of a few individuals, or even of a nation, but of a whole world of human intelligences, of accountable beings. It is to be held in the presence of other worlds, that the love, the integrity, the service, of man for God, may be honored to the highest degree. There will be no lack of glory and honor. . . . The law of God will be revealed in its majesty; and those who have stood in defiant rebellion against its holy precepts will understand that the law that they have discarded and despised . . . is God's standard of character. . . .

In this speck of a world the heavenly universe will manifest the greatest interest, for Jesus paid an infinite price for the souls of its inhabitants. . . .

God designed that the Prince of sufferers in humanity should be judge of the whole world. He who came from the heavenly courts to save man from eternal death; . . . He who submitted to be arraigned before an earthly tribunal, and who suffered the ignominious death of the cross—He alone is to pronounce the sentence of reward or of punishment. He who submitted to the suffering and humiliation of the cross here, in the counsel of God is to have the fullest compensation, and ascend the throne acknowledged by all the heavenly universe as the King of saints. He has undertaken the work of salvation, and shown before unfallen worlds and the heavenly family that the work He has begun He is able to complete. . . . In that day of final punishment and reward both saints and sinners will recognize in Him who was crucified the Judge of all living. . . .

Probationary time is granted us, opportunities and privileges are given us, to make our calling and election sure. How we should prize this precious time and improve every talent God has given, that we may be faithful stewards over ourselves! [24]

Solemn will be the day of final decision! [24]

359

JUSTICE TRIUMPHANT

And I saw the dead, small and great, stand before God; and the books were opened: and another book was opened, which is the book of life: and the dead were judged out of those things which were written in the books, according to their works. Rev. 20:12.

As the artist takes on the polished glass a true picture of the human face, so the angels of God daily place upon the books of heaven an exact representation of the character of every human being.[25]

When we become children of God, our names are written in the Lamb's book of life, and they remain there until the time of the investigative judgment. Then the name of every individual will be called, and his record examined. . . . If in that day it shall appear that all our wicked deeds have not been fully repented of, our names will be blotted from the book of life, and our sins will stand against us.[25]

Can we not understand that the most costly thing in the world is sin? It is at the expense of purity of conscience, at the cost of losing the favor of God and separating the soul from Him, and at last losing heaven. . . . What a scene will be presented when the judgment shall sit and the books shall be opened to testify the salvation or the loss of all souls! It will require the unerring decision of One who has lived in humanity, loved humanity, given His life for humanity, to make the final appropriation of the rewards to the loyal righteous, and the punishment of . . . the disloyal, and the unrighteous.[26]

The work of our salvation lies between God and our own souls. Though all nations are to pass in judgment before Him, yet He will examine the case of each individual with as close and searching scrutiny as if there were not another being on earth. . . .

The Judge of all the earth will render a just decision. He will not be bribed; He cannot be deceived. He who made man, and whose are the worlds and all the treasures they contain—He it is who weighs character in the balance of eternal justice. . . . Every individual has a soul to save or to lose. Each has a case pending at the bar of God. Each must meet the great Judge face to face.[27]

LIFE OR DEATH?

For the wages of sin is death; but the gift of God is eternal life through Jesus Christ our Lord. Rom. 6:23.

"All have sinned, and come short of the glory of God" (Rom. 3:23). But Christ gave His life to save the sinner from the death sentence. He died that we might live. . . . By His death He brought salvation within the reach of all. . . .

The abundant evidence given by God that He desires the salvation of all, will be the condemnation of those who refuse the gift of heaven. At the last great day, when all will be rewarded or punished according to their obedience or disobedience, the cross of Calvary will appear plainly before those standing before the Judge of all the earth to receive sentence for eternity. They are made capable of comprehending something of the love that God has expressed for fallen human beings. They see how greatly He has been dishonored by those who have continued in transgression, choosing sides with Satan and showing contempt for the law of Jehovah. . . .

Today angels are sent to minister to those who shall be heirs of salvation, to help them to escape from the thralldom of Satan's power. . . . Each human being is given the freedom of choice. It is his to decide whether he will stand under the black banner of rebellion or under the blood-stained banner of Prince Emmanuel. With deep solicitude Heaven watches the conflict between good and evil. None but the obedient can enter the gates of the city of God. Upon those who choose to continue in transgression the death sentence must at last be pronounced. The earth will be purified from their misdoings, their defiance of God. . . .

God's law is the transcript of His character, and those only who obey this law will be accepted by Him. Every departure from obedience to the law of God is rebellion. It is for the highest interest of man to obey the law of God, for conformity to the principles of this law is essential to the formation of a righteous character. The rules of life that the Lord has given will make men pure and happy and holy. Those only who obey these rules can hear from the lips of Christ the words, "Come up higher." [28]

TOO LATE!

While it is said, To day if ye will hear his voice, harden not your hearts, as in the provocation. Heb. 3:15.

Oh, who will describe to you the lamentations that will arise when at the boundary line which parts time and eternity the righteous Judge will lift up His voice and declare, "It is too late." Long have the wide gates of heaven stood open and the heavenly messengers have invited and entreated "Whosoever will, let him take the water of life freely" (Rev. 22:17). "To day if ye will hear his voice, harden not your heart." But at length the mandate goes forth, "He that is unjust, let him be unjust still: and he which is filthy, let him be filthy still: and he that is righteous, let him be righteous still: and he that is holy, let him be holy still" (Rev. 22:11).

The heavenly gate closes, the invitation of salvation ceases. In heaven it is said, "It is done." Such a time is not far distant. I plead with you to make sure work for eternity, to lay hold on the hope set before you in the gospel. Strive to enter in at the strait gate, for if you merely seek, you will not be able.

The world is loaded down with the curse which sin brings. It is literally deluged with sin, with violence and corruption, as in the days of Noah. And yet at this fearful period of our world's history many are asleep. They cease to make efforts to become Christians. . . .

Honesty, nobility, purity of soul, fellowship with God and angels, the heavenly hope, the eternal inheritance, the joys unspeakable and the bliss immeasurable, are your birthright, and will you barter away these treasures for sinful pleasure? . . . What shall worldly pleasures avail you when all the world shall be overwhelmed as was Sodom and destroyed like Gomorrah? . . .

Too late will sinners realize that they have sold their birthright. The crown that they might have had shines upon the brow of another. The inheritance which they might have had is lost. Beware how you trifle with temptation. Beware how you boast of your strength. Christ is your everlasting strength; confide in God, lay hold of His strength, and He will bring you off conqueror and you will wear the crown of victory.[29]

CONFESSING OUR FAITH

Whosoever therefore shall confess me before men, him will I confess also before my Father which is in heaven. Matt. 10:32.

If ever there was a period of time when the words of Christ should be heard, it is now. . . . Through the sanctification of the truth, we may bear a decided testimony for righteousness both before believers and before unbelievers.

We are far behind what we should be in our experience. We are backward in pronouncing the testimony that should flow from sanctified lips. Even when sitting at the table Christ taught truths that brought comfort and courage to the hearts of His hearers. Whenever it is possible we are to present the words of Christ. If His love is in the soul, abiding there as a living principle, there will come forth from the treasure house of the heart, words suitable to the occasion, not light, trifling words, but uplifting words, words of truth and spirituality. . . . Confessing Christ openly and bravely, exhibiting in the choice of words the simplicity of true godliness, will be more effective than many sermons. There are but few who give a true representation of the meekness of Christ. Oh, we need, and we must have, His meekness. Christ is to be formed within, the hope of glory.

We are preparing for translation to the heavenly world. Our conversation should be in heaven, from whence we look for the Lord Jesus. He is to be acknowledged as the Giver of every good and perfect gift, the Author of all our blessings, in whom is centered our hope of eternal life.[30]

Never for one moment should the impression be given to anyone that it would be for his profit to hide his faith and doctrines from the unbelieving people of the world, fearing that he may not be so highly esteemed if his principles are known. Christ requires from all His followers open, manly confession of faith. Each must take his position and be what God designed he should be, a spectacle to the world, to angels, and to men. The whole universe is looking with inexpressible interest to see the closing work of the great controversy between Christ and Satan. . . . Never, from cowardice or worldly policy, let the truth of God be placed in the background.[31]

THE SOUL WINNER'S REWARD

And they that be wise shall shine as the brightness of the firmament; and they that turn many to righteousness as the stars for ever and ever. Dan. 12:3.

When I think of those words of Daniel, I find myself waking up in the night and repeating them over and over: "And they that be wise shall shine as the brightness of the firmament; and they that turn many to righteousness as the stars for ever and ever." Look at the sun and the stars marshaled in the heavens, and known by their names. The Lord says, They that turn many to righteousness shall shine as the stars forever and ever.[32]

In order to determine how important are the interests involved in the conversion of the soul from error to truth, we must appreciate the value of immortality; we must realize how terrible are the pains of the second death; we must comprehend the honor and glory awaiting the ransomed, and understand what it is to live in the presence of Him who died that He might elevate and ennoble man, and give to the overcomer a royal diadem.

The worth of a soul cannot be fully estimated by finite minds. How gratefully will the ransomed and glorified ones remember those who were instrumental in their salvation! No one will then regret his self-denying efforts and persevering labors, his patience, forbearance, and earnest heart yearnings for souls that might have been lost had he neglected his duty or become weary in well-doing.

Now these white-robed ones are gathered into the fold of the Great Shepherd. The faithful worker and the soul saved through his labor are greeted by the Lamb in the midst of the throne, and are led to the tree of life and to the fountain of living waters. With what joy does the servant of Christ behold these redeemed ones, who are made to share the glory of the Redeemer! How much more precious is heaven to those who have been faithful in the work of saving souls! "And they that be wise shall shine as the brightness of the firmament; and they that turn many to righteousness as the stars. . . ."[33]

What is done through the cooperation of men with God is a work that shall never perish, but endure through the eternal ages.[34]

TO SEE THE KING

Thine eyes shall see the king in his beauty: they shall behold the land that is very far off. Isa. 33:17.

If we desire to see the King in His beauty we must here behave worthily. We must outgrow our childishness. When provocation comes let us be silent. There are times when silence is eloquence. We are to reveal the patience and kindness and forbearance that will make us worthy of being called sons and daughters of God. We are to trust Him, and believe on Him, and rely upon Him. We are to follow in Christ's steps. "If any man will come after me," He says, "let him deny himself, and take up his cross daily, and follow me" (Luke 9:23). . . . It may be a heavy cross to keep silent when you ought to. It may be a painful discipline, but let me assure you that silence does much more to overcome evil than a storm of angry words.

Here in this world we are to learn what we must be in order to have a place in the heavenly courts. We are to learn the lessons that Christ desires to teach us, that we may be prepared to be taken to the higher school in the courts above, where the Saviour will lead us beside the river of life, explaining to us many things that here we could not comprehend. . . . There we shall see the glory of God as we have never seen it here. We get but a glimpse of the glory now, because we do not follow on to know the Lord.[35]

Every right principle, every truth learned in an earthly school, will advance us just that much in the heavenly school. As Christ walked and talked with His disciples during His ministry on this earth, so will He teach us in the school above, leading us beside the river of living waters, and revealing to us truths that in this life must remain hidden mysteries because of the limitations of the human mind, so marred by sin. In the heavenly school we shall have opportunity to attain, step by step, to the greatest heights of learning. There, as children of the heavenly King, we shall ever dwell with the members of the royal family; there we shall see the King in His beauty, and behold His matchless charms.[36]

Long have we waited, but our hope is not to grow dim. If we can but see the King in His beauty we shall be forever blessed.[37]

365

GLORIES OF THE FUTURE WORLD

For since the beginning of the world men have not heard, nor perceived by the ear, neither hath the eye seen, O God, beside thee, what he hath prepared for him that waiteth for him. Isa. 64:4.

Many have longed to penetrate into the glories of the future world and to have the secrets of eternal mysteries disclosed to them, but they knock in vain. That which is revealed is for us and for our children. . . . The Great Revealer hath opened to our intelligence many things that are essential in order that we may understand the heavenly attractions and have respect to the recompense of the reward. . . .

The unfoldings of Jesus in reference to heavenly things are of a character that only the spiritual mind can appreciate. The imagination may summon its utmost powers in order to picture the glories of heaven, but "eye hath not seen, nor ear heard, neither have entered into the heart of man, the things which God hath prepared for them that love him" (1 Cor. 2:9). The heavenly intelligences are all around us. . . . Angels of light create a heavenly atmosphere about the soul, lifting us toward the unseen and eternal. We cannot behold their forms with our natural sight; only by the spiritual vision can we discern heavenly things. Our human powers would be extinguished by the inexpressible glory of the angels of light. The spiritual ear alone can distinguish the harmony of heavenly voices. It is not Christ's plan to excite the emotions by brilliant descriptions. . . . He has with sufficient distinctness presented Himself, the way, the truth, and the life, as the only means whereby salvation is to be obtained. No more than this is really required.

He might bring the human soul to the threshold of heaven, and through the open door show us its inner glory flooding the heavenly sanctuary and shining out through its portals; but we must behold it by faith, not with the natural eyes. He does not forget that we are His human agents, to work the works of God in a world all seared and marred with the curse. It is in this world, that is clothed with moral darkness like the pall of death, where darkness covers the earth and gross darkness the people, that we are to walk in the light of heaven.[38]

"COME, YE BLESSED"

But as it is written, Eye hath not seen, nor ear heard, neither have entered into the heart of man, the things which God hath prepared for them that love him. 1 **Cor.** 2:9.

Those who truly love God will desire so to improve the talents that He has given them, that they may be a blessing to others. And by and by the gates of heaven will be thrown wide open to admit them, and from the lips of the King of Glory the benediction will fall upon their ear like richest music, "Come, ye blessed of my Father, inherit the kingdom prepared for you from the foundation of the world" (Matt. 25:34). Thus the redeemed will be welcomed to the mansions that Jesus is preparing for them. There their companions will not be the vile of earth, but those who through divine aid have formed perfect characters. Every sinful tendency, every imperfection, has been removed by the blood of Christ; and the excellence and brightness of His glory, far exceeding the brightness of the sun in its meridian splendor, is imparted to them. And the moral beauty, the perfection of His character, shines through them in worth far exceeding this outward splendor. They are without fault before the great white throne, sharing the dignity and privileges of the angels.

"Eye hath not seen, nor ear heard, neither have entered into the heart of man, the things which God hath prepared for them that love him." In view of the glorious inheritance which may be his, "What shall a man give in exchange for his soul?" (Matt. 16:26). He may be poor; yet he possesses in himself a wealth and dignity that the world could never bestow. The soul, redeemed and cleansed from sin, with all its noble powers dedicated to the service of God, is of surpassing worth.[39]

To dwell forever in this home of the blest, to bear in soul, body, and spirit, not the dark traces of sin and the curse, but the perfect likeness of our Creator, and through ceaseless ages to advance in wisdom, in knowledge, and in holiness, ever exploring new fields of thought, ever finding new wonders and new glories, ever increasing in capacity to know and to enjoy and to love, and knowing that there is still beyond us joy and love and wisdom infinite—such is the object to which the Christian's hope is pointing.[40]

LONGING FOR HEAVEN

My soul longeth, yea, even fainteth for the courts of the Lord: my heart and my flesh crieth out for the living God. Ps. 84:2.

When God's people take their eyes off the things of this world and place them on heaven and heavenly things they will be a peculiar people, because they will see the mercy and goodness and compassion that God has shown to the children of men. His love will call forth a response from them, and their lives will show to those around them that the Spirit of God is controlling them, that they are setting their affections on things above, not on the things of the earth.

In thinking of heaven, we may put our imagination to the utmost stretch and think the loftiest thoughts that we are capable of thinking, and our minds will grow weary in the effort to comprehend the breadth and depth and height of the subject. It is impossible for our minds to take in the great themes of eternity. It is impossible for us even to make an effort to understand these things without the effort affecting our whole character for good and having an uplifting influence on our minds. As we think of how Christ came to our world to die for fallen man, we understand something of the price that was paid for our redemption, and we realize that there is no true goodness or greatness apart from God.

Only by the light shining from the cross of Calvary can we know to what depths of sin and degradation the human race has fallen through sin. Only by the length of the chain let down from heaven to draw us up can we know the depths to which we had sunk. And it is only by keeping the unseen realities in view that we can understand anything of the wonderful theme of redemption.[41]

We are almost home; we shall soon hear the voice of the Saviour richer than any music, saying, Your warfare is accomplished. Enter into the joy of thy Lord. Blessed, blessed benediction; I want to hear it from His immortal lips. I want to praise Him; I want to honor Him that sitteth on the throne. I want my voice to echo and re-echo through the courts of heaven. Will you be there? . . . God help us, and fill us with all fullness and power, and then we can taste of the joys of the world to come.[42]

368

BY THE TREE OF LIFE

And they sung a new song, saying, Thou art worthy to take the book, and to open the seals thereof: for thou wast slain, and hast redeemed us to God by thy blood out of every kindred, and tongue, and people, and nation. Rev. 5:9.

Do we expect to get to heaven at last and join the heavenly choir? Just as we go into the grave we will come up, as far as the character is concerned. . . . Now is the time for washing and ironing. . . .

John saw the throne of God and around that throne a company, and he inquired, Who are these? The answer came, "These are they which . . . have washed their robes, and made them white in the blood of the Lamb" (Rev. 7:14). Christ leads them to the fountains of living waters, and there is the tree of life and there is the precious Saviour. Here is presented to us a life that measures with the life of God. There is no pain, sorrow, sickness, or death there. All is peace and harmony and love. . . .

Now is the time to receive grace and strength and power to combine with our human efforts that we can form characters for everlasting life. When we do this we will find that the angels of God will minister unto us, and we shall be heirs of God and joint heirs with Jesus Christ. And when the last trump shall sound, and the dead shall be called from their prison house and changed in a moment, in the twinkling of an eye, the crowns of immortal glory shall be placed upon the heads of the overcomers. The pearly gates will swing back for the nations that have kept the truth and they will enter in. The conflict is ended.

"Come, ye blessed of my Father, inherit the kingdom prepared for you from the foundation of the world" (Matt. 25:34). Do we want this benediction? I do, and I believe you do. May God help you that you may fight the battles of this life and gain a victory day by day and at last be among the number that shall cast their crowns at Jesus' feet and touch the golden harps and fill all heaven with sweetest music. I want you to love my Jesus. . . . Do not reject my Saviour, for He has paid an infinite price for you. I see in Jesus matchless charms, and I want you to see these charms.[43]

369

BREATHING THE ATMOSPHERE OF HEAVEN

These are they which came out of great tribulation, and have washed their robes, and made them white in the blood of the Lamb. Rev. 7:14.

John, while in vision, saw a company clothed in white robes. . . . They were seen in the temple of God. This will be the result for all who will lay hold of the merits of Christ and wash their robes in His blood. Every provision has been made so that we can sit with Christ upon His throne, but the condition is that we be in harmony with the law of God. . . .

We cannot afford to lose heaven. We ought to have our conversation on heavenly things. There there is no death nor pain. Why are we so reluctant to talk of these things? Why do we dwell upon earthly things? The apostle exhorts us to have our conversation in heaven. "For our conversation is in heaven; from whence also we look for the Saviour, and the Lord Jesus Christ" (Phil. 3:20). . . . Christ will soon return to gather those who are prepared, and take them to this glorious place. "So Christ was once offered to bear the sins of many; and unto them that look for him shall he appear the second time without sin unto salvation" (Heb. 9:28).

Do we love to think of this event or do we want to put it off? . . . The more we talk of Jesus, the more we shall reflect His divine image. By beholding we become transformed. We need to bring Christ into our religious experience. When you assemble together, let the conversation be on Christ and His salvation. . . . The more we talk of Jesus the more of His matchless charms we shall behold.⁴⁴

Those who take no pleasure in thinking and talking of God in this life, will not enjoy the life that is to come, where God is ever present, dwelling among His people. But those who love to think of God will be in their element, breathing in the atmosphere of heaven. Those who on earth love the thought of heaven will be happy in its holy associations and pleasures. . . . "And there shall be no more curse: but the throne of God and of the Lamb shall be in it; and his servants shall serve him: and they shall see his face; and his name shall be in their foreheads" (Rev. 22:3, 4).⁴⁵

JOY EVERMORE

After this I beheld, and, lo, a great multitude, which no man could number, of all nations, and kindreds, and people, and tongues, stood before the throne, and before the Lamb, clothed with white robes, and palms in their hands. Rev. 7:9.

All classes, all nations and kindreds and people and tongues will stand before the throne of God and the Lamb with their spotless robes and jeweled crowns. Said the angel, These are they that have come up through great tribulation and have washed their robes and made them white, while the lovers of pleasure more than lovers of God, the self-indulgent and disobedient, have lost both worlds. They have neither the things of this life nor the immortal life.

That triumphant throng, with songs of victory and with crowns and harps, have trodden in the fiery furnace of earthly affliction when it was heated and intensely hot. From destitution, from hunger and torture, they come, from deep self-denial and bitter disappointments. Look upon them now as conquerors, no longer poor, no longer in sorrow, in affliction and hatred of all men for Christ's sake. Behold their heavenly garments, white and shining, richer than any kingly robe. Look by faith upon their jeweled crowns; never did such a diadem deck the brow of any earthly monarch.

Listen to their voices as they sing loud hosannas and as they wave the palm branches of victory. Rich music fills heaven as their voices sing forth these words: "Worthy, worthy is the Lamb that was slain and rose again forevermore. Salvation unto our God which sitteth upon the throne, and unto the Lamb." And the angelic host, angels and archangels, covering cherub and glorious seraph, echo back the refrain of that joyous, triumphant song saying, "Amen: Blessing, and glory, and wisdom, and thanksgiving, and honour, and power, and might, be unto our God for ever and ever" (Rev. 7:12).

Oh, in that day it will be discovered that the righteous were the wise ones, while the sinful and disobedient were fools. . . . Shame and everlasting contempt is their portion. Those who have been colaborers for Christ will then be near the throne of God, girt with purity and the garments of eternal righteousness.[46]

371

KINGDOM OF HOLY LOVE

The kingdoms of this world are become the kingdoms of our Lord, and of his Christ; and he shall reign for ever and ever. Rev. 11:15.

The government of the kingdom of Christ is like no earthly government. It is a representation of the characters of those who compose the kingdom. . . . His court is one where holy love presides and whose offices and appointments are graced by the exercise of charity. He charges His servants to bring pity and loving-kindness, His own attributes, into all their office work. . . .

The power of Christ alone can work the transformation in heart and mind that all must experience who would partake with Him of the new life in the kingdom of God. . . . In order to serve Him aright, we must be born of the divine Spirit. This will purify the heart and renew the mind and give us a new capacity for knowing and loving God. It will give us willing obedience to all His requirements. This is true worship.[47]

"Thine eyes shall see Jerusalem a quiet habitation, a tabernacle that shall not be taken down; not one of the stakes thereof shall ever be removed, neither shall any of the cords thereof be broken. But there the glorious Lord will be unto us a place of broad rivers and streams. . . . For the Lord is our judge, the Lord is our lawgiver, the Lord is our King; he will save us. . . . And the inhabitant shall not say, I am sick: the people that dwell therein shall be forgiven their iniquity" (Isa. 33:20-24).

"Be ye glad and rejoice for ever in that which I create," the Lord exhorts; "for, behold, I create Jerusalem a rejoicing, and her people a joy. And I will rejoice in Jerusalem, and joy in my people: and the voice of weeping shall be no more heard in her, nor the voice of crying. . . . And they shall build houses, and inhabit them; and they shall plant vineyards, and eat the fruit of them. They shall not build, and another inhabit; they shall not plant, and another eat: for as the days of a tree are the days of my people, and mine elect shall long enjoy the work of their hands. . . . They shall not hurt nor destroy in all my holy mountain, saith the Lord" (Isa. 65:18-25).[47]

KEY TO ABBREVIATIONS

AA—*Acts of the Apostles, The*
1BC—Ellen G. White Comments in
   SDA Bible Commentary, vol. 1
   (2 BC, etc. for vols. 2-7)
CH—*Counsels on Health*
COL—*Christ's Object Lessons*
CT—*Counsels to Parents, Teachers,*
   and Students
Crisis—Ellen G. White MS 7, 1888,
   quoted in *Through Crisis to Vic-*
   tory, by A. V. Olson
Ev—*Evangelism*
FE—*Fundamentals of Christian Edu-*
   cation
GCB—General Conference *Bulletin*
GW—*Gospel Workers*
Letter—Ellen G. White Letter
MB—*Thoughts From the Mount of*
   Blessing (1956)

MH—*Ministry of Healing, The*
MM—*Medical Ministry*
MS—Ellen G. White Manuscript
PUR—*Pacific Union Recorder*
RH—*Review and Herald*
SC—*Steps to Christ*
SL—*Sanctified Life, The*
1SM—*Selected Messages,* book 1 (2
   SM for book 2)
Sp.T—*Special Testimonies*
ST—*Signs of the Times, The*
Sufferings—*Sufferings of Christ, The*
1T—*Testimonies for the Church,* vol.
   1 (2T, etc., for vols. 2-9)
TM—*Testimonies to Ministers and*
   Gospel Workers
Und. MS—Undated Ellen G. White
   Manuscript
YI—*Youth's Instructor*

SOURCE REFERENCES

JANUARY

1 RH March 31, 1904
2 RH May 30, 1907
3 RH Oct. 15, 1908
4 RH Feb. 15, 1912
5 Letter 43, 1875
6 MS 76, 1903
7 *Crisis,* 246-248
8 ST May 21, 1902
9 ST Feb. 27, 1901
10 1 BC 1084
11 RH March 9, 1905
12 MS 132, 1902
13 4T 461, 462.
14 MS 31, 1911
15 YI Sept. 29, 1892
16 YI Sept. 22, 1892
17 RH June 9, 1910
18 YI Sept. 22, 1892
19 MS 8, 1914
20 RH July 7, 1904
21 RH July 7, 1904
22 RH July 27, 1897
23 RH May 5, 1896
24 RH May 12, 1896
25 Letter 4, 1889
26 Letter 42, 1879
27 RH Aug. 23, 1892
28 RH Oct. 15, 1908
29 Letter 135, 1898
30 4 BC 1154
31 MS 121, 1902
32 RH May 26, 1904
33 RH Nov. 19, 1908
34 RH Jan. 14, 1904
35 RH Jan. 7, 1909
36 RH Jan. 14, 1909
37 SL 16, 17

38 RH May 16, 1907
39 RH Oct. 15, 1908
40 MS 75a, 1900
41 MS 20, 1899
42 RH Oct. 15, 1908
43 MS 9, 1883
44 RH Nov. 21, 1912
45 RH Nov. 28, 1912

FEBRUARY

1 MS 48, 1893
2 *Sufferings* 7-10
3 MS 75, 1886
4 Letter 276, 1904
5 MS 11, 1885
6 MS 6, 1897
7 MS 127, 1899
8 RH April 4, 1912
9 MS 75, 1886
10 6T 230, 231
11 RH Aug. 6, 1889
12 RH March 8, 1892
13 TM 139
14 RH Nov. 24, 1885
15 6 BC 1087, 1088
16 RH Dec. 21, 1886
17 YI June 10, 1897
18 Letter 30a, 1892
19 MS 154, 1898
20 RH May 31, 1906
21 RH May 5, 1910
22 RH Nov. 3, 1904
23 RH May 23, 1899
24 MS 61, 1895
25 RH Oct. 23, 1900
26 TM 388, 389
27 Letter 66, 1878
28 9T 181

29 MS 194, 1898
30 RH Sept. 18, 1900
31 RH May 30, 1907
32 MS 31, 1911
33 FE 234
34 4 BC 1168
35 MS 21, 1911
36 RH April 14, 1904
37 Letter 23, 1890
38 RH May 17, 1906
39 RH Jan. 5, 1911
40 RH April 7, 1904
41 MB 49
42 RH March 31, 1904
43 MS 13, 1892
44 Letter 25a, 1895

MARCH

1 RH March 4, 1909
2 RH July 4, 1907
3 RH Oct. 30, 1900
4 RH Jan. 9, 1900
5 ST Nov. 18, 1903
6 Letter 48, 1903
7 RH June 30, 1910
8 4T 533-535
9 MS 8, 1892
10 5T 200, 201
11 Letter 123, 1904
12 MS 19, 1892
13 RH March 24, 1904
14 Letter 121, 1901
15 RH Jan. 28, 1904
16 MS 9, 1906
17 MS 139, 1898
18 Letter 22, 1898
19 ST Nov. 18, 1903
20 MS 91, 1901

²¹ Letter 92, 1895
²² COL 147
²³ ST April 18, 1892
²⁴ RH April 22, 1884
²⁵ 4 BC 1184
²⁶ RH Oct. 30, 1900
²⁷ ST Nov. 18, 1903
²⁸ COL 174
²⁹ ST Oct. 27, 1881
³⁰ Letter 1, 1904
³¹ GW 254, 255
³² Ibid., 254
³³ MS 194, 1898
³⁴ RH Nov. 10, 1910
³⁵ CH 362
³⁶ MB 131
³⁷ Letter 110, 1893
³⁸ MS 6, 1889
³⁹ 6T 51
⁴⁰ RH Jan. 9, 1900
⁴¹ RH Nov. 19, 1895
⁴² ST Aug. 7, 1884
⁴³ RH June 30, 1896
⁴⁴ SC 98
⁴⁵ 2T 578, 579
⁴⁶ Ibid., 268
⁴⁷ SC 101, 102
⁴⁸ 7T 195
⁴⁹ 4 BC 1183
⁵⁰ 6T 175
⁵¹ 4T 107
⁵² RH Jan. 3, 1907
⁵³ RH April 30, 1908
⁵⁴ RH Jan. 3, 1907
⁵⁵ 3 BC 1148
⁵⁶ 4 BC 1153, 1154
⁵⁷ YI March 29, 1904
⁵⁸ RH Aug. 5, 1890
⁵⁹ RH Sept. 16, 1890
⁶⁰ MS 120, 1898
⁶¹ RH July 7, 1910

APRIL

¹ 6 BC 1120
² 7 BC 967
³ RH Feb. 5, 1895
⁴ 7 BC 923
⁵ MS 8, 1905
⁶ RH Aug. 5, 1890
⁷ RH June 30, 1896
⁸ YI June 12, 1902
⁹ MS 38, 1895
¹⁰ MS 152, 1898
¹¹ RH Aug. 6, 1889
¹² Letter 257, 1904
¹³ RH March 19, 1901
¹⁴ YI Feb. 14, 1901
¹⁵ 6 BC 1073
¹⁶ MS 6, 1889
¹⁷ Letter 355, 1904
¹⁸ Und. MS 43
¹⁹ MS 10, 1883
²⁰ ST June 23, 1887
²¹ Letter 11, 1897
²² Und. MS 23
²³ Letter 24, 1888
²⁴ Letter 57, 1887
²⁵ Letter 130, 1898
²⁶ 1 SM 334
²⁷ RH March 17, 1910
²⁸ MS 32, 1894
²⁹ Letter 4, 1889
³⁰ RH March 17, 1910
³¹ RH Feb. 28, 1907
³² 4T 523

³³ MS 19, 1886
³⁴ MS 15, 1912
³⁵ Address at Goguac Lake, leaflet, 1878, p. 10
³⁶ Ibid., 9, 10, 14, 16
³⁷ Ibid., 16, 17
³⁸ Letter 98b, 1896
³⁹ MS 156, 1907
⁴⁰ MS 5, 1886
⁴¹ Letter 17, 1862
⁴² MH 199
⁴³ Letter 123, 1904
⁴⁴ Letter 150, 1903
⁴⁵ MS 40, 1892
⁴⁶ MS 161, 1897
⁴⁷ RH Feb. 11, 1890
⁴⁸ RH April 7, 1904
⁴⁹ RH Nov. 19, 1895
⁵⁰ RH May 5, 1891
⁵¹ Letter 10, 1893
⁵² Letter 30, 1893

MAY

¹ RH June 23, 1910
² RH March 15, 1906
³ RH Dec. 31, 1908
⁴ RH March 19, 1895
⁵ RH Feb. 28, 1907
⁶ RH March 22, 1906
⁷ RH March 29, 1906
⁸ RH March 22, 1906
⁹ ST Jan. 30, 1893
¹⁰ RH June 11, 1908
¹¹ MS 30a, 1896
¹² RH June 11, 1908
¹³ Ibid.
¹⁴ Letter 1, 1904
¹⁵ 8T 322, 323
¹⁶ CT 139
¹⁷ MS 15, 1898
¹⁸ RH June 11, 1908
¹⁹ 5T 273
²⁰ Letter 144, 1898
²¹ RH March 29, 1906
²² RH July 6, 1911
²³ RH Feb. 14, 1899
²⁴ MS 16, 1896
²⁵ MS 130, 1897
²⁶ MS 13, 1897
²⁷ CT 64-66
²⁸ Letter 11, 1897
²⁹ MS 5, 1886
³⁰ ST July 23, 1902
³¹ Und. MS 73
³² RH July 7, 1904
³³ MS 16, 1896
³⁴ MS 3, 1885
³⁵ Ibid.
³⁶ MS 3, 1879
³⁷ Letter 180, 1902
³⁸ RH Jan. 11, 1912
³⁹ Und. MS 73
⁴⁰ RH March 8, 1906
⁴¹ ST Feb. 27, 1901
⁴² Letter 179, 1902

JUNE

¹ RH April 28, 1910
² RH May 28, 1901
³ RH June 3, 1884
⁴ MS 13, 1897
⁵ Letter 10, 1894
⁶ Letter 178, 1899
⁷ CT 544
⁸ Letter 8, 1891

⁹ 2T 267
¹⁰ RH April 21, 1885
¹¹ Letter 123, 1904
¹² Letter 10, 1894
¹³ MS 21, 1898
¹⁴ RH Nov. 23, 1905
¹⁵ RH March 9, 1905
¹⁶ MS 8, 1894
¹⁷ RH Oct. 23, 1888
¹⁸ RH Aug. 23, 1892
¹⁹ RH Dec. 4, 1894
²⁰ RH Jan. 2, 1900
²¹ MS 21, 1898
²² Letter 71, 1893
²³ Letter 26d, 1887
²⁴ MS 61, 1898
²⁵ RH May 12, 1910
²⁶ GCB April 23, 1901
²⁷ RH May 12, 1910
²⁸ MS 151, 1898
²⁹ RH Jan. 5, 1911
³⁰ Letter 1, 1904
³¹ RH Dec. 22, 1896
³² GCB April 4, 1901
³³ Und. MS 144
³⁴ MS 82, 1900
³⁵ Letter 20, 1903
³⁶ MS 139, 1898
³⁷ ST July 16, 1902
³⁸ Ibid.
³⁹ Letter 179, 1902
⁴⁰ RH May 9, 1907
⁴¹ RH Jan. 8, 1884
⁴² RH Oct. 23, 1900
⁴³ Letter 123, 1904
⁴⁴ RH Nov. 24, 1904
⁴⁵ RH Oct. 6, 1904
⁴⁶ Letter 329a, 1905
⁴⁷ 8T 17

JULY

¹ MS 82, 1900
² Letter 128, 1897
³ RH Dec. 31, 1908
⁴ Letter 90, 1898
⁵ Letter 27, 1872
⁶ Sufferings 10-12
⁷ CT 103
⁸ Letter 26d, 1887
⁹ Ibid.
¹⁰ Ibid.
¹¹ COL 326
¹² MS 1, 1888
¹³ CT 225
¹⁴ Letter 26d, 1887
¹⁵ Letter 139, 1898
¹⁶ AA 563, 564
¹⁷ Letter 117, 1896
¹⁸ MS 16, 1899
¹⁹ Letter 76, 1894
²⁰ Letter 10, 1894
²¹ Letter 24, 1870
²² Letter 76, 1894
²³ Letter 27, 1872
²⁴ Letter 76, 1894
²⁵ RH Oct. 12, 1911
²⁶ RH Jan. 12, 1911
²⁷ RH Oct. 5, 1911
²⁸ RH Nov. 23, 1905
²⁹ RH Jan. 28, 1904
³⁰ RH Nov. 23, 1905
³¹ RH Oct. 12, 1911
³² ST Aug. 7, 1884
³³ RH Oct. 24, 1899
³⁴ RH Oct. 12, 1911

³⁵ RH Oct. 5, 1911
³⁶ MS 67, 1909
³⁷ RH Oct. 28, 1909
³⁸ RH May 16, 1912
³⁹ MS 9, 1863
⁴⁰ MS 10, 1863
⁴¹ MS 78, 1886
⁴² RH Oct. 12, 1911

AUGUST

¹ MS 182, 1903
² RH Dec. 1, 1904
³ MS 139, 1898
⁴ RH July 11, 1907
⁵ RH Oct. 26, 1911
⁶ RH Feb. 29, 1912
⁷ RH April 25, 1912
⁸ RH Feb. 29, 1912
⁹ RH Dec. 29, 1910
¹⁰ Letter 1, 1904
¹¹ MS 15, 1898
¹² Letter 36, 1901
¹³ MS 36, 1891
¹⁴ 5T 200
¹⁵ Letter 6, 1894
¹⁶ RH May 2, 1907
¹⁷ RH Feb. 24, 1891
¹⁸ Letter 123, 1904
¹⁹ MH 487
²⁰ Letter 123, 1904
²¹ RH July 13, 1886
²² MS 99, 1902
²³ RH March 10, 1904
²⁴ MS 11, 1885
²⁵ 2T 132, 133
²⁶ RH July 21, 1910
²⁷ MM 51, 52
²⁸ MS 94, 1899
²⁹ Letter 187, 1902
³⁰ ST May 21, 1902
³¹ RH Aug. 22, 1899
³² *The Watchman,* May 5, 1908
³³ *Ibid.*
³⁴ RH May 11, 1897
³⁵ YI Sept. 29, 1892
³⁶ Letter 1, 1904
³⁷ *The Watchman,* May 26, 1908
³⁸ RH Jan. 4, 1887
³⁹ RH Dec. 21, 1886
⁴⁰ RH Jan. 4, 1887
⁴¹ Letter 28, 1897
⁴² Letter 27, 1886
⁴³ Letter 131, 1904
⁴⁴ MS 102, 1901
⁴⁵ *Ibid.*
⁴⁶ Letter 28, 1907
⁴⁷ *The Watchman,* April 7, 1908
⁴⁸ RH July 20, 1897

SEPTEMBER

¹ ST March 12, 1912
² *Ibid.*
³ 7T 213.
⁴ 6 BC 1119
⁵ 1T 345, 346
⁶ RH Aug. 8, 1907
⁷ MS 14, 1893
⁸ Letter 96, 1900
⁹ MS 15, 1908
¹⁰ RH June 9, 1910
¹¹ Letter 71, 1898
¹² RH Dec. 17, 1908

¹³ MS 82, 1900
¹⁴ MS 51, 1898
¹⁵ RH April 18, 1907
¹⁶ MS 5, 1886
¹⁷ RH Nov. 19, 1908
¹⁸ Sp.T Ser. B, No. 6, pp. 5-7
¹⁹ RH Oct. 23,1900
²⁰ RH March 7, 1912
²¹ *Ibid.*
²² ST Nov. 5, 1902
²³ RH March 8, 1892
²⁴ Letter 10, 1879
²⁵ MB 30
²⁶ Letter 71, 1878
²⁷ Address at Goguac Lake, leaflet, 1878, p. 26
²⁸ *Ibid.,* 25-27
²⁹ *Ibid.,* 23-25
³⁰ RH April 7, 1904
³¹ 2T 358
³² RH March 10, 1904
³³ MS 194, 1898
³⁴ MS 11, 1911
³⁵ MS 19, 1909
³⁶ MS 126, 1907
³⁷ MS 49, 1909

OCTOBER

¹ RH Dec. 4, 1900
² TM 17
³ Letter 43, 1899
⁴ RH Jan. 14, 1904
⁵ TM 18
⁶ *Ibid.,* 17, 18, 19
⁷ MS 193, 1898
⁸ MS 157, 1899
⁹ MS 63, 1901
¹⁰ RH April 30, 1908
¹¹ TM 15, 16
¹² *Ibid.,* 19, 20
¹³ RH Dec. 5, 1912
¹⁴ Letter 21, 1901
¹⁵ RH May 13, 1909
¹⁶ RH Oct. 24, 1899
¹⁷ MS 33, 1885
¹⁸ ST May 21, 1902
¹⁹ RH Feb. 26, 1895
²⁰ 5T 603
²¹ MS 31, 1911
²² Letter 16a. 1895
²³ RH Aug. 10, 1905
²⁴ MS 126, 1907
²⁵ RH April 26, 1887
²⁶ RH April 29, 1884
²⁷ RH Sept. 8, 1885
²⁸ MS 53, 1905
²⁹ RH April 12, 1898
³⁰ MS 23, 1910
³¹ Letter 52, 1897
³² RH Sept. 16, 1884
³³ MS 63, 1901
³⁴ RH May 9, 1893
³⁵ *Ibid.*
³⁶ RH May 16, 1893
³⁷ Letter 65, 1884
³⁸ RH May 9, 1893
³⁹ RH May 16, 1893
⁴⁰ RH March 8, 1892
⁴¹ RH Feb. 2, 1897
⁴² *Ibid.*
⁴³ RH Jan. 2, 1900
⁴⁴ RH Feb. 26, 1895
⁴⁵ RH Jan. 9, 1900
⁴⁶ RH Aug. 25, 1910
⁴⁷ RH July 27, 1905

NOVEMBER

¹ RH Jan. 2, 1900
² RH Oct. 23, 1888
³ RH March 31, 1910
⁴ RH Nov. 23, 1905
⁵ MS 63, 1912
⁶ YI March 4, 1897
⁷ MS 104, 1898
⁸ RH July 27, 1905
⁹ RH April 29, 1909
¹⁰ RH Aug. 12, 1909
¹¹ RH Jan. 14, 1904
¹² Letter 8, 1901
¹³ MS 21, 1895
¹⁴ RH Jan. 14, 1904
¹⁵ RH Oct. 30, 1894
¹⁶ RH Jan. 6, 1910
¹⁷ RH April 29, 1909
¹⁸ MS 38, 1901
¹⁹ MS 126, 1902
²⁰ RH April 29, 1909
²¹ MS 2, 1905
²² PUR March 24, 1904
²³ 6T 261-263
²⁴ Address at Goguac Lake, leaflet, 1878, pp. 12-14
²⁵ MS 70, 1897
²⁶ RH Feb. 18, 1904
²⁷ RH April 29, 1909
²⁸ MS 41, 1890
²⁹ RH May 2, 1907
³⁰ MS 79, 1886
³¹ RH Nov. 23, 1905
³² RH April 30, 1908
³³ 7T 32
³⁴ RH Feb. 10, 1903
³⁵ RH Nov. 23, 1905
³⁶ RH April 30, 1908
³⁷ RH June 10, 1902
³⁸ Ev 615
³⁹ RH May 5, 1896
⁴⁰ RH Dec. 5, 1912
⁴¹ RH May 17, 1906
⁴² RH March 24, 1910
⁴³ RH Nov. 14, 1912
⁴⁴ 2 SM 402-408

DECEMBER

¹ RH March 14, 1912
² MS 161, 1897
³ RH Nov. 19, 1908
⁴ RH Oct. 11, 1906
⁵ RH Oct. 18, 1906
⁶ RH Oct. 11, 1906
⁷ MS 161, 1897
⁸ SC 34
⁹ RH Sept. 28, 1911
¹⁰ RH Nov. 19, 1908
¹¹ RH Aug. 19, 1909
¹² RH July 22, 1909
¹³ RH April 3, 1888
¹⁴ RH Nov. 29, 1892
¹⁵ RH Aug. 25, 1885
¹⁶ *The Watchman,* Jan. 7, 1908
¹⁷ Letter 9, 1856
¹⁸ MS 80, 1886
¹⁹ *Ibid.*
²⁰ MS 11, 1885
²¹ GCB April 6, 1903
²² Letter 90, 1898
²³ *Ibid.*
²⁴ RH Nov. 22, 1898
²⁵ 7 BC 987

[26] MS 36, 1890
[27] RH Jan. 19, 1886
[28] RH March 15, 1906
[29] Letter 21, 1867
[30] MS 127, 1907
[31] 6T 144, 145
[32] MS 83, 1886
[33] 5T 620, 621

[34] FE 199
[35] RH July 20, 1905
[36] CT 208, 209
[37] 8T 253
[38] Letter 30, 1893
[39] *The Watchman,* March 31, 1908
[40] CT 55

[41] MS 17, 1888
[42] MS 8, 1888
[43] MS 84, 1886
[44] MS 60, 1886
[45] RH May 13, 1890
[46] Letter 71, 1878
[47] MS 9, 1908

SCRIPTURE INDEX

Inasmuch as no subject index is provided for this book, the Scripture Index has been expanded to include not only quoted texts but many that are suggested by, or related to, the comments. While not exhaustive, it will be found helpful to the student desiring to refer to the various statements that may be traced by means of these texts Memory texts are in bold-face type.